Lecture Notes in Control and Information Sciences

Edited by A. V. Balakrishnan and M. Thoma

Lecture Notes in Control and Information Sciences

Edited by A.V. Balakrishnan and M. Thoma

IFIP

18

Modelling and Optimization of Complex System

Proceedings of the
IFIP-TC 7 Working Conference
Novosibirsk, USSR, 3–9 July, 1978

Edited by G. I. Marchuk

Springer-Verlag Berlin Heidelberg GmbH

Editor
Prof. Guri Ivanovich Marchuk
Computing Center, Novosibirsk 630090, USSR

ISBN 978-3-540-09612-2 ISBN 978-3-540-34781-1 (eBook)
DOI 10.1007/978-3-540-34781-1

Originally published by Springer-Verlag Berlin Heidelberg New York in 1979.

2060/3020-543210

PREFACE

These Proceedings contain most of the papers presented at the IFIP TC-7 Working Conference on Modelling and Optimization of Complex Systems held in Novosibirsk on 3-9 July, 1978.

The Conference was organized by the IFIP Technical Committee on Optimization with the Computing Center of the Siberian Branch of the USSR Academy of Sciences and sponsored by the USSR Academy of Sciences.

The Conference was attended by 70 scientists from 10 countries. The program offered a broad view of optimization techniques currently in use and under investigation. Major emphasis was on recent advances in optimal control and mathematical programming and their application to modelling, identification and control of large systems, in particular, recent applications in areas such as biological, environmental and socio-economic systems.

The International Programme Committee of the Conference consisted of:

A.V.Balakrishnan (Chairman, USA), C.Bruni (Italy), J.L.Lions (France), K.Malanowski (Poland), G.I.Marchuk (USSR), R.R.Mohler (USA), L.S.Pontryagin (USSR), J.Stoer (FRG).

TABLE OF CONTENTS

MAXIMUM LIKELIHOOD IDENTIFICATION OF AN IMMUNE RESPONSE MODEL (*)

Alessandro Bertuzzi[(1)], Carlo Bruni[(2,1)]

Alberto Gandolfi[(1)], Giorgio Koch [(3,1)]

(1) Centro di Studio dei Sistemi di Controllo e Calcolo Automatici del CNR, Via Eudossiana 18, 00184 ROMA, ITALY

(2) Istituto di Automatica dell'Università di Roma, Via Eudossiana 18, 00184 ROMA, ITALY

(3) Istituto Matematico "G.Castelnuovo" dell'Università di Roma, Città Universitaria, Piazzale delle Scienze 5, 00185 ROMA,ITALY.

1. INTRODUCTION

In a previous work a model for the humoral immune response was established, based on the clonal selection theory (Bruni et al.1974, 1975). This model was tested against available data in the literature (Eisen and Siskind, 1964; Siskind et al.,1968;Werblin et al., 1973) giving the parameters some reasonable values, with rather satisfactory results. In order to achieve a more thorough validation of the model, it appeared necessary to a) obtain a more complete and homogeneous set of experimental data, b) achieve a better knowledge of the values of the model parameters.

As far as the first point is concerned, an *ad hoc* experimental program was carried out, in which the population of antibodies generated in the primary and secondary immune response triggered by inoculation of a suitable antigen was tested at different times (Oratore, 1977). Inbred Guinea pigs (strain 13) were inoculated by doses of 0.1 mg and 1 mg of DNP-RNAase in Freund's complete adjuvant. Bleedings were performed weekly and the adopted titration procedure was the Farr technique.Also, some experiments were made to get information about the time evolution of the free antigen concentration in the blood during the maturation of the immune response (Oratore, unpublished results).

The aim of this paper is to deal with the second point, namely to identify the unknown parameters of the model.

(*) This work was partially supported by C.N.R.. The experiments which are referred to in this paper were conducted at Oregon Regional Primate Research Center, under a joint scientific program between the Centro di Studio dei Sistemi di Controllo e Calcolo Automatici and the Oregon State University, supported by Italian National Research Council and the U.S. National Science Foundation (Grant n. ENG-74-15330 AOI).

2. AN IDENTIFICATION ORIENTED MODEL

A first problem was to revise the previously proposed model in order to get an identification oriented version of it. This primarity led to assume as input and output variables the free antigen concentration and respectively the antibody concentration density, i.e. those quantities which were experimentally observed. With reference to the original model, this means to consider only the phenomena of stimulation, differentiation and duplication of lymphocytes, and of antibody production and removal, while the feedback phenomena of antigen removal by the antibodies was cut off (see Fig. 1). In addition, the term which in the original model described a burst of antibody synthesis by immunocompetent cells immediately after their duplication was disregarded, since it was found to be not quantitatively relevant. By this way we arrived at the following simplified model equations:

$$\frac{\partial C(K,t)}{\partial t} = \alpha_c \frac{1}{1+KH(t)} p_s(KH(t))C(K,t) - \alpha_c \frac{KH(t)}{1+KH(t)} p_s(KH(t))C(K,t) + - \frac{1}{\tau_c} C(K,t) + \beta p_c(K) \tag{2.1}$$

$$\frac{\partial C_p(K,t)}{\partial t} = 2\alpha_c \frac{KH(t)}{1+KH(t)} p_s(KH(t))C(K,t) - \frac{1}{\tau_p} C_p(K,t) \tag{2.2}$$

$$\frac{\partial S_T(K,t)}{\partial t} = \alpha_s C_p(K,t) + \alpha_s' C(K,t) - \frac{1}{\tau_B} \frac{KH(t)}{1+KH(t)} S_T(K,t) - \frac{1}{\tau_s} \frac{1}{1+KH(t)} S_T(K,t) \tag{2.3}$$

where:

K is the *association constant* between antigen and antibody sites ranging in the interval $[0,\infty)$ (antigen is considered functionally univalent)

$H(t)$ is the *free antigen concentration* in the circulating fluids

$C(K,t)$ is the *concentration density*, with respect to K, *of immunocompetent cells*

$C_p(K,t)$ is the *concentration density of plasmacells*

$S_T(K,t)$ is the *total* (free and bound) *antibody sites concentration density*

$p_s(KH(t))$ is the probability that a cell of affinity K is stimulated; in (Bruni et al., 1975) it is shown that this is a smooth window function, which takes value very close to 1 if $\frac{\sigma_1}{1-\sigma_1} \leq KH(t) \leq \frac{\sigma_2}{1-\sigma_2}$ and very close to zero otherwise

$p_c(K)$ is the original distribution of immunocompetent cells and it is assumed to be lognormal and known.

The parameters which appear in the model, are:

α_c proliferation rate constant of stimulated immunocompetent cells

β rate of production of new immunocompetent cells from stem cells

τ_c mean lifetime of immunocompetent cells

τ_p mean lifetime of plasmacells

τ_B mean lifetime of the immune complex

τ_s mean lifetime of free antibody sites

α_s rate constant of antibody production by plasmacells

α_s' rate constant of antibody production by immunocompetent cells

σ_1, σ_2 endpoints of the interval of occupied receptor site ratio causing stimulation.

To these parameters we must add suitable initial conditions for equations (2.1)-(2.3).

While the input H is directly measured at different times, the total antibody sites concentration density is indirectly measured through the concentration $Y(X,t)$ of bound antibody sites in the titration assay made on the circulating fluids at different times and for fixed free hapten concentration X:

$$Y(X,t) = \int_0^\infty \frac{KX}{1+KX} \frac{S_T(K,t)}{1+KH(t)} dK \tag{2.4}$$

Noting that the free antibody site concentration density in the circulating fluids is given by the term $\frac{S_T(K,t)}{1+KH(t)}$, the previous relation provides under mild assumptions (Bruni et al., 1976) a one to one correspondence between the free antibody site concentration density itself at time t and the behaviour of $Y(X,t)$ as a function of X. Thus $Y(X,t)$ plays the role of actual model output (Fig. 1).

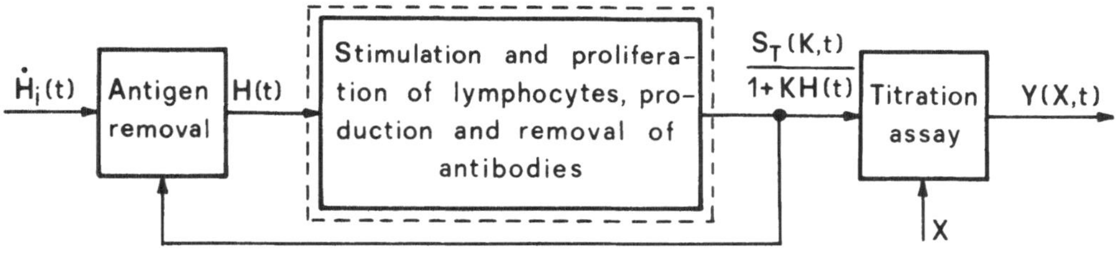

Fig. 1 - Block diagram showing connection among quantities relevant for identification purpose. The dashed square includes the identification oriented immune response model; $\dot{H}_i(t)$ denotes the rate of injection of antigen in the organism.

Now the second problem is to choose those parameters in the model which are to be identified. Indeed, if all parameters and initial conditions appearing in the model were assumed to be unknown in the identification procedure, then we would face: a) difficulties in meeting possible a priori (or experimental) information about relationships among some of them, b) possible non identifiability problems due to low sensitivity of the output with respect to some parameters and/or equivalent effect on the output itself, c) an excessive computational burden. With the purpose of overcoming these difficulties, only the primary response was considered, so that the initial conditions reduce to:

$$C(K,0) = C_o p_c(K) = \tau_c \beta p_c(K)$$

$$C_p(K,0) = 0 \qquad (2.5)$$

$$S_T(K,0) = \tau_s \alpha'_s C(K,0)$$

In the first equation (2.5), C_o denotes the initial total number per unit volume of immunocompetent cells which turns out to be equal to $\tau_c\beta$, since $C(K,0)$ must be a stationary solution of (2.1) in absence of stimulation.By simulation of the model it appeared that variations in C_o may be (output) compensated by suitable variations of α_s , α'_s. Therefore C_o was fixed to the biologically reasonable value:

$$C_o = 8 \cdot 10^{-16} \text{ moles/liter}$$

Information reported in the literature (Weigle, 1961; Gowans, 1970; Mattioli and Tomasi, 1973) further suggest to assume the following values:

$$\tau_p = 6 \text{ days} = 144 \text{ h}$$

$$\tau_c = 300 \text{ days} = 7200 \text{ h}$$

$$\tau_s = 2\ \tau_B$$

$$\beta = C_o/\tau_c = 1.1 \cdot 10^{-19} \text{ moles/liter} \cdot \text{h}$$

Finally, the parameters which are considered as unknown in the identification procedure are :

$$\sigma_1, \sigma_2, \alpha_c, \alpha_s, \alpha'_s, \tau_B$$

This selection seems to meet some remarks (Mohler, 1978) about the sensitivity of the model with respect to various parameters.

As a matter of fact, in order to take the positivity constraint for all six parameters into account, the unknown parameter vector was defined as:

$$\gamma \triangleq \left[\ln \sigma_1 \quad \ln \sigma_2 \quad \ln \alpha_c \quad \ln \alpha_s \quad \ln \alpha'_s \quad \ln \tau_B\right]^T \tag{2.6}$$

3. PROBLEM FORMULATION

We first note that the experimental data presently available for H are constituted by its value at a very limited number of times, so that an interpolation procedure is required to simulate the model. Simple interpolating functions were chosen constituted by the sum of two exponentials which for the two doses of 1 mg and 0.1 mg are respectively (Fig. 2, solid lines), H moles/liter, t hours:

$$H(t) = 8.16\cdot 10^{-7}\left[e^{-t/85} - e^{-t/11}\right] \tag{3.1}$$

$$H(t) = 10^{-7}\left[e^{-t/100} - e^{-t/14}\right] \tag{3.2}$$

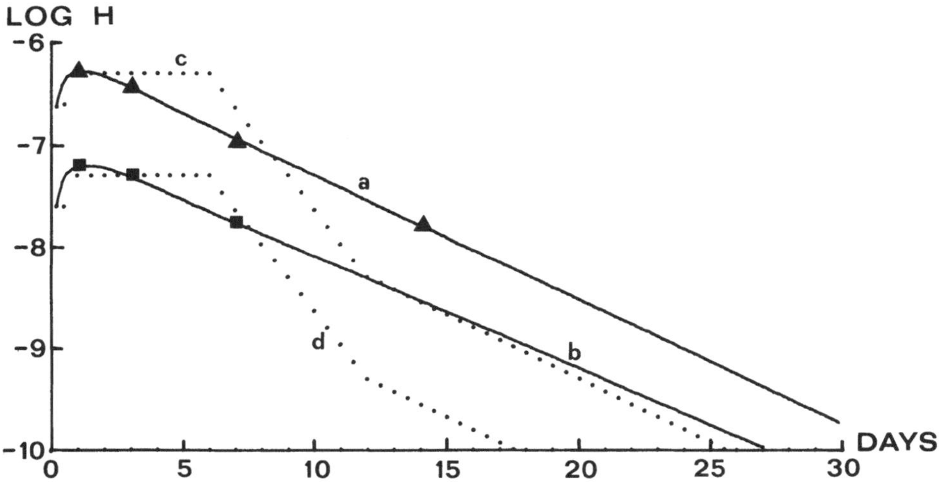

Fig. 2 - Time evolution of free antigen: experimental points (▲, ■), exponential interpolation (solid lines), piecewise exponential behaviour (dotted lines) for 1 mg dose (lines a-c) and 0.1 mg dose (lines b-d).

As a matter of fact, equations (3.1),(3.2) differ from the real behaviour of free antigen not only because of interpolation errors but also because of random measurement errors which affect the data.These errors influence the output function (2.4) both directly and indirectly through the dependence of S_T on H itself (taking the dynamics of the model into account). However, if one linearizes the functional dependence of $Y(X,t)$ on H for fixed X and t, as described by (2.4) and the model equations, one finds that the first order approximation of the influence on $Y(X,t)$ of the random errors of H is negligible with respect to those experimental errors which affect $Y(X,t)$ itself in the titration assays. As far as interpolation errors on H, it is not possible to evaluate their magnitude with such a low number of data. For sake of simplicity their effect on $Y(X,t)$ was also neglected, while some considerations about possible consequences of this fact are reported in the concluding section.

Let now $t_1, t_2, \ldots, t_N$ be the bleeding times and $X_j(t_i)$, $j = 1,2,\ldots,n_i$, $i = 1,\ldots,N$, be the j-th hapten concentration in the i-th titration assay. Let $Y(X_j(t_i), t_i; \gamma)$ be the corresponding bound antibody site concentration given by (2.4) in which the dependence of the model output on γ is evidentiated. Denoted by x and $y(x,\gamma)$ the vectors of all $X_j(t_i)$ and $Y(X_j(t_i), t_i; \gamma)$, respectively, and by z_x, z_y the vectors of the measured values for the same quantities, the measurement equations may be written as:

$$z_x = x + u \tag{3.3}$$

$$z_y = y(x,\gamma) + v \tag{3.4}$$

where u,v are respectively the measurement errors on x,y. A detailed analysis of the statistics of u,v was carried out (Koch and Oratore, 1978), taking the various error sources into account. The conclusions were that u,v may be taken to be zero mean gaussian variables whose variances and covariances at each titration point are deducible from approximate formulas, while errors at different points are incorrelated. Quantitatively speaking, the mean square error on X data is approximately 2 - 3%, while the same error on Y data increases from 2% up to 20-30% as X increases.

Consequently, the maximum likelihood functional for x,γ is given by:

$$J(x,\gamma) = \begin{bmatrix} z_x - x \\ z_y - y(x,\gamma) \end{bmatrix}^T \Psi^{-1} \begin{bmatrix} z_x - x \\ z_y - y(x,\gamma) \end{bmatrix} \tag{3.5}$$

where:

$$\Psi = E\left\{ \begin{bmatrix} u \\ v \end{bmatrix} \begin{bmatrix} u^T & v^T \end{bmatrix} \right\} = \begin{bmatrix} \Psi_u & \Psi_{uv} \\ \Psi_{uv} & \Psi_v \end{bmatrix} \tag{3.6}$$

is a known block-diagonal non singular matrix. Due to small values of Ψ_u entries, we may linearize $y(x,\gamma)$ around z_x. Then minimizing $J(x,\gamma)$ with respect to x and substituting back the obtained value for x leads to the reduced functional:

$$J_1(\gamma)=\left[z_y-y(z_x,\gamma)\right]^T \Psi_e^{-1}(z_x,\gamma)\left[z_y-y(z_x,\gamma)\right] \tag{3.7}$$

where:

$$\Psi_e(z_x,\gamma) = \Psi_v-2\,\frac{\partial y(z_x,\gamma)}{\partial z_x}\,\Psi_{uv}+\left[\frac{\partial y(z_x,\gamma)}{\partial z_x}\right]^2\Psi_u \tag{3.8}$$

It can be proved (see Bruni and Germani, to appear) that Ψ_e is always nonsingular, since the absolute value of the correlation coefficient between u and v values is always less than one.

4. IDENTIFIABILITY

The problem now arises of identifiability of γ, namely of the existence and uniqueness of an optimal estimate $\hat{\gamma}$ of γ with respect to the loss functional (3.7). Of course, local identifiability of γ is equivalent to the existence of an isolated minimum of (3.7) within a suitable neighbourhood $D(\gamma^o,\delta)\subset\mathbb{R}^6$ of the initial guess γ^o.

Since our functional $J_1(\gamma)$ is continuously differentiable with respect to γ, this problem may be regarded as the problem of local existence and uniqueness of a solution of the equation:

$$P(\gamma) = \frac{dJ_1(\gamma)}{d\gamma} = 0 \tag{4.1}$$

and therefore studied by adapting well-known Kantorovich theorems (Kantorovich and Akilov, 1964). Specifically, let $\gamma^o,\delta_R,\delta_I,B_o,\eta_o$ be such that:

(i) $|P'(\gamma^o)| \neq 0$

(ii) $\|[P'(\gamma^o)]^{-1}\| \leq B_o$

(iii) $\|[P'(\gamma^o)]^{-1}P(\gamma^o)\| \leq \eta_o$

(iv) $\Omega = D(\gamma^o,\delta_R)\times D(0,\delta_I)$ is contained in the complex region of $\mathbb{C}^6$ in which $P(s)=P(\gamma+j\omega)$ is holomorphic.

Then the following theorem may be proved (Bruni and Germani, to appear):

*Thm.*1. Let $M_{\partial\Omega} = \sup_{s \in \partial\Omega} \|P(s)\|$.

a) If: $h_o = \dfrac{\eta_o B_o M_{\partial\Omega}}{\delta_I^2} \leq 1/4$

$$r_o \leq \delta_R < r_1 \quad , \quad \text{with} \quad r_o = \frac{1-\sqrt{1-4h_o}}{2h_o}\,\eta_o \quad , \quad r_1 = \frac{1+\sqrt{1-4h_o}}{2h_o}\,\eta_o$$

or

b) if: $h_o = 1/4$

$$r_o \leq \delta_R \leq r_1$$

then a unique optimal estimate $\hat{\gamma}$ exists in $D(\gamma^o, \delta_R)$.

The estimate $\hat{\gamma}$ may be looked for through a suitable minimization algorithm. If one adopts the Newton method, the following result turns out to be useful:

Thm. 2. Under the same assumptions of Thm.1, the Newton method for the solution of (4.1), starting from γ^o, yields a sequence quadratically convergent to $\hat{\gamma}$.

Remark 1. It is possible to prove that if the function P is that defined by our problem, for each $\delta_R > 0$, and γ^o satisfying (i) above, a $\delta_I > 0$ exists such that (iv) is satisfied.

Remark 2. The results of Thm.1,2 allow to set in a rigorous framework the identification problem under both aspects of identifiability and of numerical determination of the optimal estimate. However, we must say that checking conditions of Thm.1, and specifically computing $M_{\partial\Omega}$, is not at all an easy task. Furthermore in our case, due to the high degree of nonlinearities and to the dimensionality of the problem, the Newton method implementation requires heavy computational effort.

Therefore to obtain the results reported in the following section, a simpler direct search method (Hooke and Jeeves) was adopted.

5. IDENTIFICATION AND VALIDATION OF THE MODEL

In the minimization of functional $J_1(\gamma)$, as initial guess γ^o we assumed those parameter values which in a previous work (Bruni et al., 1975) were selected according to information available directly or indirectly from the literature. In particular we assumed:

$$\sigma_1^o = 0.01 \ ; \quad \sigma_2^o = 0.9 \ ; \quad \alpha_c^o = 0.06 \ h^{-1} \qquad (5.1)$$

$\alpha_s^o = 10^8$ molecules$\cdot$cell$^{-1}\cdot$h^{-1}; $\alpha_s'^o = 2\cdot10^6$ molecules$\cdot$cell$^{-1}\cdot$h^{-1}; τ_B^o=100h.

Bleeding times (Oratore, 1977) were:

14;21;28;35;42;49;56;70;77;84;113 days after inoculation, for 1mg dose
14;21;28;35;42;49;56;63;93 days after inoculation, for 0.1 mg dose.

Minimization was performed including in the functional only a part of the available data, that is the data for the input dose of 1 mg and at 14,21,28,35,42,49,56,70 days after inoculation; the remaining part of the data was left for testing the predictive capabilities of the identified model. As input functions,the exponential interpolations (3.1),(3.2) were used.

After about 700 evaluations of $J_1(\gamma)$, the minimization algorithm yielded the final value of the parameters:

$$\hat{\sigma}_1 = 0.0120 \quad ; \quad \hat{\sigma}_2 = 0.499 \quad ; \quad \hat{\alpha}_c = 0.0452$$

$$\hat{\alpha}_s = 0.861\cdot10^8 \text{ molecules}\cdot\text{cell}^{-1}\cdot\text{h}^{-1}; \tag{5.2}$$

$$\hat{\alpha}_s' = 0.485\cdot10^6 \text{ molecules}\cdot\text{cell}^{-1}\cdot\text{h}^{-1}; \quad \hat{\tau}_B = 48.4 \text{ h}$$

while the functional decreased from $J_1(\gamma^o) = 3.03\cdot10^6$ to $J_1(\hat{\gamma}) = 2.10\cdot10^4$.

To illustrate how the identified model fits the experimental data, in Fig. 3 some diagrams are reported, which show the experimental titration points along with the corresponding output of the model for the initial and final choice of the parameters, for the 1 mg dose and 21,49 days after inoculation.

Then the model was validated by checking its predictive ability with respect to the remaining part of the data. In Fig. 4 similar diagrams are reported, for the 1 mg dose 84 days after inoculation, and for the 0.1 mg dose 21 and 56 days after inoculation.

It is convenient now to point out that going on with the minimization algorithm would have led to a negligible decrease in the functional value but with a loss in the biological significance of the parameter values and a worse predictive ability.

6. DISCUSSION AND CONCLUDING REMARKS

The adopted procedure allowed to confirm a good behaviour of the model with respect both to its fitting and predicting ability. The fact that, as an average, fitting errors at low values of X are less than at high values of X, may be explained recalling that the weighting matrix Ψ_e^{-1} enhances the relevance of the former with respect to the second ones.

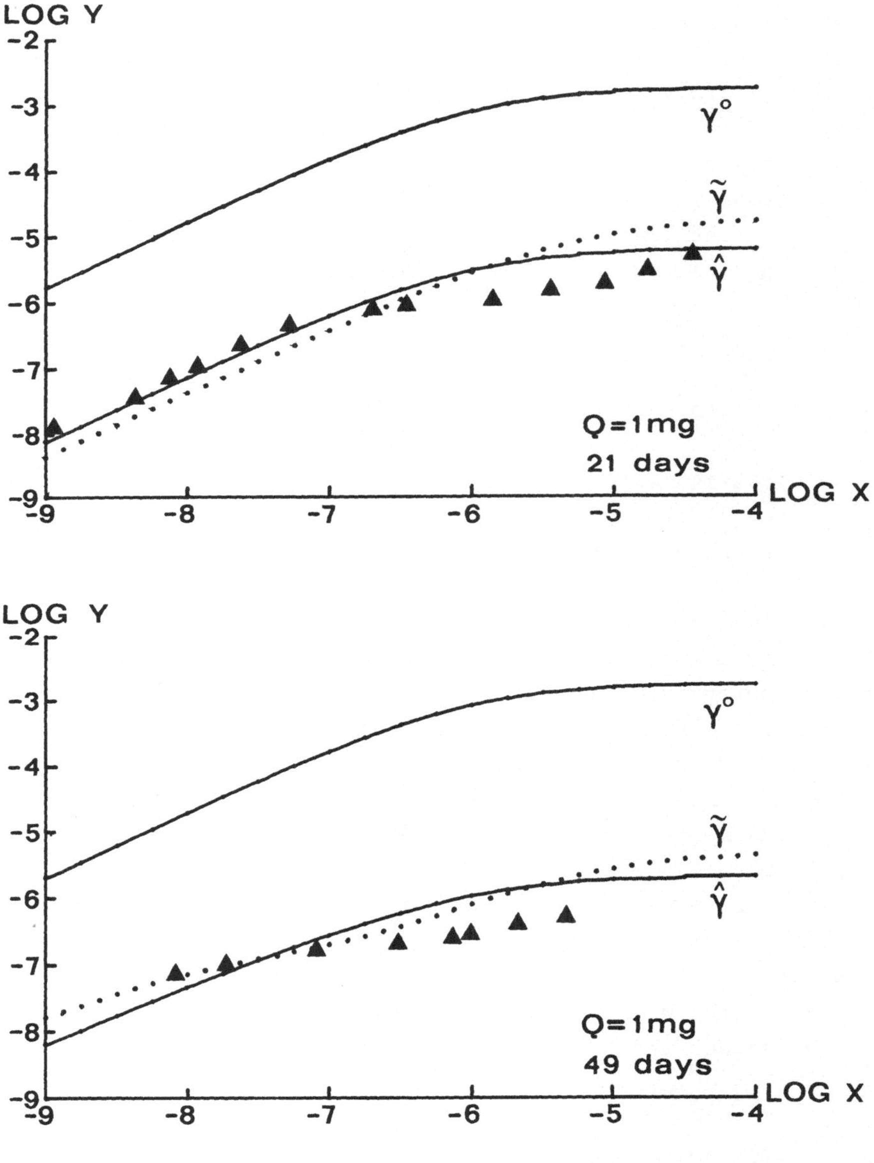

Fig. 3 - Titration diagrams showing experimental points (▲), model outputs with exponentially interpolated input and parameter value $\gamma^o, \hat{\gamma}$ (solid lines), model outputs with piecewise exponential input and parameter value $\tilde{\gamma}$ (dotted lines).

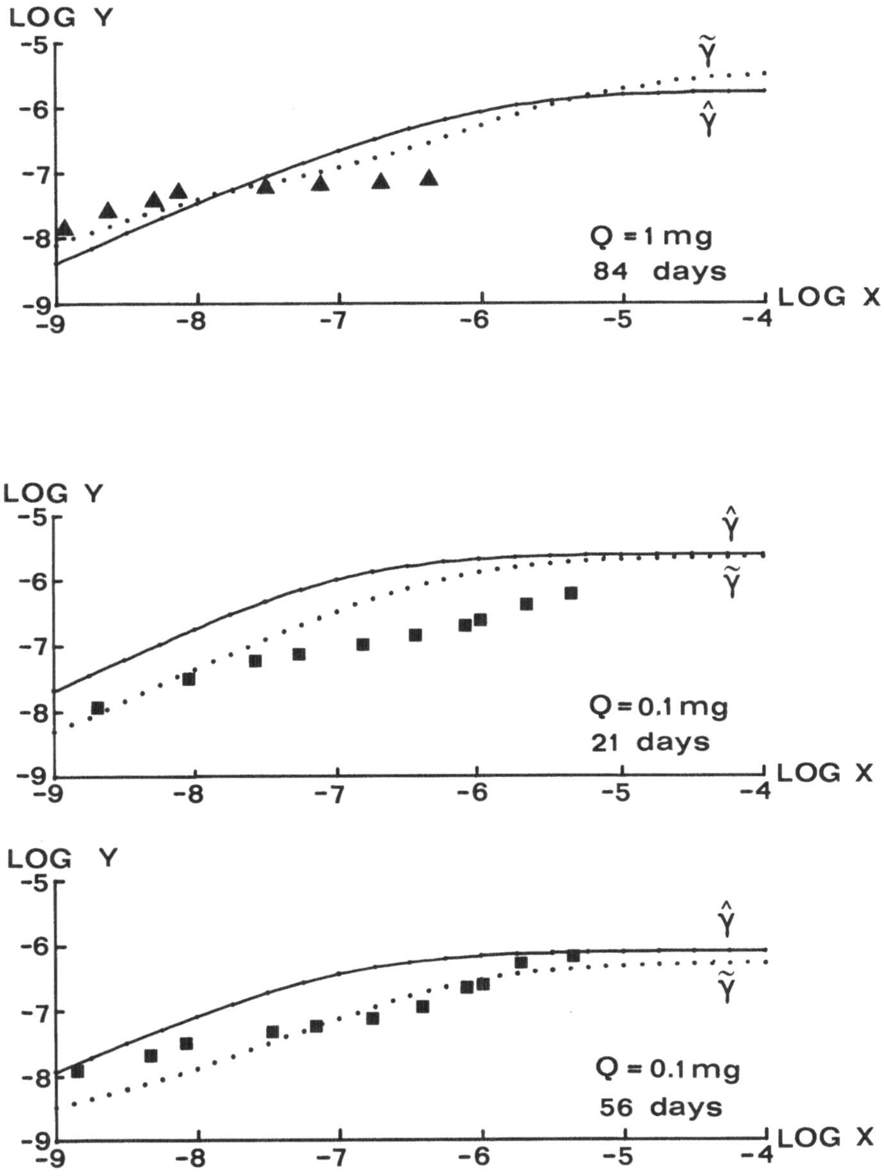

Fig. 4 - Titration diagrams showing experimental points (▲, ■), model outputs with exponentially interpolated inputs and parameter values $\hat{\gamma}$ (solid lines), model outputs with piecewise exponential inputs and parameter value $\tilde{\gamma}$ (dotted lines).

We observed that the functional value exhibits a very small sensitivity to variations in the parameters around their optimal values, with the exception of α_c ; this was also confirmed by direct simulation of the model with γ varying in a wide region around $\hat{\gamma}$. This fact on one side creates some difficulty in the determination of the optimal value of γ according to our functional; on the other side it stresses a positive feature of the model, namely that its behaviour is not sensitive to minor changes in the individual characters within a given biological species.

A further important remark is that the shape of the model output is somehow stiff with respect to parameter variations. In fact it appears not to be able to exhibit the inflection in the central part, which on the contrary appears in the experimental data and is directly connected with the bimodal character of the antibody site population with respect to affinity K, as claimed in (Bruni et al.,1976) and (Oratore, 1977). Indeed, several simulation experiments (Gandolfi, 1974; Bruni et al., 1975) proved that the shape of the model output is strongly influenced by the time behaviour of the input H, and in particular that the model is able to generate a bimodal antibody affinity distribution once the input H is represented by a function which after an initial plateau quickly drops to slowly decreasing values. Such a behaviour for H may also be explained if one considers both the effect on the free antigen concentration in the blood due to the release mechanism of the Freund's adjuvant (Herbert, 1967) and that one of the uprising of the immune response. Following this line, we tried to identify the model with the same data but assuming as input function that one depicted as curve c in Fig. 2. Starting from the same γ^o above, the optimal estimate turned out to be:

$$\tilde{\sigma}_1 = 0.00945 \; ; \quad \tilde{\sigma}_2 = 0.886 \; ; \quad \tilde{\alpha}_c = 0.0489 \; ;$$

$$\tilde{\alpha}_s = 6.17 \cdot 10^8 \text{ molecules} \cdot \text{cell}^{-1} \cdot \text{h}^{-1}; \qquad (6.1)$$

$$\tilde{\alpha}_s' = 1.92 \cdot 10^6 \text{ molecules} \cdot \text{cell}^{-1} \cdot \text{h}^{-1}; \quad \tilde{\tau}_B = 94.9 \text{ h}$$

while the functional decreased to the value $J_1(\tilde{\gamma}) = 1.72 \cdot 10^4$. The resulting model output[(1)] is shown in Fig. 3,4 (dotted lines). The sought inflection is now evident in most diagrams, with a better

(1) The 0.1 mg dose was simulated by assuming as input function the curve c in Fig. 2 divided by a factor 10 (curve d in Fig. 2).

qualitative agreement with experimental data, both in the fitting and prediction cases. Furthermore, the asymptotic ordinate of the diagrams as X increases, which yields the total free antibody sites concentration (Bruni et al., 1977; Oratore, 1977) is closer to that value which can be extrapolated by the data.

The previous results yield as a conclusion that a more precise and exaustive experimental analysis of the input time evolution is required.

Also the problem can be raised whether it is sufficient and adequate to look at the free antigen concentration only in the blood. As a matter of fact considering this concentration in different organs (like spleen, lymphonodes, etc.) would require a reformulation of the model itself to include compartmentation effects. Indeed an attempt to reconstruct the total antigen quantity $H_i(t)$ injected in the organism up to time t (see Fig. 1), exploiting the output of the identified model and the considered interpolations for H(t), seems to confirm that a part of the injected antigen is trapped in compartments different from the blood.

Another important validation to be carried out for the identified model is against the experimental results of the secondary response. This will be an area of possible future work.

REFERENCES

Bruni,C., Giovenco,M.A., Koch,G., and Strom,R. II U.S.-Italy Seminar on Variable Structure Systems, Portland, Oregon, May 1974.

Bruni,C., Giovenco,M.A., Koch,G., and Strom,R. Math. Biosci. 27, 191-211 (1975).

Bruni,C., Germani,A., Koch,G., and Strom,R. J. Theor. Biol. 61, 143-170 (1976).

Bruni,C., Germani,A., and Koch,G. 8th IFIP Conference on Optimization Techniques, Würzburg, 1977.

Bruni,C., Germani,A. Rept. Ist. Automatica, Università di Roma, to appear.

Eisen,H.N., and Siskind,G.W. Biochemistry 3, 996-1008 (1964).

Gandolfi,A. Doctoral dissertation, Università di Roma (1974).

Gowans,J.L. Harvey Lectures 1968-1969 p.87, Academic Press, New York and London, 1970.

Herbert,W.J. Symp. Series Immunobiol. Standard 6, 213-220 (1967).

Kantorovich,L.V., and Akilov,G.P. Functional analysis in normed spaces, McMillan, 1964.

Koch,G., and Oratore,A. J. Immunol. Math., in press (1978).

Mattioli,C.A., and Tomasi,T.B. J. Exp. Med. 138, 452-460 (1973).

Mohler,R.R. IFIP Working Conference on Modelling and Optimization of Complex Systems, Novosibirsk, 1978.

Oratore,A. Rept. Ist. Automatica, Università di Roma R.77-17(1977).

Weigle,G.O. Adv. Immunol. 1, 283-317 (1961).

Werblin,T.P., and Siskind,G.W. Immunochemistry 5, 171-183 (1968).

Werblin,T.P., Young Tai Kim, Quagliata,F., and Siskind,G.W. Immunology 24, 473-492 (1973).

STOCHASTIC MODEL OF THE IMMUNE RESPONSE

Miloš Jílek and Petr Klein
Department of Immunology, Institute of Microbiology, Czech.Acad.Sci.
Prague, Czechoslovakia

I. INTRODUCTION

The immune system includes a number of developmentally established mechanisms: phagocytosis (by macrophages), specific cellular response (effected by T cells), and humoral antibody formation by B cells.

Under the natural conditions, all mechanisms cooperate to provide the most effective immune response. However, experimental results indicate that under appropriate conditions B cells can be stimulated directly by antigen and undergo the differentiation process leading to antibody formation.

The mathematical model of the humoral immune response is thus based, for the sake of simplicity, on the following assumptions, concerning only the B cell line (see e.g. Šterzl 1967):

(1) In the organism a spontaneous maturation of stem cells into cells immunologically competent for various antigens takes place even in the absence of antigen; the immunological competence of a lymphatic B cell for a given antigen is determined by the number, character and localization of its surface receptors, i.e. immunoglobulin molecules built into the membrane, which possess the ability to bind with the antigen.

(2) The immunologically competent cell has not yet encountered the antigen with which it is capable of binding; however, after an adequate stimulation (i.e. after the binding of a critical amount of immunogenic antigen) it can enter the irreversible differentiation process which leads eventually to its transformation into the antibody forming cell. If the contact of the immunologically competent cell with antigen does not occur, this cell remains for a long time in a relatively quiescent state and does not take part in the immune response. On the other hand, the gradual drain of immunologically competent cells does usually not lead to the exhaustion of their supply as new cells from precursor sources are provided by a feedback mechanism.

(3) Subsequent to its stimulation by the antigen, the immunologically competent cell undergoes metabolic and morphological changes (e.g. increased transport of ions and other metabolites into the cell, rise in the rate of RNA and DNA synthesis), and becomes the immunologically activated cell which does not yet secrete antibodies. The immunologically activated cell is characterized by an active proliferation which lasts for a certain number of generations. The fate of the immunologically activated cell depends on a possible further antigenic stimulus which leads to its conversion into the producing cell; if this contact does not occur, the proliferative activity is gradually lost, the cell changes also morphologically and stays in the organism for a long time as a memory cell which is potentially prepared to react to another antigenic stimulus and hence to be transformed into the antibody forming cell.

(4) The generation of the terminal, short-lived cell, which during its existence secretes specific antibody molecules against a given antigen at a rate of 12 to 20 thousand molecules per a second, is the final state of the differentiation process.

The following diagram provides an illustration of the development of one B cell clone:

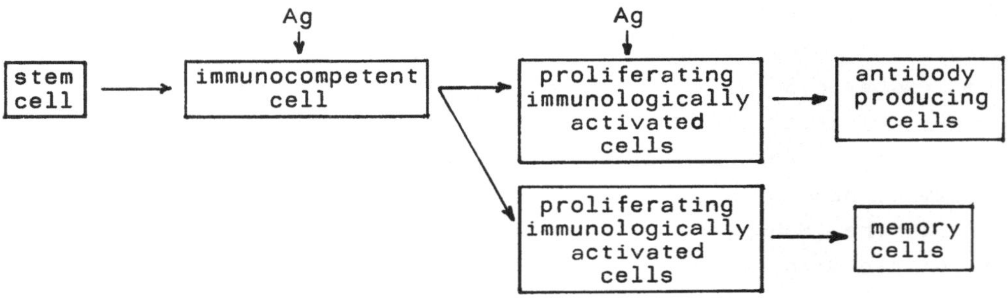

II. MODEL

1. Cell Types

According to the above hypothesis, three populations of B cells, viz. immunocompetent (X), immunologically activated (Y), and antibody producing (Z) cells, are involved in the process of differentiation and proliferation triggered by the antigenic stimulus.

An immunocompetent cell stimulated by antigen needs some time to change into a proliferating Y cell. We call the cell in this intermediate period "Y_a cell" and include it, for the purpose of the mathematical model, in the population of Y cells. The inhomogeneous population of Y cells thus consists of Y_a cells, of several generations of proliferating cells, of cells which received the second antigenic stimulus and therefore undergo transformation into antibody producing cells, and of long-lived memory cells. Although the antibody producing cells are assumed to have restricted proliferative capacity, their population may admittedly consist of more than one generation.

Thus the following B cell types were taken into account:

X... immunocompetent cell,

Y_a... cell in the intermediate state between X and Y_1,

Y_g... proliferating Y cell of the g-th generation (the last generation of these cells represents the subpopulation of memory cells),

Y_b... stimulated Y cell (2nd stimulus) which is just being transformed into antibody producing cell,

Z_h... Z cell of the h-th generation.

We denote as X(t), Y(t), and Z(t) the sizes of respective populations at time t.

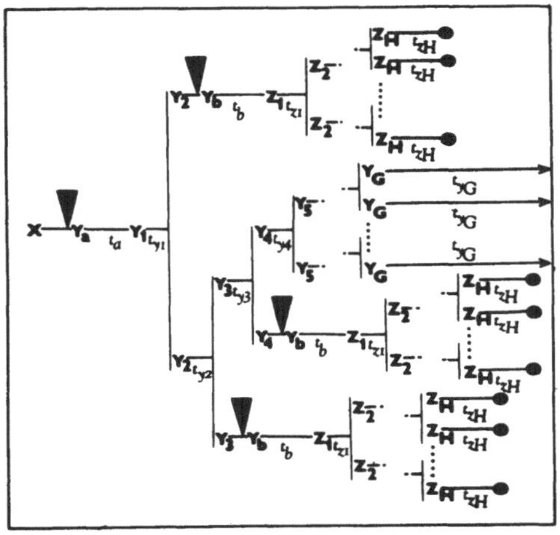

Figure 1.
Scheme of B cell differentiation and proliferation (Jílek 1976)

2. Parameters

The constant model parameters are as follows:

t_a... duration of the intermediate state Y_a,

t_{yg}... generation time of a Y_g cell,

t_{yG}... lifetime of a memory cell,

t_b... intermediate period after the second stimulus and before the production of antibodies,

t_{zh}... generation time (or lifetime if $h = H$) of a Z_h cell,
G... number of generations of proliferating Y cells,
H... number of generations of Z cells (usually $H = 1$).

Furthermore there are parameters characterizing the antigen; its decrease in the organism is generally expressed by the function Ag(t). Usually

$$Ag(t) = A\ e^{-Bt} \tag{1}$$

where A is proportional to the amount of antigen injected, and B is the rate of its elimination due to phagocytosis and metabolic decay.

3. Transitions between Cell Types

There are several hypotheses on the stimulation of an immunocompetent cell. This model is based on the assumption of a direct stimulating effect of antigen, and other possible factors, as T cells or macrophages, were thus neglected. The event that triggers the differentiation of a cell is its contact with the antigen. As a matter of fact, the term contact represents the events necessary for the stimulation (e.g. the cross-linking of receptors). The probability of the contact is assumed to depend solely on the amount of the antigen present.

Two kinds of transitions of a cell from one type into another are possible in this model and both of them are the consequences of the stimulating encounter with the antigen. Transitions $X \rightarrow Y_a$ and $Y_g \rightarrow Y_b$, $g = 1, \ldots, G$, are random and their execution coincides with the contact. The occurrence of either of these transitions implies that the transition $Y_a \rightarrow Y_1$ or $Y_b \rightarrow Z$, respectivelly, follows after a constant time interval (for the sake of simplicity we restrict ourselves to the case of $H = 1$). Similarly, the proliferation of Y cells (i.e. the division of one Y_g cell into two Y_{g+1} cells) is determined once the contact of an cell with antigen has taken place and only those Y cells which are once again stimulated by the antigen do not reach memory cell state because they are changed into producing Z cells via intermediate Y_b cells.

In Table 1 possible transitions are denoted by "+". "O" denotes transitions which cannot occur. $H = 1$ for the sake of simplicity. Type D was included to point out the short life of antibody producing cells.

TABLE 1

	X	Y_a	Y_1	Y_2	...	Y_g	Y_{g+1}	...	Y_G	Y_b	Z	D
X	+	+	0	0	...	0	0	...	0	0	0	0
Y_a	0	+	+	0	...	0	0	...	0	0	0	0
Y_1	0	0	+	+	...	0	0	...	0	+	0	0
⋮	⋮	⋮	⋮	⋮	⋮	⋮	⋮	⋮	⋮	⋮	⋮	⋮
Y_g	0	0	0	0	...	+	+	...	0	+	0	0
⋮	⋮	⋮	⋮	⋮	⋮	⋮	⋮	⋮	⋮	⋮	⋮	⋮
Y_G	0	0	0	0	...	0	0	...	+	+	0	0
Y_b	0	0	0	0	...	0	0	...	0	+	+	0
Z	0	0	0	0	...	0	0	...	0	0	+	+
D	0	0	0	0	...	0	0	...	0	0	0	+

III. RESULTS

It was assumed (Jílek and Šterzl 1970, 1971) that the contact between a cell and an antigen is an event of the nonhomogeneous Poisson process with the intensity function Ag(t), and that X cells as well as Y cells are independent and have the same access to the antigen. On this basis probabilities of transitions in certain time intervals were evaluated and two approaches were used to describe the time development of the populations of X, Y, and Z cells. On the one hand, formulae for mean value functions of these populations were expressed analytically, and, on the other hand, Monte Carlo method was employed to calculate the variability. The results of these two approaches were compared and a good fit of the mean value functions was obtained.

1. Analytical Approach

The time development of the mean number of cells of each individual type was derived from infinitesimal probabilities of transitions between cell types (Jílek and Ursínyová 1970a, b). Mean value functions of inhomogeneous populations Y(t) and Z(t) were obtained as sums:

$$E[Y(t)] = E[Y_a(t)] + \sum_{g=1}^{G} E[Y_g(t)] + E[Y_b(t)], \quad E[Z(t)] = \sum_{h=1}^{H} E[Z_h(t)].$$

Formulae for $E[X(t)]$, $E[Y(t)]$, and $E[Z(t)]$ were derived by Jílek and Šterzl (1970, 1973). For example, under the assumption that Z cells do not proliferate (H = 1)

$$E[Z(t)] = \sum_{g=1}^{G} E[Z_{1,g}(t)],$$

where $E\,Z_{1,g}(t)$ denotes the mean value function of the number of Z cells having arisen by differentiation of Y_g cells, and

$$E[Z_{1,g}(t)] = \begin{cases} 2^{g-1}\big[K(t-t_b-t_{z1})J(\theta_g,\theta_{g-1}) - K(t-t_b)J(k_g,k_{g-1}) + \\ \quad + J_{g-1}(\theta_{g-1},k_{g-1}) - J_g(\theta_g,k_g)\big],\ g = 1, 2, \ldots, G-1 \\ 2^{G-1}\big[K(t-t_b-t_{z1})J(0,\theta_{G-1}) - K(t-t_b)J(0,k_{G-1}) + \\ \quad + J_{G-1}(\theta_{G-1},k_{G-1})\big],\ g = G, \end{cases}$$

where

$$A(u,v) = \int_u^v Ag(x)\,dx,$$

$$J(u,v) = \int_u^v Ag(x)\exp\big[A(x,x+t)\big]\,dx,$$

$$J_g(u,v) = \int_u^v Ag(x)\exp\big[A(x,x+t_a) - A(0,x+t_a+T_g)\big]\,dx,$$

$$k_g = \max(0,t-t_a-t_b-T_g),$$

$$\theta_g = \max(0,t-t_a-t_b-t_{z1}-T_g),$$

$$T_g = \sum_{j=1}^{g} t_{yj}$$

(see Jílek and Šterzl 1973, Tab. 3).

The general intensity function Ag(t) can be replaced in the formulae by any suitable integrable function; we have mostly assumed that it is equal to the mean value function of the pure death process given by (1). This assumption is in accordance with some experimental findings (Franzl and Morello 1965, Franzl 1972). Figure 2 shows the typical mean course of X, Y, and Z population sizes in the primary response (formulae are given in Jílek and Šterzl 1973, Tab. 4).

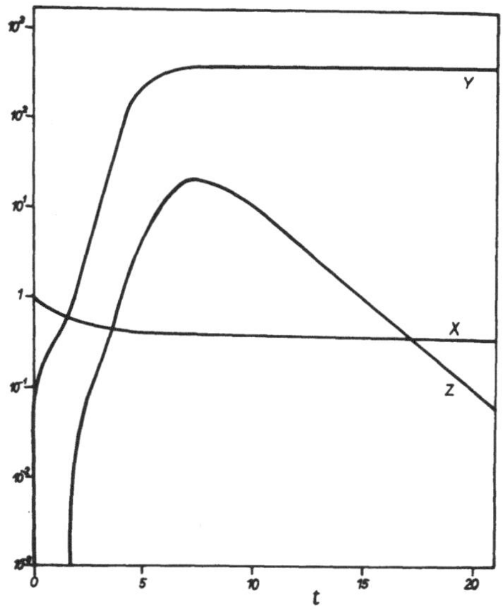

Figure 2.
Mean value functions of X, Y, Z populations (Jílek and Šterzl 1973)

In numerous model experiments the effect of parameters on the immune response was studied. It was concluded that antigen-characterizing parameters influence the response more than the rest of parameters (Jílek and Šterzl 1973, Jílek 1973a). As an example, Fig. 3 shows the effect of the first dose of antigen on the primary and secondary responses.

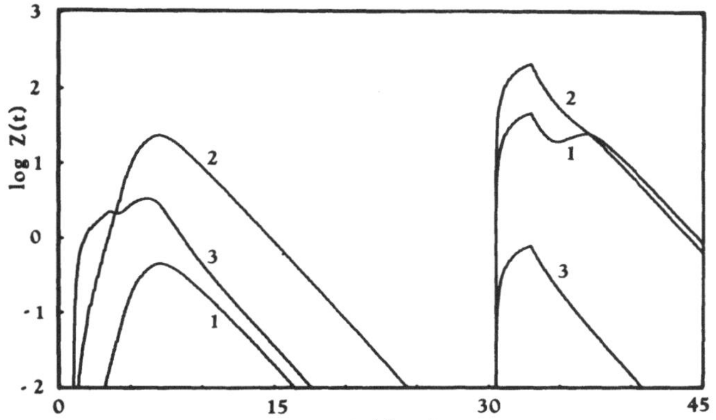

Figure 3. Influence of the first dose of antigen on the primary and secondary responses. A = 0.002 (1), 0.02 (2), 0.2 (3) in the primary response and 0.02 in the secondary response.

2. Monte Carlo Method

The computer simulates the behaviour of individual cells in discrete steps (the step is, e.g., an hour) exactly according to the assumptions of the model (Fig. 1). When the decision is to be made whether the random contact occurs or not during the next 1-h interval, the probability of the occurrence of the contact in that interval is compared with a random number. In this procedure each cell must be followed separately. Thus the first X cell is taken and every hour the decision concerning the contact with the antigen is made. If the contact takes place the transition $X \rightarrow Y_a \rightarrow Y_1$ follows inevitably in due time. When two Y_2 cells are born, one of them is stored in the memory and every hour we inquire on the fate of the second one to choose between proliferation and differentiation, etc. (Jílek and Šterzl 1970).

The clone development (see Fig. 4) was simulated many times over and used to estimate mean value functions, covariance functions, skewness and kurtosis of distribution of cell population sizes, etc. (Jílek 1975a, 1976).

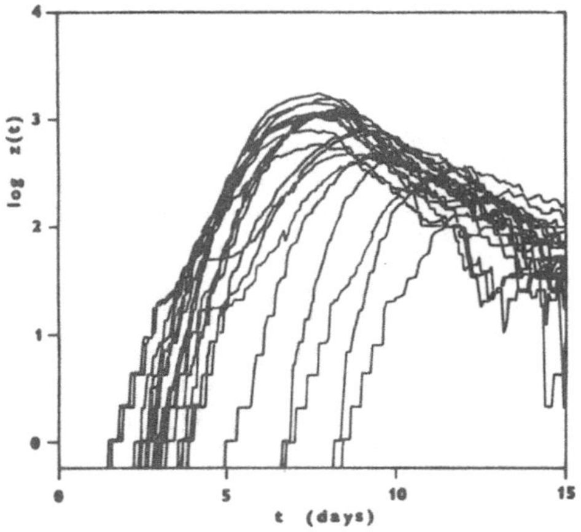

Figure 4.
20 clones of Z cells
(Jílek 1976)

IV. OTHER PROBLEMS

1. Maintenance of immunological capacity after immunization

Under normal steady state (in the absence of antigen), spontaneously dying immunocompetent cells are replaced by new cells arising by differentiation from stem cells and a relatively constant number of immunocompetent cells is maintained. Stem cells are capable of self-renewal (they proliferate extensively); however, this ability is gradually lost during the differentiation process consisting of several stages and, thus, the renewal of immunocompetent cells depends on the activity of less differentiated cells. (The situation is similar in other haemopoietic lines.)

Immunization represents the evoking from the resting steady state. Immunocompetent cells specific for the given antigen are stimulated and an increased demand of new immunocompetent cells is countered by an increased production of precursors. There is a certain delay between the termination of the main part of the immune response and the return to the original number of immunocompetent cells.

We used a branching process to model the control of replacement of immunocompetent cells (Klein, in preparation). The transition probabilities of this branching process are subject to the action of regulatory mechanism.

When included in the model of X → Y → Z differentiation, the model of renewal of immunocompetent cells is expected to influence the immune response to the long persisting antigen. Some authors (Bell 1970, Bruni et al. 1975, 1978, Dibrov et al. 1977, Mohler et al. 1978) assume a constant generation of new immunocompetent cells.

2. Some Marginal Problems

Attention was paid also to some questions that arose when the model of immune response was constructed. An attempt was made to employ a discrete birth-and-death process to the modelling of proliferation of Y cells (Jílek 1973b, 1974, 1975b), the number of memory cells after repeated immunizations was studied (Jílek 1971b), and a generalization of the assumption that one encounter with an antigen is sufficient to stimulate an X cell was made (Jílek 1971a).

V. DISCUSSION

In this paper a stochastic model of the process of differentiation and proliferation of B cells during a humoral immune response is described. Its plausibility has been supported earlier by comparison with experimental results (Jílek and Šterzl 1970, 1971).

The model differs from other models of the immune response dynamics especially in the assumption that two contacts with antigen are necessary for terminal differentiation of an immunocompetent cell. The first contact brings about a change into a proliferating cell. Out of these cells only those which receive the second stimulus differentiate into antibody producing cells, the rest stays as long-lived memory cells amenable to the second stimulus. Other authors do not attempt to describe the mechanism causing the differentiation of stimulated immunocompetent cells into two lines. In his model, Bell (1970, 1971) assumes that when the antigen is in excess, the symmetric division of proliferating cells prevails and when the amount of antigen decreases, the proliferating cells divide asymmetrically to produce antibody forming and memory cells, their ratio being constant. Bruni et al. (1975, 1978) and Mohler et al. (1978) assume that this ratio varies with the changing amount of the antigen present. Dibrov et al. (1977) do not specify the factor controlling the choice between differentiation of immunocompetent cells into memory or antibody forming cells, and Waltman and Butz (1977) do not distinguish between the two populations. Perelson (1978) assessed optimal strategies of switching between antibody forming and memory cell production used by the organism to ensure the most effective handling of a twofold antigenic assault.

A stochastic approach, used in this model, has its merits and shortcomings in comparison with the deterministic one. It can account for variations in the response while the solution of deterministic differential equations corresponds to the mean course of the immune response. On the other hand, the deterministic model is more flexible and its adaptation - if addition of some population or parameter is required - usually does not cause much difficulty in the numerical solution of a system of nonlinear differential equations. This is connected with the unavoidable adjustment of the assumptions of this model, especially in the regulation of the immune response. Although the antigen is an important regulating factor, the role of other participating factors (the presence of antigen-binding antibodies, the role of macrophages and T cells in the presentation of antigen to B cells, intercellular interactions with helper and suppressor T cells) must also be taken into account (see Richter 1975, 1978, Hoffmann 1975, 1978, Mohler et al. 1978).

REFERENCES

Bell, G.I. J. theor. Biol. 29, 191-232 (1970)

Bell, G.I. J. theor. Biol. 33, 339-378 (1971)

Bruni, C., Giovenco, M.A., Koch, G., and Strom, R. Math. Biosci. 27, 191-211 (1975)
Bruni, C., Giovenco, M.A., Koch, G., and Strom, R. In: Theoretical Immunology, Marcel Dekker, New York, pp. 379-414 (1978)
Dibrov, B.F., Livshits, M.A., and Volkenstein, M.V. J. theor. Biol. 65, 609-631 (1977)
Franzl, R.E., and Morello, J.A. In: Exchange Group No. 5, Scientific Memorandum No. 59 (1965)
Franzl, R.E. Infection and Immunity 6, 469-482 (1972)
Hoffmann, G.W. Eur.J.Immunol. 5, 638-647 (1975)
Hoffmann, G.W. In: Theoretical Immunology, Marcel Dekker, New York, pp. 571-602 (1978)
Jílek, M. Folia microbiol. 16, 12-23 (1971a)
Jílek, M. Folia microbiol. 16, 83-87 (1971b)
Jílek, M. In: Identification and System Parameter Estimation, North-Holland, Amsterdam, pp. 209-212 (1973a)
Jílek, M. Biometr. Z. 15, 485-494 (1973b)
Jílek, M. In: Progress in Statistics, North-Holland, Amsterdam, pp. 365-371 (1974)
Jílek, M. In: Simulation of Non-technical Dynamical Systems, Czech. Sci.-Techn.Soc., Prague, pp. 182-191 (1975a)
Jílek, M. Acta biotheor. 24, 108-119 (1975b)
Jílek, M. In: Natl.Conf.Cybernetics, Czech.Soc.Cybernetics, Prague, pp. 99-111 (1976)
Jílek, M., and Šterzl, J. In: Developmental Aspects of Antibody Formation and Structure, Academia, Prague, pp. 963-981 (1970)
Jílek, M., and Šterzl, J. In: Morphological and Functional Aspects of Immunity, Plenum Publishing Corp., New York, pp. 333-349 (1971)
Jílek, M. and Šterzl, J. In: Trans. 6th Prague Conf. on Information Theory, Statistical Decision Functions, Random Processes, Academia, Prague, pp. 275-289 (1973)
Jílek, M., and Ursínyová, Z. Folia microbiol. 15, 294-302 (1970a)
Jílek, M., and Ursínyová, Z. Folia microbiol. 15, 492-499 (1970b)
Mohler, R.R., Barton, C.F., and Hsu, C.-S. In: Theoretical Immunology, Marcel Dekker, New York, pp. 415-435 (1978)
Perelson, A.S., Mirmirani, M., and Oster, G.F. J. math. Biol. 5, 213-256 (1978)
Richter, P.H. Eur. J. Immunol. 5, 350-354 (1975)
Richter, P.H. In: Theoretical Immunology, Marcel Dekker, New York, pp. 539-569 (1978)
Šterzl, J. Cold Spring Harbor Symp. Quant. Biol. 32, 493-506 (1967)

A COMPUTATIONAL METHOD FOR HIERARCHICAL OPTIMIZATION OF COMPLEX SYSTEMS

A. Kalliauer

Österreichische
Elektrizitätswirtschafts-
Aktiengesellschaft
1010 Wien, AUSTRIA

1. Introduction:

Control problems which deal with the optimization of complex systems often result into problems of large-scale mathematical programming when they are discretisized. Special methods of compactification and decomposition have been developed for the solution of such problems (e. g. [4]). Decomposition methods require a special structure in the constraints. This is given by most of the usual control problems. Often nested decomposition can be applied. In this case a problem of "Hierarchical Optimization" arises. Such ideas were already described for example in [2] or [3]. Till now few is reported about the realisation of such concepts and methods for nested decomposition (as reported e.g. in [1]).

In our electricity supply company we have come across with such methods discretisizing the problem of optimal control of our hydro power system. This yields a structured problem - varying upon the given question - with multilevel structure of up to 4 levels with coupling variables. The structure is defined by subdividing the domain with respect to time and system. The problem arising has a nonlinear objective function and linear constraints.

For this type of problems we have developed an optimization algorithm which uses the concept of primal partitioning for several times and which is suitable for nested structured problems. We will concentrate on problems with nested structures with coupling variables. An example of such a constraint matrix is shown in Fig. 1. For our investigations let the constraint system be linear. Thus coupling constraints can be transformed into local constraints by adding coupling variables. The objective function may be nonlinear.

2. Development of the partitioning algorithm:

Without loss of generality we are going to develop the algorithm applied to an unstructured problem. We partition the total constraint matrix A_{tot} into two submatrices A and E and analogously the total vector x_{tot} into vectors x and y. Let the optimization problem be given by maximizing the nonlinear objective function $f(x_{tot}) = f(x,y)$ subject to the constraints $a^i_{tot}\, x_{tot} \leqslant b_i$ for $i \in I$, where $a^i_{tot} = [a^i, e^i]$ denotes the i-th row vector of matrix A_{tot} and where a^i belongs to A and e^i belongs to E.

Thus the optimization problem is given by

$$\left.\begin{aligned} &\max_{x_{tot}} f(x_{tot}) \\ &\text{subject to } A_{tot}\, x_{tot} \leqslant b \end{aligned}\right\} \quad (2.1)$$

or

$$\left.\begin{aligned} &\max_{x,y} f(x,y) \\ &\text{subject to } Ax + Ey \leqslant b \end{aligned}\right\} \quad (2.2)$$

We now like to define a subproblem to (2.2) as follows: optimize system (2.2) for x to a fixed vector y:

$$\left.\begin{aligned} &z(y) = \max_{x} f(x,y) \\ &\text{subject to } Ax \leqslant (b - Ey) \end{aligned}\right\} \quad (2.3)$$

This we call the "inner" optimization to (2.2).

We define as the "outer" problem to increase in the objective function with a change of the vector y. This is done in accordance with the results from the inner optimization. Considering a primal method the change of vector y implies a change of the inner vector x. In this way we keep the feasibility of the total variable vector. Thus the outer problem uses the variables to the whole problem (2.2). In terms of decomposition the outer problem can be called the master problem to the subproblem (2.3).

Let (x^o, y^o) be a feasible point to problem (2.2) and $\{[a^i, e^i],\ i \in I_a\}$ be a maximum set of linearly independent constraint vectors which belong to constraints active at point (x^o, y^o).

Considering now the inner problem at (x^o, y^o) the active constraints are the same as for problem (2.2). Thus we always can define a maximum set of linearly independent active constraint vectors $\{a^i, i \varepsilon I_a^A\}$ for the inner problem such that $I_a^A \subset I_a$.

To solve the inner problem we use the same primal iterative method. Let the feasible and usable direction vector to this problem be denoted by p_x^A. Let the column vector $p = [p_x, p_y]^T$ be a feasible and usable direction vector for the outer problem.

In order to be feasible p has to fulfil

$$[a^i, e^i]\ p \leq 0 \qquad \text{for all } i\ \varepsilon I_a.$$

Assuming positive Lagrangian multipliers for each of these active constraints we may keep to stay within the corresponding hyperplanes. Thus we can require that holds

$$[a^i, e^i]\ p = 0 \qquad \text{for all } i\ \varepsilon I_a. \tag{2.4}$$

These conditions can be divided into two sets according to the following subdivision of the vectors $[a^i, e^i]$ for $i\ \varepsilon I_a$:

(i) $\{[a^i, e^i]\ ,\ i\ \varepsilon I_a^A\}$..... vectors corresponding to the inner problem,
(ii) $\{[a^i, e^i]\ ,\ i\ \varepsilon I_a - I_a^A\}$.... vectors corresponding to the outer problem.

Either the a-component of a vector $[a^k, e^k]$ for $k\ \varepsilon I_a - I_a^A$ is linearly dependent on the vectors a^i, $i\ \varepsilon I_a^A$, or the vector equals the null vector. Thus the vectors $[a^k, e^k]$ for $k\ \varepsilon I_a - I_a^A$ can be transformed into vectors $[\tilde{a}^k, \tilde{e}^k]$ with $\tilde{a}^k = o$ by a linear combination of the vectors $[a^i, e^i]$ with $i\ \varepsilon\ I_a^A$. That gives

$$[\tilde{a}^k, \tilde{e}^k] = [o, \tilde{e}^k] = [a^k, e^k] - \sum_{i\ \varepsilon I_a^A} \bar{\gamma}_{ki}\ [a^i, e^i] \tag{2.5}$$

$$\text{for } k\ \varepsilon I_a - I_a^A.$$

Now we define A_a as the matrix of row vectors a^i for $i \varepsilon I_a$ and E_a as the matrix of the vectors e^i, $i \varepsilon I_a^A$. Furthermore A_e be the matrix of vectors a^i for $i \varepsilon I_a - I_a^A$ and E_e the matrix of vectors e^i for $i \varepsilon I_a - I_a^A$. We denote by $\tilde{E}_e$ the matrix of the transformed vectors $\tilde{e}_i$, $i \varepsilon I_a - I_a^A$ and by $\Gamma_e^A = (\bar{\gamma}_{ki})$ the corresponding coefficient matrix.

Then we write

$$\left.\begin{aligned} \tilde{E}_e &= E_e - \Gamma_e^A E_a \\ \text{where} \quad \Gamma_e^A &= A_e A_a^T (A_a A_a^T)^{-1} \\ \text{or} \quad \Gamma_e^A &= A_e A_a^{\dagger}, \end{aligned}\right\} \tag{2.6}$$

where we denote by $A_a^{\dagger} = A_a^T (A_a A_a^T)^{-1}$ the pseudoinverse matrix of A_a.

Instead of (2.4) we are now able to write the conditions for a feasible direction vector p as

$$a^i p_x + e^i p_y = 0 \text{ for } i \varepsilon I_a^A \tag{2.7}$$

and

$$\tilde{e}^i p_y = 0 \text{ for } i \varepsilon I_a - I_a^A, \tag{2.8}$$

or, taking matrix notation

$$A_a p_x + E_a p_y = o$$
$$\tilde{E}_e p_y = o.$$

The relations (2.7) define the interdependence between the p_x - and p_y - component of vector p. We now try to express p_x by p_y:

First let U^A denote the subspace of the active constraints a^i, $i \varepsilon I_a^A$. We know that each feasible direction vector p_x^A is a vector in the orthogonal subspace $O(U^A)$. Each vector of the given space can uniquely be determined by the sum of two vectors, one out of U^A and the other one out of $O(U^A)$. Applying this to vector p_x we write p_x as a sum of vector $(p_x - p_x^A) \varepsilon U^A$ and of vector $p_x^A \varepsilon O(U^A)$.

Thus

$$p_x = (p_x - p_x^A) + p_x^A. \tag{2.9}$$

Vector $(p_x - p_x^A)$ can be represented as a linear combination of basis vectors of U^A:

$$p_x - p_x^A = \sum_{L \in I_a^A} \beta_L \, (a^L)^T \tag{2.10}$$

with $\beta = (A_a \, A_a^T)^{-1} \, A_a \, p_x$, because of $A_a p_x^A = o$.

Using (2.7) we write

$$\beta = - (A_a \, A_a^T)^{-1} \, E_a \, p_y. \tag{2.11}$$

Combining (2.10) and (2.11) this yields

$$p_x - p_x^A = - A_a^T (A_a \, A_a^T)^{-1} \, E_a p_y$$

or
$$p_x = p_x^A - A_a^+ \, E_a \, p_y. \tag{2.12}$$

Doing so we get a feasible direction vector p beginning with a feasible vector p_y which satisfies (2.8) and computing p_x using (2.12).

Now we concentrate on the usability of vector p. Thus we require that

$$\nabla_x \, f(x^o,y^o) \, p_x + \nabla_y \, f(x^o,y^o) \, p_y > 0. \tag{2.13}$$

Writting $g_x = \nabla_x \, f(x^o,y^o)$ and $g_y = \nabla_y \, f(x^o,y^o)$ and using (2.12) we get

$$g_x p_x^A - g_x \, (A_a^+ \, E_a \, p_y) + g_y \, p_y > 0.$$

After the inner problem has been optimized, the first term equals zero because of $p_x^A = o$. If $p_x^A \neq o$, then $g_x \, p_x^A > 0$ according to the definition of p_x^A as usable direction vector. Tightening up (2.13) we can require that

$$(g_y - g_x \, A_a^+ \, E_a) \, p_y > 0. \tag{2.14}$$

Concerning the outer problem to search a direction vector which satisfies (2.8) and (2.14) is just the same as finding a usable and feasible direction vector p_y for a problem with gradient g_e defined by

$$g_e := g_y - g_x A_a^{+} E_a \tag{2.15a}$$

and with the active constraints be given by

$$\tilde{e}^i \; p_y = 0 \text{ for } i \in I_a - I_a^A. \tag{2.15b}$$

In a situation, where $p_y = o$ and $p_x^A = o$ (which implies $p_x = o$), we have to check by means of the Kuhn-Tucker conditions whether we have reached an optimum point. This is done by examining the sign of the Lagrangian multipliers. If there is at least one multiplier with - in our case - negativ sign, we have not yet reached on optimum solution for the given problem. In this case the corresponding active constraints are inactivated and further iteration steps can be done.
At the optimum we get $g_x = \alpha_a^A A_a$ and $g_e = \tilde{\alpha}_e \tilde{E}_e$.
Defining $\tilde{\alpha} := [\alpha_a^A, \tilde{\alpha}_e]$ and

$$\Gamma := \begin{bmatrix} 1_a & 0 \\ -\Gamma_e^A & 1_e \end{bmatrix},$$

(where 1_a is the identity matrix of order of vector α_a^A and 1_e the identity matrix of order of vector $\tilde{\alpha}_e$).

The vector of the Lagrangian multipliers α can be derived as

$$\alpha = \tilde{\alpha}\, \Gamma. \tag{2.16}$$

After the partitioning step just described we can show the structure of the problem as the following graph:

2nd level	S_2	y	outer problem (master problem)
1st level	S_1	x	inner problem (subproblem)

At the second partitioning step we partition the former outer problem itself, especially given by (2.15a and b), into a second inner and a new outer problem. Let the column vector y be partitioned as $[x_2, y_2]$.

After the second partitioning step the structure of problem (2.1) appears as follows:

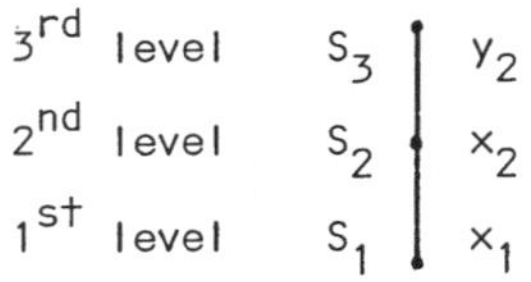

Now let the optimization problem be a structured two level problem with coupling vector y and with the local variable vectors corresponding to the subsystems given by x_k, $k=1,\ldots\ldots,r$. Now the inner optimization belongs to the variable vector $(x_1,\ldots\ldots,x_r)$.

$$\left.\begin{aligned} &\max f\,(x,y) = \max f\,(x_1,x_2,\ldots\ldots,x_r,y) \\ &\text{subject to} \\ &\quad A_k\, x_k + E_k\, y \leqslant b_k \text{ for } k=1,\ldots r \\ &\quad\quad E_{r+1}\, y \leqslant b_{r+1}. \end{aligned}\right\} \quad (2.17)$$

Applying the partitioning concept as described before the inner optimization can be splitted into r independent subproblems each of them concerning the variable vector x_k:

$$\left.\begin{aligned} &\max_{x_k} f(x_1,\ldots,x_k,\ldots\ldots,x_r,y) \\ &\text{subject to } A_k\, x_k \leqslant (b_k - E_k\, y) \end{aligned}\right\} \quad (2.18)$$

Thus we can draw the structure of our optimization problem (2.17) as the following tree:

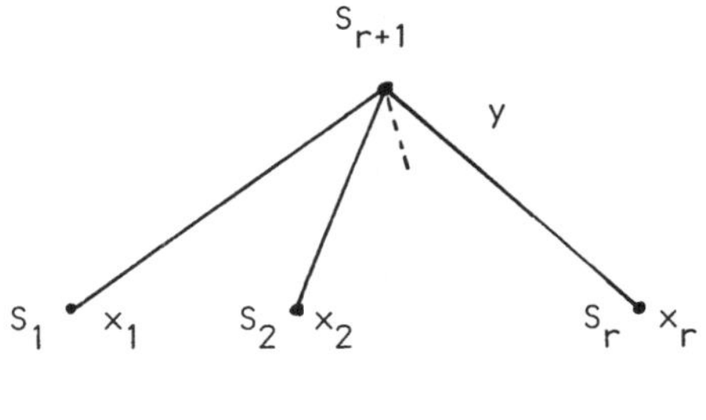

The same concept can be used for every problem of multilevel structure with coupling variables as for example shown in Fig. 2. For such general structures we need a method of partitioning which allows us a simple handling of the constraint matrix. This we are going to set up in the next chapter.

3. A special Gradient Projection Method (GPM) used as direction generator:

Up to now we have not defined the algorithm used as generator for a feasible and usable direction vector to the considered problems.

Remembering formulas (2.6) and (2.12) we already have to compute the pseudo-inverse matrix A_a^{+} as a working matrix. It would be advantageous, if this matrix is also applicable to the direction generator algorithm.

This can be realized using Rosen's GPM (see [7]). We can consider now the application of this method to our inner problem.

This is also suggested by Grigoriadis in [5]. In principle the Grigoriadis partitioning concept is the same, but the outer problem - there called "MEP" - is slightly differing.

Let g_x be the gradient vector. The projection matrix P_a is given by

$$P_a = 1_a - A_a^T (A_a A_a^T)^{-1} A_a = 1_a - A_a^{+} A_a \tag{3.1}$$

(where 1_a denotes the identity matrix of order of vector x).

The direction vector p_x^A is the projection vector:

$$p_x^A = P_a (g_x)^T. \tag{3.2}$$

On account of the uniformity of the algorithm we like to use the same direction generator for all levels considered. In particular the GPM used for the second level problem gives

$$p_y = P_e (g_e)^T \tag{3.3}$$

$$\text{where } P_e = 1_e - \tilde{E}_e^T (\tilde{E}_e \tilde{E}_e^T)^{-1} \tilde{E}_e.$$

Let us now try to improve the concept for updating of the working matrices when constraints are activated or inactivated during the iteration process. For this purpose we use at each level an orthogonal basis representation for the active constraints. This idea originally was developed in [6].

This enables us to write formulas (2.6), (2.12), (2.15a, b), (3.1) and (3.2) as shown below.

Let the orthogonal basis to the inner problem be given by $\{\tilde{a}^i,\ i \in I_a^A\}$ forming matrix $\tilde{A}_a$. The relationship between matrix A_a and matrix $\tilde{A}_a$ let be given by a coefficient matrix Γ_a.

This gives

$$\tilde{A}_a = \Gamma_a A_a. \tag{3.4}$$

The elements of Γ_a result from the orthogonalisation process. In the same way we transform the e-components yielding matrix $\tilde{E}_a$:

$$\tilde{E}_a = \Gamma_a E_a.$$

Computing p_x^A we use now matrix $\tilde{A}_a$ instead of A_a. Then (3.2) and (3.1) are replaced by the following formulas

$$\left.\begin{aligned} (p_x^A)^T &= g_x - \tilde{\alpha}^A \tilde{A}_a \\ \text{with } \tilde{\alpha}^A &= g_x \tilde{A}_a^T (\tilde{A}_a \tilde{A}_a^T)^{-1}. \end{aligned}\right\} \tag{3.5}$$

Matrix $(\tilde{A}_a \tilde{A}_a^T)^{-1}$ is a diagonal matrix because of the orthogonality of the vectors $\tilde{a}^i$. Therefore the components of $\tilde{\alpha}^A$ can be easily computed by

$$\tilde{\alpha}_i^A = \frac{\tilde{a}^i g_x^T}{|\tilde{a}^i|^2} \quad \text{for} \quad i \in I_a^A. \tag{3.6}$$

Thus the orthogonal basis $\{\tilde{a}^i,\ i \in I_a^A\}$ forms at the same time the working matrix for the algorithm.

The subdivision of the active constraints $[a^i, e^i]$, $i \in I_a$ into two disjunct subsets corresponding to the index sets I_a^A and $I_a - I_a^A$ is effected within the orthogonalization process applied to the a-components. Vectors which yield $\tilde{a}^i = o$ within this process are assigned to $I_a - I_a^A$.

We can write the resulting vectors in matrix notation as

$$[\tilde{A}_e, \tilde{E}_e] = [0, \tilde{E}_e] = [-\Gamma_e^A, 1_e] \begin{bmatrix} A_a & E_a \\ A_e & E_e \end{bmatrix} \tag{3.7}$$

The coefficient matrix results from the orthogonalization applied to the 1st level.

Let us now consider the relationship (2.12) between p_x and p_y. (2.12) is written as

$$\left.\begin{aligned} p_x &= p_x^A + \tilde{A}_a^T \tilde{\beta} \\ \text{with} \quad \tilde{\beta} &= -(\tilde{A}_a \tilde{A}_a^T)^{-1} \tilde{E}_a p_y. \end{aligned}\right\} \quad (3.8)$$

The elements of vector $\tilde{\beta}$ are easily computed by

$$\tilde{\beta}_i = \frac{\tilde{e}^i p_y}{|\tilde{a}^i|^2} \quad \text{for} \quad i \in I_a^A. \qquad (3.9)$$

Instead of (2.15a) we get

$$g_e = g_y - g_x \tilde{A}_a^T (\tilde{A}_a \tilde{A}_a^T)^{-1} \tilde{E}_a$$

and using (3.5)

$$g_e = g_y - \tilde{\alpha}^A \tilde{E}_a. \qquad (3.10)$$

Applying this method using an orthogonal basis as direction generator for each level we can succeed with the orthogonalization of the vectors $\tilde{e}^i$ after having transformed them by formula (3.7). Let this procedure yield the orthogonal vectors $\tilde{\tilde{e}}^i$, $i \in I_a - I_a^A$.

Thus we can write

$$\tilde{\tilde{E}}_e = \Gamma_e^E \tilde{E}_e. \qquad (3.11)$$

Combining this with formula (3.7) we get

$$\tilde{\tilde{E}}_e = \Gamma_e \begin{bmatrix} E_a \\ E_a \end{bmatrix} \text{with } \Gamma_e := \left[-\Gamma_e^E \Gamma_e^A, \Gamma_e^E \right].$$

Now the total working matrix for both the inner and the outer problem can be shown as the following matrix product:

$$\begin{bmatrix} \tilde{A}_a & \tilde{E}_a \\ 0 & \tilde{\tilde{E}}_e \end{bmatrix} = \begin{bmatrix} \Gamma_a & 0 \\ & \Gamma_e \end{bmatrix} \begin{bmatrix} A_a & E_a \\ A_e & E_e \end{bmatrix}. \qquad (3.12)$$

In the whole optimization process we need only the matrices

$$\begin{bmatrix} \tilde{A}_a & \tilde{E}_a \\ 0 & \tilde{\tilde{E}}_e \end{bmatrix} \quad \text{and} \quad \Gamma = \begin{bmatrix} \Gamma_a & 0 \\ & \Gamma_e \end{bmatrix} .$$

The advantage of the partitioning algorithm using the special GPM as direction generator as shown above consists in its uniform representation for each level of a nested structured problem.

The developments made up to now announce the idea of the following specialised concept of partitioning. This idea is the application of the partitioning concept column by column to a chain-like structure. (This concept can be accordingly generalized to tree-like systems.) Here the a^k -components are one element vectors. Thus after total partitioning over all columns one constraint vector at maximum is assigned to each level. This successive application of the partitioning concept makes the direction generating problem a trivial one constraint problem. No special algorithm is needed for this purpose. The main algorithm consists now only of simple transformations of vectors from one level to a subsequent one. We like to call this concept "successive partitioning".

The concept of the successive partitioning method can be used without generalizations for any tree-like structured problems with coupling variables. A greater number of coupling variables does not mean major difficulties. If the problem is not structured, the method behaves as an elimination process.

4. Realisational aspects:

The method shown so far is a primal iteration algorithm. An iteration step determines a feasible and usable direction vector to some subproblem. In principle such a step occurs as in case of a method for unstructured problems. The diagram in Fig. 3 shows the main parts of an iteration step.

Now let us consider an iteration step to some subproblem of our structured system. As example we take the matrix given in Fig. 1 and the structure shown in Fig. 2. When optimizing the subproblem S_4 we only need the rows of the working matrices corresponding to the following nodes: S_4 itself, the subnodes of S_4, that are

S_1, S_2, S_3 and all the master nodes of S_4 up to the vertex, that is in our case only S_9. The other parts of the working matrices are not needed within the procedures for determining vector p to subproblem S_4 and for updating. We can minimize the data access operations, if we make a sequence of local optimization steps within the subproblem S_4 and if it is possible to store the row vectors to the above mentioned nodes in core storage. In this way we can save computer time.

On the other hand considering one node the maximum increase of the objective function can be expected to be at the first iteration steps. In our case using the primal partitioning algorithm it is possible to perform only one or more steps for the subproblems. The algorithm does not require the suboptimizations of the subproblems. Thus it seems to be advantageous to take influence on the iteration process by choosing the right sequence of nodes, where the optimization is performed, and by limiting the iteration number per node.

When we realized the successive partitioning method, we have provided a special routine which enables us to control the iteration process. If no local iterations are allowed for all subproblems to a given node, the algorithm behaves as a compactification method for the subproblem corresponding to this node. Using an appropriate iteration control we can define our algorithm within the range of compactification and decomposition methods.

5. References:

[1] Beer, K.:
Lösung großer linearer Optimierungsaufgaben.
1977 - Berlin VDW

[2] Bensoussan, A., R. Glowinski, J.L. Lions:
Methode de decomposition appliquee au control optimal de systemes distribues.
5. IFIP Conference on Optimization Techniques, Rom, 1973

[3] Cambon, Ph., L. le Letty:
Applications of decomposition and multi-level techniques to the optimization of distributed parameter systems.
ibid.

[4] Geoffrion, A.M.:
Elements of Large-scale Mathematical Programming, Part I and II.
Management Sci., Vol. 16, No. 11 (1970)

[5] Grigoriadis, M.D.:
A Projective Method for structured Nonlinear Programs. Math. Programming (1971)

[6] Kalliauer, A.:
Ein Optimierungsalgorithmus für verschachtelt strukturierte Probleme. Forschungsbericht Nr. 10, Inst. f. OR, TU-WIEN, 1978

[7] Rosen, J.B.:
The Gradient Projection Method for Nonlinear Programming,
Part I: Linear Constraints.
SIAM 8 (1960)

[8] Winkler, C.:
Basis Factorization for Block Angular Linear Programs:
Unified Theory of Partitioning and Decomposition using the Simplex Method.
IIASA-Research Report 74-22 (1974)

Fig. 1: Example of a constraint matrix with a two level structure with coupling variables

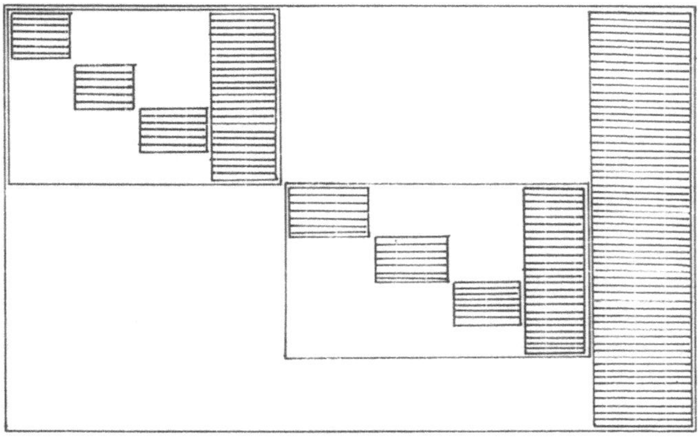

Fig. 2: Structure of matrix in Fig. 1

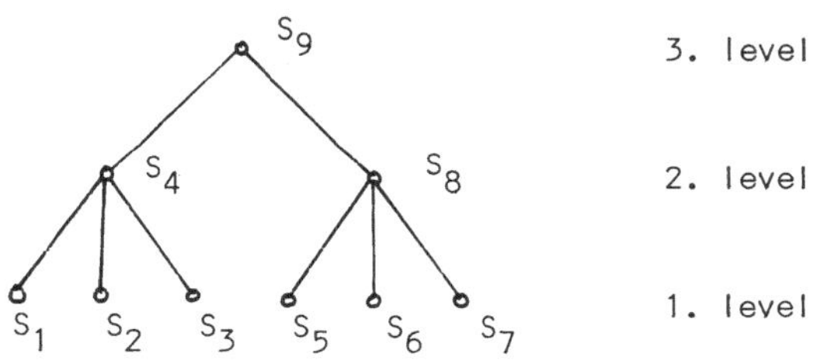

Fig. 3: Schematic Diagram of an iteration step

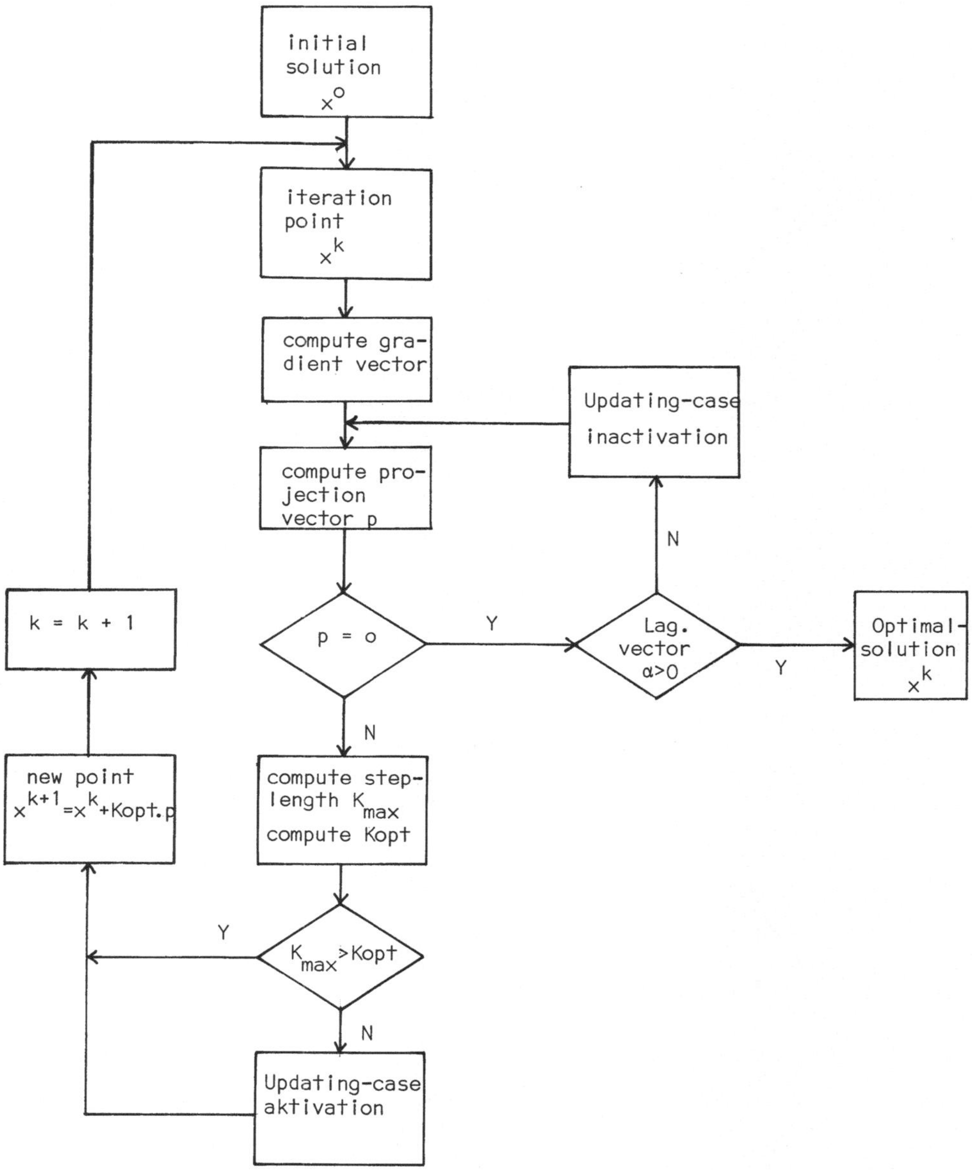

ON REGULARITY OF SOLUTIONS TO CONSTRAINED OPTIMAL CONTROL PROBLEMS FOR SYSTEMS WITH CONTROL APPEARING LINEARLY

Kazimierz Malanowski

Polish Academy of Sciences
Systems Research Institute
ul. Newelska 6, 01-447 Warszawa

INTRODUCTION

It is well known that the regularity of solutions to optimal control problems for continuous systems plays crucial role in investigating of the convergence of finite dimensional approximations to these problems. It referes to such methods of approximation as finite-difference or finite-element methods.

Not very much has been done in studying of the regularity of solutions to constrained optimal control problems. One has to mention here the pioneer paper by W.W.Hager [3] who propose a the general method of investigating regularity of solutions to such problems. This method is based on some results of convex programming stability with respect to a parameter. Using this idea Hager proved Lipschitz continuity of primal and dual optimal variables for convex optimal control problems with linear dynamics subject to convex constraints of both controls and state, providing that these constraints satisfy some regularity conditions.

In this paper there is given a straight-forward generalization of Hager's result to the class of systems described by nonlinear ordinary differential equation with the right-hand side being an affine function of control. This class contains in particular bilinear systems which play important role in modelling of bio-medical processes. Such a generalization is possible since for such a class of systems appropriate Lagrangian is a function convex with respect to control. It enables us to use the idea of Hager. The whole paper is devoted to problems of regularity. Only in the last section some results concerning the convergence of finite-difference approximations to considered optimal control problem are presented as an illustration of applications of the regularity results.

The full proves of all presented results can be found in [8,9].

The following notations will be used in the sequel:

R^n - n-dimensional Euclidean space with the usual inner product denoted by $\langle\cdot,\cdot\rangle$ and the norm $|\cdot|$.

$L^2(0,T)$ - Hilbert space of functions square integrable on (0,T) with the inner product denoted by $(\cdot,\cdot)$ and the norm $\|\cdot\|$.

AC(0,T) - space of absolutely continuous functions.

BV(0,T) - space of left continuous functions with bounded variations.

$$[\nu,y] = \int_0^T y(t)^T \, d\nu(t) \quad \text{- a Stieltjes integral.}$$

For the sake of simplification of the notation we write

$$\partial_x \varphi(x,y) \overset{\text{def}}{=} \frac{\partial \varphi(x,y)}{\partial x}, \quad \partial^2_{x,y} \varphi(x,y) \overset{\text{def}}{=} \frac{\partial^2 \varphi(x,y)}{\partial x \partial y}$$

If f(.) is a r-dimensional function of s-dimensional argument then $\partial_x f(x)$ denotes $r \times s$-dimensional matrix whose rows are gradients of components of f(.) evaluated at x.

We write $f(x) \leqslant 0$ if $f_i(x) \leqslant 0$ for $i = 1,2,\ldots,r$.

1. OPTIMAL CONTROL PROBLEM

We consider the following problem of optimal control

(P) find $$J^o = \inf \left\{ J(u,y) = \int_0^T \varphi(u(t),y(t))dt \right\} \tag{1.1}$$

subject to constraints

$$\dot{y}(t) = A(y(t)) + B(y(t))u(t), \tag{1.2}$$

$$y(0) = y^P, \tag{1.3}$$

$$u \in L^2(0,T),$$

$$\psi(u(t)) \leqslant 0 \quad \text{for almost all} \quad t \in [0,T], \tag{1.4}$$

$$\vartheta(y(t)) \leqslant 0 \quad \text{for all} \quad t \in [0,T], \tag{1.5}$$

where

$$y(t) \in R^n, \quad u(t) \in R^m; \quad \varphi: R^m \times R^n \to R^1, \; A: R^n \to R^n;$$
$$B: R^n \to R^{n \times m}, \quad \psi: R^m \to R^p; \quad \vartheta: R^n \to R^q.$$

Denote

$$D^c = \{ v \in R^n: \; \varphi(v) \leqslant 0 \}, \tag{1.6a}$$
$$D^s = \{ z \in R^m: \; \vartheta(z) \leqslant 0 \}. \tag{1.6b}$$

The following conditions are assumed to be satisfied

(i) $\varphi(\cdot,\cdot)$ is two times continuously differentiable with respect to both arguments and there exists $\alpha > 0$ such that

$$[v^T, z^T] \begin{bmatrix} \partial^2_{u,u}\varphi(u,y), \; \partial^2_{u,y}\varphi(u,y) \\ \partial^2_{y,u}\varphi(u,y), \; \partial^2_{y,y}\varphi(u,y) \end{bmatrix} \begin{bmatrix} v \\ z \end{bmatrix} \geqslant \alpha |v|^2 \tag{1.7}$$
$$\forall u \in D^c, \quad \forall y \in D^s, \quad \forall [v^T, z^T] \in R^{m+n}$$

(ii) $A(.)$ and $B(.)$ are continuously differentiable.

(iii) there exist constants $a, b < \infty$ such that

$$|\langle y, A(y) + B(y)u \rangle| \leqslant a|y|^2 + b|u|^2, \; \forall u \in D^c, \; \forall y \in D^s.$$

(iv) there exist $\hat{u}$ and $\hat{y}$ satisfying (1.2) through (1.5).

(v) $\psi(.)$ and $\vartheta(.)$ are two times continuously differentiable convex functions.

(vi) $\vartheta(y^p) < 0$.

(vii) the following constraints regularity condition is satisfied:

there exists $\delta > 0$ such that

$$\left| \left[-B^T(z)\, \partial_z \vartheta^T_{b(z)}(z),\ \partial_v \psi^T_{b(v)}(v) \right] w \right| \geq \delta |w|, \tag{1.8}$$
$$\forall w, \quad \forall v \in D^c, \quad \forall z \in D^s$$

where $\vartheta_{b(z)}$ and $\psi_{b(v)}$ denote components of constraints functions ϑ and ψ binding at z and v respectively.

Taking advantage of (i) through (v) and using the same argument as in [6] (Theorem 8, Chapter 4) we get

Lemma 1.1

There exists an optimal pair (u^o, y^o) *satisfying constraints* (1.2) *through* (1.5) *and such that*

$$J^o = J(u^o, y^o) \tag{1.9}$$

Let us define a Lagrangian

$$L_1 : L^2(0,T) \times AC(0,T) \times L^2(0,T) \times BV(0,T) \longrightarrow R^1$$

given by

$$L_1(u,y;p,\nu) \overset{def}{=} J(u,y) + (p, \dot{y} - A(y) - B(y)u) + [\nu, \vartheta(y)]. \tag{1.10}$$

Lemma 1.2.

Let u^o *and* $y^o = y(u^o)$ *be an optimal solution of* (P) *then there exist Lagrange multipliers* p^o *and* ν^o *- nondecreasing and satisfying* $\nu^o(T) = 0$ *- such that at* (u^o, y^o, p^o, ν^o) *Lagrangian* L_1 *assumes its stationary point with respect to* y *and its minimum with respect to control functions* u *satisfying* (1.4) *and the following complement-*

ary slackness condition holds

$$[\nu^o, \vartheta(y^o)] = 0. \tag{1.11}$$

Stationary condition implies that p^o satisfies the following adjoint equation

$$p^o(t) = \int_t^T \{[\partial_y A^T(y^o(t)) + u^{oT}(t)\,\partial_y B^T(y^o(t))]p(t) + - \partial_y \varphi(u^o(t), y^o(t))\}dt - \int_t^T \partial_y \vartheta^T(y^o(t))d\nu^o(t). \tag{1.12}$$

On the other hand since constraints (1.4) are of the local type condition of minimum of L_1 with respect to u reduces to

$$\varphi(u^o(t), y^o(t)) - \langle B^T(y^o(t))p^o(t), u^o(t)\rangle = = \min_{u \in D^c} \{\varphi(u, y^o(t)) - \langle B^T(y^o(t))p^o(t), u\rangle\} \quad \text{a.e. in } [0,T] \tag{1.13}$$

Proof

Condition (1.13) together with (1.12) and (1.11) constitute well known weak maximum principle [1]. The only non-trivial point is that the coefficient corresponding to function φ is different from zero (put equal to 1). It corresponds to the so called normality of Lagrange multipliers [4] for Problem (P). It is shown in [7] and [9] that constraints regularity condition (vii) implies such normality. q.e.d.

2. CONTINUITY OF OPTIMAL CONTROL AND OF LAGRANGE MULTIPLIERS

Following Hager [3] we introduce a new variable q given by

$$q(t) = \partial_y \vartheta^T(y^o(t))\, \nu^o(t) - p^o(t) \tag{2.1}$$

It is easy to check that q satisfies the following equation

$$\dot{q}(t) = -\left[\partial_y A^T(y^o(t)) + u_0^T(t)\,\partial_y B^T(y^o(t))\right]q(t) +$$

$$+ \left\{\left[\partial_y A^T(y^o(t)) + u_0^T(t)\,\partial_y B^T(y^o(t))\right]\partial_y \vartheta^T(y^o(t)) +\right.$$

$$\left.+ \partial^2_{y,y}\vartheta^T(y^o(t))\dot{y}^o(t)\right\}\nu^o(t) - \partial_y\varphi(u^o(t),y^o(t)), \qquad (2.2)$$

$$q(T) = 0, \qquad (2.2a)$$

hence it is an absolutely continuous function.

Condition (1.13) can be rewritten in terms of q as follows

$$c(u^o(t),z(t)) = \min_{u\in D^c} c(u,z(t)) \quad \text{a.e. in } [0,T] \qquad (2.3)$$

where

$$z^T(t) \overset{\text{def}}{=} (y^{oT}(t), q^T(t), \nu^{oT}(t)) \qquad (2.3a)$$

$$c(u,z(t)) \overset{\text{def}}{=} \varphi(u,y^o(t)) + \langle B^T(y^o(t))q(t) +$$

$$- B^T(y^o(t))\,\partial_y\vartheta^T(y^o(t))\,\nu^o(t),u\rangle. \qquad (2.3b)$$

Thus the values $u^o(t)$ of optimal control u^o are solutions to parametric, finite-dimensional convex programming problem (2.3). By (1.7) this problem has a unique solution.

Note that optimal control u^o must satisfy (2.3) almost everywhere on $(0,T)$. However, parameter $z(t)$ is well defined for all $t\in(0,T)$. Hence we can define u^o as the solution of (2.3) for every $t\in(0,T)$. The function u^o defined in this way on $(0,T)$ is still an optimal control. In the sequel by optimal control we shall understand such a function.

Using some stability results for convex programming problems as well as the fact that z is a function with bounded variation we obtain (cf. [3,8]) from (2.3)

Lemma 2.1

Optimal control u^o is continuous and uniformly bounded on $(0,T)$.

Let us denote by $\vartheta_{b(t)}(\cdot)$ and $\psi_{b(t)}(\cdot)$ subvectors of vector functions $\vartheta(\cdot)$ and $\psi(\cdot)$ respectively, containing all components of these vectors binding at the points $y^o(t)$ and $u^o(t)$, i.e.

$$\vartheta_{b(t)}(y^o(t)) = 0, \quad \psi_{b(t)}(u^o(t)) = 0 \tag{2.4}$$

It can be shown [8] that Lemma 2.1 yields

Corollary 2.2

For every $t \in (0,T)$

$$\partial_y \vartheta_{b(t)}(y^o(t))\left[A(y^o(t)) + B(y^o(t))u^o(t)\right] = 0\,. \tag{2.5}$$

Now we shall introduce Lagrange multiplier λ corresponding to constraints (1.4) in problem (P).

To this end first we introduce Lagrange multiplier $\lambda(t)$ corresponding to constraints $u \in D^c$ in finite-dimensional convex programming problem (2.3).

It follows from (vii) that for this problem Kuhn-Tucker conditions (cf. [2]) are satisfied. Hence there exists a vector $\lambda^o(t) \in R^p$ such that

$$\partial_u \varphi(u^o(t),y^o(t)) + B^T(y^o(t))(q(t) - \partial_y \vartheta^T(y^o(t))\, \nu^o(t)) +$$
$$+ \partial_u \psi^T(u^o(t))\, \lambda^o(t) = 0, \tag{2.6}$$
$$(\lambda^o(t), \psi(u^o(t))) = 0, \quad \lambda^o(t) \geqslant 0 \tag{2.6a}$$

or

$$\partial_u \varphi(u^o(t),y^o(t)) + B^T(y^o(t))(q(t) - \partial_y \vartheta^T(y^o(t)))\, \nu^o(t) +$$
$$+ \partial_u \psi^T_{b(t)}(u^o(t))\, \lambda^o_{b(t)}(t) = 0, \tag{2.7}$$

where $\lambda^o_{b(t)}$ is the subvector of λ^o corresponding to $\psi_{b(t)}(u^o(t))$.

It follows from (2.6a) that the vector $\lambda^o_{n(t)}(t)$ containing all components of $\lambda^o(t)$ not belonging to $\lambda^o_{b(t)}(t)$ is a zero vector:

$$\lambda^o_{n(t)}(t) = 0. \tag{2.8a}$$

Condition (vii) and (2.8a) imply that $\lambda^o(t)$ is defined uniquely.

By (vii) there exists left inverse $\mathcal{H}(t)$ of the matrix

$$\partial_u \psi^T_{b(t)}(u^o(t)).$$

Hence from (2.6) we get

$$\lambda^o_{b(t)}(t) = -\mathcal{H}(t)\left[\partial_u \varphi(u^o(t),y^o(t))+ \right.$$
$$\left. + B^T(y^o(t))(q(t) - \partial_y \vartheta^T(y^o(t))\,\nu^o(t))\right]. \tag{2.8b}$$

Let us consider the function λ^o defined on (0,T) by (2.8).It can be easily checked that $\lambda^o_{n(t)}$ is a measurable function [5].Similarly $\mathcal{H}(t)$ can be chosen in such a way that $\mathcal{H}$ is measurable and, due to (vii), uniformly bounded on (0,T). Therefore λ^o is a measurable and uniformly bounded function on (0,T).

Now if we introduce a new Lagrangian

$$L:\ L^2(0,T)\times AC(0,T)\times L^2(0,T)\times BV(0,T)\times L^2(0,T) \longrightarrow R^1$$

given by

$$L(u,y;p,\nu,\lambda) \overset{\text{def}}{=} L_1(u,y;p,\nu)+(\lambda,\psi(u)) \tag{2.9}$$

then (2.6) implies that $L(u,y^o;p^o,\nu^o,\lambda^o)$ assumes its minimum with respect to all control functions $u\in L^2(0,T)$ at u^o.

<u>Lemma 2.3</u>

<u>Functions λ^o and ν^o are continuous and uniformly bounded on</u> (0,T).

Proof

Suppose that λ^o is discontinuous at $\sigma \in (0,T)$. Since λ^o is uniformly bounded there exist a sequence $\{t_k\} \subset (0,T)$ and a number μ such that

$$t_k \xrightarrow[k \to \infty]{} \sigma^+, \quad \lambda(t_k) \xrightarrow[k \to \infty]{} \mu, \quad \mu \neq \lambda(\sigma). \qquad (2.10)$$

From condition of optimality (2.6) we have

$$\partial_u \varphi(u^o(t_k), y^o(t_k)) + B^T(y^o(t_k))(q(t_k) - \partial_y \vartheta^T(y^o(t_k))\, \nu^o(t_k)) +$$
$$+ \partial_u \psi^T(u^o(t_k))\, \lambda^o(t_k) = 0.$$

Using Lemma 2.1 we get for $k \to \infty$

$$\partial_u \varphi(u^o(\sigma), y^o(\sigma)) + B^T(y^o(\sigma))(q(\sigma) - \partial_y \vartheta^T(y^o(\sigma))\, \nu^o(\sigma^+)) +$$
$$+ \partial_u \psi^T(u^o(\sigma))\mu = 0. \qquad (2.11)$$

Combining condition of optimality at σ and (2.11) we obtain

$$-B^T(y^o(\sigma))\partial_y \vartheta^T(y^o(\sigma))(\nu^o(\sigma^+) - \nu^o(\sigma)) +$$
$$+ \partial_u \psi^T(u^o(\sigma))(\mu - \lambda^o(\sigma)) = 0. \qquad (2.12)$$

By (1.11) $\nu_j^o(\sigma^+) \neq \nu_j^o(\sigma)$ only if $\vartheta_j(y^o(\sigma))=0$, similarly by continuity of u^o and condition (2.6a) $\mu_j \neq \lambda_j(\sigma) \neq 0$ only if $\psi_j(u^o(\sigma))$ $= 0$. Hence we can rewrite (2.12) in the form

$$-B^T(y^o(\sigma))\partial_y \vartheta^T_{b(\sigma)}(y^o(\sigma))(\nu^o_{b(\sigma)}(\sigma^+) +$$
$$- \nu^o_{b(\sigma)}(\sigma)) + \partial_u \psi_{b(\sigma)}(u^o(\sigma))(\mu_{b(\sigma)} - \lambda^o_{b(\sigma)}(\sigma)) = 0 \qquad (2.13)$$

where $\mu_{b(\sigma)}$ denotes the subvector of μ corresponding to $\vartheta_{b(\sigma)}(y^o(\sigma))$.

Assumption (vii) together with (2.13) give

$$\nu^o_{b(\sigma)}(\sigma^+) - \nu^o_{b(\sigma)}(\sigma) = 0, \quad \mu_{b(\sigma)} - \lambda^o_{b(\sigma)} = 0.$$

Since ν^o is left continuous and the above argument can be repeated for left limit at σ Lemma 2.3 holds. q.e.d.

Now let us consider the end point $t = 0$. It is obvious that without destroing optimality we can put

$$u^o(0) = \lim_{t \to 0} u^o(t) \tag{2.14a}$$

and

$$\lambda^o(0) = \lim_{t \to 0} \lambda^o(t). \tag{2.14b}$$

On the other hand from (vi) and (1.11) it follows that

$$\nu^o(0) = \lim_{t \to 0} \nu^o(t). \tag{2.14c}$$

From (2.14) Lemma 2.4 and Lemma 2.3 as well as from (1.2) and (2.2) we get

Corollary 2.4

Functions u^o, λ^o, ν^o, $\dot{y}^o$ and $\dot{q}$ are continuous and uniformly bounded on $[0,T)$.

3. LIPSCHITZ CONTINUITY OF OPTIMAL CONTROL AND OF LAGRANGE MULTIPLIERS

Now we are in the position to prove the following basic result of the paper:

Theorem 3.1

Optimal control u^o and optimal Lagrange multipliers ν^o and λ^o are Lipschitz continuous functions on $[0,T)$.

Proof

For simplification of notations let us put

$$x^T \overset{def}{=} (u^{oT}, \nu^{oT}, \lambda^{oT}) \tag{3.1}$$

Since we already proved that x^T is a continuous function than by Hager's result [3] (cf. also [8]) in the proof of Lipschitz continuity we can restrict ourself to so called compatible pairs. By compatible pair we understand any pair of points $\tau, \sigma \in (0,T)$ such that at τ and σ the same constraints (both of control and state) are binding while in the whole segment $[\tau,\sigma]$ none other constraints are binding. Strictly speaking to prove that x is Lipschitz continuous with the Lipschitz constant c it is enough to show [8] that if (τ,σ) is any compatible pair such that

$$|\sigma-\tau| \leq \varepsilon \tag{3.2}$$

then

$$|x(\sigma) - x(\tau)| \leq c\,|\sigma-\tau| \tag{3.3}$$

where $\varepsilon > 0$ is a fixed positive number independent of τ and σ.

Let (τ,σ) be a compatible pair. To simplify notation let us write

$$b(\tau) = b(\sigma) = b; \quad n(\tau) = n(\sigma) = n.$$

At the points $t = \tau$ and $t = \sigma$ the equations (2.6),(2.5) and (2.6a) can be rewritten in the form of the following system

$$\partial_u \varphi^T(u^o(t),y^o(t)) - B^T(y^o(t))\,\partial_y \vartheta_b^T(y^o(t))\,\nu_b^o(t) +$$
$$+ \partial_u \psi_b^T(u^o(t))\,\lambda_b^o(t) + B^T(y^o(t))q(t) - B^T(y^o(t))\,\partial_y \vartheta_n^T(y^o(t))\,\nu_n^o(t) = 0, \tag{3.4a}$$

$$-\partial_y \vartheta_b(y^o(t))B(y^o(t))u^o(t) - \partial_y \vartheta_b(y^o(t))A(y^o(t)) = 0, \tag{3.4b}$$

$$\psi_b(u^o(t)) = 0. \tag{3.4c}$$

For the sake of simplification of notations let us put

$$w^T(t) \overset{def}{=} (u^{oT}(t),\nu_b^{oT}(t),\lambda_b^{oT}(t)); \quad k^T(t) \overset{def}{=} (y^{oT}(t),q^T(t),\nu_n^{oT}(t)) \tag{3.5}$$

and rewrite (3.4) as

$$\Phi(w(t),k(t)) = 0 \tag{3.6}$$

In this equation we shall treat $w(t)$ as an unknown and $k(t)$ as a parameter.

We introduce an auxiliary equation depending on scalar parameter s putting

$$\bar{\Phi}(\bar{w},s) \overset{\text{def}}{=} \Phi(\bar{w},(1-s)k(\tau)+sk(\sigma)) = 0, \quad 0 \leqslant s \leqslant 1 . \tag{3.7}$$

It is obvious that for s = 0 and s = 1 equation (3.7) reduces to (3.6) for τ and σ respectively.

From (3.7) we shall find $\bar{w}$ as a function of the parameter s using implicite function theorem.

To do that we must find $\partial_w \bar{\Phi}(w,s)$. From (3.4) we have

$$\partial_w \bar{\Phi}(\bar{w},s) =$$

$$= \begin{bmatrix} \partial^2_{u,u}\varphi(\bar{u},\bar{y}^o(s))+\partial^2_{u,u}\psi^T_b(\bar{u})\bar{\lambda}_B, & -B^T(\bar{y}^o(s))\partial_y\vartheta^T_b(\bar{y}^o(s)), & \partial_u\psi^T_b(\bar{u}) \\ -\partial_y\vartheta_b(\bar{y}^o(s))B(\bar{y}^o(s)), & 0, & 0 \\ \partial_u\psi_b(\bar{u}), & 0, & 0 \end{bmatrix} \tag{3.8}$$

where $\bar{k}(s) = (1 - s)k(\tau) + sk(\sigma)$.

Using (i), (v) and (vii) it can be shown [8] that if

$$|y^o(\sigma) - \overset{o}{y}(\tau)| \leqslant \xi \tag{3.9}$$

and

$$|\bar{w} - w(\tau)| \leqslant \zeta, \tag{3.10}$$

where $\xi > 0$ and $\zeta > 0$ are some constants independent of τ, then $\partial_w \bar{\Phi}(\bar{w},s)$ is nonsingular and has a uniformly bounded inverse

$$|[\partial_w \bar{\Phi}(\bar{w}, s)]^{-1} \leqslant c_0. \tag{3.11}$$

Hence by implicite function theorem there exists a continuous function $\bar{w}(s)$ such that

$$\bar{\Phi}(\bar{w}(s), s) = 0.$$

On the other hand from (3.4) we get

$$\partial_s \Phi(\bar{w},s) = \begin{bmatrix} r_{1,1}(s) + r_{1,2}(s)\,\bar{\nu}_b \\ r_{2,4}(s) + r_{2,2}(s)\,\bar{u} \\ 0 \end{bmatrix} \tag{3.12}$$

where

$$r_{1,1}(s) = \partial^2_{u,y}\varphi(\bar{u},\bar{y}(s))(y(\sigma)-y(\tau)) + \partial_s B^T(\bar{y}(s))[\bar{q}(s)+$$
$$-\partial_y \vartheta_n^T(\bar{y}(s))\bar{\nu}_n^o(s)] + B^T(\bar{y}(s))[(q(\sigma)-q(\tau)) - \partial^2_{y,s}\vartheta_n^T(\bar{y}(s))\,\bar{\nu}_n^o(s)], \tag{3.12a}$$

$$r_{1,2}(s) = -\partial_s B^T(\bar{y}(s))\partial_y \vartheta_b^T(\bar{y}(s)) - B^T(\bar{y}(s))\partial^2_{y,s}\vartheta_b^T(\bar{y}(s)), \tag{3.12b}$$

$$r_{2,1}(s) = -\partial^2_{y,s}\vartheta_b(\bar{y}(s))A(\bar{y}(s)) - \partial_y \vartheta_b(\bar{y}(s))\,\partial_s A(\bar{y}(s)), \tag{3.12c}$$

$$r_{2,2}(s) = -\partial^2_{y,s}\vartheta_b(\bar{y}(s))B(\bar{y}(s)) - \partial_y \vartheta_b(\bar{y}(s))\,\partial_s B(\bar{y}(s)). \tag{3.12d}$$

From implicite function theorem it follows that

$$\partial_s \bar{w}(s) = -[\partial_w \bar{\Phi}(\bar{w},s)]^{-1}\,[\partial_s \bar{\Phi}(\bar{w},s)].$$

Hence

$$|\partial_s \bar{w}(s)| \leq |[\partial_w \bar{\Phi}(\bar{w},s)]^{-1}|\,|\partial_s \bar{\Phi}(\bar{w},s)|. \tag{3.13}$$

Taking into account (i),(ii) and (v) as well as Lemma 2.3 and definition of $\bar{k}(s)$ we obtain from (3.12):

$$|\partial_s \bar{\Phi}(\bar{w},s)| \leq c_1(|y^o(\sigma)-y^o(\tau)| + |q(\sigma)-q(\tau)|) + c_2|\bar{w}(s)|\,|y^o(\sigma)-y^o(\tau)|. \tag{3.14}$$

It follows from (3.11),(3.13) and (3.14) that if conditions (3.9) and (3.10) hold then

$$|\partial_s \bar{w}(s)| \leq c_3(|y^o(\sigma)-y^o(\tau)| + |q(\sigma)-q(\tau)|) + c_4|\bar{w}(s)|\,|y^o(\sigma)-y^o(\tau)|.$$

Hence taking into account that by definition (3.5) $\bar{w}(0)=w(\tau)$ is uniformly bounded on (0,T) and using Gronwall's inequality we get

$$|\partial_s \bar{w}(s)| \leq c_5(|y^o(\sigma)-y^o(\tau)| + |q(\sigma)-q(\tau)|) \tag{3.15}$$

where c_s does not depend on τ and σ .

From definition $\bar{w}(s)$ and from (3.15) we have

$$|w(\sigma)-w(\tau)| = |\bar{w}(1)-\bar{w}(0)| \leqslant \int_0^1 |\partial_s \bar{w}(s)|\, ds \leqslant$$
$$\leqslant c_5(|y^o(\sigma)-y^o(\tau)|+|q(\sigma)-q(\tau)|). \tag{3.16}$$

Since by Corollary 2.4 functions y^o and q are Lipschitz continuous, then from (3.16) we eventually get

$$|w(\sigma) - w(\tau)| \leqslant c\,|\sigma-\tau| \tag{3.17}$$

where c does not depend on τ and σ.

It follows from the definition of w, that to prove Lipschitz continuity of $x^T = (u^{oT}, \nu^{oT}, \lambda^{oT})$ it remains to show that ν_n^o and λ_n^o are Lipschitz continuous. But from the definition of compatible pair and from (1.11) and (2.8a) we immediately have

$$\nu_n^o(\sigma) - \nu_n^o(\tau) = 0, \quad \lambda_n^o(\sigma) = \lambda_n^o(\tau) = 0$$

what completes the proof of (3.3).

Still the assumptions (3.9) and (3.10) have to be verified.

It follows from (3.16) that (3.10) will be satisfied if

$$|y^o(\sigma)-y^o(\tau)| + |q(\sigma) - q(\tau)| \leqslant \frac{\xi}{c_5}. \tag{3.18}$$

But from Lipschitz continuity of y^o and q it follows that there exists a constant $\varepsilon > 0$ such that if (3.2) holds then also (3.9) and (3.18) are satisfied.

In this way it was shown that (3.3) is satisfied for every compatible pair satisfying (3.2). q.e.d.

Using the state equation (1.2) and the adjoint equation (2.2) as well as (2.1) we obtain

<u>Corollary 3.2</u>

<u>Functions $\dot{y}^o$ and p^o are Lipschitz continuous on $[0,T)$.</u>

4. ESTIMATION OF THE CONVERGENCE OF FINITE-DIFFERENCE APPROXIMATIONS TO PROBLEM (P)

In this section as an example of application of obtained regularity, there will be presented some results concerning the rate of convergence of finite-difference approximations to Problem (P). The proof of this results can be found in [9] and in this proof Theorem 3.1 plays the crucial role.

First let us introduce a finite-difference approximation to (P). To this end let us divide the interval $[0,T)$ into $M(\tau)$ subintervals $[i\tau,(i+1)\tau)$, $i = 0,1,\dots M(\tau)-1$. The length τ of subintervals will be treated as the parameter of approximation destinated to tend to zero.

Let $\chi_i(t)$ denote the characteristic function of $[i\tau,(i+1)\tau)$.

By $E_\tau(0,T)$ we denote the space of step functions of the form

$$z_\tau(t) = \sum_{i=1}^{M(\tau)-1} z_\tau(i\tau)\,\chi_i(t) \tag{4.1}$$

where $z_\tau(i\tau)$ belong to some finite-dimensional space.

In a similar way we introduce the space $E_\tau(0,T+\tau)$ putting $M(\tau)$ instead of $M(\tau)-1$ in (4.1).

On the space $E_\tau(0,T+\tau)$ we introduce the operator of finite differences given by

$$\nabla z_\tau(t) \overset{\text{def}}{=} \frac{1}{\tau}\sum_{i=0}^{M(\tau)-1} \left[z_\tau((i+1)\tau)-z_\tau(i\tau)\right]\chi_i(t). \tag{4.2}$$

A finite dimensional problem of optimization (P_τ) approximating (P) is defined as follows

(P_τ) <u>find</u>

$$J^o = \inf \left\{ J(u_\tau, y_\tau) = \int_0^T \varphi(u_\tau(t), y_\tau(t))dt \right\} \tag{4.3}$$

subject to constraints

$$u_\tau \in E_\tau(0,T), \quad y_\tau \in E_\tau(0,T+\tau) \tag{4.4}$$

$$\nabla y_\tau(t) = A(y_\tau(t)) + B(y_\tau(t))u_\tau(t) \tag{4.5}$$

$$y_\tau(0) = y^p$$

$$\psi(u_\tau(t)) \leqslant 0 \quad \text{for all} \quad t \in [0,T) \tag{4.6}$$

$$\vartheta(y_\tau(t)) \leqslant 0 \quad \text{for all} \quad t \in [0,T]\,. \tag{4.7}$$

Using Theorem 3.1 as well as some results of Slater's type condition following from assumption (vii) the following estimation of the convergence rate of J^o_τ to J^o as a function of τ was obtained in [9]:

Theorem 4.1

If assumptions (i) *through* (vii) *are satisfied then*

$$|J^o - J^o_\tau| \leqslant O(\tau)\,. \tag{4.8}$$

REFERENCES

1. Girsanov I.V.: *Lektsi po matematicheskoy teorii ekstremalnykh zazadach*. Izd. Moskovskogo Universiteta. Moskva 1970.
2. Hadley G.: *Nonlinear and dynamic programming*. Addisson Wesley. Reading Ma. 1964.
3. Hager W.W.: Lipschitz continuity for constrained processes (to appear).
4. Kurcyusz S.: On existence and nonexistence of Lagrange multipliers in Banach spaces. *JOTA* *20*, 81-110, 1976.

5. Lasiecka I., Malanowski K.: On regularity of solutions to convex optimal control problems with control constraints for parabolic systems. Control a. Cybernetics 6, no. 3/4, 57-74 (1977).

6. Lee E.B., Markus L.: Foundations of optimal control theory. J. Wiley a. Sons. New York 1967.

7. Malanowski K.: On normality of Lagrange multipliers for state and control constrained optimal control problems. Bull.Acad. Pol.Sci. Ser. tech. 26, 529-535 (1978).

8. Malanowski K.: On regularity of solutions to optimal control problems for systems with control appearing linearly. Arch. Autom. i Telemech. 23, 227-242 (1978).

9. Malanowski K.: On convergence of finite difference approximations to optimal control problems for systems with control appearing linearly (to appear in Arch. Autom. i Telemech.).

BILINEAR CONTROL STRUCTURES IN IMMUNOLOGY†

R.R. Mohler

Department of Computing and Control≠
Imperial College of Science and Technology
180 Queens Gate
London SW7 2BZ
United Kingdom

ABSTRACT

The structure of various immune processes are studied. While the overall feedback systems are seen to be highly nonlinear, distributed and stochastic, the basic open-loop processes in many cases are bilinear. This opens the door for the application of numerous new theories and methodologies which are being derived or have been developed for bilinear systems BLS and so-called affine systems which are a subclass of BLS.

INTRODUCTION

Mathematical models of the humoral immune system were introduced by Huge and Cole (1966) with a very preliminary model. Bell (1970, 1971, 1974) and Bell and DeLisi (1974) presented more comprehensive immunological models. Jilek and Sterzl (1971) and Jilek (1974) developed probability models of different cell types undergoing repeated antigen constants. Poisson processes and Monte Carlo simulations were used here. More recently, Bruni, Giovenco, Koch and Strom (1975, 1978) and Mohler, Barton and Hsu (1976,1977, 1978) have developed comprehensive mathematical models and joint experimentation which in the latter case includes cell-mediated as well as humoral actions. And, the analysis here follows that of Mohler,Barton and Hsu (1978). A slightly different approach to humoral immune structure from that studied here is presented by Bruni, et al (1975). In other immune-system analyses Waltman (1978), Gatica and Waltman (1979) and Merrill (1977) analyze the threshold phenomenon of antibody-antigen interactions and limit cycles. The latter analysis includes an interesting geometrical intrepretation via catastrophe theory.

The recent book edited by Bell,Perelson and Pimbley (1978) surveys the state of immunological modeling in about 1977. DeLisi (1976) presents a good survey of experimental analyses related to verification of these models. Jerne (1974), Hoffmann(1975, 1979) and Richter (1975) introduce an interesting network topology for the immune system. This provides a general approach to activation and suppres-

---

† Research reported here is supported by US National Science Foundation Grant No. ENG-74-15530-A01

≠ On leave from Oregon State Uni., Corvallis, OR97331,USA, until June 1979.

sion of different classes of antibody through an idiotype-anti-idiotype network. But, care must be followed in blindly applying superposition to the network as is done normally.

Perhaps the recent work of Marchuk (1977) and his associates (see these proceedings) best shows the real motivation for all this work by their application to virus disease control.

BASIC B-CELL MODEL

Following the work of Mohler, Barton and Hsu (1978), the B-cell model has the following form:

$$\frac{d\underline{x}}{dt} = A\underline{x} + (\underline{b}_1 u_1 + \underline{b}_2 u_2) x_1 + \underline{b}_3 u_3 x_3 + \underline{c}_4 v_1 + \underline{c}_5 v_2 \tag{1}$$

where state vector, $\underline{x} \epsilon R^5$, and control vector, $\underline{u} \epsilon R^5$, have components:
x_1, population density of immunocompetent cells (ICC), which are sensitized lymphocyte cells with particular surface receptors for antigen according to k. They may differentiate into plasma cells or may differentiate into memory cells. The latter, which may further divide, and enter the pool of immunocompetent cells. x_2, population density of plasma cells, which are non-reproducing offspring of stimulated immunocompetent cells. x_3, population density of "antibody sites" which are free. x_4, population density of immune complex which individually includes antibody site and antigen. x_5, antigen concentration which triggers the response mechanism. u_1, ICC multiplication. u_2, plasma cell multiplication. u_3, binding multiplication. v_1, stem-cell source rate (from bone marrow). v_2, inoculation rate of antigen. k is specificity or association constant.

$$A = \begin{bmatrix} -1/\tau_1 & 0 & 0 & 0 & 0 \\ 0 & -1/\tau_2 & 0 & 0 & 0 \\ \alpha'' & \alpha' & -1/\tau_3 & c_k & 0 \\ 0 & 0 & 0 & -(c_k+1/\tau_4) & 0 \\ 0 & 0 & 0 & Nc_k & -1/\tau_5 \end{bmatrix}$$

$$\underline{b}_1 = \begin{bmatrix} \alpha \\ 0 \\ \cdot \\ \cdot \\ 0 \end{bmatrix}, \underline{b}_2 = \begin{bmatrix} 0 \\ 2\alpha \\ 0 \\ 0 \\ 0 \end{bmatrix}, \underline{b}_3 = \begin{bmatrix} 0 \\ 0 \\ -c_k \\ c_k \\ -Nc_k \end{bmatrix}, \underline{c}_4 = \begin{bmatrix} 1 \\ 0 \\ \cdot \\ \cdot \\ 0 \end{bmatrix}, \underline{c}_5 = \begin{bmatrix} 0 \\ \cdot \\ \cdot \\ 0 \\ 1 \end{bmatrix} .$$

The immune parameters are defined as follows:
α is birthrate constant of stimulated ICC; c_k is dissociation rate; N is a weighting constant (to account for total number of association constants); α' is plasma-cell antibody production rate; α'' is ICC antibody production; τ_1 is the mean lifetime of immunocompetent cells; and $\tau_2, \tau_3, \tau_4, \tau_5$ are the appropriate life times.

The additive control v_1 is independent of the multiplicative control variables, (u_1, u_2, u_3) and is significant in immunotherapy, since certain cancers (e.g., leukemia) have been treated by "injection" of healthy bone marrow cells into the blood stream of the patient. The model can be used to further analyze the effectiveness of such treatment by consideration of deterioration of the infected process or organs as an added component to the model. Though this source of stem cells, v_1 is distributed according to affinity k (usually to be Poisson or Gaussian), an average k seems representative in most practical cases.

The other additive control, rate of inoculation of antigen v_2, is independent of the other control variables and has significance in disease prevention (or more correctly, disease control) by vaccination as well as in simulation of experiments whereby certain animal strains may be inoculated with antigens of particular characteristics.

While $u_3 = kx_5$, u_1 and u_2 are dependent stochastic parameters which may be approximated by

$$u_1 = p_s(1-2p_d),$$

$$u_2 = p_s p_d.$$

Here the probability that antigen stimulates the cell of affinity k is derived as follows.

$p_s = \sum_n p^n(kx_5)$, where $p^n(.)$ represents the binomial distribution. Then due to the large m, number of receptors (about 10^5), it is readily seen that

$$p_s \simeq \begin{cases} 1, \text{ on some sensitive interval } \gamma_1 \leq kx_5 \leq \gamma_2 \\ 0, \text{ elsewhere.} \end{cases} \tag{2}$$

The probability that ICC with n occupied receptors, differentiates into a plasma cell is about n/m or

$$p_d \simeq \frac{kx_5}{1+kx_5}. \tag{3}$$

The binding multiplicative control is:

$$u_3 = kx_5.$$

It is evident that the multiplicative control variables (u_1, u_2, u_3) are not independent and are generated as nonlinear functions of state. In many cases, this closed-loop control system could be approximated by a multilinear control system which may be decomposed into a feedback combination of bilinear systems, or directly approximated by BLS.

From our analysis of the simulation of this model, it is shown that the system is quite insensitive with respect to variations in dissociation constant over some broad range, but not zero. This is convenient, since its exact value is not accurately established. On the other hand, the system is quite sensitive with respect to net association constant due to its effect on probability of cell stimulation. Also, immune-complex lifetime τ_4, immunocompetent-cell generation rate α, and antibody generation rate α' and lifetime τ_3 are somewhat critical parameters in the model.

By a series of steps including this sensitivity information, the above fifth-order B-cell model can be approximated by a series of time lags shown below where gains or time constants may be adjusted according to the output, free antigen concentration. In Figure 1,

$$\alpha_1' \simeq \begin{cases} -\alpha, & \alpha_1 \le kx_5 \le \alpha_2 \\ 1/\tau_1, & \text{elsewhere} \end{cases}, \quad s = \frac{d}{dt}(\cdot),$$

$$\alpha_2 \simeq 2\alpha kx_5, \ \alpha_3 \simeq c_k kx_5, \ \alpha_3' \simeq \alpha_3 + 1/\tau_3,$$

$$\alpha_4' \simeq c_k + 1/\tau_4, \ c_{45} \simeq \text{appropriate constant.}$$

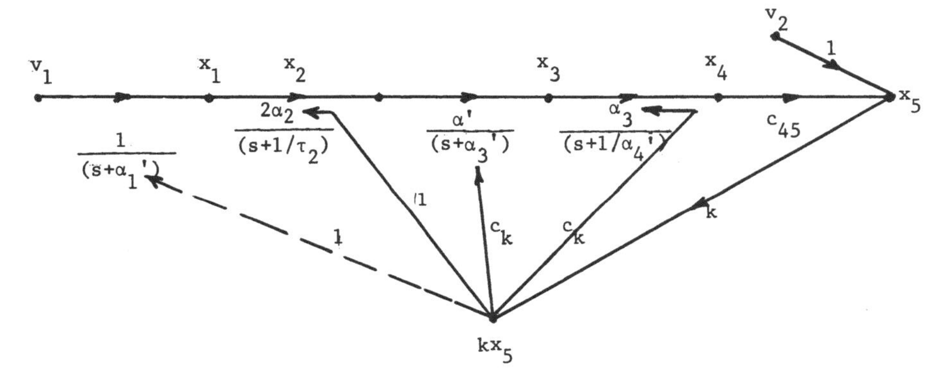

Figure 1 Approximating Signal Flow Diagram

Further approximation yields a somewhat more manageable but more crude second-order time-variant model of the form:

$$\frac{dx_1'}{dt} = 2\alpha k u_1' y - x_1'/\tau_2, \tag{5}$$

$$\frac{dx_2'}{dt} = c_k k y x_2' + \alpha' x_1' \tag{6}$$

and the output:

$$y = v_2 - c_{35}x_2' \tag{7}$$

Here, $x_1' = x_2$, $x_2' = x_3$, $y = x_5$ and $u_1' = x_1$ with x_1 assumed independent of x_5.

It is seen that the control structure is not at all of a traditional engineering nature. The parametric control structure and role of BLS is quite apparent.

Typical parameter values are given in Table 1. Here $\beta_k = v_1$ is constant and v is the volume of injected antigen solution.

α	5.780×10^{-2}	hr^{-1}
β_k	1.627×10^{-22}	mole/hr
τ_1	7140	hr
τ_2	71	hr
k	10^6	$mole^{-1}$
c_k	3.5×10^3	hr^{-1}
α'	10^8	hr^{-1}
α''	0.2×10^7	hr^{-1}
τ_3	200	hr
τ_4	50	hr
τ_h	100	hr
Q	3.33×10^{-8}	mole
V	0.2	liter
T_u	1000	hr
τ_u	100	hr
γ_1	0.01	
γ_2	0.10	
$x_1(0)$	0.8262×10^{-20}	mole/liter

TABLE 1

Parameters Used in the Simulation

It is shown by Mohler and Hsu (1979) that the above model of the humoral immune system (1) has a unique positive-invariant solution which is asymptotically stable for positive constant input v_1, v_2.

T CELL KINETICS

It is commonly accepted in immunology that various classes of T cells (thymus derived lymphocytes) respond to most antigens to cooperate in their overall control with B cells. While some T cells (T helper cells, called T-plasma cells here) do emit an antibody like substance (called T-Ab here), they do not bind an appreciable amount of antigen in the sense that B cell Ig does. There is experimental evidence to the existence of T suppressors (deactivators) as well as T helpers (activators). Again, the process is similar to that given for B cells with bilinear structure in the open-loop cellular and chemical processes.

However, the probability of stimulation and differentiation may be changed to approximate the effect of T-cell control as follows with added T-complex density, $x_{4T}(t,k,k')$.

$$p_s = \begin{cases} 1 & \gamma_1' \le kx_5 + \gamma_T \dfrac{x_{4T}}{x_3} \le \gamma_2',\ x_3 > 0 \\ 0 & \text{elsewhere} \end{cases} \tag{8}$$

and

$$p_d = \begin{cases} \dfrac{kx_5 + \gamma x_{4T}/x_3}{1+kx_5+\gamma_T(x_{4T}/x_3)} & x_{4T} \le x_{4M},\ x_3 > 0 \\ \dfrac{kx_5+\gamma_T[(2x_{4M}-x_{4T})/x_3]}{1+kx_5+\gamma_T(x_{4T}/x_3)} & x_{4T} \ge x_{4M},\ x_3 > 0 \end{cases} \tag{9}$$

k' is affinity of T-Ab for antigen.

γ_1', γ_2' are limits of distribution of p_s.

γ_T is a T-B coupling coefficient to account for T-complexes lost to bridging, and for increased stimulation of B-cell activity relative to that from simple antigen binding.

x_{4M} represents the finite limitation of binding that can be made with available macrophage surface.

Similar to the B-cell subsystem, the rate of generation of T-ICC population of density $x_{1T}(t,k')$ is

$$\frac{dx_{1T}}{dt} = \alpha_T p_{sT}(1-2p_{dT})x_{1T} - \frac{x_{1T}}{\tau_{1T}} + \beta_{k'} \tag{10}$$

where τ_{1T} is T-ICC mean lifetime, α_T is T-ICC birth-rate constant, $\beta_{k'}$ is the rate of generation of new T-ICC (from bone marrow through thymus),

$$p_{sT} = \begin{cases} 1 & \gamma_{1T} \le k'x \le \gamma_{2T} \\ 0 & \text{elsewhere} \end{cases} \tag{11}$$

$$p_{dT} = \frac{k'x}{1+k'x} \tag{12}$$

and γ_{1T} and γ_{2T} are limits of distribution.

Then it is assumed that T-plasma cells of population density $x_{2T}(t,k')$, T-Ab of molecular density $x_{3T}(t,k')$ and T-complexes of density $x_{4T}(t,k,k')$ are generated similarly to the way that B clones are generated, so that

$$\frac{dx_{2T}}{dt} = 2\alpha_T p_{sT} p_{dT} x_{1T} - \frac{x_{2T}}{\tau_{2T}} \tag{13}$$

$$\frac{dx_{3T}}{dt} = \alpha'_T x_{2T} - \frac{x_{3T}}{\tau_{3T}} + c_{k'} x_{4T} - k' c_{k'} x_5 x_{3T} + \alpha''_T x_{1T} \tag{14}$$

$$\frac{dx_{4T}}{dt} = k' \, c_{k'} x_5 x_{3T} - c_{k'} x_{4T} - \frac{x_{4T}}{\tau_{4T}} . \tag{15}$$

The above T-B model accounts for stimulation (T-helper) by the effect on p_s and p_d, and for inhibition by the T-antibody-antigen capping of B-Antibody. But more active suppression can be introduced by addition of a term $-\gamma_{sB} x_1 x_{2T}$ to the $\dot{x}_1$ equation. Here γ_{sB} is a suppression coupling coefficient. However, it should be noted that this is only a crude approximation which is being refined as more evidence becomes available as to the nature of this mechanism.

Other complexities to the model can be appropriately introduced as more experimental data becomes available to justify such additions. E.g., the above equations can be written for each individual k and k' which would result in an extremely large system order, or just a few average values might be used. Indeed, experimental data sometimes suggests two relevant peaks in the distribution. Switch over of antibody generators can be introduced by merely introducing a switch in certain parameters with some appropriate switch or delay time as discussed by Mohler, Barton and Hsu (1976).

It should be noted that the system involves relatively fast and relatively slow modes of response creating a very stiff process with interesting numerical integration problems. Conventional Runge-Kutta integration algorithms were not found effective unless instant equilibrium in association and dissociation are assumed for the immune complex. An adaptive Gear (1971) algorithm, however, was found to be very effective.

IMMUNE REGULATION AND IDENTIFICATION

The above T-cell model assumes that the macrophages are available in sufficient quantity and neglects their dynamics. This could represent an added "mode" in the overall system with its stem cells derived from bone marrow as for B and T cells. But again it adds no new structure. Even the addition of complement adds more parametrically controlled (nearly BLS) modes of response. Complement includes approximately nine protein-enzyme stages in cascade. According to the chemical law of mass action, each stage generates an increased concentration of enzyme cascaded in such a manner that bilinear amplification leads to a deterioration of a target cells membrane permeability and its lysis. The first stage of the cascade is originally triggered by an antigen-antibody complex.

Antigen replication, though not difficult to include by an added birth term in the antigen equation, is neglected above. Also, the destruction of antigen by T-cytotoxic cells and macrophages as well as by complement is not analyzed by the above model. However, these additions do not change the structure but only add more variables to the already complex system. In summary, the system may be envisioned as a combination of BLS (humoral process, cell-mediated process, complement and antigen replication) all coupled together (with the first three controlling the latter by parametric feedback controls).

Parameter identification of the humoral system from joint experiments conducted in Oregon through cooperation with University of Rome is presented by Bruni, et al in these proceedings. Suitability of a Walsh function method for this problem is studied by Mohler and Rao (1976). The latter study shows that Walsh functions, as a consequence of their convenient group properties, are effective for identification of certain BLS and certain immune functions. This work, however, is far from complete.

CONCLUSION

BLS structures are seen to evolve naturally for B-cell kinetics, T-cell kinetics, generation of antibody and immune complexes. Their closed-loop processes are more highly nonlinear, and, also may be modeled by stochastic differential equations. High-zone and low-zone tolerance may be expressed through the probability of stimulation terms given by (2) or (8) and (11).

It is indicated that such further complications as antibody switch over, complement, and macrophage dynamics and antigen killers do not alter the BLS structure which is basic throughout the model. Of course, other approximations such as to the chemical law of mass action are available but it is quite apparent that linear system is not at all adequate.

Consequently, newly developed methodology for BLS may be quite useful for immune system analysis; the reader who may be uninitiated in BLS is referred to Mohler (1973). E.g., Lie algebraic techniques, which were developed by Brockett (1975) are used by Mohler and Hsu (1979) to analysze reachable zones for a simplified B-cell model. Compartmental BLS techniques and identifiability conditions, which were derived by Mohler (1974) and Smith and Mohler (1976), can be used to model and to estimate parameters for compartmental immune processes which include such compartmental organs as bone marrow, spleen, thymus, lymph, lymph nodes, gut-associated tissue and blood. Such a B-cell models is introduced by Mohler and Barton (1977).

In terms of practical considerations in studying the immune process dynamics, stiffness due to broad differences in response times for cellular division and differentiation, and chemical reactions, while most studies assume instant chemical equilibrium, present studies do not substantiate this. Indeed, a great deal of effort has gone into efficient numerical techniques for computer simulation. Some preliminary comparison of the basic model with experimental data is presented by Mohler, Barton and Hsu (1978).

REFERENCES

Bell, G.I., "Mathematical Model of Clonal Selection and Antibody Production", J. Theor. Biol. 29, 191-232, (1970).

Bell, G.I., "Mathematical Model of Clonal Selection and Antibody Production, II", J. Theor. Biol. 33, 339-378, (1971).

Bell, G.I., "Model for the Binding of Multivalent Antigen to Cell", Nature 248, 430-431, (1974).

Bell, G.I., and DeLisi, C.P., "Antigen Binding to Receptors on Immunocompetent Cells. I. Simple Models and Interpretation of Experiments", Cell Immunol. 10, 415-431, (1974).

Bell, G.I., Perelson, A.S., and Pimbley, G.H., Jnr., Eds. Theoretical Immunology, Marcel Dekker, New York, (1978).

Brockett, R.W.,"On the Reachable Set for Bilinear Systems", in Variable Structure Systems (Ruberti and Mohler, Eds.),Springer-Verlag, New York, 54-63, (1975).

Bruni, C., Giovenco, M., Koch, G., and Strom, R., "The Immune Response as a Variable Structure System", in Variable Structure Systems with Application to Economics and Biology, (A. Ruberti and R.R. Mohler, Eds.), Springer-Verlag, New York, (1975).

Bruni, C., Giovenco, M., Koch, G. and Strom, R., "Modeling of the Immune Response: A System Approach", in Bell, G.I., et al, Eds., 379-414, (1978).

DeLisi, C., Antigen-Antibody Interactions, Springer-Verlag, New York, (1976).

Gatica, S.A. and Waltman, P., "A threshold Model of Antigen - Antibody Dynamics", Proc. IEEE Decision and Control Conf., San Diego, (1979).

Gear, C.W., "DIFSUB for Solution of Ordinary Differential Equations", Comm. ACM 14, 185-190, (1971).

Hege, J.S., and Cole, L.J., "Mathematical Model Relating Circulating Antibody and Antibody Forming Cells", J. Immunol. 94, 34-40, (1966).

Hoffmann, G.W., "A Theory of Regulation and Self-Nonself Discrimination in an Immune Network", Eur. J. Immunol. 5, 50-75, (1975).

Hoffmann, G.W., "A Theory of Regulation and Self-Nonself Discrimination in an Immune Network", Proc. IEEE Decision and Control Conf., San Diego, (1979).

Jerne, N.K., "Clonal Selection in a Lymphocyte Network", in Cellular Selection and Regulation in the Immune Response (Edelman, Ed.), Raven, New York, (1974).

Jilek, M. and Sterzl , J., "Modeling of Immune Response", in Morphological and Functional Aspects of Immunity, Plenum, New York, 333-349, (1971).

Jilek, M., "Immune Response and Its Stochastic Theory", Proc. IFAC Sympos. Sys. Identif., the Hague, 209-212, (1973).

Merril, S.J., "A Geometric Study of B-Cell Stimulation and Humoral Response", Proc. Int'l Conf. Nonlin. Sys. and Applic., Academic Press,(1977).

Marchuk, G.F., "An Immunological Model of Virus and Bacterial Diseases", Proc. 8th IFIP Conf., Optimization Techniques, Würzburg , Springer-Verlag, New York,(1977).

Mohler, R.R., "Bilinear Control Processes, Academic Press, New York, (1973).

Mohler, R.R., "Biological Modeling with Variable Compartmental Structure", IEEE Trans.Auto. Control AC19, 922-926, (1974).

Mohler, R.R., Barton, C.F. and Hsu, C.S., "System Theoretic Models in Immunology", Proc. 1975 IFIP Optimization Conf., Nice, Springer-Verlag, New York, (1976).

Mohler, R.R., Barton, C.F., "Compartmental Control Model of the Immune Process", Proc. 8th IFIP Conf. Optimization Tech., Würzburg , Springer-Verlag, New York, (1977).

Mohler, R.R., Barton, C.F., and Hsu, C.S., "T and B-Cell Models in the Immune System", in Bell, G.I., et al, Eds., 415-436, (1978).

Mohler, R.R., and Hsu, C.S., "T-B Cell Control Processes in Immunology", IEEE Decision and Control Conf., San Diego, (1979).

Mohler, R.R., and Rao, V.K., "BLS Identification by Orthogonal Functions with Application to Immunology", Proc. IEEE Decision and Control Conf., Clearwater Beach, Florida, (1976).

Richter, P.H., "A Network Theory of the Immune Response", Eur. J. Immunol. 5, 350-354, (1975).

Smith, W.D., and Mohler, R.R., "Necessary and Sufficient Conditions in the Tracer Determination Compartmental System Order", J. Theoret. Biol. 57, 1-21,(1976).

Waltman, P., "A Threshold Model of Antigen-Stimulated Antibody Production", in G.I. Bell, et al, Eds., 437-454, (1978).

MATHEMATICAL MODEL OF A DISEASE AND SOME RESULTS OF NUMERICAL EXPERIMENTS

A.L.Asachenkov, G.I.Marchuk

Computing Center, Novosibirsk, USSR

1. Introduction

The present paper deals with a mathematical model of the infectious disease describing the interaction between reproducing pathogenic antigen, on the one hand, (viruses, bacteria) and the immune system, on the other hand.

Let us assume that:

a) stem cells differentiate only into T-,B-lymphocytes and macrophages. Their concentration in a healthy organism is constant and determines constant levels of all the components of the immune process;

b) antigen and lymphocyte react together to form "free" and "bound" complexes. A "free" complex is a combination of antigen with the receptors torn off the lymphocyte. "Free" B-complexes and part of "free" T-complexes stimulate the bone marrow. The other part of the "free" T-complexes, having coated macrophages, take part in stimulation of B-cells. A bounded complex is a combination of antigen with the receptors fixed on the lymphocyte. After a division it differentiates into plasma cells, which are killer and antibody producers;

c) T-lymphocyte-killers are responsible only for destruction of antigen and T-lymphocytes-helpers take part in stimulation of B-cells though it is known that T-killers can fulfil both functions. Such an assumption is justifiable, since, first, it simplifies equations of a model, second, the T-killer is unlikely to fulfil both functions simultaneously;

d) plasma B-cells produce antibodies of only two types, i.e. I_gM and I_gG; switchover is performed by threshold means as specific T- and B-lymphocytes accumulate;

e) all the considered populations of cells and molecules are homogeneous;

f) damage of any organ disturbs normal functioning of the whole organism that results in failure of the immune response;

g) the organism has enough of the enzymes and non-specific immunity factors of different kind participating in the reaction described above.

The model under consideration is a system of nonlinear differential equations of sufficiently high order. Investigation of the model is performed by numerical methods. Differential equations are approximated by the fourth order Runge-Kutta scheme with a constant step. A specific feature of the models of this kind is the presence of a large number of parameters whose value is difficult to estimate from the available statistical data. The parameters were so chosen that the main characteristics (the mean lifetime of various cell populations, antibody production rate, etc.) have plausible values. It is important to note that we did not try to have calculation results coincide exactly with some concrete statistical data. Since the high order of equations and a large number of parameters generate a great variety of trajectories, it allows one to select such values of the parameters that they satisfactorily approximate any statistical curve. Therefore, the main problem we set in calculations was to reproduce the principal qualitative features characteristic of the immune system.

2. Model equations

Introduce the following notation

x_1 - the number of T-cells-helpers
x_2 - the number of B-cells
x_3 - the number of I-cells-killers
x_4 - the number of IgM antibodies
x_5 - the number of IgG antibodies
x_6 - the number of T-plasma cells
x_7 - the number of B-plasma cells
x_8 - the number of macrophages
x_9 - the number of stem cells
x_{10} - the number of antigen
x_{11} - relative characteristics of the rate of damage of an organ.

Constant levels of all the components of the process are marked by the asterisk.

Antigen

Let antigen multiply at some constant rate β. The decrease of the antigen is due to its neutralization by antibodies and killer-cells and due to formation of "free" and "bound" complexes.

For simplicity, the cell and molecule reaction to the antigen is assumed to occur according to the biomolecular reaction laws. We arrive at

$$\frac{dx_{10}}{dt} = (\beta - R)x_{10}, \qquad (1)$$

where

$$R = \sum_{i=1}^{5} \delta_i x_i, \qquad \delta_i \geq 0 \qquad (i = \overline{1,5}).$$

Stem cells

It is known that daily approximately two per cent of undifferentiated cells of the bone marrow, which are lymphocyte and macrophage precursors, enter the circulation, but this figure becomes tens of times as high with the injection of antigen. We suppose that the signal to intensified reproduction of the stem cells is recognition by the immune system of "free" T- and B-complexes whose concentrations on the interval dt is proportional to the product of the antigen and the lymphocyte

$$\frac{dx_9}{dt} = (\gamma_1 x_1 + \gamma_2 x_2)x_{10} - \gamma_3(x_9 - x_9^*). \qquad (2)$$

T-lymphocyte-helpers

The indifferentiated precursors (the bone marrow cells), on passing through the thymus, become specific T-lymphocytes. The increase of T-lymphocytes is likely to be proportional to the number of stem cells, whereas the decrease, on the one hand, is due to the natural death $\frac{1}{\tau_T} x_1\, dt$ where τ_T is the mean lifetime of T-lymphocyte, on the other, it is due to the formation of "free" and "bound" complexes.
Finally,

$$\frac{dx_1}{dt} = \rho_T x_9 - \gamma_4 x_1 x_{10} - \frac{1}{\tau_T} x_1. \qquad (3)$$

B-lymphocytes

The equation of the B-lymphocytes dynamics is derived in a similar way. It should be noted that "bound" B-complexes can form either directly after reaction to the antigen or by means of T-cells and macrophages. Hence, we have the following equation

$$\frac{dx_2}{dt} = \rho_B x_9 - \gamma_5 x_1 x_2 x_8 x_{10} - \gamma_6 x_2 x_{10} - \frac{1}{\tau_B} x_2. \qquad (4)$$

Plasma cells

From (3) and (4) one can see that a healthy organism $(x_{10} \equiv 0)$ has constant levels of T- and B-cells, equal to $x_1^* = \rho_T \tau_T x_9^*$, and $x_2^* = \rho_B \tau_B x_9^*$, which cause constant levels of T- and B-plasmacytes x_6^* and x_7^*. The balance equation is of the form

$$\frac{dx_6}{dt} = P_T(t - \tau_1) - \frac{1}{\tau_{CT}} (x_6 - x_6^*), \qquad (5)$$

$$\frac{dx_7}{dt} = P_B(t - \tau_2) - \frac{1}{\tau_{CB}} (x_7 - x_7^*), \qquad (6)$$

where

$$P_T(t) = p_1 x_1 x_{10},$$

$$P_B(t) = p_2 x_2 x_{10} + p_3 x_1 x_2 x_8 x_{10}.$$

Antibodies, killer cells

Balance equations for antibodies and T-killers are of the same structure

$$\frac{dx_3}{dt} = \rho_K x_6 - \gamma_9 x_3 x_{10} - \frac{1}{\tau_K} x_3, \tag{7}$$

$$\frac{dx_4}{dt} = \rho_M x_7 - \gamma_7 x_4 x_{10} - \frac{1}{\tau_M} x_4, \tag{8}$$

$$\frac{dx_5}{dt} = \rho_G x_7 - \gamma_8 x_5 x_{10} - \frac{1}{\tau_G} x_5, \tag{9}$$

where

$$\rho_M = \begin{cases} \rho_M & \text{if } x_1 x_2 \le (TB)^* \\ 0 & \text{otherwise} \end{cases} \tag{10}$$

$$\rho_G = \begin{cases} 0 & \text{if } x_1 x_2 \le (TB)^* \\ \rho_G & \text{if } x_1 x_2 > (TB)^* \end{cases} \tag{11}$$

where $(TB)^*$ is the product of concentration of T- and B-lymphocytes at which switchover of I_gM-I_gG antibody synthesis can occur.

Macrophages

In the model described here, the notion of macrophages includes a class of cells that are able to participate in specific immune reactions and utilize immune reaction products and obsolete components of the immune system. Introduce the following values

$$S = \sum_{i=1}^{8} \nu_i (x_i - x_i^*), \quad \nu_i \ge 0 \quad (i = \overline{1, 8}) \tag{12}$$

$$Q = \sum_{i=1}^{5} n_i x_i x_{10}, \quad n_i \ge 0 \quad (i = \overline{1, 5}) \tag{13}$$

where ν_i and n_i are coefficients characterizing the number of macrophages wanted for utilization of the immune reaction products. Taking into account the fact that part of the macrophages participate in stimulation of B-cells and adding the term describing natural death of the macrophages, we arrive at

$$\frac{dx_8}{dt} = \rho_\Lambda x_9 - (Q + S)x_8 - \gamma_{10} x_1 x_2 x_8 x_{10} - \frac{1}{\tau_\Lambda} x_8. \tag{14}$$

As in the earlier models [1,2] we add an equation for relative characteristics of the organ's damage. Then the system of model equations becomes

$$\frac{dx_1}{dt} = \rho_T\, \xi(m)x_9 - \gamma_4 x_1 x_{10} - \frac{1}{\tau_T} x_1,$$

$$\frac{dx_2}{dt} = \rho_B\, \xi(m)x_9 - \gamma_5 x_1 x_2 x_8 x_{10} - \gamma_6 x_2 x_{10} - \frac{1}{\tau_B} x_2,$$

$$\frac{dx_3}{dt} = \rho_K x_6 - \gamma_9 x_3 x_{10} - \frac{1}{\tau_K} x_3$$

$$\frac{dx_4}{dt} = \rho_M x_7 - \gamma_7 x_4 x_{10} - \frac{1}{\tau_M} x_4$$

$$\frac{dx_5}{dt} = \rho_G\, x_7 - \gamma_8 x_5 x_{10} - \frac{1}{\tau_G} x_5$$

$$\frac{dx_6}{dt} = P_T(t - \tau_1) - \frac{1}{\tau_{CT}} (x_6 - x_6^*)$$

$$P_T(t) = p_1 x_1 x_{10} \qquad (15)$$

$$\frac{dx_7}{dt} = P_B(t - \tau_2) - \frac{1}{\tau_{CB}} (x_7 - x_7^*)$$

$$P_B(t) = p_2 x_2 x_{10} + p_3 x_1 x_2 x_8 x_{10}$$

$$\frac{dx_8}{dt} = \rho_\Lambda\, \xi(m)x_9 - (Q + S)x_8 - \gamma_{10} x_1 x_2 x_8 x_{10} - \frac{1}{\tau_\Lambda} x_8$$

$$S = \sum_{i=1}^{8} \nu_i\, (x_i - x_i^*), \qquad \nu_i \geq 0 \qquad (i = \overline{1,\ 8})$$

$$Q = x_{10} \sum_{i=1}^{5} n_i x_i, \qquad n_i \geq 0 \qquad (i = \overline{1,\ 5})$$

$$\frac{dx_9}{dt} = (\gamma_1 x_1 + \gamma_2 x_2)x_{10} - \gamma_3 (x_9 - x_9^*)$$

$$\frac{dx_{10}}{dt} = (\beta - R)x_{10}$$

$$R = \sum_{i=1}^{5} \delta_i x_i, \qquad \delta_i \geq 0 \qquad (i = \overline{1,5})$$

$$\frac{dx_{11}}{dt} = \sigma x_{10} - \mu_m x_{11}.$$

The initial data are

$$x_i = x_i^o \quad (i = 1,10), \qquad x_{11} = 0, \qquad t = 0.$$

3. Immunodeficiency modelling

The structure of the model makes it possible to reject some blocks and build simple models. This is very valuable for the analysis of the solution adequacy to real processes taking place in the organism, since by switching off one or another block we can model immunodeficiencies. Figure 1 illustrates the stages of formation of T- and B-immune systems. Possible genetic blocks including one or another part of the immune response system are shown in the figure. The presence of a genetic defect at the stem cell level leads to complete anaplasia of both hemopoietic and lymphoid systems. Such a regime can be achieved in our model setting $x_9^o = x_9 = 0$. In this case concentrations of T-, B-cells, macrophages, plasma cells and antibodies at $t \to \infty$ are $x_i(t) \to x_i^*$ $(i = \overline{1, 9})$ and that of antigen is $x_{10}(t) \to e^{\beta t}$.

Normal functioning of B-system of cells with complete blockade of T-system

System of equations (15) is written as follows

$$\frac{dx_2}{dt} = \rho_B\, \xi(m)x_9 - \gamma_6\, x_2\, x_{10} - \frac{1}{\tau_B}\, x_2$$

$$\frac{dx_4}{dt} = \rho_M\, x_7 - \gamma_7\, x_4\, x_{10} - \frac{1}{\tau_M}\, x_4$$

$$\frac{dx_7}{dt} = P_B(t - \tau_2) - \frac{1}{\tau_{CB}}\,(x_7 - x_7^*)$$

$$P_B(t) = p_2\, x_2\, x_{10}$$

$$\frac{dx_8}{dt} = \rho_\Lambda\, \xi(m)x_9 - (\tilde{Q} + \tilde{S})x_8 - \frac{1}{\tau_\Lambda}\, x_8$$

$$\tilde{S} = \sum_{i\in\tilde{A}} \nu_i(x_i - x_i^*), \qquad \nu_i \geq 0, \qquad \tilde{A} = \{2,4,7,8\} \tag{16}$$

$$\tilde{Q} = x_{10} \sum_{i\in\tilde{B}} n_i\, x_i, \qquad n_i \geq 0, \qquad \tilde{B} = \{2,4\}$$

$$\frac{dx_9}{dt} = \gamma_2\, x_2\, x_{10} - \gamma_3(x_9 - x_9^*)$$

$$\frac{dx_{10}}{dt} = (\beta - \tilde{R})x_{10}$$

$$\tilde{R} = \sum_{i \in \tilde{B}} \delta_i \, x_i, \qquad \delta_i \geq 0$$

$$\frac{dx_{11}}{dt} = \sigma \, x_{10} - \mu_m \, x_{11}$$

In this case reactions according to T-system are completely absent. Reactions according to B-system are also deficient since in stimulation of B-cells the term $p_3 x_1 x_2 x_8 x_{10}$ is absent. Switchover to the synthesis of I_gG does not take place since $0 = x_1 x_2 < (TB)^*$. On account of that the maximum value of the antigen concentration in the course of reaction markedly increases which causes the increase of the maximum value of relative characteristics of the organ's damage. In the response to the thymus-dependent antigen (this situation can be modelled by selecting a small enough coefficient p_2) $m_{max} \gg m^*$ and $\xi(m) \to 0$, respectively, which causes unlimited growth of the antigen concentration.

<u>Normal functioning of T-system with complete blockade of B-system</u>

System (15) is of the form

$$\frac{dx_1}{dt} = \rho_T \, \xi(m) x_9 - \gamma_4 \, x_1 x_{10} - \frac{1}{\tau_T} \, x_1$$

$$\frac{dx_3}{dt} = \rho_K x_6 - \gamma_9 x_3 x_{10} - \frac{1}{\tau_K} \, x_3$$

$$\frac{dx_6}{dt} = P_T(t - \tau_1) - \frac{1}{\tau_{CT}} (x_6 - x_6^*)$$

$$P_T(t) = p_1 x_1 x_{10}$$

$$\frac{dx_8}{dt} = \rho_\Lambda \, \xi(m) x_9 - (\bar{Q} + \bar{S}) x_8 - \frac{1}{\tau_\Lambda} \, x_8$$

$$\bar{S} = \sum_{i \in A} \nu_i (x_i - x_i^*), \quad \nu_i \geq 0, \quad A = \{1, 3, 6, 8\}$$

$$\bar{Q} = x_{10} \sum_{i \in B} n_i x_i, \quad n_i \geq 0, \qquad B = \{1, 3\}$$

$$\frac{dx_9}{dt} = \gamma_1 x_1 x_{10} - \gamma_3 (x_9 - x_9^*)$$

$$\frac{dx_{10}}{dt} = (\beta - \bar{R})x_{10}$$

$$\bar{R} = \sum_{i \in B} \delta_i x_i, \qquad \delta_i \geq 0$$

$$\frac{dx_{11}}{dt} = \sigma x_{10} - \mu_m x_{11}$$

In this case reactions according to B-system are completely absent. Reactions according to T-system remain normal. Fig. 2 shows antigen dynamics in the course of the immune response in the case of T- and B-deficiencies . One can see that deficiency of one or another type qualitatively changes the process, the maximum value of the antigen concentration is more than in T-B-response, besides, T-deficiency causes persistent forms of a disease. In Figure 3 the situation is quite contrary. In T-B-response we have a stationary solution which can be interpreted as a persistent or chronic form of a disease. (T or B) deficiency causes "aggravation" of the disease and the antigen concentration tends to zero. This situation is known to immunologists and is associated with the blockade of antigen receptors by antibodies.

4. Conclusions

Modelling of immuno-deficient states shows that:

a) Switch off of T- or B-system causes qualitative changes of the immune response.

b) T-and B-systems unequally contribute to the immune response dynamics. The immune system is more sensible to the suppression of the T-system.

c) "Recovery" is possible only in case antigen has a low rate of damage of the organ σ.

d) The maximum value of the antigen concentration in the immuno-deficient state is much higher than in the T-B-response.

e) In the course of the immune response with T-or B-immunodeficiency the system tends to compensate the absence of the missing components of the process at the expense of higher concentrations of the functioning components.

To conclude, let us note that the present paper is the first stage of research. Many model relations are, in fact, working hypotheses and need future analysis and refinement. The research will be continued. We are planning to widely use available statistical data and results of experimental immunological and medical research.

REFERENCES

1. Belykh, L.N., and Marchuk, G.I. Chronic forms of a disease and their treatment according to mathematical immune response models. (In this volume).
2. Marchuk, G.I. Some mathematical models in immunology. Proc.of the 8th Conf.on Opt.Tech. Springer-Verlag, Heidelberg, 41-62 (1978).
3. Marchuk, G.I. Mathematical immune response models and their interpretation. (In this volume).

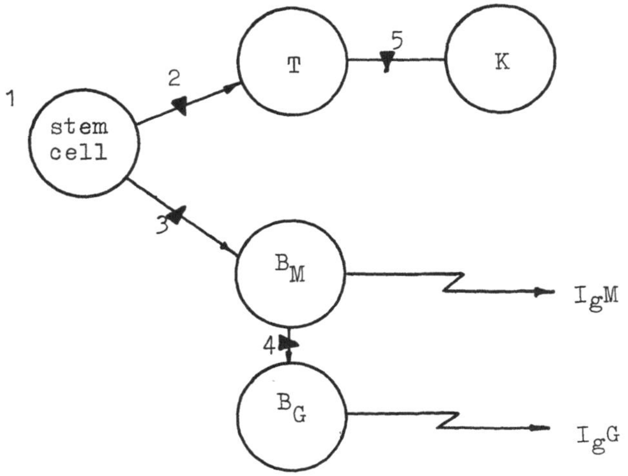

Fig. 1

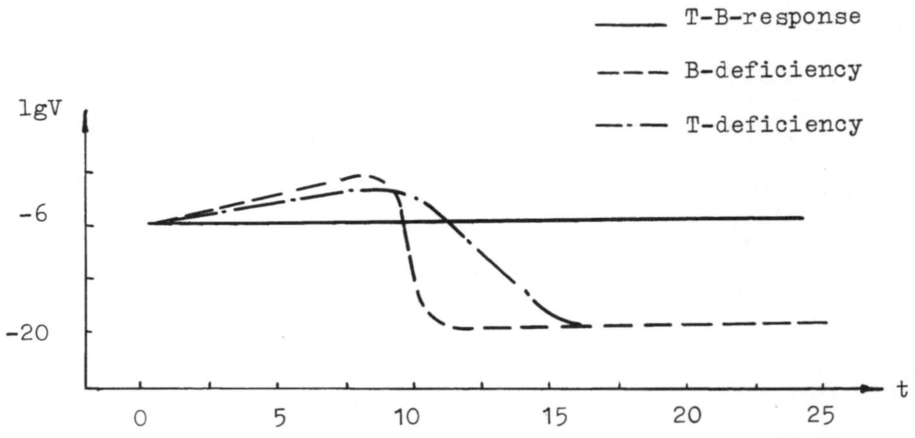
T-B-response
B-deficiency
T-deficiency
lgV
-6
-20
t
0
5
10
15
20
25

Fig. 3

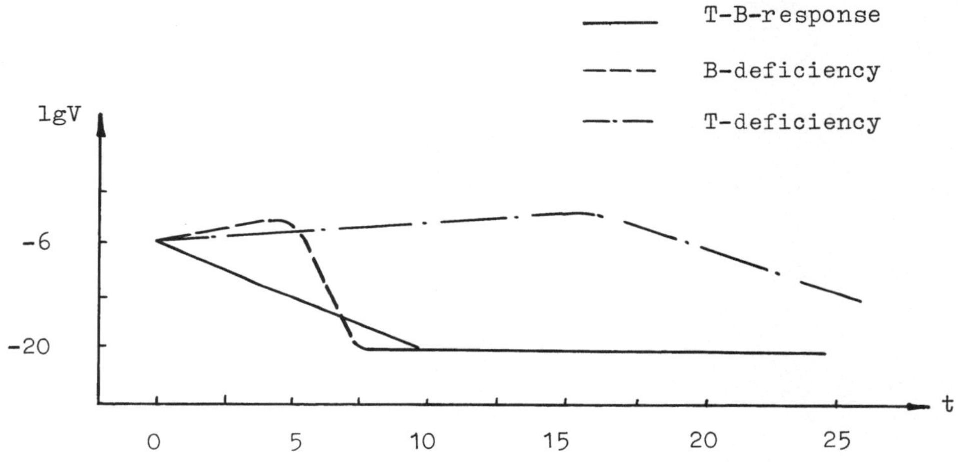
T-B-response
B-deficiency
T-deficiency
lgV
-6
-20
t
0
5
10
15
20
25

Fig. 2

CHRONIC FORMS OF A DISEASE AND THEIR TREATMENT ACCORDING TO MATHEMATICAL IMMUNE RESPONSE MODELS

L.N.Belykh, G.I.Marchuk

Computing Center, Novosibirsk, USSR

1. Introduction

Mathematical modeling of a virus disease as immune response to pathogene reproducing antigen /1-4/ has shown that chronic disease is a stable form of the immune process. It is due to the ineffective immune system stimulation and has either cyclic or time independent dynamics (periodic solutions or stationary solutions of the model, respectively). Studying the solutions dependence upon the initial conditions /3/ enabled us to find mechanism for the treatment of chronic disease. Great increase in the initial virus concentration (infected dose) seems to lead to a more effective immune system stimulation and to an effective immune response. The latter in turn leads to the entire removal of viruses from the body. These facts became the foundation of a method for chronic disease treatment the main idea of which is great increase in the virus concentration in the body. We called this method disease aggravation.

2. Immunological scheme of the chronic disease treatment

As chronic process proceeds in the body, stable equilibrium between the viruses removal caused by their interaction with antibodies and viruses birth is achieved. In this case all immune components are in a stationary state which is almost the same as in a healthy organism. Injection of increasing doses of any biostimulator (e.g., polysaccharides) induces the immune system to form its response to this new antigen. If the inoculating doses permanently increase the immune system will use its resources for the struggle with the new enemy and appears to produce mainly T- and B-lymphocytes specific for the polysaccharides rather than viruses. Thus organism "forgets" the old "chronic" antigen and switches itself on to the new one. This leads to intensive viruses reproduction and to the increase of their concentration in the body and of the pathological effect in the tissue. Disease aggravation begins. Some days later injections are over and polysaccharides are rapidly removed from the body due to their interaction with antibodies specific for them. The organism is switched on to the viruses again but the situation has already changed. While the treatment course has been applied the viruses concentration in the body has greatly increased. This concentration now may stimulate the immune system very strongly. Therefore free T- and B-complexes concentrations are greatly increased in comparison with those of the previous chronic process. This leads to the effective immune response and as the consequence of that - to the entire viruses removal from the body. Thus recovery begins.

3. The origin of the chronic disease forms according to the simple mathematical model of a disease.

We need a simple mathematical model of a virus disease /4/ to investigate the conditions of the chronic disease forms origin and to characterize mathematically the process described above.

This model is known to be described by the following system of equations :

$$\frac{dV}{dt} = (\beta - \gamma F)V$$

$$\frac{dC}{dt} = \xi(m) \cdot \alpha V(t - \tau)F(t - \tau) - \mu_c(C - C^*) \tag{1}$$

$$\frac{dF}{dt} = \rho C - \eta\gamma FV - \mu_f F$$

$$\frac{dm}{dt} = \sigma V - \mu_m m$$

with the initial data taken at $t = 0$

$$V(0) = V^\circ, \quad C(0) = C^*, \quad F(0) = \frac{\rho C^*}{\mu_f} = F^*, \quad m(0) = 0. \tag{2}$$

Variables V, C, F mean respectively concentrations of the viruses, plasma cells and antibodies, m is a value of the characteristic of the damaged tissue, $\xi(m)$ is a function characterizing the overall organism state, τ is the time interval necessary for the transformation of the immunocompetent lymphocyte into plasma cells (see /2/).

This model is known to have two types of stationary solutions. The solution of the first type is characteristic of the healthy state:

$$V_1 = 0, \quad C_1 = C^*, \quad F_1 = F^*, \quad m_1 = 0. \tag{3}$$

The solution of the second type characterizes the chronic form

$$V_2 = \frac{\mu_c(\mu_f\beta - \gamma\rho C^*)}{\beta(\alpha\rho - \mu_c\eta\gamma)},$$

$$C_2 = \frac{\alpha\mu_f\beta - \eta\mu_c\gamma^2 C^*}{\gamma(\alpha\rho - \mu_c\eta\gamma)}, \tag{4}$$

$$F_2 = \frac{\beta}{\gamma}, \qquad m_2 = \frac{\sigma}{\mu_m} V_2.$$

We are interested in the origin conditions of the chronic forms. They are the same as those of the stability of the second type solution. In order to find them the model was linearized near this stationary solution. Using some simplifications and Mikhailov's criterion we obtained the conditions :

$$\alpha\rho > \eta\gamma\mu_c,$$
$$0 < \beta - \gamma F^* = \left.\frac{d(\ln V)}{dt}\right|_{t=o} < \frac{1}{\tau + \dfrac{1}{\mu_c + \mu_f}}. \tag{5}$$

In our study the initial concentration of viruses V^o (or the infected dose) was assumed to be a very small value in comparison with that at the disease peak. Under this assumption we estimated the maximal viruses concentration in the body which seemed to be independent of the infected dose V^o.

$$V_{max} = \frac{4a(\mu_f + a)(\mu_c + a)}{(\beta + \gamma F^*)\quad [\alpha\rho e^{-\tau a} - \eta\gamma(\mu_c + a)]}$$

where $a = 0.5(\beta - \gamma F^*)$.

The chronic process was shown to be really stable when the conditions (5) are valid and $V^o < V_{max}$. It is the result of the simulation rather than a theoretical result. So V_{max} seems to be a boundary of the initial data stability area.

It should be noted that all the constants in the right-hand side of the second inequality in (5) are known from immunological literature. This enabled us to estimate analytically the time interval necessary for the disease aggravation. This interval seems to be equal to several weeks. From this we concluded that chronic antigen had slight dynamics.

4. Treatment of the chronic disease

According to our immunological scheme mentioned above the treatment process may be described by the following system of equations :

$$\frac{dV}{dt} = (\beta - \gamma_V F)V$$
$$\frac{dC}{dt} = \varphi_V(V, P)\xi(m)\alpha_V V(t-\tau)F(t-\tau) - \mu_c(C - C^*)$$
$$\frac{dF}{dt} = \rho C - \eta_V\gamma_V FV - \mu_f F \tag{6}$$
$$\frac{dm}{dt} = \sigma V - \mu_m m$$

$$\frac{dP}{dt} = -\gamma_P \Phi P + f(t)$$

$$\frac{dS}{dt} = \varphi_P(V, P)\,\alpha_P P(t-\tau)\,\Phi(t-\tau) - \mu_c(S - S^*)$$

$$\frac{d\Phi}{dt} = \rho S - \eta_P \gamma_P \Phi P - \mu_f \Phi$$

with the initial data at $t = t^*$

$$V(t^*) = V_2, \quad F(t^*) = F_2, \quad C(t^*) = C_2, \quad m(t^*) = m_2,$$

$$P(t^*) = P^\circ, \quad \Phi(t^*) = \Phi^* = \frac{\rho S^*}{\mu_f}, \quad S(t^*) = S^*. \tag{7}$$

The variables V, C, F, m are the same as previously described and P, S, Φ mean respectively the concentrations of polysaccharides, plasma cells and antibodies specific for the polysaccharides. Thus the set $\{V, C, F, m\}$ characterizes the chronic process and the set $\{P, S, \Phi\}$ is characteristic of the immune response to the polysaccharides.

Function $f(t)$ describes the polysaccharides injection and has the form

$$f(t) = Q(n)\,\delta(t - n\Delta t), \tag{8}$$

where δ is Dirak function,

$$Q(n) = Q_o + \alpha n, \quad Q_o > 0, \quad \alpha > 0, \quad n = \overline{1, N},$$

N is the number of injections, Δt is a time interval between the two injections.

Functions $\varphi_V(V, P)$ and $\varphi_P(V, P)$ describe the immune resources distribution between two antigens V and P and have the following form in the simplest case

$$\varphi_V = \frac{V}{V+P}, \quad \varphi_P = \frac{P}{V+P}. \tag{9}$$

Model (6) describes the following process. When polysaccharides are absent from the organism $(P = 0)$ it is subjected to the stable chronic process $V = V_2$, $C = C_2$, $F = F_2$, $m = m_2$, i.e. conditions (5) are valid and $V_2 < V_{max}$. Thus system (6) is in the initial data stability area. Beginning from the moment $t = t^*$ one injects the polysaccharides into the organism according to (8). When the polysaccharides concentration becomes much greater than that of viruses, i.e.

$P(t) \gg V(t)$, the immune system reacts only to polysaccharides due to the resources distribution (9) since there is no stimulation of the immune system by viruses $(\alpha_V\, \varphi_V(V, P) \approx 0)$. The viruses concentration begins to grow and as already known it takes several weeks to achieve its effective concentration $V_{ef} \approx 10^p V_2$, where $p \geq 2$.

As such aggravation of a disease proceeds the pathological effect caused by viruses grows too. When polysaccharides are absent from the body again, i.e. the treatment course has finished conditions (5) are valid again but now $V(t) \geq V_{ef} \gg V_{max} > V_2$ and system (6) is in the initial data instability area. Thus it does not return to the chronic state. There exist two possible ways out of this situation. They are recovery and death. The recovery is due to the effective stimulation of the immune system but if in the course of treatment the tissue is entirely damaged ($\xi(m) \approx 0$) the death comes, since there is no stimulation at all. As simulation has shown it is possible to apply the treatment course so that the recovery may occur.

It should be noted that our model (6) takes into consideration neither polysaccharides reproduction nor an organ damaged by them because we consider the polysaccharides to be non-reproducing and non-pathogene antigen.

5. The simulation results and discussion

Now let us discuss the simulation results.

Fig. 1 demonstrates the independence of our estimate V_{max} of the initial data. The $\log V_{max}$-level is parallel to the time axis t. The processes shown in this figure are different from one another only by the initial data V^o.

Fig. 2 is a basis for chronic disease treatment by aggravation. The $\log V_{max}$-level is parallel to the time axis t again. Two processes shown are different from one another by initial data V^o too. The conditions (5) hold for them. As we see, when $V^o < V_{max}$ the chronic process is stable indeed but when $V^o > V_{max}$ the chronic process is not stable though the stability conditions (5) are valid in this case.

Fig. 3 represents the results of the simulation of the chronic disease treatment by aggravation. In this figure the chronic process aggravation is shown by the continuous line and dynamics of the immune response to polysaccharides is shown by the dotted line. This figure confirms our theoretical results that it takes several weeks for the successful treatment (i.e. the treatment ended in recovery).

So in the course of our investigation we have found the following.

1. Stability of a chronic process depends on both the known constants of the model (properly on the time lag τ and lifetime of the plasma cells and of antibodies) and on the initial value of viruses concentration V^o.

2. Viruses causing the chronic disease have slight dynamics.

3. Our theoretical, independent of V^o, estimate of maximal viruses concentration V_{max} seems to be the boundary of the initial data stability. The chronic process is stable indeed when conditions (5) are valid and $V^o < V_{max}$. When $V^o > V_{max}$ (to be more exactly, $\lg V^o > \lg V_{max} + P$, where $P \geq 2$) it is unstable though (5) is valid. These facts are the mathematical basis for the chronic disease treatment by means of its aggravation.

4. Our analytical prediction that the treatment course should be applied during several weeks has been confirmed by the simulation of

the model for the disease aggravation treatment.

The results presented enable us to conclude that chronic forms are due to the ineffective stimulation of the immune system. It follows that it is not beneficial for the organism to response to small doses of viruses. Our investigation appears to explain the validity of the low-dose tolerance. If this is true we may say that the chronic forms are due to T-immunodeficience since T-suppressors are known to be responsible for the tolerance.

It should be noted that the main simulation results are valid for our more complex models /4/.

REFERENCES

1. Asachenkov, A.L., and Marchuk, G.I. Investigation of the Mathematical Model of a Disease and Some Results of Computer Simulation. (In this volume).
2. Marchuk, G.I. A Simple Mathematical Model of a Virus Disease. Preprint of the Computing Center, Novosibirsk (1975).
3. Marchuk, G.I. Some Mathematical Models in Immunology. Proceedings of the 8th Conference on Optimization Techniques. Springer-Verlag, Heidelberg, 41-62 (1978).
4. Marchuk, G.I. Mathematical Immune Response Models and Their Interpretation. (In this volume).

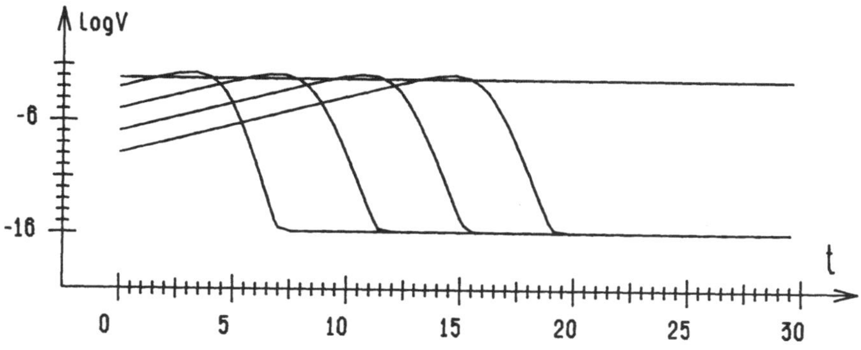

Fig. 1

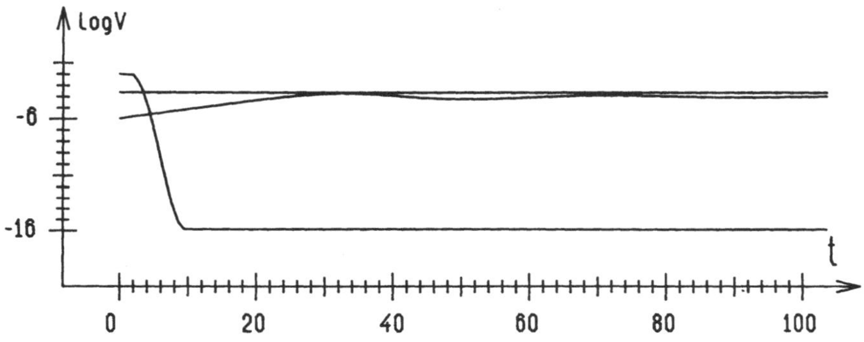

Fig. 2

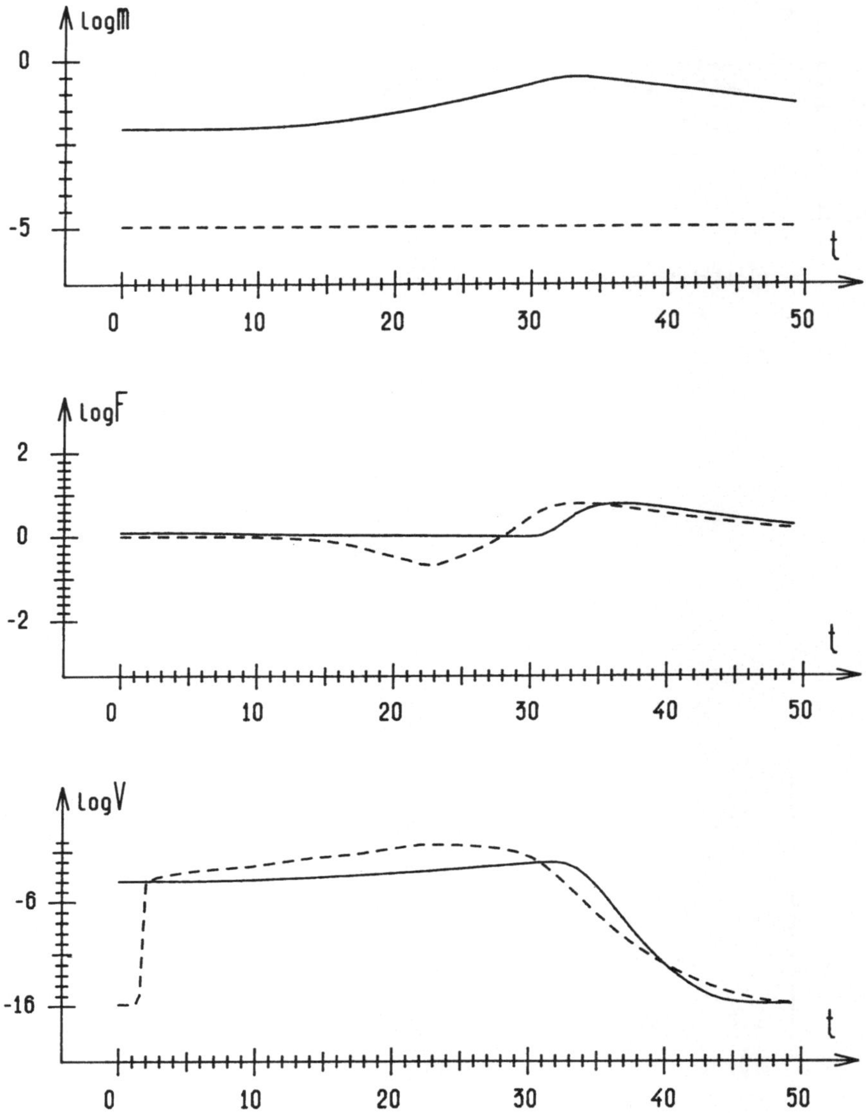
log M
0
-5
t
0
10
20
30
40
50
log F
2
0
-2
t
0
10
20
30
40
50
log V
-6
-16
t
0
10
20
30
40
50

Fig. 3

THE EFFECT OF A TIME LAG IN THE IMMUNE REACTION

B.F. Dibrov, M.A. Livshits, M.V. Volkenstein

Institute of Molecular Biology of the USSR Academy of Sciences, Moscow

The immune system of a vertebrate exhibits two types of specific responses on the antigen challenge. The mediators of the responses are either specific effector cells (cell mediated response) or specifically reacting antibody molecules (humoral response). The reaction of these agents with the antigen leads to its extinction. The main producers of specific antibodies are mature plasma cells, which are developed from the antigen stimulated B-lymphocytes. Since the differentiation of stimulated B-cells into clones of plasma cells takes appreciable time there is a retardation in antibody production with respect to the moment of B-cell stimulation. A similar delay is involved in the formation of immune memory cells responsible for the increased immune reactivity under recurrent expositions of the antigen. The memory cells are functionally equivalent to the virgin B-lymphocytes and so the two types of antigen sensitive cells (target cells) will not be distinguished in further consideration. In the present paper we focus our attention on the model of humoral immune reaction but since in the case of cell mediated reaction the main features of the interrelations of the immune system with antigen are the same the generalization to the latter case is straightforward.

In our model (Dibrov, Livshits & Volkenstein, 1977a, 1978a) the delay in the immune response is taken into account explicitly in simplified form of discrete time lag.

$$\frac{dg(t)}{dt} = Kg(t) - Qg(t)a(t)$$

$$\frac{da(t)}{dt} = A_r x(t-T_r)g(t-T_r)\theta(t-T_r) - Rg(t)a(t) - Ea(t) \qquad (1)$$

$$\frac{dg(t)}{dt} = J - \tau^{-1}x(t) - Px(t)g(t) + A_m x(t-T_m)g(t-T_m)\theta(t-T_m)$$

Here $g(t)$ is the antigen quantity, K is the effective rate of the antigen reproduction in the organism assumed further positive, $a(t)$ is the quantity of specific antibodies, the terms $-Qg(t)a(t)$ and $-Rg(t)a(t)$ describe the decrease of the antigen and antibody quantities as result of their interaction, $-Ea(t)$ describes the decay and antigen independent removal of the antibodies. $A_r x(t-T_r)g(t-T_r)\theta(t-T_r)$ represents the appearance of the specific antibodies at moment t which is determined by the number of target cells stimulated at the moment $t-T_r$, T_r is the time lag approximately equal to the time interval needed for differentiation of the stimulated target cells into clones of plasma cells. $\theta(t)$ is a step function:

$$\theta(t)=\begin{cases}1, & \text{if } t \geq 0\\ 0, & \text{if } t<0\end{cases}$$

$x(t)$ is the number of specific target cells. J is the rate of appearance of the specific target cells as the result of differentiation of stem cells, $-x(t)/\tau$ is the decay rate of target cells, term $-Px(t)g(t)$ describes the decrease of the number of specific target cells due to the interaction with the antigen, the term $A_m x(t-T_m)g(t-T_m)\theta(t-T_m)$ describes the delayed appearance of the memory cells, T_m is the time lag of immune memory formation.

This minimal model as we believe describes the main features of real immune processes, though some simplifications are apparent. The humoral immune response accomplished by specific B-lymphocytes is known to be controlled by the regulatory T-cells (helpers, suppressors). This means that the parameters A_r, A_m (and possibly P, T_r, T_m) considered further as constant can be in fact dependent on the dynamics of regulatory cells populations. The ignorance of these dependences is not crucial for main qualitative predictions of the model.

The simplified form of the description of retardation in the form of discrete time lag provides us a possibility to use ordinary differential equations instead of the integro-differential equations required in the case of continuous time lag. Continuous time lag can be used for the detailed description of immune response (cf. Dibrov, 1978).

Assuming further the constancy of the effective rate of the antigen reproduction (K) is also a simplification. In reality the effective rate can be dependent on the antigen quantity due to the interplay of nonspecific immunity factors. Infectious agents can suppress the nonspecific immune system in which case the effective rate of the antigen reproduction can happen to be negative at low concentrations of the antigen and positive for high concentrations. This can manifest itself as a threshold dependence of the infectious process on the antigen dose (Dibrov et al., 1978b).

It is reasonable to consider first the simplest case of the constant number of specific target cells $x(t) = x(0) = x_0$:

$$\frac{dg(t)}{dt} = Kg(t) - Qg(t)a(t)$$
$$\frac{da(t)}{dt} = A_r x_0 g(t-T_r)\theta(t-T_r) - Rg(t)a(t) - Ea(t). \qquad (2)$$

In the framework of equations (2) the antigen quantity grows infinitely if:

$$\frac{A_r x_0 Q}{KR} < 1 \qquad (3)$$

or if

$$\frac{A_r x_0 Q}{KR} > 1 \qquad (4)$$

and

$$\frac{A_r x_0 Q}{KR} T_r K \exp(-T_r K + 1) < 1 \ , \quad T_r K > 1. \qquad (5)$$

The antigen quantity is bounded above if inequality (4) is fulfilled but at least one of the conditions (5) is violated.

The singular point (0,0) of the equations (2) is always repulsive ($K > 0$). If inequality (4) is fulfilled there is another singular point:

$$a_{st} = K/Q \ , \ g_{st} = E/R(A_r x_0 Q/KR - 1). \qquad (6)$$

The character of this point depends on the values of parameters of the system. The analytical stability conditions of the singular point (6) presented in Dibrov et al. (1976, 1977b) show the crucial role of the magnitude of the time lag T_r . In particular for all $T_rK < 1$ the stationary point (6) is attractive and for all $T_rK > \pi/2$ it is repulsive. Fig. 1 shows the separation of the parameters space into domains which correspond to different regimes of the reaction:

1) singular point (6) is attractive, the antigen quantity is bounded above (damped oscillations lead to the stable carrier state)
2) singular point (6) is repulsive, the antigen quantity is bounded above (self-sustaining oscillations)
3) singular point is repulsive, the antigen quantity grows infinitely.

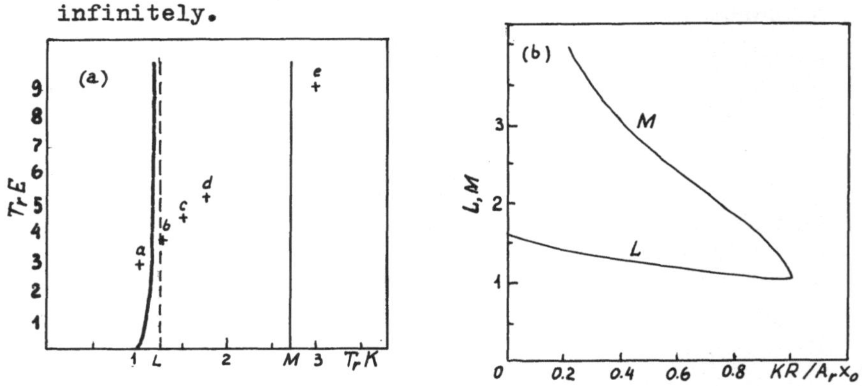

Fig. 1. (a) The separation of the parameters plane (T_rK, T_pE) into the domains, corresponding to different regimes of the reaction for KR/A_rx_oQ = 0.5. The points a, b, c, d and e correspond to different phase trajectories shown in Fig. 2. (b) The values of the characteristic points L and M of the separation versus KR/A_rx_oQ.

With increase of the time lag T_r the system goes from the domain 1 to 2 and further into 3. The computed phase trajectories of the system (2) corresponding to the points a, b, c, d and e (see Fig. 1) of the parameters space are shown in Fig. 2.

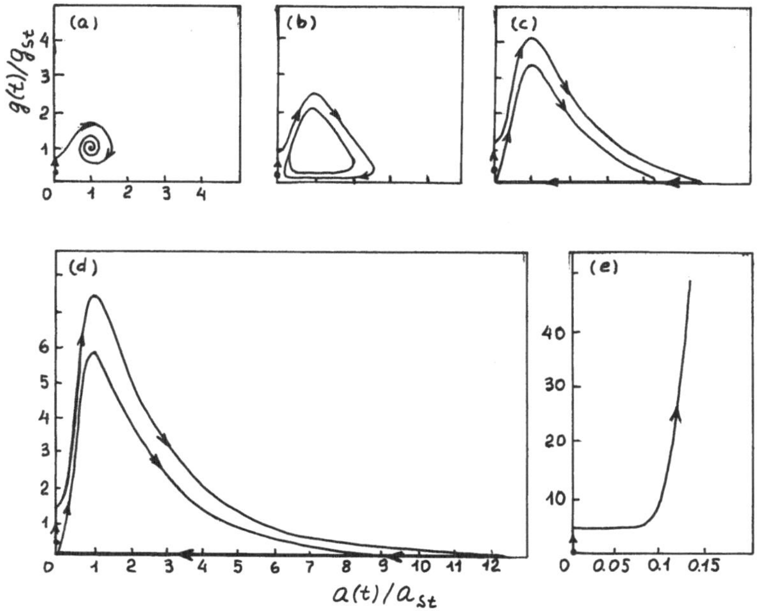

Fig. 2. Phase trajectories for equations (2) in dimensionless variables $a(t)/a_{st}$, $g(t)/g_{st}$ (see (6)) for $KR/A_r X_0 Q$ = 0.5; E/K = 3; $g(0) = 0.25 g_{st}$; $a(0)$ = 0 and for different values of the time lag T_r : (a) 1; (b) 1.25; (c) 1.5; (d) 1.75; (e) 3.

Very small bottom antigen quantity in most cases corresponds to complete antigen elimination because of the discrete stochastic character of the real birth and death processes. In Dibrov et al. (1977b,c) a method of evaluation of the probability of the antigen extinction was suggested. For the cases corresponding to phase trajectories b, c, d of Fig. 2 and g_{st} = 1000 the probabilities of the antigen extinction are 3.10^{-16}; 0.48; 0.99998. The striking fact is that the probability strongly depends on the time lag. The biological reasonability requires the time lag to be not too small since otherwise either the probability of a relapse of the desease can be too high or carrier state can be formed.

The optimal tactics of antibiotic and specific antibody treatment as to avoid the relapses can be worked out by computer simulation of the reaction (Dibrov et al., 1977c).

The main features of the antigen and antibody dynamics according to equations (1) are similar to those for equations (2). For ($A_m > P$) the equations (1) have only one nonzero stationary state. The stability conditions for this state are violated by sufficiently high values of the time lag T_r (see (2, 3)). If

$$\sqrt{J\tau A_r Q/KR - 1} < \sqrt{(P - A_m)E\tau/R} \qquad (7)$$

which corresponds to a high rate of specific B-lymphocyte consumption the antigen quantity increases infinitely independently of the initial data. If (7) is violated and

$$P > A_m \qquad (8)$$

then there are two nonzero stationary states, one of which is always repulsive and the other is attractive (repulsive) for sufficiently small (large) time lags (see Fig. 3 and Fig. 4).

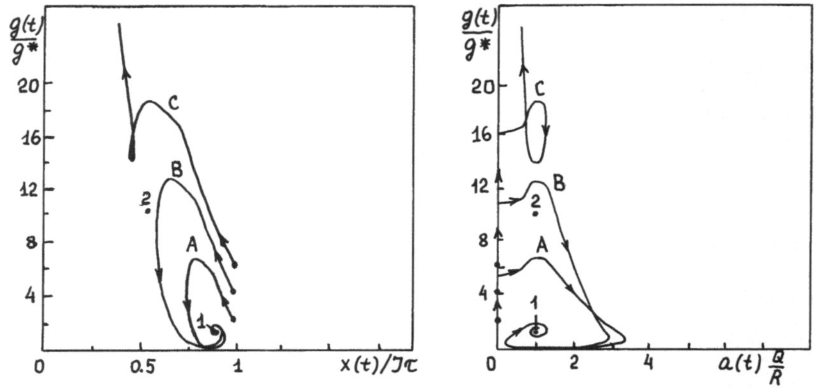

Fig. 3. Projections of the phase trajectories of the system (1) on the planes (x,g) and (a,g). The trajectories are computed for $T_r K = 1$, $x(0) = J\tau$; $a(0) = 0$, $J\tau A_r Q/KR = 2$, $K\tau = 2$, $PE/RK = 0.04$, $A_m = 0$, $E/K = 3$ and different initial antigen quantities $g(0)/g^*$: A 2, B 4, C 6: $g^* = E/R(J\tau A_r Q/KR - 1)$ 1 and 2 are stationary points

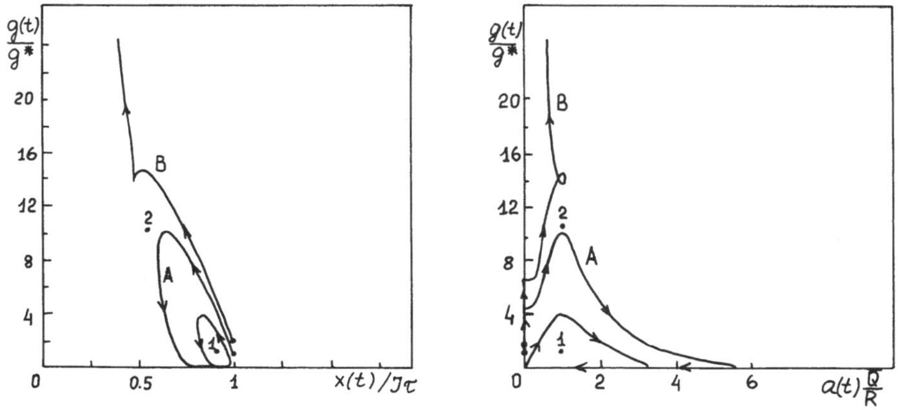

Fig. 4. Projections of the phase trajectories of equations (1) on the planes (x,g) and (a,g). The trajectories are computed for $T_r K = 1.5$. The values of other parameters and initial data are the same as in Fig. 3.

A new feature of the solutions of equations (1) is the dependence of the asymptotic behaviour on the initial data. The solutions can be bounded above for small initial values of the antigen quantity and unlimited for high initial values.

The model taking into account nonspecific immunity factors describes also the possibility of antigen extinction in the framework of deterministic equations (Dibrov et al., 1978b).

REFERENCES

Dibrov, B.F., Livshits, M.A., Volkenstein, M.V. Biophys. 21, 905-909 (1976) (In Russian).

Dibrov, B.F., Livshits, M.A., Volkenstein, M.V. J. Theor. Biol. 65, 609-631 (1977a).

Dibrov, B.F., Livshits, M.A., Volkenstein, M.V. J. Theor. Biol. 69, 23-39 (1977b).

Dibrov, B.F., Livshits, M.A., Volkenstein, M.V. Biophys. 22, 313-317 (1977c) (In Russian).

Dibrov, B.F., Ph.D. thesis, Moscow Physical Technical Institute, Moscow, 1978 (In Russian).

Dibrov, B.F., Livshits, M.A., Volkenstein, M.V., Biophys. 23, 143-147 (1978a) (In Russian).

Dibrov, B.F., Livshits, M.A., Volkenstein, M.V., Biophys. 23, 494-500 (1978b) (In Russian).

IMMUNOLOGICAL ASPECTS OF NEOPLASTIC GROWTH.

Gruntenko Evgeniy V.

Institute of Cytology and Genetics,
Siberian Department of the USSR Academy of Sciences,
Novosibirsk, USSR

Among diseases, affecting man and animals, a large group can be identified. All the diseases of this group have a common feature, an obligatory development of an immunological conflict based on the response of the organism's lymphoid system to an antigenic challenge. The last decades have witnessed dramatic developments in immunology, a science concerned with the patterns and mechanisms of such responses. The large body of data now accumulated permits to identify features common to the nature of all immunological conflicts.

Participation in seminars conducted by Academician G.I.Marchuk has fortified the idea that the aim of mathematical simulation is not only to formally describe the immunological conflict itself,but also to predict the general course of the disease. Any influence on the course of the disease is, to a large extent, determined by the role of the conflict in the development of a pathological condition. In some cases the presence of the conflict is the result of the defense response of the organism and is a guarantee of cure; in other cases, it is the very cause of the disease. However, there are all transitional forms between these two extremes of the immunological conflict. The contribution of an immunological response of the organism to the development of an outwardly seeming identical disease may be quite different depending upon a whole set of factors. This is brought out by comparing the results of immunodepressive interference with the arisal of mammary tumours in laboratory animals.

In the experiments, the same approach was used to affect immunity, namely surgical removal of the thymus, the most influential organ of the lymphoid system, during the first week of life. It is known that this operation, early thymectomy, is an efficient means of suppressing immunological reactivity. In all the experiments,the occurrence of mammary tumours in animals was recorded. An oncogenic virus, the so-called Bittner's virus, or, synonymously, the mammary tumour virus, the milk factor, is involved in the development of these tumours in mice.

Females of the high-mammary-tumour mouse strain,C3H/HE, were thymectomized on day 6 of life. The control group was composed of unoperated female mice in all of which tumours arose on days 238 ± 15. In thymectomized females, tumours arose two months later, 299 ± 17 days, on the average, after birth.

Another high-mammary-tumour mouse strain, DD, was subjected to early thymectomy. The operation also had a clear- cut suppressive effect on tumour arisal. During the entire period of observation (18 months), the percentage of tumour-bearing females was consistently lower in the operated group. The differences between the thymectomized and control mice were statistically significant.The tumours developed in 92 of 110 females of the control group, 327 ± 9 days, on the average, after birth, and only in 34 of 72 females of the thymectomized group. The latent period for mammary tumour development in the thymectomized group was 359 ± 12 days. It is pertinent to note that doctor Squartini has reported that early thymectomy has a depressive effect on the arisal of mammary tumours in BaLB/c mice fostered by females of the C3H strain carrying Bittner's virus in the milk.

Thus, thymectomy inhibits carcinogenesis, induced by Bitther's virus, in three different strains of mice (C3H, DD, BaLB/c). However, doctor Squartini has not observed such an effect in the high-mammary-tumour strain R111; in this strain with the milk factor, tumours developed with the same frequency and time as in mice of the control group.

This prompted to study the effect of early thymectomy on the development of such tumours in females of the low-mammary-tumour strain, C57BL, which acquired Bittner's virus with the milk. The thymus was removed from a part of mice on day 6 of life; on the same day, the operated and control mice were removed from their mothers and placed with foster mothers of the high-mammary-tumour strain C3H which had Bittner's virus in the milk. Over a 22-month period the mice were observed: tumours developed in 19 of 75 unoperated females and only in 1 of 32 thymectomized ones.

Another experimental series was carried out on hybrid females obtained by crossing C57BL males to C3H females. These hybrids carried the milk factor. Like in the preceding experiments, mice of the experimental group were thymectomized on day 6 after birth and those of the control group were not operated. The mice were under constant observation for 25 months. In hybrid females with the milk factor, thymectomy had no effect on the occurrence frequencies of the tumours (86.7 and 86.2 % in the control and thymectomized mice, respectively), nor on the latent period (247.1 $\pm$ 9.3 and 247.5 $\pm$9.1 days, respectively).

Hence, the effect of early thymectomy on the arisal of tumors induced by Bittner's virus is definitely related to mouse genotype. In mice of strains C3H, D/D, BaLB/c and C57BL, removel of the thymus suppresses the development of malignant processes of the mammary gland; by contrast, in Hybrids of the first generation from crosses between mice of C3H and C57BL strains, as well as in females of strain R111, thymectomy has no effect on these processes.

Animals of the high-mammary-tumour strain were infected with Bittner's virus as a result of its transmission through the mother's milk. A mouse substrain without the mammary tumour virus was derived from mouse strain C3H; this substrain was not infected with Bittner's virus. After a special hormonal stimulation, tumours developed in 15 of 25 females without the milk factor; the average latent period was 463 ± 17 days. Of 25 females, which had been thymectomized at the age of 6 days, tumours developed in 12 with a latent period of 437 ± 18 days. Mice of the thymectomized group lived, on the average, 2 months less than those of the control group. This decreased longevity was the possible reason why the number of tumour-bearers was somewhat lower in the thymectomized group. In fact, the percentage of tumour-bearing mice in this group, as compared with the number of mice survived to this age, was even larger than in the control group.

Based on these experimental results, it may be stated that early thymectomy has no inhibitory effect on the arisal of mammary tumours in C3H mice, unless thay were infected with Bittner's virus.

Furthermore, data were obtained indicating that the effect of thymectomy is inhibitory only when animals were infected with Bittner's virus at an early age.

Females of BALB/c strain without the mammary tumour virus were infected with it at the age of 3.5 months. Half of the mice were prethymectomized on day 6 after birth. Mammary tumours arose in almost all of the mice observed; their developmental rates were even higher in thymectomized females than in those of the control group. When estimates of tumours arisen were based per mouse in a group, the differences in the number of tumours arisen were largest between the thymectomized and control groups. This index was 0.97 in the control group (one tumour per mouse developed in 32 mice of the 33 observed for 22 months); the index was 1.70 ± 0.29 in the thymectomized group (multiple tumours arose in 39 % of thymectomized females).

Consequently, the effect of early thymectomy in mice is largely related to the presence of Bittner's virus in the organism, as well as to the age at which they were infected with it. In mice without the mammary tumour virus, genetically predisposed to tumour development, thymectomy does not affect the occurrence frequencies and growth rates of the tumours; in mice which were infected with the virus at an early age, thymic removal results in an inhibition of tumour development; in mice, which were experimentally infected with Bittner's virus at an adult age, thymectomy stimulates malignant processes of the mammary gland.

Mammary tumours can be induced by chemical carcinogens, dimethylbenzanthracene, DMBA, for example. In the following experimental series, 3-day old females were subjected to thymectomy. Intact females served as controls. At the age of 3.5 months, each female received orally a single dose of 20 mg DMBA in olive oil. At the age of 2.5 years, tumours developed in 69% of unoperated mice(in 18 of 26) and in 79% of thymectomized ones (in 19 of 24). The average latent period was 584 ± 35 days in the control group and 490 ± 27 days in the experimental group. Clearly, early thymectomy stimulates tumour induction by the chemical carcinogen DMBA.

The influence of Bitter's virus on mammary tumour development was also studied in intact and thymectomized rats of strain Sprague-Dowley characterized by hereditary predisposition to these tumours. Neonatal rats of the experimental group received an extract containing Bittner's virus. The rats were observed for the appearance of mammary tumours to day 900 of life. At this age, tumours arose in 14 of 64 intact females with a latent period of 653 ± 44 days.

In the group, infected with the virus, tumours arose in 24 of 58 rats at the age of 706 $\pm$ 17 days. In the virus-free thymectomized group, tumours developed in 16 of 44 rats 626 $\pm$ 23 days after birth. Comparison of this group with the control shows that early thymectomy stimulates the arisal of spontaneous mammary tumours. Malignant processes were most pronounced in the virus-infected thymectomized group; tumours developed in 15 of 25 rats of this group and the average latent period was 609 $\pm$ 32 days.

From these data it may be concluded that the same interference with the lymphoid system (early thymectomy) has a different, sometimes quite opposite, effect on the development of malignant processes of the mammary gland. These processes depend upon tumour etiology, the species and the strain of the animal, the involvement of Bittner's virus in oncological processes, as well as upon the degree to which the experimental system conforms with natural conditions. The experimental results were subdivided into 3 groups. Group I. Early thymectomy results in an inhibition of the development of mammary tumours. Group II. Inhibition of the thymus-dependent system has no statistically significant effect on the tumours. Group III. The same inteference stimulates malignant processes. What factors determine the presence and the direction of the effects on tumours?

The effects are not related to the level of hormonal stimulation. In each group, there were experiments in which the effects of early thymectomy were studied in the presence of hormonal stimulation and in its absence. Hence, it was not hormonal stimulation that determined the direction of the effects. All the experiments, in which early thymectomy was found to be inhibitory, had a common feature, the experimental mice were infected with Bittner's oncogenic virus during the first days of life, just like under natural conditions. The presence of the virus from the very first days of postnatal life is the necessary condition for the manifestation of the inhibitory effect of early thymectomy. In virus-free mice, thymectomy does not cause a delay in tumour appearance, while in mice, infected with the virus when adult, it enhances the development of malignant processes. However, this condition is insufficient to provide the inhibitory effect. The relationship patterns between the tumour and the lymphoid system in the organism, quite obviously, depend upon mouse genotype.

How to explain the whole set of data obtained? The theory of immunological surveillance suggests that the lymphoid system of the organism is capable of destroying any antigenically modified variant of somatic cells arising during development. Tumour cells, as a rule, have tumour-specific antigens. The major function of immunological surveillance is to destroy such cells. It may be reasonably concluded that immunodepression (early thymectomy in the case considered here) has a stimulatory effect on tumour arisal. This prediction of the immunological surveillance theory does not always conform with reality. There are several reasons to explain this discrepancy. The first reason seems to be that not all the spontaneously arisen tumours are sufficiently antigenic for the organism. This also appears to be the reason why early thymectomy has no effect on mammary tumours that arise in virus-free mice. In the rat, such tumours are, probably more antigenic and, hence, the results obtained in this animal species are in accord with the predictions of the surveillance theory. Tumours, induced by chemical carcinogens and oncoviruses, show more expressed tumour-specific antigenicity, as compared with spontaneously arisen tumours. The antigenicity of tumours, induced by carcinogens, differs from that of virus-induced tumours, because the set of tumour-specific antigen is unique to each particular tumour in the former and it is virus-determined, identical in all the virus-induced tumours in the latter. Infection of animals with a xenogenic (foreign) virus (mouse tumour virus in the model suggested) gives rise to tumours with marked antigenic properties, normally subjected to destruction by the lymphoid system. In this case, immunodepression stimulates the induction of tumours. A stimulatory effect is also provided by experimental infection of an adult animal with its own virus. True, the virus is its own, but it gains access to the organism when the lyphoid system is established without provision for any possible future encounter with this virus. The situation is quite different when an animal is infected with its own virus promptly after birth. In the course of evolution, the virus has adapted itself to existence in the organism of natural hosts. This adaptation is based on selection of particular viruses. Infection with this virus does not elicit an immune response fatal to the virus in the host. It may be assumed that, during the selection of animals for high incidence of tumours induced by oncoviruses, there might have occurred a concomitant selection of viruses for their capacity to resist the effect of immunological surveillance, as well as of animals for their genetically determined tolerance to the virus. In fact, early thymectomy exerts a stimulatory influence on the arisal of mammary tumours in mice of different strains, which were infected neonatally with Bittner's virus, and it has an inhibitory effect on mammary tumour development in mice of certain genotypes.

Therefore, mathematical models of antitumour immunity have to take into account that the relationship patterns of the lymphoid system and the tumour depend upon: 1) the etiological nature of the tumours; 2) the preceding evolution of the virus and the host (own virus and xenogenic); 3) the approach used for viral infection (the age of the host); 4) the genotype of the tumour-bearer.

STRUCTURE FUNCTIONAL ARRANGEMENT OF THE IMMUNE SYSTEM

V.P.Lozovoy, S.M.Shergin
Novosibirsk, USSR

Clinical immunology at present is at the joint of many science fields: on the one hand, there is an experimental theoretical immunology, and on the other hand, there are impetuously differentiating purely medical disciplines with their centrifugal tendency to organ and anatomic system private pathology (diseases of blood, kidney, heart and vessels, liver, lungs, etc.). Including its clinical applied aspects immunology differentiates quickly and as a result such divisions as allergology and infection immunology have been out of the main course of theoretical immunology.

Clinical immunology problem includes a lot of tasks. The first is to work out the pathogenesis models of the processes, with the immune system playing the leading role in disease development mechanism, to reveal links of aetiological factors with pathologic reaction development. Comparison of pathogenesis, clinical and laboratory tests, affected organ and system pathomorphologic manifestation and functional characteristics permits us to formulate a complete immunologic diagnosis. A concept of complete diagnosis includes data about the disease causal factors, anatomophysiologic features, signs, development rate and activity, but always implies the prognosis of a disease development. The main purpose of the diagnosis is to make a logical sequence in the diagnosis steps, namely, to introduce an algorithm into the diagnosis and prognosis. A comparative method in the immunologic diagnostics implies an analysis of data concerning patient's immune system in comparison to a certain standard (taking into account geography, age, sex, pathology presence or absence, some life peculiarities, nutrition, season, virus-bacterial environment, etc.). It is rather important to make out so-called typological (group) characteristics of norm. What is the situation concerning the human immunological status estimation in health and disease at present? It is necessary to work out methodological grounds for the assessment of immune and related pathological processes to use them in diagnosis, prognosis and treatment of diseases with immunopathological reactions and immune system diseases.

It is much more difficult to work out the immune disease pathogenesis models. This difficulty depends on the necessity to registrate not only the immune status itself but in its connection to basic pathologic processes such as inflammation, sclerogenesis, and restoration of the tissue and organ structure and function. With more and more information on the immune response mechanisms at our disposal and expansion of our knowledge regarding the immune system arrangement and function, immunologists must put this huge volume of contemporary immunology facts in good order. It is necessary to formalize our knowledge for the purpose of modelling the functions and regulation processes in the immune system. It seems to be perspective in this sense to use the principles and methods of systemic analysis and cybernetic approaches.

Certain conditions (input data) that can be presented as postulates of the immune system structure-functional arrangement are necessary for mathematical modelling of the immune system, namely, making descriptive cybernetic graph-models.

In brief, the basic formalized principles of the immune system arrangement and function are the following:

1. Antigen-structure homeostasis (ASH), that is antigenic constancy of organism internal environment, its accordance with given species and an individual in ontogeny, its anti-infectious defence are provided by total complex of temporal and spatial concorded stages

in the mechanisms of recognition, regulation and the effector functions of the immune system. It can be characterized as a multicomponent system, possessing a great freedom in the choice of response variants and the presence of intra- and extrasystem relations, conditioning its homeostatic function safety.

2. Antigen-structure homeostasis is realized due to the presence in the immune system of totality of control modes for the antigenic structure and by the defence mechanisms from foreign antigenic information or from modifications of the body itself.

3. The basic homeostatic immune system function is the possibility to recognize foreign structures and to respond by developing specific complement structures in the form of the immunocompetent cell membrane modification ("cellular antibodies"), by synthesizing and secreting specific proteins - immunoglobulins, or by their combination.

4. Hierarchy is the most important structural and functional feature of the immune system (thymus, T- and B-dependent areas, regulator cells).

5. Discreteness is characteristic of the immune system arrangement. It is displayed in the building of structure hierarchy (basic proteins), in the presence of two main classes of lymphocyte subpopulations, immunoglobulin classes (M, G, A, E, D), groupings in the pattern of histocompatibility antigen, allotypes and idiotypes of immunoglobulins, etc.

6. The presence of discreteness in the immune system structure needs integration of its functions.

7. Integration of the immune system functions is provided by autoregulation processes and links via other (e.g. nervous and endocrine) regulation systems, that is why the autonomy is relative.

8. Integration of the immune system functions and the intersystem integration are built on the principles of quantitative, spatial, and

temporal accordance of the stimulus (antigen) and the effect of the action.

9. The immune system has many variants of the behaviour, it is dependent on some features of antigen, preceding antigen stimulation, the system condition and other pheno- and genotype characteristics of an organism.

10. The system's safety is explained by its complex structure, the possibility of a wide choice of responding means, steps in the reactions of control and response to foreign antigen.

11. Recirculation, far and near migration and location in certain areas of lymphoid organs realized by immunocompetent cells and their precursors are one of the main ways of integration of the functions in the immune system.

12. The other important way of the function integration is creation of transient cooperative interactions (distant ones via lymphokines or contact ones) between the immune system discrete units, namely, regulator and effector lymphocytes.

13. Apart from the direct links there are feedbacks and cascade feature of the effector functions in the immune system function regulation.

14. The organism has always immune system readiness (the so-called antigen-independent way of differentiation, proliferation, and migration of immunocompetent cells and their precursors) to reception and response to antigen stimulation (the so-called antigen-independent way of lymphocyte differentiation).

15. The immune system start into specific work and the response type are largely dependent on biological features and the magnitude of antigen stimulation (optimal immune response, high or low zone tolerance, allergic reaction).

16. Specific response products, e.g. antibodies and their frag-

ments, immune complexes, accumulation of committed cells are important autoregulators in the immune system.

17. The lymphocyte membrane functional state and influence (distant via humoral and contact factors) are the basic factors in regulation of the immune system functions.

18. The immunologic memory development and keeping are important features in response to repeated antigen exposure.

19. There is an evolution-mediated functional link between specific individual labelling (histocompatibility antigen system, allotypes and idiotypes of immunoglobulines and lymphocytes) of the organism cells and tissues, and capacity for a type of the immune responsiveness.

20. Prolonged excessive explosure of antigen and other extreme environmental factors is characterized by the presence of phases in immune adaptability reactions, a wide possibility of modulations to a change of neuro-endicrine background for the sake of antigen-structural homeostasis maintenance.

21. Destabilization of ASH is first of all characterized by some changes of spatial-temporal immune system features.

22. There is a clear functional link between the specific immunity system and the system of nonspecific defence, namely, the mononuclear phagocyte and complement systems.

23. Inflammation, inflammatory-proliferative and sclerotic processes are structurally interrelated with the specific immune defence at the expense of common cellular and humoral components.

To work out a basic model of the immune system, it is necessary to mark out its functional links:

- a link of reception and processing of antigenic information
- a link of the immune response regulation
- a link of the immune response enhancement

- a link of the follow-up
- an effector link
- a memory link.

Lymphocyte and macrophage subpopulation is the basic structural unit of these links. At present the mechanisms of their functioning are explained. The structure-functioning arrangement of the immune system is shown in Fig. 1.

The feature complex of the immune system adaptability reactions is revealed as destabilization of its functions at the expense of some changes in the self-regulation system and forms an adaptation complex according to the following indicators:

1. Changes in the ratio of basic peripheral blood lymphocyte subpopulations:

a) T-lymphocytopenia;

b) "O"-and B-lymphocytosis.

2. Augmentation of low differentiated T-lymphocytes:

a) increase of thymosin-sensitive T-cell level;

b) change in response to T-mitogens and allogeneic cells;

c) reduction of mitogen-induced cytotoxicity.

3. B-lymphocyte activation:

a) predisposition to spontaneous blast transformation;

b) increase of response to B-mitogens;

c) increase of serum IgM level, phase changes of IgA and IgG concentrations.

4. K-cell ("O"-lymphocyte) function changes:

a) suppression of antibody-dependent cytotoxicity.

5. Development of autoimmune phenomena:

a) increase of isoantibody titres to connective tissue antigen;

b) augmentation of the content of lymphocytes carrying receptors to connective tissue antigen ;

c) increase of lymphocyte cytotoxic action against allogenetic cells.

6. Complement system depletion.

7. Development of acute phase proteins:

a) heparin-precipitated fraction of blood;

b) C-reactive protein.

8. Change of the immune system sensitivity to glucocorticoid hormone actions:

a) increase of T-lymphocyte sensitivity to cortisol;

b) changes in the ratio of cortisol-resistant/cortisol-sensitive cells;

c) changes in circadian and seasonal rhythms of the basic lymphocyte subpopulation content in peripheral blood.

9. Phase changes of mononuclear phagocyte system activity.

In addition, the changes in the direction and the rate of polypotent stem hemopoietic cell differentiation during the acute phase tension to myelopoiesis, rapid maturation and going granulocytes out of the bone marrow, and erythropoiesis activation have been demonstrated in experiments on animals.

According to our findings, the bone marrow hemopoiesis in the acute hypoxia (an experiment in an altitude chamber, using mice of different genotypes) mainly switches over to erythropoiesis, at that time lymphopoiesis is inhibited, the number of circulating stem cells diminishes, the number of antibody-producing cells in the spleen decreases.

Thus, the extreme environmental factor influence is accompanied by profound changes of the immune system, and, firstly, by changes in migration of immunocompetent cells and their precursors (blood - tissues - lymphoid organs - bone marrow). It is noteworthy to mention a wide opportunity of function modulations in the immune system, its relative autonomy and compensation mechanisms to a changing hormonal regime. Apart from the effects of the immune reactivity change during prolonged exposure of the extreme factors with danger of its breakdown or deficiency of regulation (predisposition both to allergic and autoimmune reactions, change of the level in control of tissue self-antigen), one could expect some changes in trophic influences provided by immunocompetent cells, some changes in the course of the inflammatory and sclerogenic processes. The danger to turn into pathology is more possible by maintaining these functional changes in the immune system during 1.5 - 2 years (the so-called risk group) or by rapid progress of the concomitant pathologic process.

Apart from reversible functional changes in the immune system characterized as being adaptive and sometimes as prepathologic states immunopathologic processes may be considered as diseases of the immune system.

Some systemic disturbances and defects of the immune system, namely, inherited and acquired immunodeficiencies may be attributed to the following processes:

- the loss of control for the cell proliferation and differentiation;
- immune complex diseases;
- allergic diseases;
- disturbances in the macrophage system;
- disorders in the complement system.

In the development mechanisms of immunopathologic processes it is necessary to distinguish such disorders in the ASH system and outside of the system.

Lymphoproliferative diseases, some types of autoimmune diseases can serve as an example of intrasystem disorders. The extrasystem immunopathologic processes include secondary immunodeficiencies, immunopathologic complications of some infectious diseases (chronic pneumonia, tuberculosis, lepra), helminthic invasion, viral diseases (progressing hepatitis and other, especially latent, infections).

Systemic diseases, autoimmune diseases of connective tissue (collagen diseases), autoimmune lesion of kidney (Bright disease), endocrine glands (Hashimoto thyroiditis, Addisson disease) are characterized by disturbances of all levels of ASH regulation, and by disturbances of intra- and extrasystemic relations of ASH.

Our long-term investigations have revealed that in systemic autoimmune diseases, apart from functional shifts mediated by disorders of lymphoid and endocrine system relationships, autoregulation process, molecular-genetic mechanisms of functioning, genetic control for receptor molecules on the lymphocyte membrane, synthesis of immunoglobulins and lymphokines are disturbed. We consider such profound discordance of the immune functions to be the mechanism of autoimmune progression and self-maintenance of a pathologic process. These mechanisms are responsible for the chronic course of a disease and demand active cytostatic therapy.

Thus, for immunologic diagnosis and examination, prognosis for health and disease, a clinical immunologist has to possess a peculiar algorithm and system in thinking and action, namely, a complex estimation of the immunologic status according to separate links of the immune system. As to the current immunology, he must possess a complex functional estimation of the T- and B-cell system, humoral regulators of the immunity and functional units formed in the immune system.

On the basis of systemic analysis of ASH functions, one can pick out the main complexes of both functional and organic signs, permitting evaluation of the immune homeostatic state, and determine the prognosis of its functions and the choice of drugs affecting the sites of the ASH breakdown of a patient.

It is clear that at a phase of function destabilization such influences as vaccination can be less effective and fraught with serious complications including some allergic and autoimmune reactions.

The mathematical model of the immune response autoregulation with due regard for the dynamics of the regulator and effector cells interaction, the use of systemic analysis to study the reaction evolution during phylogenesis are listed in the Abstracts of the Working Conference on Modelling and Optimization of Complex Systems held in Novosibirsk, on 3 - 9 July, 1978.

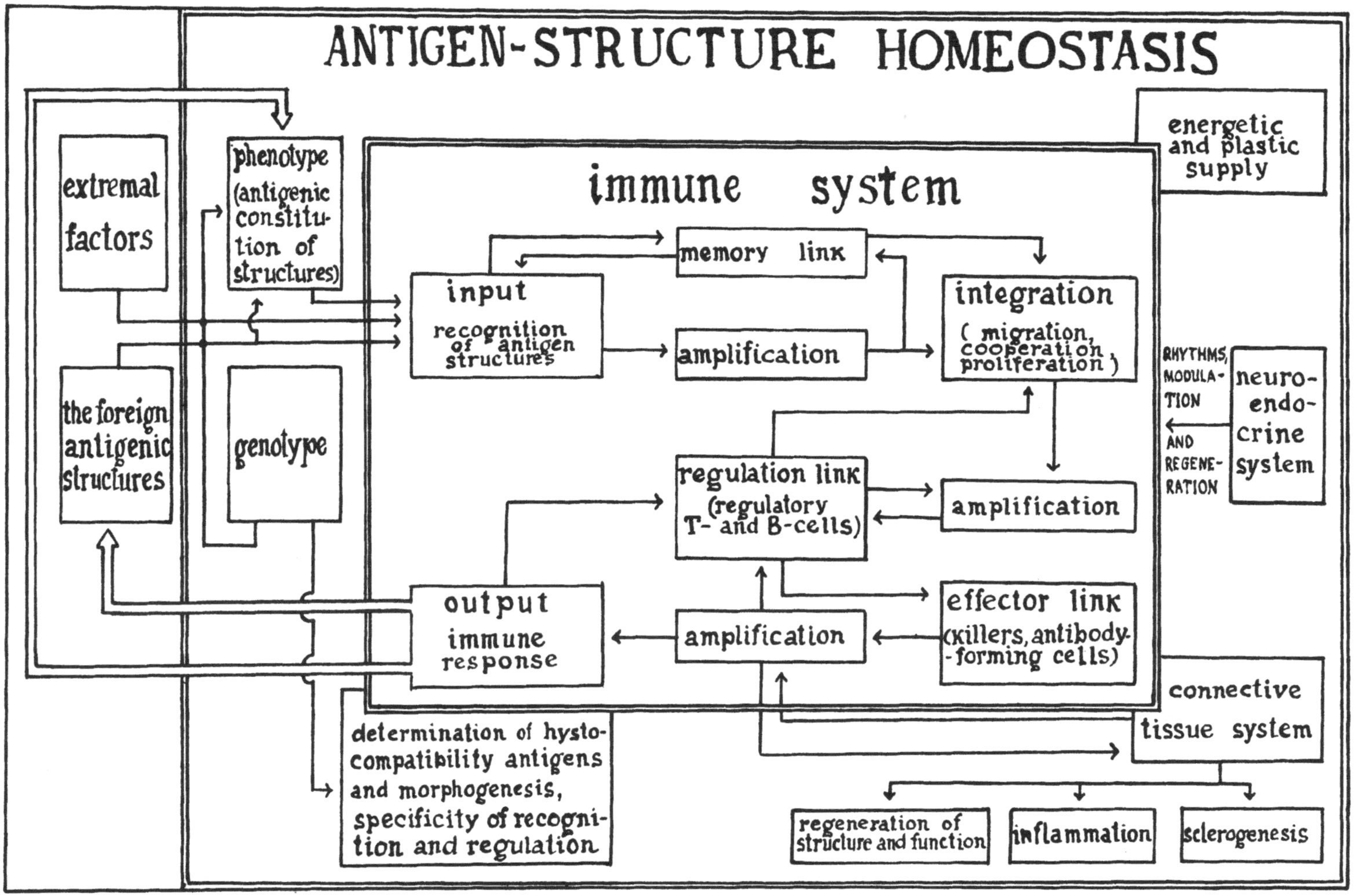

Figure 1. Structure - functional arrangement of the immune system.

MATHEMATICAL MODELS IN IMMUNOLOGY AND THEIR INTERPRETATION

G.I.Marchuk

Computing Center, Novosibirsk, USSR

1. Introduction

At the present time immunology is developing so fast that basic concepts constituting this science are literally changing before our eyes and our knowledge of the immune process is being enriched by new facts and hypotheses that completely change or refine some aspects of the theory. At the same time it should be stressed that most important immunological processes have been studied in detail by Burnet, Nossal, Feldmann, Good, Hasek, Petrov and others. These studies constitute a solid basis on which one can develop models simulating fundamental features of the immune process.

This evolution of theoretical and experimental immunology makes it possible to regard immune processes as a complex dynamic system where optimization is a natural component. Recently many interesting studies (by Hege, Cole (1966, USA), Jilek (1970-1971, ČSSR), Bell (1970-1973, USA), Bruni et al.(1974, Italy), etc) were devoted to modelling of immune processes. Most important was a study by Mohler (1975, USA) dealing with modelling of the immune system in terms of the theory of bilinear systems.

The present paper is concerned with mathematical models of a disease which have been developed at the Computing Center of the Siberian Branch of the USSR Academy of Sciences. Our models are based on the following assumptions:

1. A disease is regarded as an immune response of an organism to multiplying pathogenic antigen (virus, bacterium), i.e. the immune system is the only defensive means of the organism against infection. The outcome of the disease depends on the result of struggle between antigen and defensive means of the immune system, which include antibodies,killers, phagocytes, etc.

2. All model equations take into account the balance between the increase and decrease of every component of the process on a short time interval Δt, i.e. for every component one writes an equation in variations. When Δt approaches zero the latter become ordinary differential equations.

3. Interaction between several components of the process on a small time interval Δt is proportional to their concentrations multiplied by the length of Δt. Nonlinear terms of this type describe probability of contact of these components and quite accurately define the essence of the process.

4. All coefficients in model equations are supposed to be constant positive values, if not otherwise specified.

Now, let us consider a simple mathematical model of a disease.

2. A simple mathematical model of a disease

Let us assume that a small population of viruses has invaded a human organism and after a time reached an organ which they are able to affect. Let t_0 be the average time of the invasion. Having invaded the cell the viruses undergo neutralizing effect of interferon. On overcoming this effect, at the expense of albuminous and genetic material of the cell, the viruses begin to multiply and as a consequence hit different cells of the organ. The multiplication goes on until all reserves of the cell are exhausted.

Having injured the cell the viruses hit blood and lymphatic ducts. Some of them again invade healthy cells and continue multiplying while the others hit lymphatic nodes where there are concentrated lymphocytes specific for different antigen.

Thus, the antigen that invades the lymphatic nodes has some probability to meet with lymphocytes that react to antigen of a given kind.

As a result of binding and the catalytic reaction that follows the lymphocyte divides and transforms into antibody-producing plasmacytes. The time of formation of plasmacytes is approximately 12 to 18 hours.

In this manner, in principle, there develop defensive mechanisms of the organism stimulated by antigen.

In accordance with our model we assume that the following are basic factors of a virus disease:

V the number of viruses in an organism,

C the number of plasma cells producing antibodies F,

m relative characteristics of the damaged part of the tissue.

Let us construct model equations. The first equation will describe variation of the number of viruses in the organism

$$dV = \beta V dt - \gamma F V dt. \tag{1.1}$$

The first right-hand term of the equation represents the increase of the number of viruses dV for the time dt as a result of their division. Naturally, this number is proportional to V and to some quantity β, which is called a coefficient of virus multiplication. The term $\gamma FVdt$ denotes the number of viruses neutralized by antibodies F on the interval dt. Indeed, the above number is apparently proportional to both the number of antibodies in the organism and that of $\gamma FVdt$, γ is the coefficient associated with probable neutralization of virus by antibody during their encounter. In this model the coefficient is considered a constant value.

Having divided (1.1) by dt we obtain

$$\frac{dV}{dt} = (\beta - \gamma F)V \tag{1.2}$$

Equations for plasmacytes, antibodies and characteristics of the mass of the affected tissue are derived in a similar way. The system of model equations is as follows:

$$\frac{dV}{dt} = (\beta - \gamma F)V,$$

$$\frac{dC}{dt} = \xi(m)\,\alpha F(t - \tau)V(t - \tau) - \mu_C(C - C^*),$$

$$\frac{dF}{dt} = \rho C - \eta\gamma FV - \mu_F F,$$

$$\frac{dm}{dt} = \delta V - \mu_m m.$$

Below is the meaning of the terms on the right. In the equation for plasmacytes the first term denotes the increase of plasmacytes due to the stimulation of the immuno-competent lymphocytes by bounded viruses. It is known, that for the immuno-competent lymphocyte to produce a clone of plasmacytes some time is needed for its proliferation and division. The latter fact is taken into consideration by introducing the delay term into the model, i.e. τ is the time interval from the beginning of stimulation of lymphocyte up to plasmacyte clone formation. The second term represents ageing of plasmacytes with a constant μ_C, which is the inverse of the plasmacyte mean lifetime. Here C^* is the constant level of plasmacytes in an organism.

In the equation for antibodies the first term on the right denotes generation of antibodies by plasmacytes at speed ρ, the second - the decrease of antibodies due to neutralization of viruses, the third - natural decay of antibodies with constant μ_f equal to the inverse of the antibody half-life.

Finally, in the last equation the first term on the right represents expansion of the damage due to viruses, with the degree of damage δ, and the second - regeneration of the tissue at the expense of the organism. Now, it is convenient to explain the meaning of function $\xi(m)$ in the term denoting stimulation of lymphocytes in the equation for plasmacytes. Serious damage of vital organs worsens viability of the whole organism and, as a consequence, causes failure in functioning of the immune system. Function $\xi(m)$, shown in Fig. 1, in its simplest form, takes this fact into account. Indeed, when $0 \le m \le m^*$ damage of the organ does not affect plasmacyte production because in this case $\xi(m) = 1$, whereas on the interval $m^* \le m \le 1$ there is rapid drop in productivity of plasmacytes.

On the basis of qualitative analysis of the model we can make the following conclusions.

1. The system has two types of stationary solutions.

Solution 1 : $V = 0, \quad C = C^*, \quad F = \dfrac{\rho C^*}{\mu_F} = F^*$

describes the state of a healthy organism. Here F^* is the immunological barrier maintained by productivity of plasmacytes C^*.

Solution 2 :

$$V = \frac{\mu_c(\ \mu_f\beta - \ \gamma\rho C^*)}{\beta(\alpha\rho - \mu_c\eta\gamma)} > 0,$$

$$C = \frac{\alpha\mu_f\beta - \eta\gamma^2\mu_c C^*}{\gamma(\alpha\rho - \mu_c\eta\gamma)},$$

$$F = \frac{\beta}{\gamma},$$

$$M = \frac{\delta}{\mu_m} V$$

defines a persistent or chronic form of a disease.

2. Whatever the nonzero initial number of viruses that have invaded the organism, the disease does not progress unless the immunological barrier is overcome, i.e. $\beta/\gamma < F^*$. This is a theorem of immunological barrier.

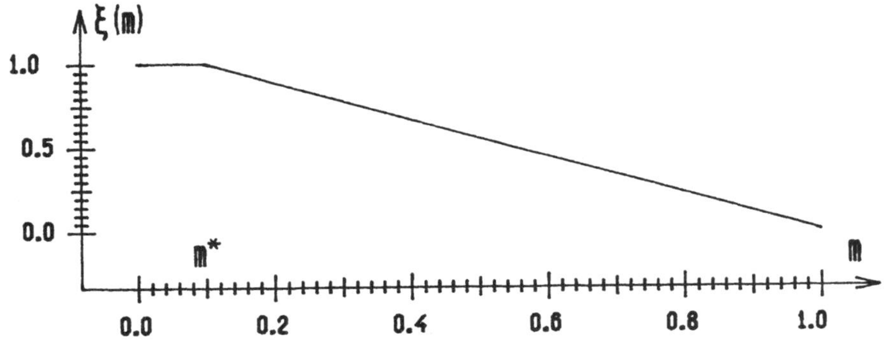

Fig. 1

Besides, as numerical experiments show, the system has purely periodic solutions interpreted as chronic forms of a disease.

3. A principal scheme of the virus disease dynamics

On the basis of the above stated mathematical model one can get a typical picture of the virus disease dynamics. It can be shown in Fig. 2.

If there is a sufficient number of functioning antibodies with respect to their antigen, the viruses that invade the organism will meet with a powerful response and their concentration will decrease and approach zero. This is a mild case of a disease (curve 1, Fig. 2).

It may so happen, however, that in the organism there goes a process of a viruses multiplication. The viruses bind with the antibodies, present in the blood plasma. Thus there establishes a balance

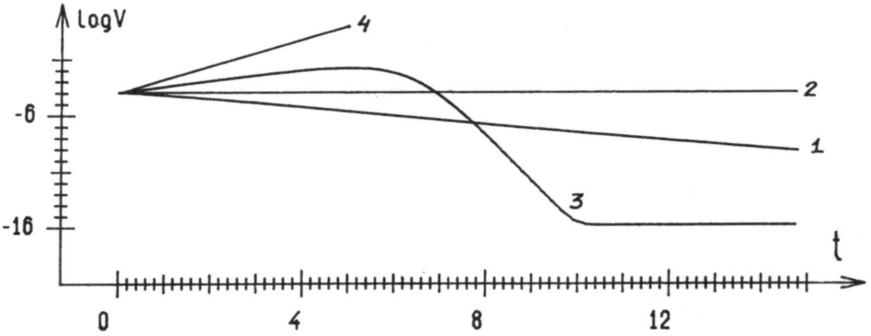

Fig. 2

between the number of viruses generated every second and those captured by antibodies. Here we deal with a stationary process which can be interpreted as a chronic or persistent form of a disease (curve 2, Fig. 2).

If the number of viruses grows more rapidly than reproduction of antibodies neutralizing the latter the curve of virus concentration begins to grow exponentially. However, after plasmacytes have formed and begun mass antibody production, the growth of the virus concentration decelerates and some time later it rapidly falls. At the same time there goes on a reproduction of new antibodies whose total number decelerates exponentially until the norman immunological level is reached. The damaged part of the organ, in which there went an evolution of the virus population, begins to recover exponentially (curve 3, Fig. 2).

Finally, it may happen that the damage of the virus-affected organ is essential. In that case the normal functioning of the organs responsible for antibody formation is seriously upset. Then the number of viruses in the organism will continuously grow, which results in a lethal issue (curve 4, Fig. 2).

Let us discuss most interesting results. The solid line in Fig. 3 shows an immune process where the effect of mass of the injured tissue is not taken into account, i.e. $\xi(m) \equiv 1$, the broken line shows the same process, with this effect taken into account. One can see that in the first case the process ends in recovery, whereas in the second case there arises a chronic form. Fig. 4 demonstrates dependence of the solution on the initial dose of viruses. It turns out that with the increase of the initial dose of viruses the chronic process (Fig. 4, solid line) degenerates into a normal response (Fig. 4, broken line). This allows us to formulate, immunologically and mathematically, a method for treatment of chronic infections by aggravation /2/.

Summing up, it will be noted that this model, abstract as it is, made it possible to determine most important mechanisms responsible for the progress of a disease, which can be used in more sophisticated models.

Now, let us consider two models generalizing the simple one and based on the scheme of the immune system functioning.

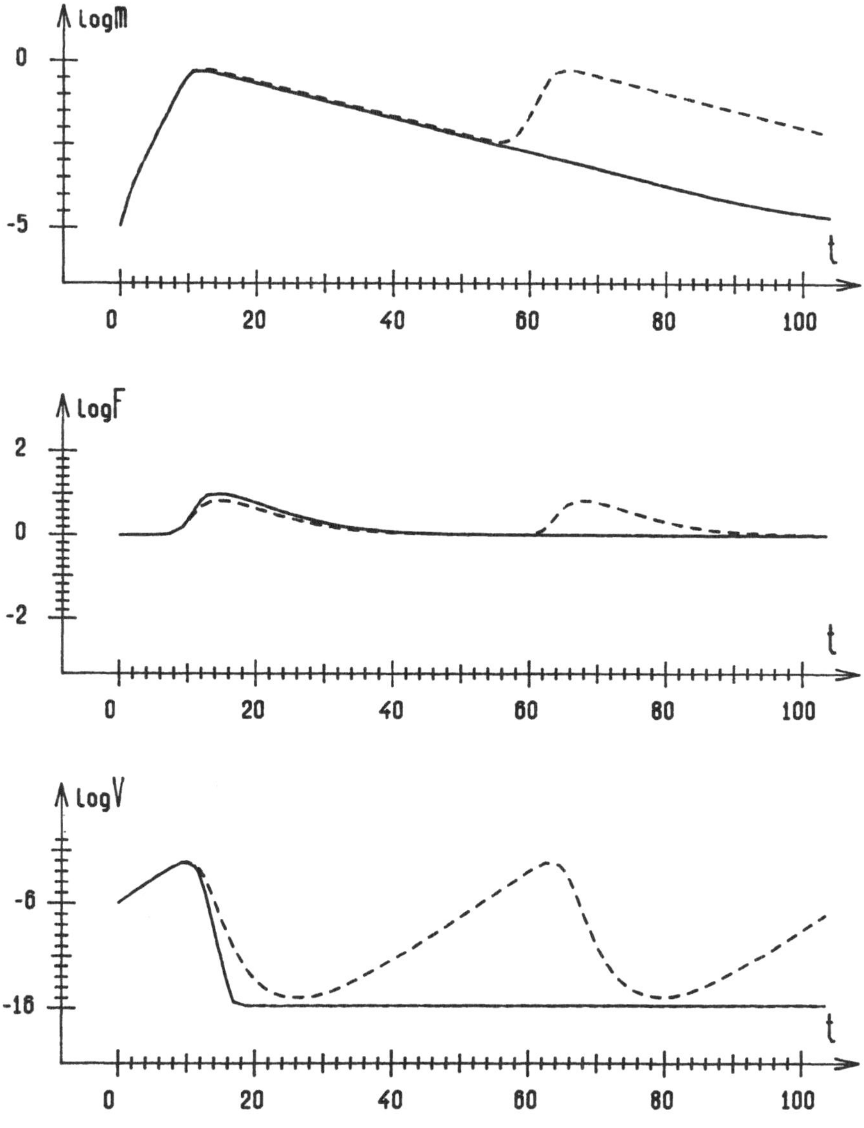
LogM
0
-5
t
0
20
40
60
80
100
LogF
2
0
-2
t
0
20
40
60
80
100
LogV
-6
-16
t
0
20
40
60
80
100

Fig. 3

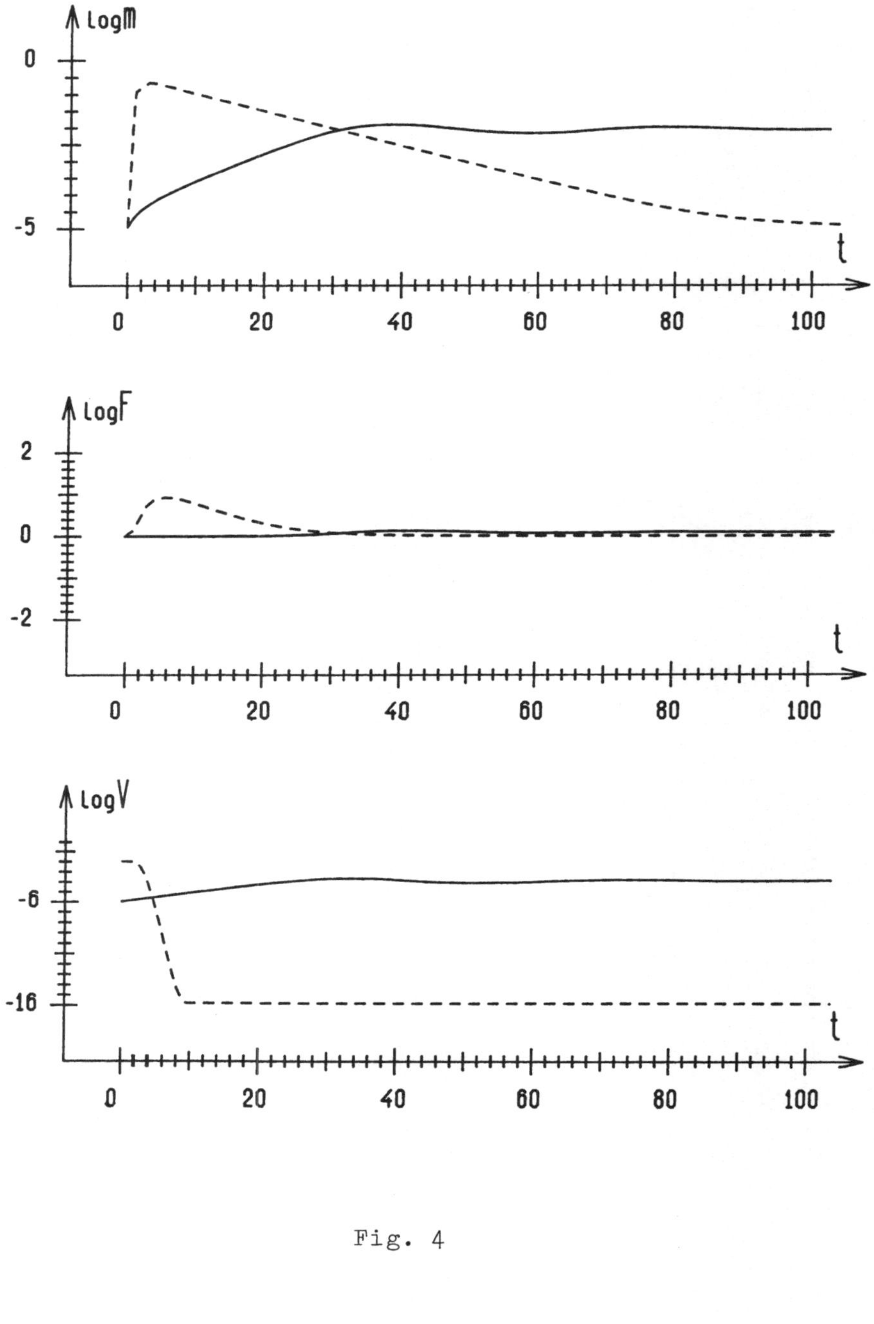

LogM
0
-5
t
0
20
40
60
80
100
LogF
2
0
-2
t
0
20
40
60
80
100
LogV
-6
-16
t
0
20
40
60
80
100

Fig. 4

4. The scheme of the immune system functioning

It is well-known at present that at least three cellular systems (T- and B-lymphocytes, macrophages) participate in antibody genesis. T- and B-lymphocytes arise according to the following scheme.Non-differentiated stem elements, generated by the bone marrow, penetrate into circulation and on passing through different lymphoid organs become immunocompetent precursors of various types. On arriving at the thymus the cells multiply and differentiate into T-lymphocytes responsible for cellular immunity. The other stem cells of the bone marrow differentiate into B-lymphocytes under the influence of Fabricius' bursa of birds or an unknown organ of mammals. The arising B-lymphocytes are precursors of plasmacytes which are antibody producers. Macrophages also arise from stem cells that have penetrated from the bone marrow into peripheral tissues. Hence, the bone marrow is one of the most important sources of "raw material" for the immune process components. About 2 percent of stem cells of the bone marrow go out into circulation every day, but their portion is tens of times higher with the injection of antigen doses. Miller and Mitchell (1968) proved that T- and B-lymphocytes must participate in antibody genesis and at present this statement arouses no doubts. There are several schemes of cooperation mechanism. Let us discuss the hypothesis formulated by Feldmann. The essence of it is as follows. On binding by their haptene parts with I_g receptors of T-lymphocytes, molecules of the antigen take I_gT off their surface (Fig. 5, steps 1 and 2). Molecules of the antigen-bound I_gT have free F_c-portions of heavy chains by which they are connected with proper receptors on the surface of macrophages (Fig. 5. step 3). There appears a concentrated "ring" of antigenic molecules whose determinant (haptene) regions are oriented outside: The "ring" is supplied to a B-lymphocyte (Fig. 5, step 4). Such an effective signal may cause the B-lymphocyte to proliferate and differentiate which leads to plasma cells formation. Binding of individual molecules of the antigen to B-lymphocytes is not an effective signal. (Generally, another non-specific signal is needed to stimulate B-lymphocytes, that is, an inducer of immunopoesis).

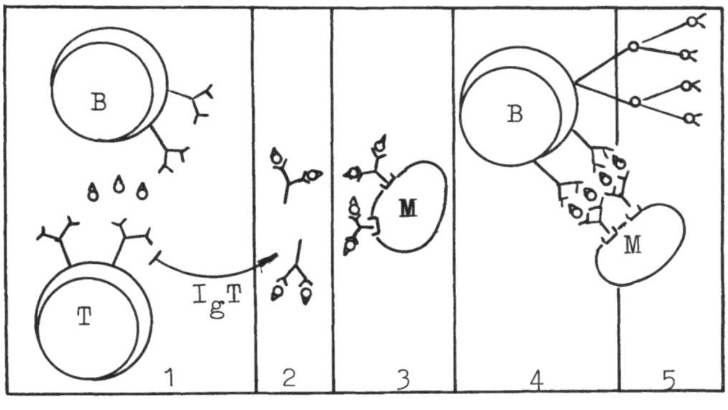

Fig. 5

Segal and Feldmann proved division of T-cells into individual subpopulations due to the fact that they have at least two functions: one is that of helpers (cooperation with B-lymphocytes) and the other of killers (cells-effectors in cellular immune reactions). They also found that T-helpers and T-killers are two different cells of different sensitivity to corticosteroids. Cortisone-sensitive lymphocytes are able to serve solely as helpers, whereas cortisone-resistent lymphocytes (or killers) have both functions. T-helpers are thymocytes and killers are mature T-lymphocytes. The sequence of events is as follows: stem cell - thymocyte (helper) - mature T-lymphocyte (killer). (The existence of cells of T-suppressors responsible for tolerance is also proved).

B-system formation goes on as follows: stem cells - immunocompetent precursors (B-cell) - antibody-producent (plasma cell). The B-cell accepts the antigen stimulus. Having reacted with the antigen and T-lymphocyte the cell begins dividing and differentiating to form antibody-producing plasma cells. It is particular feature of the B-system that antibodies even against one and the same antigen belong to different classes of immunoglobulins (I_gM, I_gG, I_gA). Moreover, it is proved that in the same cell the synthesis of I_gM is switched over to the synthesis of I_gG. Hence, there is a sequence of steps: stem cell $B_M \rightarrow B_G \rightarrow B_A$. There is a reason to assume that production of I_gG-antibodies largely depends on T-B-cooperation, because most of thymus-independent antigen (not requiring the participation of the T-system in antibody genesis) stimulate the synthesis of only I_gM, i.e. primary response, antibodies even with repeated injection of antigen.

In the course of the primary response, specific T- and B-memory cells accumulate. The immunological memory keeps on for many months or even years. This is not associated, however, with storage of high titers of antibodies in the blood.

5. Basic assumptions

Below we discuss basic assumptions used in mathematical modelling of the immune system.

Stem cells are assumed to be differenting into T- and B-lymphocytes and macrophages only. Their concentration in a healthy organism is constant which determines constant levels of all immune process components. In other words, the notion of "stem cells" includes populations of precursors of T- and B-lymphocytes and macrophages.

Antigen and (T- or B-) lymphocytes react to form free and bound (T- or B-) complexes. A free complex is a combination of antigen and receptors torn off the lymphocyte. Free B-complexes and part of free T-complexes stimulate the bone marrow performance. The other part of free T-complexes, having coated the macrophages, participate in stimulation of B-lymphocytes, thereby causing cooperation between T- and B-systems. Bound complexes (combination of antigen with fixed receptors on a lymphocyte) after a division differentiate into plasmacytes which are killer and antibody producers. We think that stimulation of B-lymphocytes may occur both directly after reaction with antigen and by means of the T-B-cooperation and that the schemes of T- and B-system formation are similar, i.e. stem cell → T-lymphocyte → T-plasma cell → killers; stem cell → B-lymphocyte → B plasma cell → antibodies. Besides, let us assume that T-lymphocytes-killers are responsible only for destruction of antigen, and plasma B-cells produce only I_gM and I_gG antibodies; switch-over to the synthesis of I_gG occurs by threshold means as soon as specific T- and B-lymphocytes accumulate. As far as macrophages are concerned, they not only participate in T-B cooperation but also utilize the exhausted components and products of the immune reaction.

Normal functioning of the organism is disturbed if one of the organs is affected by antigen (virus) and as a consequence effectiveness of the immune response falls. This means that immune reactivity depends on the normal functioning of the whole organism.

Finally, it should be noted that throughout the model we assume that in the organism there are enough of different enzymes and non-specific factors participating in the reactions described above.

6. The immune model with B-,T-antibodies

In accordance with the above stated immunological scheme and the assumptions made we suggested at first a simplified model, including

B(t) - concentration of viruses
F(t) - concentration of antibodies
$C_B(t)$ - concentration of B-plasmacytes
$C_T(t)$ - concentration of T-plasmacytes
T - concentration of T-lymphocytes
B - concentration of B-lymphocytes
Λ - concentration of macrophages
m - characteristic of the affected organ

The system of model equations is as follows:

$$\frac{dV}{dt} = (\beta - \gamma_1 F - \gamma_2 T - \gamma_3 B)V,$$

$$\frac{dF}{dt} = \mu_B \xi(m) C_B - \eta_1 \gamma_1 FV - \alpha_F(F - F^*),$$

$$\frac{dC_B}{dt} = P_B(t - \tau_B) - \alpha_{C_B}(C_B - C_B^*)$$

$$\frac{dT}{dt} = \mu_T \xi(m) C_T - \eta_2 \gamma_2 TV - \alpha_T(T - T^*)$$

$$\frac{dC_T}{dt} = P_T(t - \tau_T) - \alpha_{C_T}(C_T - C_T^*),$$

$$\frac{dB}{dt} = \gamma_6 \xi(m) BV - \gamma_7 BV - \gamma_8 VTB\Lambda - \alpha_B(B - B^*),$$

$$\frac{dA}{dt} = (\gamma_9 TV + \gamma_{10} BV)\,\xi(m) - [\gamma_{11} VT + \gamma_{12} BV + \gamma_{13} FV +$$

$$+ \gamma_{14}(C_B - C_B^*) + \gamma_{15}(C_T - C_T^*)]\,\Lambda - \gamma_{16} TVAB - \alpha_\Lambda(\Lambda - \Lambda^*),$$

$$\frac{dm}{dt} = \delta V - \alpha_m m,$$

$$P_B(t) = \gamma_4 VT\Lambda B + \gamma^1 BV, \quad P_T(t) = \gamma_5 VT.$$

This is an intermediate between the simplest model and the one to be considered below. Since stem cells are absent from this model, it is assumed that the growth of concentrations of T-,B-lymphocytes and macrophages is proportional to concentrations of free complexes. Antibodiés are not divided into classes. T-killers and T-helpers populations are joined into one population. The other aspects of the model are similar to those described in the above immunological scheme.

In terms of this model we assume that the immune B-system does not function, i.e. we "cancel" the B-system components: F-antibodies, C_B plasma cells, B-lymphocytes. Then we have

$$\frac{dV}{dt} = (\beta - \gamma_2 T)V,$$

$$\frac{dT}{dt} = \mu_T\,\xi(m)C_T - \eta_2\gamma_2 TV - \alpha_T T$$

$$\frac{dC_T}{dt} = P_T(t - \tau_T) - \alpha_{C_T}(C_T - C_T^*),$$

$$P_T(t) = \gamma_T VT$$

$$\frac{dm}{dt} = \delta V - \mu_m m.$$

Hence, we have come to the simplest model of a disease. One can see that this model is valid to describe a disease dynamics on the basis of only T-system.

Next, we assume that the T-system does not function. Again, we have the simplest model

$$\frac{dV}{dt} = (\beta - \gamma_1 F)V,$$

$$\frac{dF}{dt} = \mu_B\,\xi(m)C_B - \eta_1\gamma_1 FV - \alpha_F F,$$

$$\frac{dC_B}{dt} = P_B(t - \tau_B) - \alpha_{C_B}(C_B - C_B^*),$$

$$\frac{dm}{dt} = \delta V - \alpha_m m$$

$$P_B(t) = \gamma^1 BV.$$

Thus, the model under consideration has two limit cases essentially coinciding with the simplest scheme.

In the course of numerical analysis we have obtained forms of a disease similar to those already considered. The theorem of the immunological barrier which in this case includes normal levels of T- and B-lymphocytes, T^* and B^* correspondingly in addition to the level of antibodies F^*, is also valid.

When we analysed disagreement between T- and B-systems, i.e. when we analysed T-deficiency and B-deficiency, it appeared that in our model the major role was played by the immune T-system because with any B-deficiency the T-system coped with the infection though the dynamics of viruses could change both qualitatively and quantitatively. The T-deficiency is characterized by a persistent process, transition to chronic or lethal forms. Fig. 6 illustrates the abovesaid for the case when the immune barrier is not overcome at simultaneous response of the T-B-systems (at T-B-response).

7. The immunological model of a disease

Finally, let us consider a model that fully corresponds to the scheme of the immune system and uses the assumptions stated above. The model includes the following 11 variables: antigen, stem cells, macrophages, B-lymphocytes, T-helpers, T-killers, T- and B-plasma cells, I_gM and I_gG antibodies and characteristics of the affected organ. The dynamics of the immune response is defined by

$$\frac{dX}{dt} = \rho_T\, \xi(m)X_9 - \gamma_4 X_1 X_{10} - \frac{1}{\tau_T}X_1,$$

$$\frac{dX}{dt} = \rho_B\, \xi(m)X_9 - \gamma_5 X_1 X_2 X_8 X_{10} - \gamma_6 X_{10} X_2 - \frac{1}{\tau_B}X_2,$$

$$\frac{dX}{dt} = \rho_K X_6 - \gamma_9 X_{10} X_3 - \frac{1}{\tau_K}X_3,$$

$$\frac{dX}{dt} = \rho_M X_7 - \gamma_7 X_{10} X_4 - \frac{1}{\tau_M}X_4,$$

$$\frac{dX_5}{dt} = \rho_G X_7 - \gamma_8 X_{10} X_5 - \frac{1}{\tau_G} X_5,$$

$$\frac{dX_6}{dt} = P_T(t - \tau_1) - \frac{1}{\tau_{C_T}} (X_6 - X_6^*),$$

$$P_T(t) = \rho_1 X_{10} X_1,$$

$$\frac{dX_7}{dt} = P_B(t - \tau_2) - \frac{1}{\tau_{C_B}} (X_7 - X_7^*),$$

$$P_B(t) = p_2 X_{10} X_2 + p_3 X_1 X_2 X_8 X_{10},$$

$$\frac{dX_8}{dt} = \rho_\Lambda \xi(m) X_9 - (Q + S) X_8 - \gamma_{10} X_1 X_2 X_8 X_{10} - \frac{1}{\tau_\Lambda} X_8,$$

$$S = \sum_{i=1}^{8} \nu_i (X_i - X_i^*), \qquad Q = \sum_{i=1}^{5} n_i X_i X_{10},$$

$$\frac{dX_9}{dt} = \gamma_1 X_1 X_{10} + \gamma_2 X_2 X_{10} - \gamma_3 (X_9 - X_9^*),$$

$$\frac{dX_{10}}{dt} = (\beta - R) X_{10},$$

$$R = \sum_{i=1}^{5} \delta_i X_i ,$$

$$\frac{dX_{11}}{dt} = \delta X_{10} - \mu_m X_{11}.$$

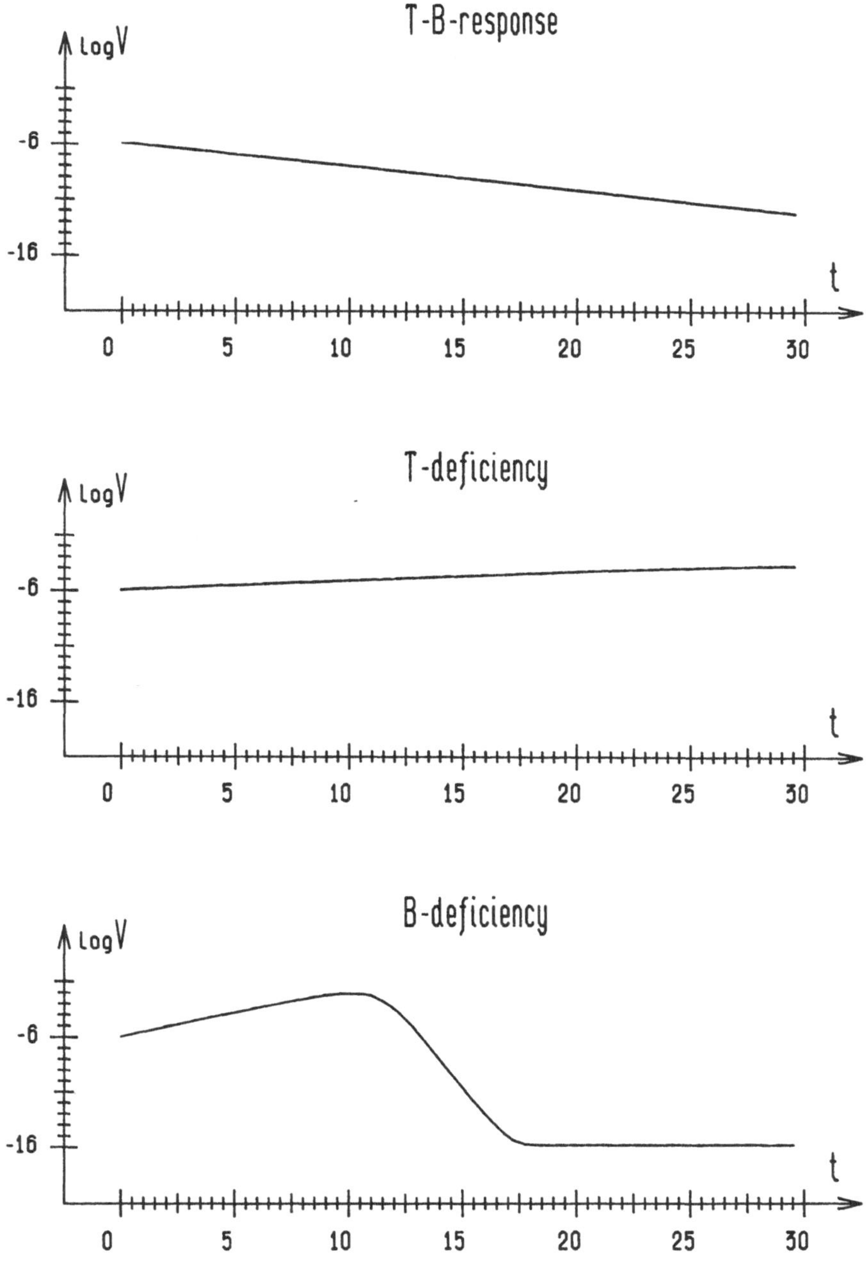
T-B-response
logV
-6
-16
t
0
5
10
15
20
25
30
T-deficiency
logV
-6
-16
t
0
5
10
15
20
25
30
B-deficiency
logV
-6
-16
t
0
5
10
15
20
25
30

Fig. 6

In /1/ one can find a detailed description of notations, equations, assumptions and results of modelling. The present paper deals with the process as a whole described by the model. If there are no viruses in the organism all components of the model have normal values (as in a healthy organism). A linear combination of these components is an immune barrier for viruses. Invading the organism a population of viruses, capable to overcome the barrier, reacts with T-helpers and B-lymphocytes to form bound and free complexes. It will be reminded that a free complex is a combination of antigen with receptors torn off the lymphocyte; a bound complex is a combination of antigen with receptors fixed on the lymphocyte. After a division, which takes time, bound (T- and B-) complexes develop a clone of T- and B-plasma cells. The latter in turn produce material substrates (cells-killers and I_gM antibodies). Free complexes stimulate the bone marrow. As a result the concentration of stem cells as well as of B-lymphocytes, T-helpers and macrophages grow. Besides, according to Feldmann, free T-complexes forming rings on macrophages, stimulate B-lymphocytes to proliferate and divide. This results in a clone of plasmacytes generating I_gM antibodies. As soon as the concentration of T-, B-lymphocytes and macrophages considerably increases and the importance of cooperation between them increases too, there occurs switch-over of I_gM- to I_gG-synthesis. In case the immune system has been stimulated effectively enough and the organ has not been seriously affected, the reaction of viruses with killers, antibodies of two kinds, as well as with B-lymphocytes and T-helpers results in recovery, i.e. in the entire removal of viruses from the organism. Products of the immune reaction and the exhausted elements will be removed from the body by macrophages. This is the process described by the model.

The model can simulate immuno-deficiency according to the scheme of T- and B- immune system formation. The scheme is shown in Fig. 7. According to Petrov, this is the main hypothesis for classification of immunodeficiency. The scheme shows the places of failure of five possible genetic blocks that switch off one or another element of the immune system. One can see that failure of stem cells has the most serious consequences. Analysis of this case by the model has shown an unlimited increase of viruses in the absence of stem cells since the latter are the source of all the immune components.

It should be noted that our model does not include memory cells responsible for the secondary immune response and T-suppressors responsible for tolerance. The secondary response can be simulated by increasing the initial data of the immune process components. First, this will cause an increase of the immune barrier. Second, the reaction will start immediately with production of I_gG antibodies which is specific for the secondary response, as concentrations of T-helpers and B-lymphocytes can be increased to levels needed for the switch-over. As for T-suppressors, their origination and the principles of action are not yet understood though it is quite clear that they should be included in the model. Our models have shown, for example, that it is inconvenient for an organism to react to small doses of viruses (there's tolerance of a low dose!) and the consequence is chronic forms of a disease /2/.

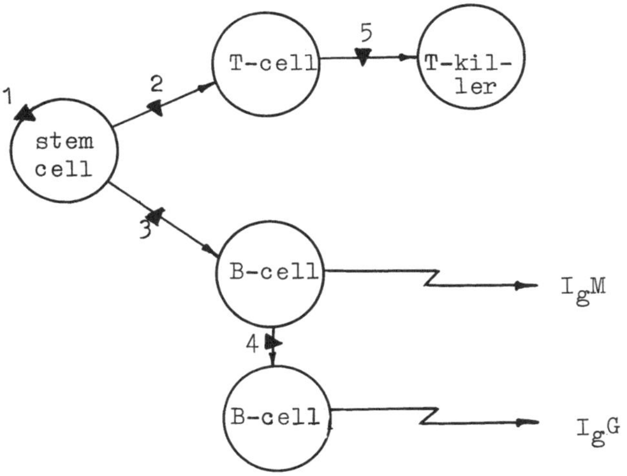

Fig. 7

To conclude with, it should be noted that if efforts of mathematicians, immunologists and physicians from different countries are joined together this will help us in solving immunological problems, problems of forecasting the progress of virus disease and, ultimately, - in finding most effective methods of treatment.

REFERENCES

1. Asachenkov, A.L., Marchuk, G.I. Investigation of the mathematical model of a disease and some results of computer simulation. In this volume.
2. Belykh, L.N., Marchuk, G.I. Chronic forms of a disease and their treatment according to mathematical immune response models.
3. Bell, G. J.Theor.Biol., 29, 191 (1970), 33, 339 (1971).
4. Bruni, C. et al. Math.Biosci., 27, 191 (1975).
5. DeLisi, C., and Perelson, A. J.Theor.Biol., 62, 159 (1976).
6. DeLisi, C., et al. Bul.of Math.Biol., 39, 201 (1977).
7. Feldmann, M.P. Erb.Cell.Immunol., 19, 356 (1975).
8. Freedman, H., and Gatica, J. Math.Biosci., 37, 113 (1977).
9. Hege, I.S., and Cole, L.I. J.Immunol., 97, 1, 34 (1966).
10. Hoffmann, G. Eur.J.Immunol.,
11. Jilek, M. Folia Microbiologica, 16, 1-3 (1971).
12. Marchuk, G.I. Proc.of the 8th IFIP Conf.on Opt.Tech. Springer-Verlag, Heidelberg, 41, 1978.
13. Mohler, R.R. et al. T- and B-cell models in the immune system. In: Theoretical Immunology, Marcel Dekker, 1978.
14. Petrov, R.V. Immunology and genetics, Moscow, Medicina, 1976.
15. Pimbly, G. Math.Biosci., 20, 27 (1974), 21, 251 (1974).
16. Pimbly, G. Arch.Rat.Mech.Anal., 55, 93 (1974).
17. Richter, P. Eur.J.Immunol., 5, 350 (1974).
18. Waltman, P., and Butz, E. J.Theor.Biol., 65, 499 (1977).

CLINICAL IMMUNOLOGY: PROBLEMS AND PROSPECTS

R.V. Petrov
Institute of Biophysics, USSR Ministry of Health, Moscow

The immune system of vertebrates encompasses two cellular subsystems clearly separable from each other in the process of differentiation but functioning cooperatively. One of them develops under the influence of the thymus and is called thymus-dependent, or T-system of immunity. It mediates cellular forms of specific reactivity, such as delayed hypersensitivity, transplantation and antitumor immunity, and other responses effected by sensitized T-lymphocytes, or killer cells. The second subsystem develops independently of the thymus and is centered around B-lymphocytes. Upon interaction with T-lymphocytes and macrophages, B-lymphocytes are transformed into plasma cells actively synthesizing immunoglobulins. The B-system is responsible for the production of antibodies, i.e. for humoral immune responses.

The populations of T-and B-lymphocytes have proved to be nonhomogeneous. Three separate subpopulations have been detected among T-lymphocytes: helper, suppressor and effector T-cells. B-lymphocytes include precursors of cells producing diverse immunoglobulin classes (IgM, IgG, IgA).

Different steps in the formation of these subpopulations have been identified, and it has become possible to outline their histogenesis. Fig. 1 shows the development of the human immune system. This schematic representation is based to a large extent on clinical immunogenetic research, i.e. studies of genetically determined immunodeficiencies in man.

Indeed, various types of genetic blocks observed in children are direct evidence demonstrating the existence of distinct steps

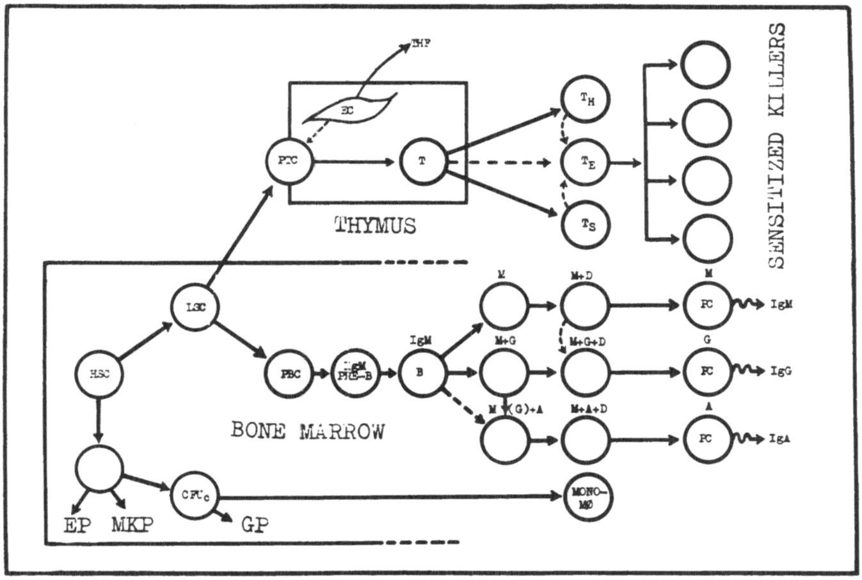

Figure 1. Schematic model of the development of the cells involved in host defence. HSC, hemopoietic stem cell; EP, erythropoiesis; MKP, megakaryocytopoiesis; GP, granulocytopoiesis; CFU$_C$, colony-forming units in culture assay; LSC, lymphoid stem cell; PTC, precursor of T-cells; EC, epithelial cell in the thymus; THF, thymic humoral factor; T, T-lymphocyte; T_H, helper T-cell; T_E, effector T-cell; T_S, suppressor T-cell; PBC, precursor of B-cells; PRE-B, pre-B cell; B, B-lymphocyte; PC, plasma cell; M,D,G,A, immunoglobulin receptors of different classes; MONO-MØ, monocyte-macrophage.

in the development and operation of the immune system. Thus, congenital agammaglobulinemia accompanied by intact cell-mediated responses proves unambiguously that the T-and B-cell systems differentiate along independent routes. Genetic defects involving both systems show that they are derived from a common progenitor. An isolated deficiency of IgA producers or suppressor T-cells indicates that the histogenesis of these cells proceeds at its final stages independently of other subpopulations.

Such decoding of immunogenetic information served as the basis for an updated model of histogenesis of human immunocytes created by a WHO Scientific Group in November 1977. Of course, the members of the Group utilized the vast amount of data accumulated by experimental immunology. Yet their main purpose was to outline the development of the human immune system. The model was prepared with utmost precision and objectivity. Every step and every cell figuring in the model were subjected to immunogenetic analysis in order to verify their existence in man.

All cells of the immune system are derived from the hemopoietic stem cell. This pluripotent self-perpetuating unit produces the lymphoid stem cell (LSC), a common progenitor of the T- and B-lymphoid cell systems. LSC generate cells of two types: PTC (precursor of T-cells) and PBC (precursor of B-cells) which give rise to the T- and B-lymphocyte populations. T-lymphocytes develop from PTC in the thymus, central organ of the immune system, under the influence of thymic epithelial cells and humoral mediators. The thymic humoral factors (thymosin, thymopoietin, etc.) are released into the bloodstream and can bring T-cells to maturity outside the thymus. Thymic lymphocytes (thymocytes) differentiate into three distinct types of T-cells: helpers, effectors and suppressors, which are delivered into the bloodstream and the peripheral lymphoid organs. Upon antigenic stimulation, effector T-cells generate a clone of sensitized lymphocytes (killers) to carry out cellular immune responses.

Under the influence of some unknown factor(s), B-cell precursors differentiate first into pre-B cells, which can already synthesize IgM but lack surface immunoglobulin receptors, and then into marrow B-lymphocytes carrying IgM receptors on their surface. The latter cells give rise to three types of B-lymphocytes homing to peripheral lymphoid organs and capable of generating plasma cells to produce, respectively, IgM, IgG and IgA antibodies. Mature

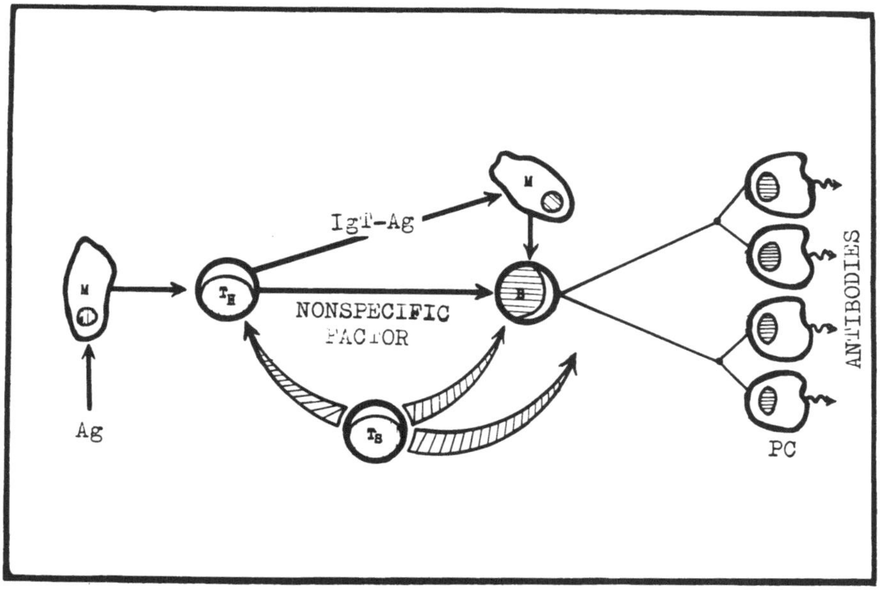

Figure 2. The sequence of events inducing antibody formation. Ag, antigen; M, macrophage; T_H, helper T-cell; T_S, suppressor T-cell; B, B-lymphocyte; PC, plasma cells; IgT-Ag, immunoglobulin receptor complexed with antigen.

B-lymphocytes carry surface immunoglobulin receptors belonging to one of these classes plus IgD.

Macrophages have their own path of development; they are not derived from LSC, but originate from a hemopoietic precursor shared with the myeloid series.

Three types of mature T-lymphocytes, three types of mature B-lymphocytes and macrophages - such are the seven principal cellular partners enacting the entire gamut of specific immune responses. These seven categories of cells are sensitive to antigenic stimulation and antigen-reactive. The sequence of events inducing antibody formation is shown in Fig. 2 according to the data presented at the Third International Congress of Immunology (1977). The antigen is processed by a macrophage and then recognized by a helper T-lymphocyte. The helper T-cell delivers two signals to trigger a B-lymphocyte. The first, specific signal is a special IgT immunoglobulin complexed with the antigen and presented to the B-cell by the macrophage. The second signal is a nonspecific stimulant of unknown nature. In other words, helper T-cells together with macrophages trigger B-cells for antibody production. Suppressor T-lymphocytes can inhibit the triggering mechanism, arrest the development of an antibody-forming clone and are responsible for the induction of tolerance. Their key function is probably to suppress autoimmune responses, to block the production of autoantibodies.

Anyway, helper and suppressor T-cells perform the main regulatory functions in the immune system.

There are at least three causes that may lead to deficient production of immunoglobulins: inadequacy of the corresponding type of B cells, inadequacy of helper T-cells and hyperactivity (or an excess) of suppressor T-lymphocytes. Formation of autoantibodies may occur, too, through different mechanisms: the appearance of an autoaggressive B-lymphocyte clone or a defect of suppressor cells. Until recently autoimmune disorders were considered to reflect hyperactivity of immunocompetent cells directed against self-antigens, but now they are assumed to be a manifestation of a suppressor T-cell deficit. Inadequacy of antitumor immunity attributed previously to a deficit of effector T-cells may actually be determined by activation of suppressor T-lymphocytes.

Together with V.A. Nasonova and her colleagues from the Institute for Rheumatism (AMS USSR), we have examined NZB mice which develop between 6 and 9 months of age an autoimmune disease similar to systemic lupus erythematosus in man. By the time of its onset the activity of marrow suppressor cells in these animals falls 10-

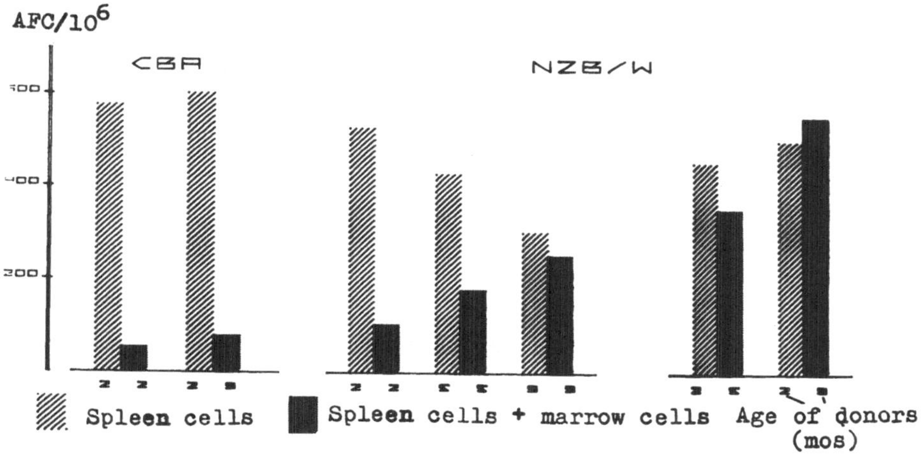

Figure 3. Disappearance of marrow suppressor cells in NZB/W mice with autoimmune disease. AFC/10^6, number of antibody-forming cells per 10^6 splenocytes.

to 15-fold, disappearing completely when the disease becomes fully established. The first two pairs of bars in Fig. 3 show the suppressive effect exerted in vitro by marrow cells from normal mice on the triggering of spleen cells for antibody production. The marrow taken from 5- and 9-month-old NZB mice is ineffective, as demonstrated by the central and right bars. When these components of the immune system were studied in mice bearing transplanted or spontaneous tumors, enhanced migration of stem cells from the marrow and activation of suppressor T-cells could be observed (Khaitov, Petrov et al., 1976).

It is possible to evaluate the numbers and functional activity of suppressor T-lymphocytes in clinical cases. The methods are already available. But they were only developed within the last few months. Therefore the world literature contains practically no factual data that would characterize various disease entities from this standpoint. Fig. 4 demonstrates the first results obtained by A. Pavlyuk (Immunology Chair of II Moscow Medical Institute) who tested the activity of suppressor T-cells in normal blood donors and in patients with multiple sclerosis, rheumatoid arthritis and acute pancreatitis. It may be seen that in acute pancreatitis these cells are preserved; yet their activity falls to an extremely low level in multiple sclerosis and is markedly decreased in rheumatoid arthritis.

Modern methodology allows to analyse quantitatively and functionally most subpopulations of cells in the human immune system. However, helper and suppressor T-cells were discovered but recently

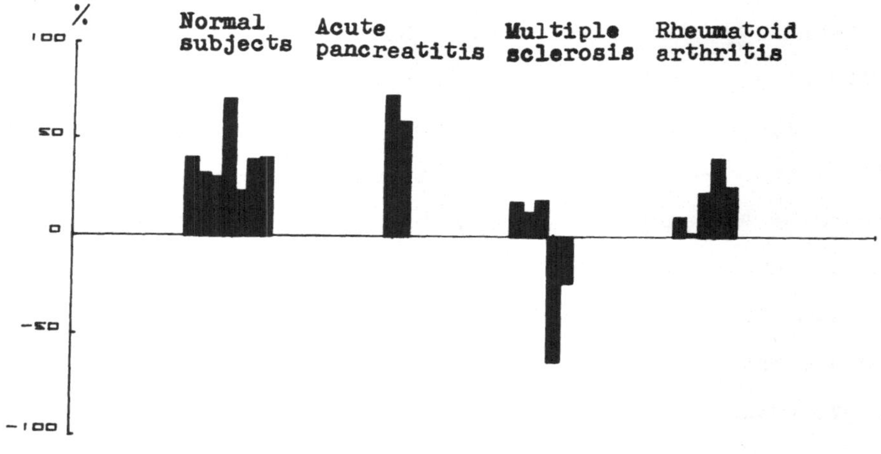

Figure 4. Indices of the activity of suppressor T-cells in the bloodstream of normal subjects and patients with different diseases.

and few of their secrets have been unravelled. On the other hand, studies carried out in the past three years have provided a large volume of information about the total populations of T-and B-lymphocytes. This information reflects quantitative and functional changes of the T-and B-systems associated with various conditions and will undoubtedly serve as a firm basis for further investigation of shifts in different compartments of cells.

First of all, I would like to present our data demonstrating the relative numbers of T; B-and null lymphocytes in the bloodstream of practically normal donors at various ages (Fig. 5). "Null cell" is the name designating lymphocytes which lack the characteristics of T-or B-cells and are probably immature. Part of null cells can be transformed into T-lymphocytes under the action of thymosin.

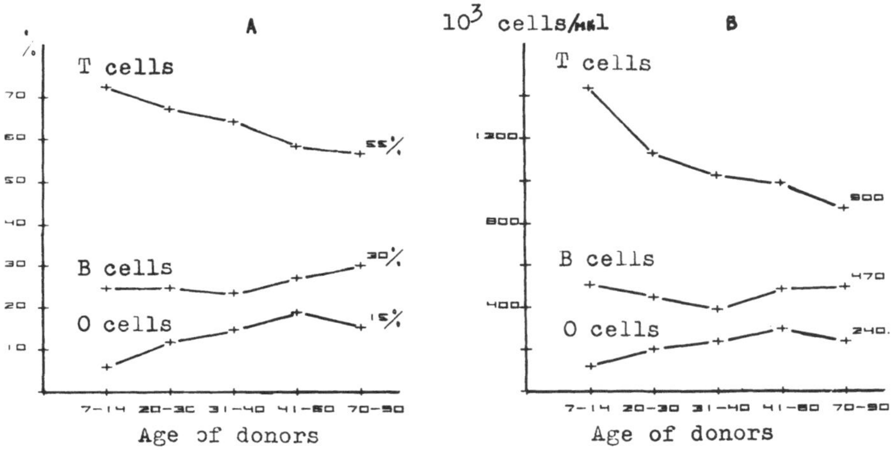

Figure 5. Relative (A) and absolute (B) numbers of T; B-and O-lymphocytes in human blood at various ages.

Fig. 5 shows that both the relative and absolute numbers of B-lymphocytes remain virtually unchanged with aging. Yet the proportions and especially the absolute content of circulating T-lymphocytes decline steadily. Old age is associated with a pronounced T-deficit. One urgent task facing contemporary gerontology is to find ways and means of compensating this deficit. In the neonatal period the numbers of T-cells are increased.

While discussing physiological, age-related changes it would be pertinent to mention another physiological condition - that of pregnancy. Fig. 6 presents data obtained in I.N. Golovistikov's laboratory and G.A. Gryaznova's clinic (II Moscow Medical Institute). It may be seen that during normal pregnancy T-cell numbers decline

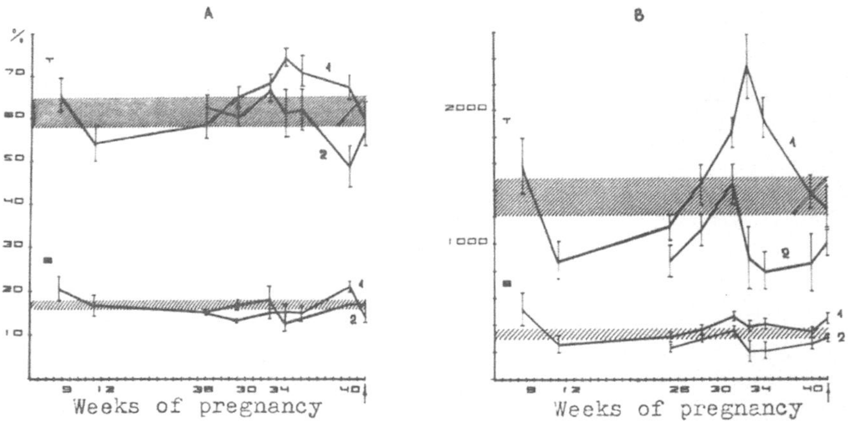

Figure 6. T-and B-lymphocytes in normal pregnancy and in nephropathy. The normal range is hatched. A, relative number of blood lymphocytes (%); B, absolute number of blood lymphocytes ($x10^3/\mu l$). 1, normal pregnancy; 2, nephropathy.

until the 32nd or 34th week and then become augmented. If pregnancy is complicated by nephropathy, this physiological change is modified: there is no secondary increase in T-lymphocytes.

A summary of information reflecting quantitative shifts in T- and B-lymphocytes during various diseases is given in Table 1. Most data were obtained by the staff of the Immunology Chair and Department of the II Moscow Medical Institute as a result of studies carried out in collaboration with the clinics of the Institute of Biophysics, I Moscow Medical Institute, Oncology Center (AMS USSR), Institute for Rheumatism (AMS USSR) and other institutions.

Much promise for the future is offered by tests for T-and B-lymphocytes in the fluids of body cavities. This approach seems to open up new possibilities for diagnosis and prediction in clinical practice. Together with researchers from V.S. Smolensky's clinic (I Moscow Medical Institute), we examined the synovial fluid in cases of rheumatoid arthritis. The percentage of T-lymphocytes (72%) was found to be higher, and that of B-cells twice lower than in the blood. Y.A. Malashhia and his colleagues from the Tbilisi Institute for Postgraduate Training developed a technique for exploring the cerebrospinal fluid. According to their results, normal CSF contains 3,000 to 6,000 lymphocytes per 1 ml, including 71% of T-cells and 9% of B-cells. In patients with cerebrovascular accidents or severe serous meningitis T-cell numbers are markedly decreased. If serous meningitis has a favorable course, there is no decline in T-lymphocytes. The test for T- and B-cells in the CSF is being introduced by E.V. Schmidt at the Institute of Neurology (AMS USSR) and has found application at other institutions in this country and abroad.

TABLE 1

T, B and O Lymphocyte Levels in Various Diseases

Disease	T	B	O
Immunodeficiency with antibody production	↓	—	↑
Agammaglobulinemia	—	⤋	↑
Di George syndrome	⤋	—	↑
Rheumatism	⇓	—	⇑
Rheumatoid arthritis	↓	—	↑
SLE	↓	↓	⤊
Multiple sclerosis	↓	⇑	—
Bronchial asthma	↓	—	↑
Contact dermatitis	—	↑	—
Pulmonary tuberculosis	↓	↑	—
Tbc meningitis	↓	↑	—
Viral hepatitis	⇓	—	↑
Pertussis	↑	⤊	—
Mycosis fungoides	↑	—	—
Nephropathy of pregnancy	⇓	—	⇑
B lymphomas and leukemias	⇓	⇑	—
T lymphomas and leukemias	⇑	⇓	—
O lymphomas and leukemias	⇓	⇓	⤊
Hodgkin's disease	↓	—	↑
Tumors (miscellaneous)	↓	—	↑
Burns, various forms of peritonitis	⇓	—	↑

— Within the normal range
↑⇑⤊ Different degrees of increase
↓⇓⤋ Different degrees of decrease

The functional status of the total T-cell population is usually evaluated at present by the intensity of blast transformation under the action of PHA and other mitogens, by production of the factor inhibiting macrophage migration and a number of skin tests.

The functional activity of the various classes of B-lymphocytes is assessed by measuring blood levels of the corresponding immunoglobulins. Such data are also of considerable diagnostic and prognostic importance in many areas of medicine. Table 2 shows how widely different are the quantitative shifts in the three principal immunoglobulin classes accompanying diverse diseases.

Quantitative and functional assays of the T-and B-systems help to monitor the effect of various therapeutic procedures and are indispensable in patients subjected to immunotherapy: immunosuppression, immunopotentiation, substitution therapy or measures directed towards restoring immune defences.

When reviewing the current status and the prospects of immunotherapy it is necessary to emphasize first of all that most efforts are aimed at and the greatest hopes placed in the treatment of autoimmune diseases, tumors and primary and secondary immunodeficiencies. The concepts, techniques and results of immunotherapy are to a large extent subject to discussion. This approach is clearly indicated and effective in two areas: transplantation of organs (immunosuppression) and immunodeficiencies (immunopotentiation or substitution therapy). As for immunosuppression in cases of autoimmune disease and immunopotentiation in tumor patients, work in these directions has been started but recently, though some results are already available. In regard to the latter two problems, which are still far from being solved, I must point out that the first advances made in the past few years bear the imprint of the not-too-distant times when knowledge of the cellular aspects of immunity

TABLE 2

IgM, IgG and IgA Levels in Various Diseases

Disease	IgM	IgG	IgA
Acute infectious hepatitis	⤊	⇑	—
Chronic hepatitis	—	⇑	—
Obstructive jaundice	—	—	⤊
Postinfectious cirrhosis	↑	⤊	—
Alcoholic cirrhosis	⇑	↑	↑
Rheumatoid arthritis	↑	—	—
SLE	—	⤊	—
Myocardial infarction	⇑	⤊	—
Glomerulonephritis	—	—	⤊
Nephrosis, protein-losing enteropathies	↓	⤋	↓
Hypoplasia of the bone marrow, myelosclerosis, metastases, tumors of the lymphoid system	⤋	⤋	⤋
Myelomas	⤊ or	⤊ or	⤊
Ataxia-telangiectasia	—	—	⤋
Hypogammaglobulinemia with IgM production	↓	⇓	⇓
Agammaglobulinemia	0	0	0

— Within the normal range

↑ ⇑ ⤊ Different degrees of increase

↓ ⇓ ⤋ Different degrees of decrease

was rather scarce. Immunosuppressive therapy has been founded on the principle of inhibiting the autoaggressiveness of immunocompetent cells with cytostatics or hormones through an attack on all the cells of the immune system, i.e. total immunosuppression. The principle underlying immunopotentiation in tumor cases is total stimulation of all the cells of the T-system which is considered responsible for antitumor defence.

Yet some palpable successes have been achieved.

G. James has listed the conditions requiring immunosuppression or immunopotentiation. The first group comprises organ transplantation, autoimmune disorders (active chronic hepatitis, rheumatoid arthritis, SLE, autoimmune hemolytic anemia, Sjögren's disease etc.), granulomatoses (including regional ileitis), primary biliary cirrhosis, sarcoidosis and various forms of dermatomyositis. Immunopotentiation is indicated in the second group of conditions, such as immunodeficiencies (Wiskott-Aldrich syndrome, candidiasis, some cases of rheumatoid arthritis, SLE and sarcoidosis), certain infections (leprosy, tuberculin-negative tuberculosis, viral diseases) and tumors (Hodgkin's disease, breast cancer, melanoma, bronchial cancer etc.).

Experience with immunostimulating therapy for chronic inflammatory processes is being accumulated.

I would like to repeat that all data pertaining to immunosuppressive or immunostimulating treatment of autoimmune disorders, tumors and infections have been obtained by methods aimed at total suppression or total stimulation. The discovery of lymphocyte subpopulations performing different functions, in particular helper and suppressor T-cells, has shed a new light on the future of immunotherapy.

Indeed, if autoantibody formation in autoimmune diseases is

caused by a defect of suppressor T-cells (and this hypothesis seems to be valid), there is a need to stimulate them, along with inhibiting antibody producers. Inhibition of suppressor T-lymphocytes with cytostatics would be dangerous. A contrasting situation exists in tumor cases: malignant neoplasias are characterized by activation of suppressor cells that may be related to the failure of antitumor immune defences. Total stimulation of the T-system may further activate suppressor T-lymphocytes and enhance the deficiency of antitumor immunity. Immunostimulating therapy is known, in fact, to accelerate the growth of the neoplasm in some patients.

A search has begun at present for ways and means of influencing selectively separate subpopulations of cells in the immune system. This is a most important and promising trend in contemporary experimental and clinical immunology. The process of data accumulation is already going on. Although this line of research is just starting to emerge, it will undoubtedly determine the immediate future of immunopharmacology. Table 3 summarizes the results of experiments done at our laboratory to elucidate the immunological sites of action of certain agents. Such studies are inspired primarily by the expectation to find means for modulating selectively the operation of the main regulatory cells, helper and suppressor T-lymphocytes, for activating or inhibiting them. Then the armamentarium of clinical medicine would be enriched with a conceptually new tool allowing purposeful regulation of immune events, since these two types of cells determine the intensity of all immune responses.

Hydrocortisone, for instance, while inhibiting all types of lymphocytes, acts preferentially on effector T-cells. Levamisole, which has attracted considerable attention in the last few years, is capable of stimulating suppressor T-lymphocytes more or less selectively. It may find wide application for treating autoimmune

TABLE 3

Effect of Certain Agents on Stem Cells, Helper, Suppressor and Effector T-cells and B-Lymphocytes

Agent	Stem cell migration	T_h	T_s	T_e	B
6-mercaptopurine	—	↓	?	↓	⇓
Hydrocortisone	⇓	↓	↓	⤋	↓
Radiation	↑	↓	⇓	↓	↓
Cyclophosphamide	—	↓	?	↓	⇓
Diodbenzotef	↓	—	↓	↓	↓
Delagil	—	↑	?	—	?
Analgin	—	—	?	—	—
Sodium salicylate	↓	—	?	↓	?
PHA	↑	↑	⇑	↓	—
Levamisole	—	—	⇑	↑	?
Thymosin	⤊	↑	?	⇑	?
Anti-IgM					
Anti-IgG					
Polyacrylic acid	⇑	⇑	?	↑	↑
Poly-4-vinylpyridine	↑	⤊	?	↑	↑
PAA-PVP copolymer	—	⇓	?	?	—

— Within the normal range
↑ ⇑ ⤊ Different degrees of increase
↓ ⇓ ⤋ Different degrees of decrease

diseases, since autoaggression is linked up with lowered activity of these cells. There was a hope that PHA, as a stimulant of the T-system, may prove useful for immunotherapy of tumors. This agent does stimulate T-lymphocytes, but it activates mostly suppressor T-cells, thereby inhibiting the immune response which is already weakened in tumor bearers.

In the nearest future the science of immunology will undoubtedly decipher the sites and character of the defects underlying diverse clinical entities. Precise definitions of diseases affecting the immune system will replace the general and quite vague terms used at present, such as "immunopathology", "autoimmune aggression" or "immunodeficiency". And the drugs with a rather unclear mode of action resulting in total immunopotentiation or total immunosuppression will give way to new agents of a highly selective nature, well suited for rational immunotherapy of various disorders and diseases.

REFERENCES

James, G. J. Mod. Geriatr. 7, 9-17 (1977)

Khaitov, R.M., Petrov, R.V., Gambarov, S.S., Norimov, A.S., and Blinov, V.A. Cell. Immunol. 22, 1-10 (1976)

Malashhia, Y.A. A population of lymphocytes in the normal cerebrospinal fluid. 11th World Congress of Neurology. Excerpta Med., Amsterdam - Oxford, 180-181 (1978)

WHO Scientific Group on Immunodeficiency, report. Geneva, 1-7 Nov., 1977

APPROXIMATE SOLUTION OF OPTIMAL CONTROL PROBLEMS

V.M.Alexandrov,
Senior Researcher

Novosibirsk, Institute of Mathematics,
the USSR Academy of Sciences, Siberian Branch

Calculative difficulties of solving optimization problems make the development of approximate methods actual. In the present paper an approximate solution approach for a series of optimal control problems is suggested. Let a controlled system be described by the equation

$$\dot{X} = A(t)x + B(t)u, \quad X(t_0) = X_0, \quad u \in V, \tag{1}$$

where $A(t)$ and $B(t)$ are the matrices of the dimensions $n \times n$ and $n \times m$ respectively; X is an n-dimensional phase state vector; u is an m-dimensional control vector with its components being limited according to the condition

$$|u_j| \leq \sum_{i=1}^{n} N_{ij} |x_i(t_0)| \leq M_j, \qquad j = \overline{1,m}, \tag{2}$$

where N_{ij} are some non-negative weight coefficients. (1) is supposed to be completely controlled.

PROBLEM 1 (highspeed one). System (1) is to be converted from the initial state $X(t_0) = X_0$ to the final zero one $x(t_1) = 0$ for the minimal time $T = t_1 - t_0$ when the control limit is (2).

Let the vector of the initial conditions $x^i(t_0)$ contain only one non-zero component - $x_i(t_0)$ for some fixed value i. The minimal time of system conversion is obtained when the function $\mathcal{H}$ takes its maximal value [1]

$$\mathcal{H} = \Psi^* A(t) X + \Psi^* B u \ , \tag{3}$$

where Ψ^* is the transposed vector of the conjugated system

$$\dot{\Psi} = - A^* \Psi . \tag{4}$$

The function $\mathcal{H}$ is maximal in the case when the control meets the expression

$$u^{(i)} = N^{(i)} x_i(t_0)\ sign\ B^*(t)\Psi^{(i)}, \quad i = \overline{1,n} . \tag{5}$$

Here $N^{(i)}$ is a diagonal matrix $m \times m$ with the conformal weight coefficients N_{ij} ; $\Psi^{(i)}$ is the vector of the conjugated system (4) for the case of initial conditions under consideration.

It can be proved that control switching moments $u^{(i)}(t)$ and time $T^{(i)}$ of the system conversion from the initial state $x^{(i)}(t_0) = (0, \ldots, 0, x_i(t_0), 0, \ldots, 0)$ to the origin of coordinates are independent of the initial condition $x_i(t_0)$, $i = \overline{1,n}$ and fixed [2] if the matrices A and B are constant.

Really, let the solution of the non-uniform equation (1) be written for the final moment $t = t_1$

$$x^{(i)}(t_1) = \Phi(t_1, t_0)\, x^i(t_0) + \int_{t_0}^{t_1} \Phi(t_1, \tau) B(\tau) u^{(i)}(\tau)\, d\tau , \quad i = \overline{1,n} , \tag{6}$$

where $\Phi(t_1, t_0)$ is the fundamental matrix of the uniform system $\dot{x} = A(t)x$ solutions. Denote as $\Gamma^{(i)}(t_1, t_0)$ the i -vector column of the fundamental matrix. Then

$$\Phi(t_1, t_0)\, x^{(i)}(t_0) = \Gamma^{(i)}(t_1, t_0)\, x_i(t_0), \quad i = \overline{1,n} . \tag{7}$$

Since at the final moment $t = t_1$ the boundary condition $x^{(i)}(t_1) = 0$ must be held from the equation (6), taking into account (5) and (7), we obtain

$$\int_{t_0}^{t_1} \Phi(t_1, \tau) B N^{(i)} x_i(t_0)\ sign\ B^* \Psi^{(i)} d\tau + \Gamma^{(i)}(t_1, t_0)\, x_i(t_0) = 0, \ i = \overline{1,n}. \tag{8}$$

As soon as $x_i(t_0) \neq 0$ is a scalar we get from (8) the following basic equation connecting control switching moments and the time $T^{(i)}$ with the matrices $A, B, N^{(i)}$

$$\int_{t_0}^{t_0+T^{(i)}} \Phi(t_1,\tau)\, B N^{(i)} \operatorname{sign} B^* \Psi^{(i)} d\tau + \Gamma^{(i)}(t_1, t_0) = 0, \quad i = \overline{1,n}. \tag{9}$$

Demand that the conversion times $T^{(i)}$ of each of phase coordinates should be equal to the value T

$$T^{(i)}(N^{(i)}, t_0) = T, \qquad i = \overline{1,n}. \tag{10}$$

For the system (1) the control vector components are formed by summarizing the order of its values for each of phase coordinates

$$u_j = \sum_{i=1}^{n} N_{ij}\, x_i(t_0) \operatorname{sign} \sum_{\xi=1}^{n} b_{\xi j}(t)\, \Psi_\xi^{(i)}(t), \quad j = \overline{1,m}. \tag{11}$$

In general case of any initial conditions the sum control (11) happens to be non-optimal. Therefore, it is called the quasioptimal one. And the question of the obtained decision closeness to the optimal one is to be solved.

It does not seem possible that these estimations might be given in the case of any matrices A and B of system (1). However, the simple estimation of the closeness can be obtained in the case of all the eigen-values of the matrix A and one-dimensional control

$$\frac{T_{quasi}}{T_{opt}} = \left[\frac{M}{\sum_{i=1}^{n} \left\{ \frac{[N_i\, |x_i(t_0)|]^n}{M^{i-1}} \right\}^{\frac{1}{n+1-i}}} \right]^{1/n} \tag{12}$$

From (12) it follows that the higher the controlled system order (n) the less is difference between quasioptimal and optimal processes.

To reach the most possible closeness it is advisable to divide the continuum of initial conditions $X(t_0) \in X$ into K subcontinua Y_ξ, $\xi = \overline{1,K}$ with a variable series of values N_{ij}^{ξ} for each subcontinuum. For instance, such a division can rather easily be realized by combining the hyperplanes and assigning in the following way

$$Y_\xi = \left\{ x_i : \sum_{i=1}^{n} \frac{|x_i|}{|x_i^{(\xi)}|} - 1 \leq 0, \quad \sum_{i=1}^{n} \frac{|x_i|}{|x_i^{(\xi-1)}|} - 1 > 0 \right\}, \tag{13}$$

where $x_i^{(\xi)}$ are boundary points on the axes of the phase space, the conversion from which into the origin of coordinates takes place for the same time $T^{(\xi)}$ in the case of the optimal control. The values N_{ij}^{ξ} are obtained from the condition

$$N_{ij}^{\xi} \, |x_i^{(\xi)}| = M_j \,, \quad j = \overline{1,m} \,. \tag{14}$$

If for arbitrary ξ both inequalities in (13) are less than zero that is just the condition of the decrease of ξ for 1. If both inequalities are more than zero ξ should be increased for 1. So, we purposefully choose ξ , and, consequently, N_{ij}^{ξ} as well, with which the formation of quasioptimal control takes place.

The points $x_i^{(\xi)}$ are chosen from the condition $T^{(\xi)}/T^{(\xi-1)} = C, \xi = \overline{1,K}$, where C has been given and it describes the admissible loss in high speed. The problem of determining $x_i^{(\xi)}$ is the inverse one of the optimal high-speed and is solved _a priori_. For the n -th order system there are $2nK$ boundary points with their quasioptimal and optimal conversion time coinciding. Therefore, such a scheme is approximating.

It should be noted that the number of the subdivisions K need not be finite.

The principle of forming control for each of phase coordinates is used when solving the "classical" problem with the minimum energetic resources.

PROBLEM 2 (minimizing the resources). It is necessary to convert

(1) from the initial state $X(t_0)=X_0$ to the origin of coordinates $x(t_1)=0$ for the fixed time $T=t_1-t_0$ ($T \geq T_{opt}$, where T_{opt} is the time of optimal high-speed conversion when the control limit is (2), and minimize the functional

$$\mathcal{J}(u) = \int_{t_0}^{t_1} \sum_{j=1}^{m} |u_j| \, d\tau \longrightarrow \min_{u \in U} . \tag{15}$$

It can also be shown that switching moments when forming control for each of phase coordinates are independent of the initial value $x_i(t_0) \, \forall i$ and are fixed for the constant matrices A and B which greatly simplifies the technical realization of the control. The components of the control vector are being formed according to the algorithm

$$u_j = \sum_{i=1}^{n} N_{ij} \, x_i(t_0) \, sign \left\{ \sum_{\xi=1}^{n} b_{\xi j} \, \psi_j^{(i)} \left[1 - sign \left(1 - \left| \sum_{s=1}^{n} b_{sj} \, \psi_j^{(i)} \right| \right) \right] \right\}, \quad j=\overline{1,m}. \tag{16}$$

Some estimations of closeness between optimal and quasioptimal processes can be obtained and the efficiency of the proposed algorithm can be shown. For instance, for the third-order system with zero proper values and one-dimensional control we have

$$\frac{\mathcal{J}(u)_{quasi}}{\mathcal{J}(u)_{opt}} = \xi_1 \frac{1 - (1-\mu_1^{-3})^{1/2}}{1-(1-\xi_1 \mu_1^{-3})^{1/2}} , \tag{17}$$

if the expressional point lies on the axis x_1 ;

$$\frac{\mathcal{J}(u)_{quasi}}{\mathcal{J}(u)_{opt}} = \xi_2 \frac{(\mu_2 K_2)^2 - \{(\mu_2 K_2)^4 - 16[(\mu_2 K_2)^2 + 1]\}^{1/2}}{(\mu_2 K_2)^2 - \{(\mu_2 K_2)^4 - 16 \xi_2^2 [(\mu_2 K_2)^2 + \xi_2]\}^{1/2}} , \quad K_2 = 2\sqrt{2+\sqrt{5}} ,$$

if the expressional point lies on the axis x_2 and

$$\frac{\mathcal{J}(u)_{quasi}}{\mathcal{J}(u)_{opt}} = \xi_3 \frac{\mu_3 K_3 - \{(\mu_3 K_3 - 1)^2 - \frac{4}{3}(\mu_3 K_3 - 1)^{-2}[6(\mu_3 K_3)^2 + 1 - 4\mu_3 K_3]\}^{1/2}}{\mu_3 K_3 - \{(\mu_3 K_3 - \xi_3)^2 - \frac{4}{3}\xi_3^2(\mu_3 K_3 - \xi_3)^{-2}[6(\mu_3 K_3)^2 + \xi_3^2 - 4\xi_3 \mu_3 K_3]\}^{1/2}} ,$$

$$K_3 = 4,3902 ,$$

if it lies on the axis x_3 .

Here the accepted denotations are $|x_i(t_0)| = \xi_i |x_i(t_0)|_{max}$; $T = \mu_i T_{quasi}$;

$N_i |x_i(t_0)|_{max} = M$. The coefficient ξ_i shows which part the current initial condition constitutes of the maximal one, and μ_i describes by how many times the assigned time exceeds that of the quasioptimal high-speed conversion. For any random location of the expressional point in the phase space the average expenditure of resources for the third-order system of quasioptimal control forms 11.7% for $\mu = 2$; 6.8% for $\mu = 3$; 4.5% for $\mu = 4$, etc. The difference between the quasioptimal and optimal control decreases with the increase of the given conversion time T and the initial conditions. For the maximal deviations for each of phase coordinates the quasioptimal and optimal controls coincide.

The permanence of the switching moments provides simple technical realization of the quasioptimal control and with an insignificant increase of expenditure of resources the above algorithm gives us an opportunity to control linear any-order system with any number of controlling parameters. Quasioptimal control is being formed of the measured initial values $x_i(t_0)$, $i = \overline{1,n}$ without wasting time for calculations. That gives us the possibility to control high-speed processes and solve the below problem of stabilization with the given accuracy for the minimal expenditure of energetic resources.

Let a controlled object be described in deviations from the basic motion trajectory or the rest state by the system of equations

$$X = A(t) + B(t)u + G\eta , \quad u \in V, \tag{18}$$

$$Z = HX + V , \tag{19}$$

where in addition to (1) we introduce: Z is the K -dimensional observation vector; V is the K -dimensional vector of measurement errors, and η is the r -dimensional perturbation vector the components of which are independent stochastic Haussian processes with zero mean values and the assigned covariance matrices. The equations (18), (19) are supposed to form a completely controlled and observed system.

Divide the half-interval $[0,\infty)$ by points t_K so that $t_{K+1} - t_K = T$.

Denote the system (18) deviations caused by the action of random perturbation on the segment $[t_{K-1}, t_K]$ as $\omega(t_K)$ and regard them as the initial state of the system

$$\dot{X} = A(t)X + B(t)u, \quad x(t_K) = \omega(t_K), \quad t \in [t_K, t_{K+1}]. \tag{20}$$

PROBLEM 3(the stabilization with the given accuracy at the minimal expenditure of resources).

System (20) should be converted from the initial state $x(t_K) = \omega(t_K)$ into the zero final state $x(t_{K+1}) = 0$ for the fixed time T ($T \geq T_{opt}$) under the influence of the limited control (2) and functional (15) should be minimized. Here: a) the dispersion value of the ℓ phase coordinates for the points $t = t_K$ must not exceed some given value μ, i.e.

$$E\left\{\sum_{i=1}^{\ell} x_i^2(t_K)\right\} \leq \mu, \qquad \ell \leq n \tag{21}$$

or: b) the maximal deviation of the phase coordinates for the points $t = t_K$ must not exceed with the probability Ω the given value ε, i.e.

$$P\left[\left(\sum_{i=1}^{\ell} x_i^2(t_K)\right)^{1/2}_{max} < \varepsilon\right] \leq \Omega. \tag{22}$$

SOLUTION. From the equation

$$\sum_{i=1}^{\ell} \sum_{\xi=1}^{r} S_\xi \int_{t_K}^{t_K+T} g_{i\xi}^2(t_K+T, \tau)\, d\tau = \mu, \tag{23}$$

where S_ξ is special density ξ of the white noise η_ξ, $g_{i\xi}$ is the weight function of the system for the i -th phase coordinate depending on the ξ -th component of the perturbation, we can determine the maximal value of the correction interval T for which the limitation (21) is satisfied for the subproblem a). In the case of the subproblem b) the maximal value of the correction interval T is obtained when solving the equation

$$\Phi\left(\frac{\varepsilon}{\left[\sum_{i=1}^{\ell}\sum_{\xi=1}^{z} s_{\xi}\int_{t_K}^{t_K+T} g_{i\xi}(t_K+T,\tau)\,d\tau\right]^{1/2}}\right)=\Omega\,, \tag{24}$$

where $\Phi(\cdot)$ is the integral of Haussian probability. From the system of the transcendental equations

$$\int_{t_K}^{t_K+T}\Phi(t_K+T,\tau)B(\tau)N^{(i)}sign\left\{\widetilde{B^*\Psi^{(i)}}\left[J-sign\left(J-|B^*\Psi^{(i)}|\right)\right]\right\}d\tau + \tag{25}$$
$$+\Gamma^{(i)}(t_K+T,t_K)=0,\quad i=\overline{1,n}$$

we obtain the values of weight coefficients N_{ij} that provide the conversion during T of every component of the initial condition vector into zero. At the same time we obtain the switching moments of quasi-optimal control which is formed according to the algorithm (16) from the estimations of phase coordinates, i.e. $x(t_o)=\hat{x}(t_o)$.

The average value of the correctional control and the average expenditure of resources for the correction are being estimated. An important quality of the suggested algorithms is being proved: the average value of the resources expenditures and the components for the correctional control are independent of the given accuracy of $\mu(\varepsilon)$ stabilization. The problem of the correct distribution of limitations and resources between the program and correctional control in the case of "strict" and integral limitations on control is being solved.

PROBLEM 4(parametric optimization). There is system (1) written in the normal form for the scalar control. The coefficients b and N_i $i=\overline{1,n}$ are fixed. Fix also one of the matrix A coefficients, for instance, a_n , which is expressed via its eigen-values λ_ξ , $\xi = \overline{1,n}$ in the following way

$$a_n = (-1)^n \prod_{\xi=1}^{n} \lambda_\xi . \tag{26}$$

The problem is set up: to obtain for quasioptimal control (5) the eigenvalues (and the rest of the coefficients) of the matrix A , for which there is obtained the minimal conversion time of system (1) from any admissible initial state $x(t_0)=x_0$ into the origin of the coordinates $x(t_1)=0$, i.e.

$$\mathcal{J} = \int_{t_0}^{t_1} d\tau \longrightarrow \min_{\lambda_\xi \in \Lambda} . \tag{27}$$

It is shown that having satisfied the conditions of complete controlability in the case of scalar control and the componentwise complete controlability for vector control, the system with arbitrary values of the matrices A and B coefficients could be converted to the normal form.

For linear systems with constant parameters without the loss of generality we may assume $t_0 = 0$ and write equation (9), connecting the constant moments of the switching of quasioptimal control with the matrices A , B and $N^{(i)}$ coefficients, in the following form:

$$\int_0^T e^{A(T-\tau)} BN^{(i)} \operatorname{sign} B^* \Psi^{(i)} d\tau + \Gamma^{(i)}(T) = 0, \tag{28}$$
$$i = \overline{1,n} .$$

For quasioptimal control the minimal time for the conversion of the system to the origin of coordinates is obtained when the intervals of control with constant terms, formed in the first phase coordinate, are equal. The minimum is singular. The validity of such a statement for $n=2$ is being proved.

For the intervals being equal the system of transcendental equations degenerates into the system of algebraic equations which, together with connection equation (26), forms the system ($n+1$) of equations relative to the unknowns T and λ_ξ, $\xi=\overline{1,n}$. For $n=2,3$ this system is solvable analytically. Optimal values of time and parameters of the object being controlled are obtained.

The minimal time is obtained for the stable dynamic system near the stability boundary which is of essential practical interest. If, while constructing the dynamic system, its parameters have been chosen to be optimal, then such a system has an additional important property - the minimal sensitivity to the parameters variations.

The equation systems are given for obtaining constant switching moments of quasioptimal control determined according to the coordinate-wise formation principle.

References

I. Л.С.Понтрягин, В.Г.Болтянский, Р.В.Гамкрелидзе, Е.Ф.Мищенко. Математическая теория оптимальных процессов. М., Изд-во "Наука", I969.

2. В.М.Александров. Квазиоптимальные процессы в автоматических системах. Известия Сибирского отделения АН СССР, серия технических наук, I975, вып. 3, № I3.

NUMERICAL SOLUTION OF ADAPTATION PROBLEMS BY MEANS OF AN EVOLUTION STRATEGY

by Klaus Bellmann[1] and Joachim Born[2]

Abstract

Adaptation problems are characterized as general extremum problems. For the numerical solution of such problems, the paper considers evolution strategies, that means direct stochastic methods being organized according to principles of the biological evolution. These strategies are assessed with special emphasis being placed on their efficiency. The paper presents a new evolution strategy simulating the "genetic load" principle - the EGL method, describing it as being efficient and convergent with probability 1. A successful application for the solution of a practically relevant adaptation problem is referred to.

---

[1] Central Institute for Cybernetics and Information Processes, Academy of Sciences of the GDR, Rudower Chaussee 5, 1199 Berlin, GDR

[2] Centre for Computing Technique, Academy of Sciences of the GDR, Rudower Chaussee 5, 1199 Berlin, GDR

1. Adaptation problems and suitable methods for their solution

The current state of the art of modern computer engineering allows the computer simulation of parameter-dependent models of scientific or technical processes or objects for the purpose of finding such parameters which govern a certain distinguished model behaviour. The adaptation task considered is of the following type:

Given:

a set of parameters	$X \subseteq R^n, \quad X \neq \emptyset$
a quality function assigning some vector of qualities y(x) to each vector of parameters $x \in X$	$y : R^n \longrightarrow R^q$
a vector of qualities	$y^o \in R^q$
and a weighting functional	$f : R^{2q} \longrightarrow R^1$

Then the following problem has to be solved:

$$\inf \left\{ f(y(x), y^o) \mid x \in X \right\} \quad (= g^*), \tag{A}$$

where it is assumed that always $g^* > -\infty$.

Generally, the quality function y will not be given explicitly. It shall however be assumed that for every vector of parameters, $x \in X$, the corresponding vector of qualities y(x) can be stated, e.g. by the realization of an algorithmic model. The vector of qualities y^o may - in the above sense - represent a distinguished model behaviour. In what follows, for the time being the parameter set X shall not be assumed to have any definite shape, but a fixed, explicit weighting functional f shall be assumed to be given.

Let the functional $g : R^n \longrightarrow R^1$ defined by

$$g(x) = f(y(x), y^o) \tag{1}$$

be called a quality functional. Then the adaptation problem (A) can be written as

$$\inf \left\{ g(x) \mid x \in X \right\} . \tag{E}$$

In the following let be g(x) the quality of the parameter vector $x \in X$.

Thus it becomes clear also formally that the adaptation problem (A) represents a general extremum problem, if the shape of the quality functional g as defined by (1) is disregarded - which shall also be done in the following considerations. But the character of the adaptation problem (A) indeed determines the type of the problem (E) as a general extremum problem inasmuch as for the parameter set X as well as for the quality functional g it is practically not possible to assume certain properties (e.g. convexity, differentiability, unimodularity) as being given. In determination of methods for the numerical solution of general extremum problems, direct or non-gradient methods are preferred because of the elimination of the numerically effortful gradient approximation. Among the direct methods, the stochastic ones distinguish themselves by the potentially existing chance of finding the global extremum. These latter methods include the evolution strategies.

2. Structure of evolution strategies

On the one hand the undertaking to simulate the evolution of natural populations for the numerical solution of extremum problems is based on the hypothesis that the mechanisms of biological evolution form an excellent strategy for adapting a population under natural conditions as closely as possible to a given environment. On the other hand the conditions for an extremum problem can be considered to be abstractions of the conditions for the evolution in natural populations. For numerical purposes it is reasonabel to utilize only the most essential evolution mechanisms. These include the principles of variation (mutation, inversion, recombination), reproduction, and selection. How important the simulation of the phenomenon of the "genetic reserve" or "genetic load" may be, shall be illustrated below.

As one of the earliest workers in this field, BREMERMANN /1/, /2/ developed evolution strategies. The evolution strategies stated by RECHENBERG /7/ for the optimization of technical systems can also be utilized in the solution of extremum problems. Recent papers on evolution strategies were published by HOLLAND /5/ and SCHWEFEL /8/.

The most evident characteristic of an evolution strategy is that it operates on a sequence of point sets - a sequence of populations - in contrast to the formation of a sequence of iteration points in the case of "usual" methods. The evolution strategies of the abovementioned authors are variants (partially with modifications) of an iterative pattern including:

A. initial step ($k = 0$).

Formation of a starting population P_1 of m ($m \geq 1$, arbitrary, but fixed)
parameter vectors in X:

$$P_1 = (x_1^1, \ldots, x_1^m);\; x_1^i \in X,\; i = 1, \ldots, m.$$

B. k-th iteration step ($k \geq 1$).

1. Variation

Starting from the k-th population P_k, l ($l \geq 1$, arbitrary, but fixed) new variants $x^{v_1}, \ldots, x^{v_l}$ are generated. Each of the new variants is determined by:

1.1. A stochastic determination of r ($r \geq 1$, arbitrary, but fixed) parents $x^{l_1}, \ldots, x^{l_r}$ from the parameter vectors $x_k^i \in P_k$, $i = 1, \ldots, m$, where every vector of parameters is selected with a certain probability (which may be determined by its quality).

1.2. Realization of the mutation (i.e. the stochastic modification) in each component of the parents x^{l_i}, $i = 1, \ldots, r$ with a certain probability and a certain spectrum of variability.

1.3. Realization of the inversion (i.e. inverson of the order of parameters within a stochastically determined component section) for the mutated parents.

1.4. Realization of the crossing-over (i.e. an interchange of parameters within stochastically determined, equal component sections) for the mutated and inverted parents, with a certain probability.

1.5. Realization of the interchromosomal recombination (i.e. stochastic selection of one of the thus modified parents as a new variant).

2. Selection

Formation of the population P_{k+1} by selecting the m best (by their qualities) new variants $x^{v_1}, \ldots, x^{v_l}$, $x^{v_i} \in X$, $i = 1, \ldots, l$, and (or else without considering) the parameter vectors $x_k^i \in P_k$, $i = 1, \ldots, m$.

3. Efficiency of evolution strategies

In the solution of practical adaptation problems, the computing time required - being rather long in most cases - for determining the quality y(x) of a parameter vector x determines an economic limit for the number of possible quality computations. For such a limited number of iterations, the object is to achieve as "close" an approximation as possible to the solution set X^*($X^* = \{ x \in X \mid g(x) = g^* \}$, $X^* \neq \emptyset$), or at least to improve the quality as much as possible.

An algorithm devised to fit this concept will always be a compromise between the object of achieving a high efficiency and the requirement to maintain a security of global convergence and a satisfactory global efficiency, respectively. For an evolution strategy, the term "efficiency" shall be understood to be a measure of the variation (improvement) of the quality of the respectively best parameter vector existing in the population after a fixed number of iterations, whereas the term "global efficiency" means a measure of the variation (improvement) of the distance of the respectively best parameter vector from the solution set X .

In particular the efficiency and the global efficiency, respectively, are influenced by:

(1) the formation of the starting populations;
(2) the power of the population; and
(3) the determination of the strategy parameters.

As regards (3), the essential point is a suitable determination of the variability spectrum for mutations.

Among the evolution strategies of the authors mentioned in Section 2, SCHWEFEL's multi-component evolution strategy (abbreviated as MCE strategy) is best suited to the abovementioned object. In the MCE strategy, during the iteration the strategy parameters (only the variability spectra for mutations) are varied by applying the evolution strategy to the strategy parameters themselves for achieving a high efficiency.

SCHWEFEL's tests certify a relatively high security of global convergence for the MCE strategy. Our own numerical tests show that the global efficiency of the MCE strategy is unsatisfactory (cf. /3/ or /4/). One cause of this deficiency consists in that the reproduction principle has been neglected. (In the MCE strategy, the elements of the population P_k are not taken into account in the selection, which may result in a reduction of quality from one iteration to another, especially for large variability spectra and a small number of descendants 1.) Another cause lies in the following fact: although a population is involved, the resultant possibilities of determining new variants are utilized only inadequately - after a few iterations the variability in the population is determined by the realization of the mutation alone. This phenomenon is observed in all of the evolution strategies of the authors mentioned in Section 2. The conception of the following evolution strategy remedies this deficiency.

4. Developing an extented evolution strategy which realizes the principle of genetic load - the EGL method

The EGL method can be considered as a variant of the general scheme mentioned in Section 2, where $l = 1$, $r = 2$, the population P_k of the k-th iteration step being taken into account in the selection. The extensions consist in

(1) operating upon strategy populations, and hence a variation of the strategy parameters in the course of the iterations by applying the evolution strategy to the strategy parameters themselves.

(2) realizing the principle of genetic load. Every population contains parameter vectors which are introduced in the initial step and never subjected to selection, irrespective of their qualities.

Practically, the genetic loads should be chosen "extrem". In the population of the parameter vectors in X - now being called the object population - they are generally chosen in the sense of a "covering" of the parameter set X, or in the sense of "bridge-heads". The genetic loads in the strategy populations are wellchosen if they form a large range of greatly different probabilities and variability spectra. Then in the course of iterations the actually favourable basic variants are selected from this permanent reserve.

In the following Block diagram, the meanings of the symbols stated are as follows:

$R_c \in R^{n+4}$ denotes the vector of strategy parameters of the probabilities of mutations, inversions, and crossing-overs in the strategy populations.

$^{V}c \in R^{n+2}$ denotes the vector of strategy parameters of the variances of normal distributed mutations in the strategy populations.

$^{R}S_k = {^{R}S_k^A} \cup {^{R}S^L}$, where $^{R}S_k^A = ({^{R}s_k^1}, \ldots, {^{R}s_k^{l_s}})$ and

$$^{R}S^L = ({^{R}s_k^{l_s+1}}, \ldots, {^{R}s_k^{m_s}}), \; l_s (\leq) m_s$$

and $^{R}s_k^l \in \{ s \in R^{n+2} \mid 0 \leq s_i \leq 1, \; i = 1, \ldots, n+2 \}, \; l = 1, \ldots, m_s$

means the k-th strategy population of the probabilities of mutations, inversion, and crossing-over in the object population having the genetic load $^{R}S^L$.

$^{V}S_k = {^{V}S_k^A} \cup {^{V}S^L}$, where $^{V}S_k^A = ({^{V}s_k^1}, \ldots, {^{V}s_k^{l_s}})$ and

$$^{V}S^L = ({^{V}s_k^{l_s+1}}, \ldots, {^{V}s_k^{m_s}}),$$

and $^{V}s_k^l \in \{ s \in R^n \mid s_i \geq 0, \; i = 1, \ldots, n \}, \; l = 1, \ldots, m_s$,

means the k-th strategy population of the variances for the normal distributed mutations in the object population having the genetic load $^{V}S^L$.

$O_k = O_k^A \cup O^L$, where $O_k^A = (x_k^1, \ldots, x_k^{l_o})$ and

$$O^L = (x_k^{l_o+1}, \ldots, x_k^{m_o}), \quad l_o (\leq) m_o$$

and $x_k^l \in X, \; l = 1, \ldots, m_o$,

means the k-th object population having the genetic load O^L.

Briefly, the quality of a strategy variant shall be understood as being the quality of the variant determined by it among the object population.

Block diagram of the algorithmic realization of the EGL method

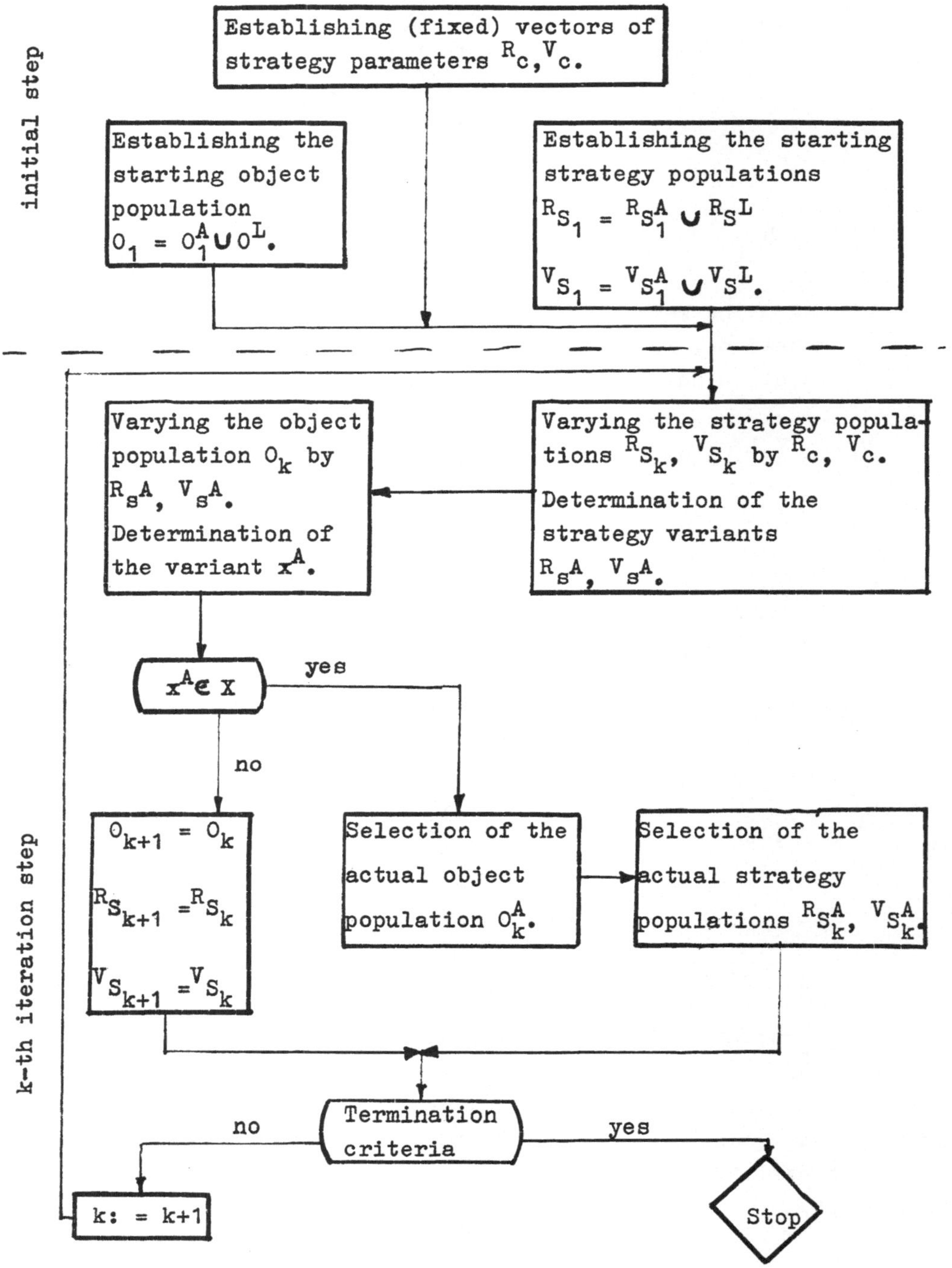

5. Convergence and efficiency of the EGL method

The convergence with probability 1 of the EGL method can be proven subject to the following condition of regularity.
Let

$$X^*_\varepsilon = \left\{ x \in X \;\middle|\; g(x) - g^* \leq \varepsilon \right\},\ \varepsilon > 0.$$

The problem (E) is called regular if the following conditions are satisfied:

(R_1) g is continuous.
(R_2) X is closed.
(R_3) For every $\bar{x} \in X$, $\tilde{X} = \left\{ x \in X \;\middle|\; g(x) \leq g(\bar{x}) \right\}$ is bounded.
(R_4) For any $\varepsilon > 0$, int $X^*_\varepsilon \neq \emptyset$[1].

The EGL method is called regular if the following conditions are satisfied:

(R_5) For the vector of strategy parameters ${}^{R}c$: $\max_{i=1,\dots,n+4} {}^{R}c_i < 1$.

(R_6) In the genetic load ${}^{R}S^L$, there exists an element ${}^{R}s$ such that $\min_{i=1,\dots,n} {}^{R}s_i > 0$ [2] and ${}^{R}s_{n+1} < 1$ [3], ${}^{R}s_{n+2} < 1$ [4].

(R_7) In the genetic load ${}^{V}S^L$, there exists an element ${}^{V}s$ such that ${}^{V}s_i = s > 0$, $i = 1,\dots,n$.

One has (cf. /3/ or /4/) the

THEOREM:
Let both the problem (E) and the EGL method be regular. Then, for a sequence of object populations $\{O_k\}$ generated by the EGL method,

$$P\left\{ \frac{1}{l_o} \sum_{i=1}^{l_o} g(x_k^i) \longrightarrow g^* \right\} = 1,$$

where $x_k^i \in O_k^A$, $i = 1,\dots,l_o$.

---

[1] For a set $M \subseteq R^n$, let int M denote the set of all interior points.

[2] Probabilities of the mutations on the individual components.

[3] Probability of inversion.

[4] Probability of crossing over.

The regularity conditions are satisfiable. For the conditions of the EGL method this is immediately obvious. But also the regularity conditions (R_1) ... (R_4) for the problem (E) are satisfied already if, say, the following conditions are met:

(1) g is continuous.

(2) X is convex, compact, and int $X \neq \emptyset$.

For the practical application of the EGL method, the following features derived from numerical tests (cf. /3/ or /4/) are of importance:

(1) The dependence of the efficiency and the global efficiency, respectively, on the starting values can be much better taken into account by the EGL method than this is possible for the evolution strategies of the authors mentioned in Section 2.

(2) The efficiency of the EGL method is at least as good as that of the MCE strategy.

(3) The global efficiency of the EGL method is much better than that of the MCE strategy.

6. Implementation and practical application of the EGL method

The EGL method was implemented for a practical utilization in FORTRAN - IV, using numerical basic modules which are available in the BESM assembler (cf. /6/). A complete description of the ADABES programme system is given in /3/. On the BESM - 6 computer, the ADABES programme occupies 662 words in the main storage without service routines; a problem with the dimensions n = 10, $m_o = m_s = 10$ takes about 0,015 sec per iteration.

The EGL method has proven successful in the solution of a practically relevant adaptation problem - the parameter identification in an algorithmic simulation model of a partial process of genetic signal transmission. For the structure of the adaptation problem given in this case (number of free parameters = 52, 4 parameters each forming a "functional unit"), the application of the EGL method with modifications appeared most suitable (cf. /4/).

References

/1/ Bremermann, H.J.: Numerical optimization procedures derived from biological evolution processes, in: Cybernetic problems in bionics, New York, 1968.

/2/ Bremermann, H.J.: A method of unconstrained global optimization, Math. Biosci. 9, 1-15 (1970).

/3/ Born, J.: Evolutionsstrategien zur numerischen Lösung von Adaptionsaufgaben (Evolution strategies for the numerical solution of adaptation problems), Dissertation (A), Humboldt University, Berlin, 1978.

/4/ Born, J.; Bellmann, K.: Numerical adaptation of parameters in simulation models by using evolution strategies, in: Modelling and simulation of molecular genetic information systems, Berlin, (to be published in 1980).

/5/ Holland, J.H.: Adaptation, in Progress in theoretical biology, vol. 4, New York, San Francisco, London, 263-293, 1976.

/6/ Hollatz, H.; Richter, D.: Programmoduln zur Erhöhung der Genauigkeit und Effektivität numerischer Algorithmen (Programme modules for improving the accuracy and efficiency of numerical algorithms), ZfR - Informationen - 78.03, Berlin, 1978.

/7/ Rechenberg, I.: Evolutionsstrategie: Optimierung technischer Systeme nach Prinzipien der biologischen Evolution (Evolution strategy: Optimization of technical systems according to principles of biological evolution), Stuttgart, 1973.

/8/ Schwefel, H.P.: Numerische Optimierung von Computer-Modellen mittels der Evolutionsstrategie (Numerical optimization of computer models by means of the evolution strategy), Interdisciplinary systems research 26, Basel and Stuttgart, 1977.

SOME MODELS OF TAKING OPTIMAL DECISIONS IN STANDARDIZATION

Vladimir Beresnev, Senior Researcher
Edward Gimady, Senior Researcher
Vladimir Dementyev, Head of Department

Novosibirsk, Institute of Mathematics,
the USSR Academy of Sciences, Siberian Branch.

1. When solving a great number of questions in quite different spheres of practical activities there often arises a problem demanding to make an optimal choice of some set of elements from a given totality of elements. Such problems arise, for instance, when choosing the type of equipment, machines and mechanisms stock, new machinery parameters, etc. Particularly great number of such questions are set up by standardization, and one of the main problems is the problem of exception of non-rational manifold of the output kinds, sorts and models.

Introduction of achievements of the scientific-technological progress into all the economy's branches is accompanied by the appearance of new and still more new goods: machines, mechanisms, apparata, equipment, materials. Here a problem of great importance arises - how to regulate the nomenclature of articles being produced, to select the best samples and regulate the quality of the output.

Standardization solves the abovementioned problem mostly by means of establishing parametric series of articles. A parametric series is some set of articles of one functional purpose, aimed at satisfying the assigned demand. Type series is defined as a specific article which differs from other specific ones by the value of one or several parameters (indices) characterizing these very articles. While constructing the series of articles one, as a rule, takes into account the basic parameters, i.e. those determining the most significant constructive and operation peculiarities of the article. Due to this a type series of an article can be identified with some set of values of basic parameters (indices).

If we accept the value of total expenditures for producing the series and satisfying by them the assigned demand as a criterion for the estimation of the articles parametric series, then the problem how to choose the optimal series arises.

In the present paper we dwell upon some of mathematical models of the optimal series choice.

2.Let us start with the description of a simple enough and at the same time one of the basic models of a series choice. Let $X=\{1,\dots,n\}$ denote the set of the demand kind, and $\mathcal{U}=\{1,\dots,m\}$ - the set of all the article's graded parameter, each of them, as a matter of principle, will do to satisfy some demand in some points $j\in X$. For any $i\in\mathcal{U}$ there is considered known a non-negative function $g_i(v), v\geq 0$ called the function of expenditures to produce the articles of the i-th graded parameter. This function characterizes all the total expenditures concerning the development of an article and its production depending on the volume of the output. Function $g_i(v)$ is assumed to be non-decreasing and semiadditive, that is, such that $g_i(v_1+v_2)\leq g_i(v_1)+g_i(v_2)$. These assumptions reflect the fact that the magnitude of expenditures increases with the series growth, and the specific expenditures, that is, the expenditures for a unit of output, decrease.

Besides, for any pair "the i-th graded parameter - the j-th kind of the demand", $i \in \mathcal{U}$, $j \in X$, the magnitudes $p_{ij} > 0$ and $g'_{ij} \geqslant 0$ are assumed to be known. The former denotes the number of articles of the i-th graded parameter, necessary to satisfy the j-th kind of the demand, and the latter corresponds to the expenditures to operate these articles.

Introduce the variables $x_{ij} \in \{0,1\}$, $i \in \mathcal{U}$, $j \in X$, indicating the articles of what types are used to satisfy each kind of the demand. $x_{ij} = 1$ if the j-th kind of the demand is satisfied by the i-th graded parameter; otherwise $x_{ij} = 0$. Then the problem of the optimal series of the articles choice might be put down in the following way:

$$\sum_{i \in \mathcal{U}} g_i(v_i) + \sum_{i \in \mathcal{U}} \sum_{j \in X} g'_{ij} x_{ij} \longrightarrow \min_{(x_{ij})} ; \tag{1}$$

Nonlinear model (N)

$$\sum_{i \in \mathcal{U}} x_{ij} = 1, \quad j \in X ; \tag{2}$$

$$v_i = \sum_{j \in X} p_{ij} x_{ij}, \quad i \in \mathcal{U} ; \tag{3}$$

$$x_{ij} \in \{0,1\}, \quad i \in \mathcal{U}, \ j \in X . \tag{4}$$

Restriction (2) means that each kind of the demand from the set should be satisfied, i.e., for each $j \in X$ there should be appointed some article.

If (x_{ij}) is the optimal solution for a given problem, then the optimal series of articles will be represented by the set $u = \{i \in \mathcal{U} \mid x_{i1} + \ldots + x_{in} > 0\}$. Denote as $X(i)$ the set $\{j \in X \mid x_{ij} = 1\}$

and call it the sphere of the articles of the i-th type application.

An important case of problem N is the problem where the expenditure functions $g_i(v)$, $i \in \mathcal{U}$, have the form:

$$g_i(v) = \begin{cases} 0, & v = 0, \\ g_i^0 + c_i v, & v > 0. \end{cases}$$

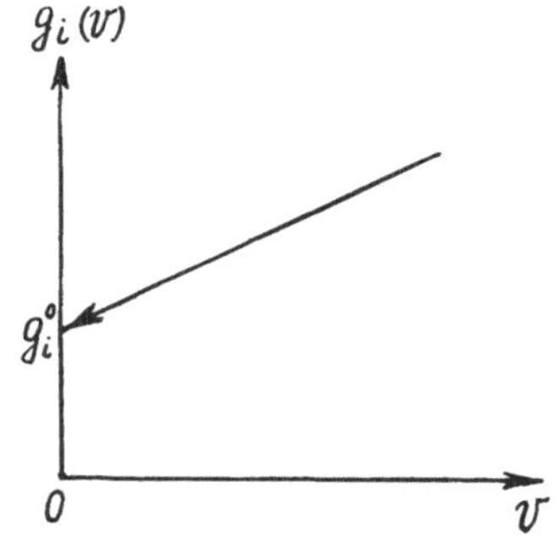

The problem (1) - (4) of the optimal series choice with such expenditure functions is called a linear one. Here the magnitude $g_i^0 \geq 0$ has the sense of initial expenditures concerning the putting into operation of the i-th graded parameter, and independent of the number of them. The magnitude $c_i \geq 0$ means the expenditures to produce a unit of output.

Introduce new variables $x_i \in \{0, 1\}$, $i \in \mathcal{U}$: $x_i = 1$, if the i-th graded parameter is being used; $x_i = 0$ otherwise. Then in the linear case problem (1) - (4) acquires the form:

$$\sum_{i \in \mathcal{U}} g_i^0 x_i + \sum_{j \in X} \sum_{i \in \mathcal{U}} g_{ij} x_{ij} \longrightarrow \min_{(x_i)(x_{ij})} ; \tag{5}$$

Linear model (L)

$$\sum_{i \in \mathcal{U}} x_{ij} = 1, \quad j \in X; \tag{6}$$

$$x_{ij} \leq x_i, \quad i \in \mathcal{U}, \ j \in X; \tag{7}$$

$$x_{ij} \in \{0, 1\}, \quad i \in \mathcal{U}, \ j \in X \tag{8}$$

where $g_{ij} = c_i p_{ij} + g'_{ij}$, $i \in \mathcal{U}$, $j \in X$. Restriction (7) means that if $x_i = 0$ (the i-th graded parameter does not enter the series), then $x_{ij} = 0$ as well (i.e., the j-th kind of the demand cannot be satisfied by the i-th graded parameter).

Problem (5) - (8) is the one of linear integral programming. It can also be expressed in the equivalent form:

Linear model (L')

$$\sum_{i\in \mathcal{U}} g_i^0 x_i + \sum_{j\in X} \min_{i/x_i=1} g_{ij} \longrightarrow \min_{(x_i)} \qquad (9)$$

$$x_i \in \{0,1\}, \quad i \in \mathcal{U}. \qquad (10)$$

If one manages to precisely enough approximate the expenditure function $g_i(V)$ for any $i \in \mathcal{U}$ by a piecewise linear function $\bar{g}_i(V)$ then a close to optimal solution of problem N can be obtained from the solution of some problem L. We point out the way of obtaining such a solution.

Let $X_i = \{j / p_{ij} < \infty,\ g'_{ij} < \infty\}$, $\bar{V}_i = \sum_{j\in X_i} p_{ij}$. Let us have for any $i \in \mathcal{U}$ a piecewise linear function $\bar{g}_i(V)$, which approximates the function $g_i(V)$ so that inequalities

$$0 \leq g_i(V) - \bar{g}_i(V) \leq \frac{\varepsilon}{m} \qquad (11)$$

hold. Besides, we consider the function $g_i(V)$ to coincide with the approximating function $\bar{g}_i(V)$ in the points of its break. Let V_i^{τ}, $\tau = 1, \dots, R_i$ be the break points of the function $\bar{g}_i(V)$ and let $\bar{g}_{i\tau}(V)$ be the τ-th, $\tau = 1, \dots, R_i$, linear part of this function, and be presented by the equation $\bar{g}_{i\tau}(V) = g_{i\tau}^0 + c_{i\tau} V$. To each pair $(i, \tau), i\in \mathcal{U}, \tau = 1,\dots,R_i$ we associate a new article $i' \in \mathcal{U}' = \{1, \dots, \sum_{i\in\mathcal{U}} R_i\}$ with parameters $g_{i'}^0 = g_{i\tau}$, $c_{i'} = c_{i\tau}$, $g'_{i'j} = g'_{ij}$. Consider the problem L with the set $\mathcal{U}'$ as a set of graded parameters. Let $(x_{i'})$ $(x_{i'j})$ be the optimal solution of this problem. We associate to it the solution (x_{ij}) of the original problem N as follows. Suppose, $x_{ij} = 1$, if for some $r = 1, \ldots, R_i$ to the pair (i, r) there corresponds the number i' for which $x_{i'j} = 1$, and suppose $x_{ij} = 0$ otherwise. There takes place the following

T h e o r e m. If for any $i \in \mathcal{U}$ inequality (11) holds, then the constructed solution (x_{ij}) of problem N differs by the purposeful function from the optimal solution of this problem for less than ε.

3. Nowadays, we do not know any efficient algorithm to solve a linear problem of the optimal series choice. Efficient are the algorithms, the number of operations and the storage capacity of which are the power functions of the length of the problem's input data. Moreover, the so-called problem of the covering by sets, referring to the list of polynomially complete problems (NP-problems), (see R.M.Karp [1]), is reduced to the problem L. The abovementioned reducibility indirectly proves that efficient precise algorithms for the solution can hardly be constructed in the general case for the problem of the optimal series choice. Therefore, the main efforts, while investigating the problem, have been aimed at: 1) seeking for specific properties of the problem, the use of which allows us to construct effective precise algorithms; 2) constructing approxiamted methods with small number of operations, which make it possible to always or nearly always obtain a solution with small error.

Let us dwell on the first direction. It often turns out possible to reduce problem L to the so-called problem of the closest neighbour formulated by R.Bellmann and being efficiently solved by the method of dynamic programming. Let $Z = [0, \beta]$ be an integral segment, and $f(x, y)$

be a real function determined on the set $Z \times Z$. The problem of the closest neighbour has the form:

$$\text{(B)} \qquad \sum_{K=1}^{N} f(z_{K-1}, z_K) \longrightarrow \min_{N, (z_K)}$$

$$0 = z_0 \leq z_1 \leq \cdots \leq z_N = \beta .$$

To solve it there can be constructed an algorithm of the number of operations $T \sim \beta^2$ at the storage capacity $\Pi \sim \beta$.

One of the conditions for the problem L being reduced to the problem B is the connectivity of application spheres $X(i)$ of the optimal series articles. Spheres $X(i)$ possess this property in the case when a matrix $(g_{ij})(i \in U, j \in X)$ satisfies the connectivity property, that is, for any $i, K \in U$ the remainder $g_{ij} - g_{Kj}$ changes the sign (like function j) not more than once for the monotone change of $j \in X$.

While performing the abovementioned property of the matrix (g_{ij}) the optimal solution of problem L can be obtained by means of $T \sim mn$ operations at the storage $\Pi \sim m+n$ by solving problem B, where $\beta = n$ and the value of the function $f(x,y)$ is calculated by the formula

$$f(x,y) = \min_{i \in U} \{ g_i^0 + \sum_{j=x+1}^{y} g_{ij} \} .$$

The property of connectivity of matrix g_{ij} can rather often be observed in real problems where for two graded parameters i, K the numbers of kinds of demand are divided into two subsets with a boundary j' , to the left side of which the graded parameter i is "better", and to the right side - the one K is.

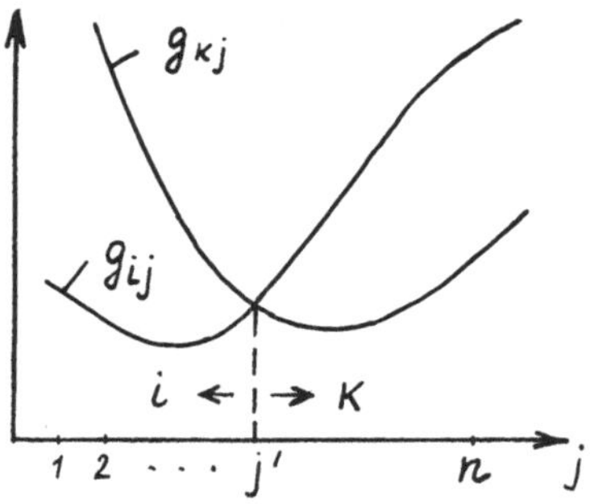

Another sufficient condition for reducing problem L to problem B is the quasiconvexity property of the matrix g_{ij}, where for any $j \in X$ and $i < k < \ell$ inequality $g_{kj} \le max\{g_{ij}, g_{\ell j}\}$ holds.

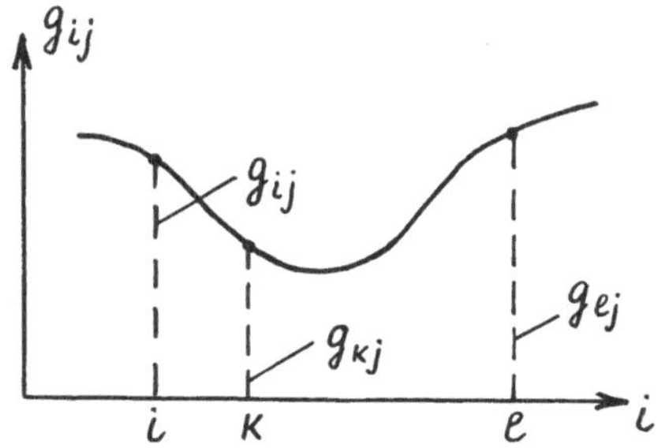

In this case, though spheres of application of the optimal series can be non-connected, the optimal solution of the problem is constructed by the optimal one of problem B, where $\beta = m+1$.

$$f(y,z) = \begin{cases} g_z^0 + \sum\limits_{j \in X} g_{zj}, & 0 = y < z \le m; \\ g_z^0 - \sum\limits_{j \in X} max\{0; g_{yj} - g_{zj}\}, & 0 < y \le z \le m; \\ 0, \; 0 < y \le z = m+1; \\ \infty, \; y = 0, \; z = m+1. \end{cases}$$

Thus we obtain the algorithm for solving problem L of $T \sim m^2 n$ number of operations for storage capacity $\Pi \sim m$.

The real function $S(y_1, \dots, y_m)$ of the variables acquiring values 0 and 1 is called a polynomial of Boolean variables. There takes place the following

T h e o r e m. The problem L(L') is equivalent to the minimization problem of the polynomial of Boolean variables.

The optimal solution of problem L(L') is constructed according to the optimal solution of minimization problem of the following polynomial:

$$S(y_1, \dots, y_m) = \sum_{i \in U} g_i^0 (1 - y_i) + \sum_{j \in X} \sum_{\ell=0}^{m-1} \Delta g_{\ell j} \, y_{i_1^j}, \dots, y_{i_\ell^j} .$$

Here $i_1^j, \dots, i_m^j$ for any j is a reset of the set U, such that

$g_{i_1^j j} \leq \cdots \leq g_{i_m^j j}$, and $\Delta g_{\ell j} = g_{i_{\ell+1}^j j} - g_{i_\ell^j}$ for any j and ℓ. If $(y_1, \ldots, y_m)$ is a vector which minimizes the given polynomial S, then (x_i), where $x_i = 1 - y_i$ is the optimal solution of problem L'.

The polynomial $S(y_1, \ldots, y_m)$ is called corresponding to the pair (g_i^o) (g_{ij}). If this polynomial also corresponds to the pair (g_i^o) (h_{ij}), then matrices (g_{ij}) and (h_{ij}) are called equivalent ones. For the problems L(L') with equivalent matrices the sets of optimal decisions coincide. Due to this problem L can efficiently be solved not only in the case when the input matrix (g_{ij}) possesses connectivity or quasiconvexity properties, but also in such cases when there exists a matrix equivalent to the input one and possessing one of these properties.

For problem L of the general kind an approximated algorithm with small number of operations is constructed which makes it possible to estimate the precision of the solution obtained. While constructing the algorithms there was considered a problem L dual to problem (5)-(8), where condition (8) was substituted for condition $x_{ij} \geq 0$. This problem has the form

Dual problem (L^*)

$$\sum_{j \in X} \min_{i \in \mathcal{U}} (g_{ij} + w_{ij}) \to \max_{(w_{ij})} ;$$

$$\sum_{j \in X} w_{ij} \leq g_i^o, \quad i \in \mathcal{U},$$

$$w_{ij} \geq 0, \quad i \in \mathcal{U}, \; j \in X .$$

The number of operations of the algorithm is $T \sim m^2 n$ for the storage capacity $\Pi \sim m + n$. The algorithm is based on the construction of the so-called impasse solution (w_{ij}), where $w_{ij} > 0$, if $g_{ij} < \min_{\kappa \in \mathcal{U}} (g_{\kappa j} + w_{\kappa j})$.

Numerical calculations have been held with matrices (g_{ij}) of the size $m = 30 \div 50$; $n = 100 \div 300$. Here, the mean relative error was within the units of per cent.

Seeking for the impasse solution for problem L^* and the calculati on with the help of it of the lower boundary of the real function for problem L allows us to construct a branch-and-bound algorithm for this problem to be solved.

Numerical calculations for this algorithm have been held with matrices (g_{ij}) of the size $m \leq 120$, $n \leq 100$. Here, less than an hour was necessary to solve the problem at the computer BESM-6.

4. It was assumed for the above considered model that the expenditures to produce the assigned article can be given independently of other articles of the series. This assumption is not valid when unified blocks are used to produce articles. In such cases the expenditures to produce the articles of a given graded parameter depend on what unified blocks are used to complete such articles and how widely these blocks are used. Thus, we approached the problem to choose such a series of articles and such sets of unified blocks used to complete the articles that the total expenditures should satisfy the assigned demand but be minimal.

Let, as in the first model, X be the set of the demand kind, and $\mathcal{U}$ - the set of graded parameters of unified blocks. $W=\{1,\dots,K\}$ denotes the set of type series of unified blocks. The number of blocks of the K -th graded parameter, necessary to complete the articles of the i-th graded parameter, is considered to equal q_{Ki} . Let for any $i \in \mathcal{U}$ there be known an expenditure function $g_i(v)$, $v \geq 0$ to produce the articles of the i-th graded parameter, with volume v , without taking the expenditures to produce completing blocks into account. The latter expenditures should be calculated separately, since a block of one and the same graded parameter is used to complete articles of different graded parameters. Therefore, for any $\kappa \in W$ we also assume as known the function $h_\kappa(w)$, $w \geqslant 0$ of the expenditures to produce κ blocks of the w-th graded parameter. For any $i \in \mathcal{U}$, $j \in X$ we consider to know the magnitudes p_{ij}, g'_{ij} , having the same sense as the ones in the first model. The former variables $x_{ij} \in \{0,1\}$, $i \in \mathcal{U}$, $j \in X$ having been used , the problem to choose the articles' optimal series and the completing blocks is put down in the following form:

$$\sum_{\kappa \in W} h_\kappa(w_\kappa) + \sum_{i \in \mathcal{U}} g_i(v_i) + \sum_{j \in X} \sum_{i \in \mathcal{U}} g'_{ij}\, x_{ij} \rightarrow \min_{(x_{ij})} ;$$

$$\sum_{i \in \mathcal{U}} x_{ij} = 1, \quad i \in \mathcal{U} ;$$

(K)

$$v_i = \sum_{j \in X} p_{ij}\, x_{ij}, \quad i \in \mathcal{U} ;$$

$$w_\kappa = \sum_{i \in \mathcal{U}} q_{i\kappa}\, v_i, \quad \kappa \in W;$$

$$x_{ij} \in \{0,1\}, \quad i \in \mathcal{U}, \ j \in X .$$

5. The above given models do not take into account possible reset of the articles' series with their functioning conditions being changed. It goes without saying that such changes at the given period of time can be insignificant, and, therefore, the series can be considered unchanged in the course of time. However, while investigating a period of time long enough this assumption may cease to be valid and it is necessary to pass from the statical articles' series to the sub-

stituting one another articles' series. We call such a sequence a dynamic series of articles.

Let the period of time under investigation be divided into T intervals with numbers $t=1,\dots,T$. X, as above, denotes the set of the demand kinds, and $X_t \subset X$ - the demand which is to be satisfied at the t-th interval. Let $\mathcal{U}$ be the totality of all the articles' graded parameters. For any pair "the i-th graded parameter - the j-th kind of the demand" we, as before, assume to know the magnitudes p_{ij}, g'_{ij}. Production of articles of a given graded parameter in the situation at hand is distributed for the intervals of the period of time under investigation, therefore, for any $i \in \mathcal{U}$ we assume to know functions $g_{it}(v)$ implying the expenditures to produce articles of the i-th graded parameter of volume v at the interval t.

If we use variables $x_{ij} \in \{0,1\}$, $i \in \mathcal{U}$, $j \in X$, indicating what kinds of demands are satisfied by what graded parameters, the problem to choose the optimal dynamic series acquires the following form:

Dynamic problem (D)

$$\sum_{t=1}^{T} \sum_{i \in \mathcal{U}} g_{it}(v_{it}) + \sum_{j \in X} \sum_{i \in \mathcal{U}} g'_{ij}\, x_{ij} \longrightarrow \min_{(x_{ij})} ;$$

$$\sum_{i \in \mathcal{U}} x_{ij} = 1, \quad j \in X;$$

$$v_{it} = \sum_{j \in X_t} p_{ij}\, x_{ij}, \quad i \in \mathcal{U}, \quad t = 1,\dots,T;$$

$$x_{ij} \in \{0,1\}, \quad i \in \mathcal{U}, \quad j \in X .$$

6. The models given above assume the kind of the demand to be known and assigned uniquely. However, sometimes the demand only becomes known after one has chosen the series and the volume of the production of the articles' series. Some set of demand alternatives has only been assigned beforehand. In such cases the choice of the

articles' series and of the volume of production should necessarily take place in such a way as to minimize the expenditures for realizing of the "worst" kind of demand with respect to the chosen series.

Let us assume that there exist K alternatives of the demand and at the realization of the K -th alternative, $K=1,\dots,K$, it is necessary to satisfy the demand in the set X_K. Denote the set X as $\bigcup_K X_K$. Let $\mathcal{U}$ be the set of all the articles' graded parameters, and let functions $g_i(v)$ and the magnitudes g'_{ij}, p_{ij} have the same sense as in the previous problems. Besides variables $x_{ij} \in \{0,1\}$, $i \in \mathcal{U}$, $j \in X$, we also introduce the ones v_i, $i \in \mathcal{U}$, indicating the volumes of the articles' production. Then the problem of the optimal series choice for the alternative demand is put down as follows:

Alternative problem (A)

$$\max\Big\{\sum_{i\in\mathcal{U}} g_i^0(v_i) + \sum_{j\in X_K}\sum_{i\in\mathcal{U}} g'_{ij}\, x_{ij}\Big\} \longrightarrow \min_{(x_{ij})\,(v_i)};$$

$$\sum_{i\in\mathcal{U}} x_{ij} = 1, \; j\in X;$$

$$v \geq \sum_{j\in X_K} p_{ij}\, x_{ij}, \; i \in \mathcal{U};$$

$$x_{ij} \in \{0,1\}, \; i\in\mathcal{U}, \; j\in X.$$

Methods of solving the above given models of standardization are contained in the authors' monograph (see V.L.Beresnev, E.Kh.Gimady, V.T.Dementyev [2]).

References

1 Karp R.M. Reducibility among Combinatorial Problems, Complexity of Computer Computations. Proc. Symp.March 20-22, 1972, p.85-103.

2 V.L.Beresnev, E.Kh.Gimady, V.T.Dementyev. Extremal problems of standardization. "Nauka", Novosibirsk, 1978, 303 p. (in Russian).

ON OPTIMAL CONTROL OF DISCRETE SYSTEMS WITH DELAYS

Jaroslav DOLEŽAL

Research Fellow
Institute of Information Theory and Automation
Czechoslovak Academy of Sciences
182 08 PRAGUE, Czechoslovakia

The previous author's results dealing with discrete systems with state-dependent control regions are extended for the case of systems with delays. In this way the necessary optimality conditions (discrete maximum principle) are obtained for the considered case.

1. INTRODUCTION

Discrete systems arise often in various technical applications. Recently rather deep results concerning necessary optimality conditions for discrete systems with state-dependent regions of admissible controls were obtained, e.g., see [2]. The method of mathematical programming was thus successfully applied to such class of discrete systems. In this contribution it is briefly reported about the possibility how to generalize this theory also to other interesting class of discrete systems. Due to the limited space only the final results are stated and briefly discussed. The more detailed treatment of the studied subject will be published elsewhere.

Discrete systems with delays were studied formerly in [6]. However, the obtained discrete maximum principle was derived only under rather strong linearity and convexity assumptions. More recently somewhat special cases of discrete systems with delays were investigated in [1, 7]. The dual decentralized approach in [7] provides an effective computational scheme for the considered special case, while in [1] the mathematical programming approach is applied to a class of systems with delays, but under the assumption of constant regions of addmissible controls.

It was briefly reported by the author in [4] that the mathematical programming approach to the optimization of discrete systems with state-dependent control regions [2] is applicable also if the discrete system in question contains various delays. Moreover, the approach described in [2] enables fairly convenient treatment of various additional constraints, e.g., the state constraints. From these reasons the reader is referred to [2], where the all here concepts and results are properly defined and derived. For convenience, the matrix notation is used. If not otherwise explicitely stated all vectors are supposed to be column-vectors except of the gradients of various functions, which are always treated as row-vectors.

2. DISCRETE SYSTEMS WITH DELAYS

In [3] it was shown that after the appropriate reformulation the problems with delays can be handled in a unified manner. It is then not very hard to see that the construction suggested in [2] applies also to such problems. However, for the sake of the notational simplicity let us consider a more concrete case for which the necessary optimality conditions will be stated. Thus only one delay in the state and/or control is assumed. The extension of these results for the case of more delays is then straightforward. Therefore let us assume a discrete system with delays described by the difference equation (upper or lower index k denotes always the current stage of the system)

$$x_{k+1} = f^k(x_k, x_{k-\alpha}, u_k, u_{k-\beta}), \quad k = 0,1, \ldots, K-1, \tag{1}$$

where positive integer K denotes the given number of stages, $x_k \in E^n$ is the state, $u_k \in E^m$ the control and $f^k : E^{2n} \times E^{2m} \to E^n$.

Further the following state and control constraints are imposed

$$S^k(x_k, x_{k-\delta}) = 0, \quad s^k(x_k, x_{k-\delta}) \le 0, \quad k = 0,1, \ldots, K, \tag{2}$$

$$Q^k(x_k, x_{k-\eta}, u_k, u_{k-\varepsilon}) = 0, \quad q^k(x_k, x_{k-\eta}, u_k, u_{k-\varepsilon}) \le 0,$$
$$k = 0,1, \ldots, K-1, \tag{3}$$

where $S^k : E^{2n} \to E^\rho$, $s^k : E^{2n} \to E^\pi$, $Q^k : E^{2n} \times E^{2m} \to E^\gamma$ and $q^k : E^{2n} \times E^{2m} \to E^\tau$. The inequality sign for vectors is to be taken componentwise.

The aim is to minimize the cost functional

$$J = g(x_K) + \sum_{k=0}^{K-1} h^k(x_k,\ x_{k-\sigma},\ u_k,\ u_{k-\theta}), \tag{4}$$

where $h_k : E^{2n} \times E^{2m} \to E^1$ and $g : E^n \to E^1$. In (1) - (4) denote $\alpha,\ \beta,\ \delta,\ \eta,\ \sigma,\ \theta,\ \varepsilon$ the positive integers less than K , which represent the various delays in (1) - (4). The initial conditions (history)

$$\begin{aligned} &\hat{x}_{-i},\ \hat{x}_{-i+1},\ \dots,\ \hat{x}_{-1}, \hat{x}, \hat{x}_0, && i = max\ (\alpha,\ \delta,\ \eta,\ \sigma), \\ &\hat{u}_{-j},\ \hat{u}_{-j+1},\ \dots,\ \hat{u}_{-1}, && j = max\ (\beta,\ \varepsilon,\ \theta), \end{aligned} \tag{5}$$

let be given. Then the problem (1) - (5) is denoted as a discrete optimal control problem with delays. Using the terminology of I2I the constraints (2) - (3) are alternatively called the explicite ones. In principle, also more abstract case could be studied, see [2, Theorem 3], however, the case considered here is more instructive from the practical point of view.

3. NECESSARY OPTIMALITY CONDITIONS

In accordance with [2] let us assume that all functions in (1) - (4) are continuously differentiable. Further let the local convexity and the mixed constraints (3) regularity assumptions be fulfilled for this problem - for the definitions and further details see [2, Assumptions 3 and 4]. Then the following theorem can be proved using the results of [2, Theorems 4 and 5]. The lower indices are used to denote the various gradients. As control process (x, u) is denoted a pair of sequences satisfying the constraints (1) - (3) and the initial conditions (5).

Theorem. Consider the discrete optimal control probelm with delays (1) - (5). If $(\hat{x},\ \hat{u})$ is an optimal control process, then there exists a scalar $\mu \le 0$ and row-vector multipliers

$$\lambda_k \in E^n,\quad \psi_k \in E^\rho,\quad \nu_k \in E^\pi,\quad k = 0, 1, \dots K,$$

$\zeta_k \in E^\gamma, \quad \xi_k \in E^\tau, \quad k = 0,1, \ldots, K-1,$

such that (arguments omitted for the sake of brevity):

(a) if $\mu = 0$, then not all $\lambda_k, \psi_k, \nu_k, k = 0,1, \ldots, K,$

are zero;

(b) the row-vectors $\lambda_k, k = 0,1, \ldots, K$ satisfy the equation

$$\lambda_k = H^{k+1}_{x_k} + H^{k+\alpha+1}_{x_k} + H^{k+\sigma+1}_{x_k} + \zeta_k Q^k_{x_k} + \xi_k q^k_{x_k} + \zeta_{k+\eta} Q^{k+\eta}_{x_k}$$

$$+ \xi_{k+\eta} + \psi_k S^k_{x_k} + \nu_k s^k_{x_k} + \psi_{k+\delta} S^{k+\delta}_{x_k} + \nu_{k+\delta} s^{k+\delta}_{x_k} ,$$

$$k = 0,1, \ldots, K-1,$$

$$\lambda_0 = 0, \quad \lambda_K = \mu g_{x_K} + \psi_K S^K_{x_K} + \nu_K s^K_{x_K} ,$$

where

$$H^{k+1}(x_k, x_{k-\alpha}, x_{k-\sigma}, u_k, u_{k-\beta}, u_{k-\theta}) = \mu h^k(x_k, x_{k-\sigma}, u_k, u_{k-\theta})$$

$$+ \lambda_{k+1} f^k(x_k, x_{k-\alpha}, u_k, u_{k-\beta}), \quad k = 0,1, \ldots, K-1;$$

(c) the expression

$$\mathrm{H}^{k+1}(u_k) = H^{k+1}(u_k) + (H^{k+\beta+1}_{u_k} + H^{k+\theta+1}_{u_k} + \zeta_{k+\varepsilon} Q^{k+\varepsilon}_{u_k} + \xi_{k+\varepsilon} q^{k+\varepsilon}_{u_k}) u_k,$$

$$k = 0,1, \ldots, K-1,$$

attains its maximum as a function of u_k subject to (3) at the point $\hat{u}_k$;

(d) $\nu_k \leq 0, \quad \nu_k s^k = 0, \quad k = 0,1, \ldots, K;$

(e) $\xi_k \leq 0, \quad \xi_k q^k = 0, \quad k = 0,1, \ldots, K-1 .$

If not otherwise stated all expressions are evaluated along the optimal process $(\hat{x}, \hat{u})$. To derive these results rather tedious manipulations were necessary to apply the scheme of [2]. From condition (c) one easily obtains the more practical characterization of optimal controls. Namely,

$$H^{k+1}_{u_k} + H^{k+\beta+1}_{u_k} + H^{k+\theta+1}_{u_k} + \zeta_k Q^k_{u_k} + \xi_k q^k_{u_k} + \zeta_{k+\varepsilon} Q^{k+\varepsilon}_{u_k} + \xi_{k+\varepsilon} q^{k+\varepsilon}_{u_k} = 0,$$

$k = 0, 1, \ldots, K-1.$

However, with this condition instead of (c) the conditions (a) - (e) in the above theorem can be derived rather straightforward applying some basic facts from the mathematical programming theory. Moreover, no convexity or regularity assumptions for such form of necessary optimality conditions are needed. On the other hand, such conditions cannot be denoted as a discrete maximum principle given by the theorem.

In this way we obtained a generalization of the results described in [6], which are valid only for the linear-convex case. It is further clear that in our general formulation the obtained conditions do not possess such a transparent form as in [6]. More deep results can be obtained under some additional assumptions, e.g., the delays being "additive" as in [1, 7]. This is shown in the forthcoming author's paper [5]. The existence question for this class of discrete optimal control problems was treated in [3] in detail.

4. CONCLUSIONS

It was shown that the existing necessary optimality conditions for discrete systems with state-dependent regions of admissible controls can be successfully applied to derive the analogous results also for systems with delays. The derived necessary optimality conditions have the form of a discrete maximum principle. The importance of the obtained results is strengthened by a number of practical problems which can be treated within the framework of the studied case.

REFERENCES

1. Burdet, C.A., Sehti, S.P.: *J. Optimization Theory Appl.* 19 (1976), 445-454.
2. Doležal, J.: *Kybernetika* 11 (1975), 423-450.
3. Doležal, J.: *Applied Math. Optimization* 3 (1976), 51-63.
4. Doležal, J.: In "*Proceedings of the 5th Symposium COMPUTERS IN CHEMICAL ENGINEERING*", 5.-9.10.1977, High Tatras, 831-834.
5. Doležal, J.: *Kybernetika* 15 (1979). To appear.
6. Mariani, L., Nicoletti, B.: *IEEE Trans. Automatic Control* AC-18 (1973), 311-313.
7. Tamura, H.: *Automatica* 11 (1975), 593-602.

ANALYSIS OF THE INFLUENCE OF A SYSTEM ON OBJECTS AS A PROBLEM OF TRANSFORMATION OF DATA TABLES

Yu.P.Drobyshev, V.V.Pukhov

Computing Center, Novosibirsk, USSR

Introduction

One of the first steps in studying complex systems such as the environment, economics, medicine is construction of a formal model. Very often the mechanism of the system's functioning reveals itself through its influence on some homogeneous set of objects, e.g. the influence of the environment as a set of factors on individuals of some population. States of the objects influenced by the system are fixed as a set of concrete characteristics and form a description in some ensemble of properties (a data table). Properties of objects can be measured in different scales. The initial ensemble of the properties being measured can be broad and contain a large number of secondary factors in an implicit form. The above factors complicate the problem of the search for an adequate model and require that preliminary analysis be made of the data so as to select and transform them and obtain new knowledge.

This paper suggests an approach to the analysis of data tables which consists in some transformation of the initial table to the derived one. The latter must preserve a list of invariants, a priori specified, and appear simpler than the first table. The invariants are fixed before the beginning of transformation. They include: cardinality of the set of objects, cardinality of sampling space of states of the table, closeness, similarity of the objects of the table; some dependence characteristics of the ensemble of properties, etc.

The above procedure of transformation includes such important problems of the analysis of data as cluster analysis, ordering, data compression, analysis of correspondences.

The approach is based on the following observation concerning the above mentioned problems. Any solution of a problem can be considered as some complex transformation consisting of two independent aspects: transformation of a set of objects in the initial table into a set of objects in the derived table; transformation of the initial ensemble of properties into the secondary one. Taking account of the fact that both the initial system, which has generated the data table, and the data themselves have uncertainties of different kind, the authors make an attempt to use the apparatus of the theory of fuzzy sets /3/.

Equivalent transformations of the table. Model I.

The given model preserves the following invariants: cardinality of a set of objects, cardinality of the initial sampling space, measure of similarity between couples of objects in the table.

1.1. Let the construction of the form

$$T = \langle M; \{\mathcal{X}_i\}; f_T \rangle \quad , i \in I$$

be table T.

Here $\mathcal{X}_i = (X_i; \mu_i; \rho_i)$ is the i-th property; I is a finite set of property indices; X_i is a finite set of property gradations; μ_i is measure of similarity*) of property gradations in

*) There is also a term "fuzzy tolerance" /2/ or a more general term "fuzzy relation" /3/.

$X_i \times X_i$($\mu_i: X_i \times X_i \rightarrow [0,1]$), characterized by

a) $\mu_i(x,y) = \mu_i(y,x), \quad \forall x,y \in X_i$;

b) $\mu_i(x,x) = 1, \quad \forall x \in X_i$;

ρ_i is the informational weight of the $\mathcal{X}_i$-property in a system of properties $\{\mathcal{X}_i\}$:

$$\rho_i > 0, \qquad \sum_{i \in I} \rho_i = 1.$$

Function f is intended for selecting the set Ω_T- the domain of admissible values of table T:

$$M \subseteq \Omega_T \subseteq \prod_{i \in I} X_i$$

$$f: \Pi X_i \rightarrow \{0,1\}$$

$$f = \begin{cases} 1, & x \in \Omega_T; \\ 0, & x \overline{\in} \Omega_T. \end{cases}$$

M is a set of concrete realizations of objects or lines of the table.

1.2. Let there be two tables, T and T', with the same cardinality of sets M and M'. Let table T' be a corollary of table T if there exists mapping

$$F: T \rightarrow T' \tag{1}$$

satisfying the following conditions:

a) there exists F_1, establishing one-to-one correspondence between subsets $\{J_k\}$ and $\{J'_k\}$, $1 \leq k \leq s$ of sets I and I',

$I = \bigcup_{k \leq s} J_k, \quad I' = \bigcup_{k \leq s} J'_k$

$$F_1: J_k \rightarrow J'_k$$

b) there exists F_2:

$$F_2 : (\Omega_T)_k \rightarrow (\Omega_{T'})_k$$

transforming for any $k \leq s$ a set of admissible gradations $(\Omega_T)_k$ into a similar set $(\Omega_{T'})_k$ of table T', $(\Omega_W)_k$ is the mapping of the set Ω_W onto the space of properties J_k of table W;

c) $\rho_k = \sum_{i \in J_k} \rho_i = \sum_{i \in J'_k} \rho'_i = \rho'_k$, $\quad \forall k \leq s$

d) $\sum_{i \in J_k} \rho_i \mu_i(x,y) = \sum_{i \in F_1(J_k)} \rho'_i \mu'_i(F_2(x), F_2(y)), \quad \forall x,y \in (\Omega_T)_k.$

Transformation (1) under conditions a)-d) will be considered as primary and denoted by $F = \langle F_1, F_2 \rangle$.

Note that if for tables T_1 and T_2 there exists primary transformation $F: T_1 \rightarrow T_2$ then there exists transformation $G: T_2 \rightarrow T_1$ which is also primary and inverse to F.

Below two special cases of the initial transformation are considered, i.e. operation of convolution and decomposition of properties.

1.3. Let there be given a set $I^o \subseteq I$. The system of properties $\{\mathcal{X}_i\}$, $i \in I_o$ can be regarded as some integral property $\mathcal{X}_{I_o}$, which has a set of gradations X_{I^o}, measure of similarity μ_o, an informational weight $\rho_{I^o} = \sum \rho_i$. Here $X_{I^o} = (\Omega_T)_{I^o}$ are gradations of a new property, including only those elements $\prod_{i \in I_o} X_i$, which have non-empty projections onto Ω_T. The measure of similarity μ_{I^o} over subset I_o is introduced analogously to measures all over the entire set of properties /2/:

$$\mu_{I^o}(x,y) = \Sigma \frac{\rho_i}{\rho_{I^o}} \mu_o((x)_i,(y)_i), \qquad \forall x,y \in X_{I^o}.$$

Let transformations of such a type be called convolution and denoted by S. In this case table T turns into T' and this transformation satisfies conditions a)-d).

1.4. Now consider the operation of R property decomposition as the inverse to convolution. In this connection one of the properties of the initial table is substituted by a group of secondary properties in such a way that certain characteristics of the initial property, e.g. measure of similarity, cardinality of a gradation set and informational weight, are preserved. The initial property is integral with respect to the secondary ones and is derived from the latter by convolution.

Let property $\mathcal{X}_{i_o}$ be decomposed into the product of properties $\{\mathcal{X}_j^{i_o}\}$, $j \in J$, if: i) $\rho_{i_o} = \sum_{j \in J} \rho_j^{i_o}$; ii) for any gradation in X_{i_o} there exists the only group of gradations in $\prod_{j \in J} X_j^{i_o}$ and iii) measures of similarity in $\mathcal{X}_j^{i_o}$ are related by

$$\mu_{i_o}(x,y) = \sum_{j \in J} \frac{\rho_j^{i_o}}{\rho_{i_o}} \mu_j^{i_o}((x)_j,(y)_j), \qquad \forall x,y \in X_{i_o}.$$

Transformation R of table T yields

$$T' = \langle M'; \{\mathcal{X}'_i\}_{i \in I} ; f' \rangle$$

where f' equals unity on the set of gradations from $\Omega_{T'}$, obtained from the set Ω_T by replacing the gradation from X_{i_o} by a corresponding group.

Properties $\{\mathcal{X}'_i\}$ for $i \in I \setminus \{i_o\}$ are identical, but the property $\mathcal{X}_{i_o}$ is replaced by a set of properties $\{\mathcal{X}_j^{i_o}\}$, $j \in J$.

It is obvious that transformation R satisfies conditions a)-d).

1.5. Let us show now that any transformation $F = \langle F_1, F_2 \rangle$ considered in 1.2 can be represented as a composition of relations of R and S types. Indeed, in a) and b) definition of F is given, where F_2 is mapping of a group of properties $\{J_k\}$ onto $\{J_k'\}$ and the objects' similarity is invariant with respect to the transformation.

Next, let us consider table T" having S number of properties

$\mathcal{X}_k'' = (X_k'', \mu_k'', \rho_k'')$, where

$$\mu_k''(G_1 x, G_1 y) = \sum_{i \in J} \rho_i \mu_i(x,y), \qquad \forall x,y \in X_k'', \qquad \rho_k'' = \sum_{i \in J_k} \rho_i .$$

Mapping G_1 establishes one-to-one correspondence with gradations of property X_k'' and $(\Omega_T)_k$ of table T.
Transformation $U = (U_1, U_2)$ is constructed in a similar way, transforming table T" into table T' satisfying conditions a)-d).

Thus, T is represented as a composition of mappings G and U. In this connection below only transformation of R and S types are considered.

1.6. Let us assume that T and T' tables are in ω relation, if there exists a sequence of $T_k (1 \leq k \leq m)$

$$T = T_1 \overset{\alpha_1}{\to} T_2 \overset{\alpha_2}{\to} \dots \overset{\alpha_{m-1}}{\to} T_m = T' \tag{2}$$

where for any k, α_k there is R or S.

1.6.1. It is easy to show that $T \omega T$ is true for any table T.

1.6.2. Let $T \omega T'$ be true, then $T' \omega T$ is true, too. Indeed, let (2) be given. Consider the sequence of transformations

$$T' = T_m \overset{\beta_{m-1}}{\to} T_{m-1} \overset{\beta_{m-1}}{\to} \dots \overset{\beta_1}{\to} T_1 = T$$

where β_k is determined as the inverse to α_k operation and, consequently β_k is R or S.

1.6.3. If $T\,\omega\,T'$ and $T'\,\omega\,T''$, then $T\,\omega\,T''$.

Indeed, if sequences

$$T = T_1 \overset{\alpha_1}{\rightarrow} T_2 \overset{\alpha_2}{\rightarrow} \dots \overset{\alpha_{m'-1}}{\rightarrow} T_{m_1} = T'$$

and

$$T' = T_1' \overset{\beta_1}{\rightarrow} T_2 \overset{\beta_2}{\rightarrow} \dots. \overset{\beta_{m_2-1}}{\rightarrow} T_{m_2}' = T''$$ are correct,

then the sequence

$$T = T_1 \overset{\alpha_1}{\rightarrow} T_2 \overset{\alpha_2}{\rightarrow} \dots \overset{\alpha_{m_1-1}}{\rightarrow} T_{m_1} \overset{\beta_1}{\rightarrow} T_2' \overset{\beta_2}{\rightarrow} \dots \overset{\beta_{m_2-1}}{\rightarrow} T_{m_2}' = T''$$

is correct as well, where $\alpha_i, \beta_i \in \{R,S\}$ and, consequently, $T\,\omega\,T''$. On the basis of 1.6.1-1.6.3 we conclude that relation ω is an equivalence relation and by the same token the class of tables [T] which is equivalent to the given one is connected with any data table T. A general problem of transformation of the initial table T is formulated as follows.

Let us find in class [T] a table T' of simpler structure than table T. In this case we do not try to formulate the criterion of simplicity and assume only that it exists at least in the majority of specific cases, and the comparison of tables can be fulfilled due to this criterion. In what follows we deal exactly with the case.

1.7. A problem of transforming table T into T', where properties are nominal, is of interst. The procedure of such transformation is based on the definition in 1.2 with the use of concepts of fuzzy relations approximation. For convenience the apparatus and results of approximation are presented in Appendix 1.

The procedure of constructing the nominal properties which characterize the structure of secondary data is as follows.

The initial table T is transformed into T' with one property. Then table T' is transformed into T", the latter possessing two properties, one of which is nominal with the maximum informational weight for any such representation. Next, T" is transformed into T"' where the nominal property in T" is presented in T"', and the nonnominal property from T"' undergoes further decomposition, and so on./1/.

The class of real tables, where analysis of this kind is possible, is small due to the presence of coefficients $S\ \rho_i$ in model 1. The next model is free of such a drawback, but it is necessarily deprived of other positive characteristics of model 1, e.g. the preciseness of conclusions, results of transformation.

Transformation of the tables. Model 2.

As the description of table M in the given model we understand the construction of the following type:

$$T = \langle M;\ U;\ V;\ \{\ \mathcal{X}_J\ \}_{j \in J}\rangle$$

M is a set of objects described in the system of properties $\{\mathcal{X}_j\}$.

$U: M \times M \rightarrow [0,\ 1]$ is fuzzy relation given on the set M.

$V: J \times J \rightarrow [0,\ 1]$ is fuzzy relation on I.

$\mathcal{X}_j = (X_j, \mu_j)$, μ_j is fuzzy relation on X_j.

As an invariant of transformation it is convenient to use the following fuzzy graph π_T, given on $\{m_{ij}\}$ and determined as follows:

$$\pi_T(m_{i_1 j_1}, m_{i_2 j_2}) = [v_{j_1 j_2} \wedge (u_{i_1 i_2} \vee \mu_{j_2}(m_{i_1 j_2}, m_{i_2 j_2}))] \vee$$

$$[v_{j_1 j_2} \wedge (u_{i_1 i_2} \vee \mu_{j_1}(m_{i_1 j_1}, m_{i_2 j_1}))].$$

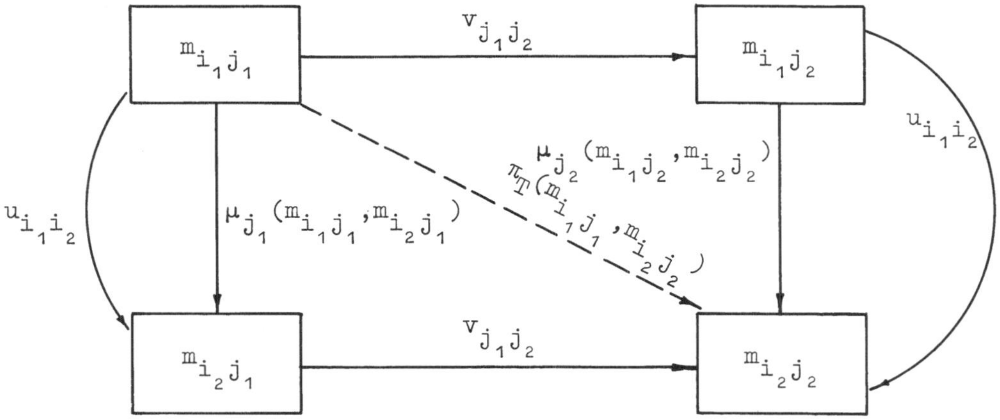

Fig. 1

Transformation of T to T' is represented as $f = (f_1, f_2)$ where f_1 and f_2 are fuzzy relations:

$$f_1 : M \times M' \to [0, 1]$$

$$f_2 : J' \times J \to [0, 1],$$

where $M = f_1 \circ M' \circ f_2$.

In this operation "$\circ$" is determined as follows:

$$m_{ij} = \underset{\alpha,\gamma}{+} \frac{m'_{\alpha\gamma}}{f^1_{i\alpha} \wedge f^2_{\gamma j}}, \text{ where "+" is enumeration.}$$

Depending on the type of the problem to be solved U and V could be sought for from the condition

i) $M = U \circ M \circ V$ or ii) $M = U \circ M$ and $M = M \circ V$.

Transformation $f = (f_1, f_2)$ of table T to table T' must meet the conditions

i) $U \circ f_1 = f_1 \circ U'$ and $f_2 \circ V = V' \circ f_2$ or ii) $U = f_1 \circ U' \circ f^*$ and $V = f_2 \circ V' \circ f_2$ depending on the type of the problem, in the given case "$\circ$" is the min-max operation of the composition of fuzzy relations.

Appendix.

Let D be a class of fuzzy relations given on the fixed set M.

$$\mu \in D \Rightarrow \mu : M \times M \to [0, 1]$$

Let us distinguish in D classes of more commonly used relations.

D is a class of equivalence relations

$$\mu \in D \Rightarrow \begin{cases} 1. \ \mu(x,y) = 0 \vee 1 & \forall x,y. \\ 2. \ \mu(x,x) = 1, & \forall x \in M \\ 3. \ \mu(x,y) = \mu(y,x) & \forall x,y \in M \\ 4. \ \mu(x,y) = 1 \ \& \ \mu(y,z) = 1 \Rightarrow & \mu(x,z) = 1. \end{cases}$$

D_t is a class of fuzzy relations of tolerance

$$\mu \in D_t \Rightarrow \begin{cases} 1. \ \mu(x,y) \leq 1 \\ 2. \ \mu(x,x) = 1 \\ 3. \ \mu(x,y) = \mu(y,x). \end{cases}$$

$D_{\geq}$ is a class of linear order

$$\mu \in D_{\geq} \Rightarrow \begin{cases} 1. \ \mu(x,y) = 0 \vee 1 \\ 2. \ \mu(x,x) = 1 \\ 3. \ \mu(x,y) = 1 \ \& \ \mu(y,z) = 1 \Rightarrow \mu(x,z) = 1. \end{cases}$$

Let us have arbitrary relations $\mu_o \in D$ and class $\bar{D}$ of precise relations defined by a certain system of axioms.

It is required to determine in $\bar{D}$ μ_R approximating μ_o most accurately.

Let number $d(\mu_1,\mu_2)$ be the distance between μ_1 and μ_2. Define the number by the formula

$$d(\mu_1,\mu_2) = \max_{(x,y)} |\mu_1(x,y) - \mu_2(x,y)|.$$

It is possible to set problem A.

Problem A: it is required to find $\{\mu^*_R\}_A/$

$$d(\mu_o,\mu_R^*) \le d(\mu_o,\mu_R) \ \forall \mu_R.$$

Let us consider now the problem of approximation of μ_o as the problem of finding the best approximation in the system

$$\begin{cases} \mu_o = \Theta_1\mu_R + \Theta_2\overline{\mu}_R \\ \mu_1 + \mu_2 = \|\mu_o\| \\ \Theta_1 \ge 0 \\ \Theta_2 \ge 0 \end{cases}$$

where the greater Θ_1, the better μ_R approximates μ_o.

Let μ_R be fixed, then

$$\Theta_1 \le \Theta_1^* = \min_{(x,y)} \{\mu_R(x,y)(1 - \mu_o(x,y)) + (1 - \mu_R(x,y))\mu_o(x,y)\}.$$

It is possible to set problem B.

Problem B: it is required to find $\{\mu_R^*\}_B /$

$$\Theta_1^*(\mu_R^*) \ge \Theta_1^*(\mu_R) \quad \forall \mu_R.$$

Statement: $\{\mu_R^*\}_A = \{\mu_R\}_B.$

On the basis of problem B it is convenient to approximate $\mu_o \in D_t$ by $\mu_R \in D_\sim$, $\mu_o \in D$ - by $\mu_R \in D_\ge$.

Algorithms have been developed for all these important cases.

REFERENCES

1. Drobyshev, Yu.P., Pukhov, V.V. Equivalent transformation of empirical data tables. Autometria, 2, 1978.

2. Orlov, A.I. Problems of stability and correctness of solution in the theory of expert evaluation. In the book:"Statistic methods of expert evaluation analysis".

3. Zadeh, L.A. Fuzzy Sets, Inf.Control., 8, 1965.

ON NON-PARAMETRIC ALGORITHMS OF OPTIMIZATION

Iljin E.V., Medvedev A.V., Novikov N.F.

Computing Center, Siberian Branch of the USSR Ac.Sci.,

Krasnojarsk, USSR

Introduction. In recent years one can observe an increasing interest in optimization problems in terms of incomplete information. This incompleteness of information is caused not only by the stochastic nature of optimized system, but by incomplete knowledge of aid function and bounds as well. A natural desire to optimize processes occurring in complex objects and systems brought into life new directions in optimization theory - multi-criterial optimization, vector--optimization, optimization by means of man-computer procedures, and so on. The lack of statistical information yielded optimization problems in terms of non-parametric indefiniteness, i.e. such problems in which the parametric structure of the investigated object or process is not known *a priori* [1,2] . In the following we shall deal with this latter class of problems.

A priori information. Let functions u,x,q (controlled, uncontrolled and output vector variables of object correspondingly) be defined on $\Omega(u,x,q)$ and take values in $U^k \times U^m \times U^n$. The object satisfies the equation $q=f(u,x)$, $\forall (u,x) \in \Omega(u,x)$, the form of which is unknown.

The measuring of variables u,x,q is made with random error ξ, such that $M\{\xi\}=0$, $M\{\xi^2\}<\infty$. The a priori information in case of non-parametric indefiniteness is such that there is no possibility to formulate the model of investigated object in form $q=\hat{f}(u,x,\alpha)$, where α is vector of parameters. Suggest that $q=f(u,x)$ is singlevalued and continuous on $\Omega(u,x)$. Suggest also, that we have a sample, consisting of statistically independent observations $\{u_i,x_i,q_i\}$, $i=\overline{1,s}$ having probability density $p(u,x,q)$ $\forall (u,x,q)\in\Omega(u,x,q)$. Let $p(u,x)>0$ for almost all $(u,x)\in\Omega(u,x)$.

Non-parametric models. Let vectors u,x,q be k-, m-, and n-dimensional correspondingly. Then the model of object on the strength of incompleteness of information about its structure may be represented in general form as follows:

$$f_j(u,x,q,\alpha)=0,\quad j=\overline{1,n1},$$
$$f_j(u,x,q)=0,\quad j=\overline{n1+1,n}, \qquad (1)$$

where the first part of the equations is represented in parametrized form (α - vector of unknown parametres), and the second part of the equations can not be parametrized (presence of non-parametric indefiniteness). Using the sample $\{u_i,x_i,q_i\}$, $i=\overline{1,s}$ one may construct algorithms of estimation of parameters α . Various algorithms of construction of parameter estimates are described, for example, in [3]. Denote these estimates as $\hat{\alpha}$. In order to obtain the second part of the equations (1) in terms of non-parametric indefiniteness, one may use non-parametric estimates [2] . Then the model (1) will take form:

$$\hat{f}_j(u,x,q,\hat{\alpha})=0, \quad j=\overline{1,n1},$$
$$\tilde{f}_j(u,x,q)=0, \quad j=\overline{n1+1,n}. \qquad (2)$$

If it is suggested for example that $\tilde{f}_n(u,x,q)=0$ may be resolved with respect to one of components, for instance q^n, then

$$\tilde{f}_n(u,x,q)=\tilde{q}^n-\frac{\sum_{i=1}^{s} q_i^n \prod_{j=1}^{k}\Phi\left(\frac{u_j^i-u_j}{c_j(s)}\right)\prod_{j=1}^{m}\Phi\left(\frac{x_j^i-x_j}{c_j(s)}\right)\prod_{j=1}^{n-1}\Phi\left(\frac{q_j^i-q_j}{c_j(s)}\right)}{\sum_{i=1}^{s}\prod_{j=1}^{k}\Phi\left(\frac{u_j^i-u_j}{c_j(s)}\right)\prod_{j=1}^{m}\Phi\left(\frac{x_j^i-x_j}{c_j(s)}\right)\prod_{j=1}^{n-1}\Phi\left(\frac{q_j^i-q_j}{c_j(s)}\right)}=0, \qquad (3)$$

where $\tilde{q}^n$ is non-parametric estimate of $M\{q^n/u,x,q^1,\dots,q^{n-1}\}$ and square integrable functions $\Phi(c_s,z)$ (z is an arbitrary element) satisfy conditions

$$0\le\Phi(c_s,z)<\infty \quad \forall z\in\Omega(z),$$
$$c_s^{-1}\int_{\Omega(z)}\Phi(c_s,z)dz=1, \quad \lim_{s\to\infty} c_s^{-1}\Phi(c_s,z)=\delta(0), \qquad (4)$$

where δ is delta-function, and the sequence $c(s)$ is such, that

$$c(s)>0, \; s=1,2,\dots, \; \lim_{s\to\infty} c(s)=0, \; \lim sc^{m+k+n-1}(s)=\infty. \qquad (5)$$

The models of the form (2) may, in particular case, be represented by both parametric relations and relations using non-parametric statistics. For given vectors u,x, arises the problem to resolve the system (2) with respect to $q\in\Omega(q)$. A method of solving a system of the type (2), i.e. of constructing the statistical estimates of solution of the system (2) is considered for several cases in [2] . Different modifications of such models may be constructed using (2). These models will be used below in optimization problems.

Optimization problem statement. Let $q^*=(q_1^*,\dots,q_n^*)$ be given value of the output of object, belonging to the domain $\Omega(q)$. We shall introduce the following criterion (function of merit, aid function)

$$R=R\{(q_1,q_1^*),\dots,(q_n,q_n^*),\beta\},$$

where β is a vector of parametres (weight coefficients) which may be *a priori* unknown. The function of merit R may be unknown expicitly. In distinction from the usual [4] formulations of optimization problem the equation of the object is not given explicitly, $q=f(u,x)$, $\forall (u,x)\in\Omega(u,x)$, but one can obtain statistically independent observations $\{u_i,x_i,q_i\}$, $i=\overline{1,s}$. Optimization problem consists in finding minimum of

$$R=R\{(q_1,q_1^*),\dots,(q_n,q_n^*),\beta\} \longrightarrow \min_{u\in\Omega(u)} \qquad (6)$$

for fixed $x\in\Omega(x)$ may be given in form of some restrictions. R is convex function.

Non-parametric algorithms of optimization I. Suppose that the function of merit is given in explicit form

$$R=\sum_{i=1}^{n}\beta_i M_\xi\{Q(q_i,q_i^*)\}, \qquad (7)$$

where Q is convex function. Consider first the situation, when the values of parameters β are known. The range of $u\in\Omega(u)$ for fixed $x\in\Omega(x)$ is given by the restrictions

$$M_\xi\{\varphi^i(u,x)\}=0,\quad i=\overline{1,\lambda},$$
$$M_\xi\{\Psi^i(u,x)\}>0,\quad i=\overline{1,\nu}, \qquad (8)$$

where form of vector-functions $\varphi(u,x)$ is prescribed and sign ξ denotes average with respect to ξ.

Thus the optimization problem consists in minimization (7) under the restrictions (8) in the presence of sample $\{u_i,x_i,q_i\}$, $i=\overline{1,s}$. Define an optimal value $u=u^*$ (in suggestion that u^* exists) in form

$$u^*=M_{\xi}\{u/R=0,\ \varphi(u,x)=0,\ \Psi(u,x)>0,\ \forall(u,x)\in\Omega(u,x)\}. \qquad (9)$$

Now in order to estimate (9) we shall use non-parametric procedure. It's easy to show [2], that the non-parametric estimate (9) will take form

$$u_t^j = \sum_{i=1}^{s} u_i^j a_{it} \Big/ \sum_{i=1}^{s} a_{it}, \quad j=\overline{1,k}, \qquad (10)$$

where

$$a_{it}=\Phi\left(\frac{\sum_{j=1}^{n}\beta_j Q(q_j,q_j^*)}{c_t}\right)\prod_{j=1}^{m}\Phi\left(\frac{x_t^j-x_i^j}{c_t}\right)\prod_{j=1}^{\lambda}\Phi\left(\frac{\varphi^j(u_i,x_i)}{c_t}\right)\prod_{j=1}^{\nu}\operatorname{sgn}\Psi^j(u_i,x_i), \qquad (11)$$

and λ and ν is dimension of vector-functions $\varphi(u,x)$ and $\Psi(u,x)$ respectively, function $\Phi(\cdot)$ and sequence c_s (the components of vector c_s in (11) are taken equal to simplify the notations) satisfy conditions (4) and (5), sgn(z)=1 for $z\geqslant 0$, sgn(z)=0 for $z<0$.

Let $q^*=(q_1^*, \ldots, q_n^*)$ be unknown, but one is informed that $q=f(u,x)$ has minimum (or maximum), and it's required to find minimum R with respect to $u\in\Omega(u)$ for $x\in\Omega(x)$ under the restrictions (8). Non-parametric algorithm of optimization takes the form

$$q_t^j=\frac{\sum_{i=1}^{s} q_i^j \prod_{j=1}^{m}\Phi\left(\frac{x_t^j-x_i^j}{c_s}\right)\prod_{j=1}^{k}\Phi\left(\frac{u_{t-1}^j-u_i^j}{c_s}\right)}{\sum_{i=1}^{s}\prod_{j=1}^{m}\Phi\left(\frac{x_t^j-x_i^j}{c_s}\right)\prod_{j=1}^{k}\Phi\left(\frac{u_{t-1}^j-u_i^j}{c_s}\right)}, \quad j=\overline{1,n}, \qquad (12)$$

$$u_t^j = \sum_{i=1}^{s} u_i^j a_{it} \Big/ \sum_{i=1}^{s} a_{it}, \quad j=\overline{1,k}, \qquad (13)$$

where as q^* in formua (11) one takes q_t from (12), $x_{t=1}=x_1$ is chosen so that the plane $q=q_1$ corresponding to x_1 intersects $q=f(u,x)$ at least in two points. For stated algorithms of optimization the following propositions are valid.

Theorem 1. Suppose in problem (7), (8) q^* is unknown, $q=f(u,x)$ satisfies Lipshitz's condition and has minimum (or maximum). Then in terms of upper conditions, algorithm (12), (13) converges to u^* in mean square sense if u^* exists.

Theorem 2. Suppose in problem (7), (8) there exists an optimal $u=u^*\in\Omega(u)$. Then in terms of upper conditions, algorithm (10) satisfies the asymptotic relation

$$\lim_{t,s\to\infty} M\{(u_t-u^*)^2\} = 0.$$

Suppose, that the values of parameters β in (7) are not known a priori. Then the search of optimal value of $u=u^*\in\Omega(u)$ may be fulfilled in dialog of computer (executing algorithms (10), (11) or (12), (13)) and PTD (person taking decision). In this situation while the computer treats the problem, PTD varying values of β finds the solution, most preferable from its point of view.

Non-parametric algorithms of optimization II. Suppose that the function of merit R is not given explicitly and the values of parameters β are also unknown. The optimization problem under n-criteria may be considered in the following form (q^* is given)

$$R=R\{M\{Q(q_1,q_1^*)\},\ldots,M\{Q(q_n,q_n^*)\},\beta\} \longrightarrow \min_{u\in\Omega(u)}, \qquad (14)$$

for $x\in\Omega(x)$ and restrictions of the type (8), Q is convex function, $q=f(u,x)$ is not parametrized, but there are statistically-independent sample values $\{u_i, x_i, q_i\}$, $i=\overline{1,s}$ at investigators' disposal. Such optimization problem may be solved only in dialog of computer and PTD (man-computer dialog) on the set of Pareto $\Omega_{\pi}(u)$, from which PTD may choose most preferable solution. This solution is found then by means of models of the type (2). The optimization algorithm is described in this case by the following scheme:

1. PTD chooses initial value of parameters $\beta_{t=1}=(\beta_1[t=1], \ldots, \beta_n[t=1])$.

2. Solution $u_{t=1}$ is calculated according to algorithm

$$u_t^j = \sum_{i=1}^{s} u_i^j \, b_{it} \Big/ \sum_{i=1}^{s} b_{it}, \quad j=1,k, \qquad (15)$$

where

$$b_{it} = \prod_{j=1}^{n} \Phi\left(\frac{Q_j(q_j^*, q_j^i)}{\beta_{jt}}\right) \prod_{j=1}^{m} \Phi\left(\frac{x_j^b - x_j^i}{c_t}\right) \prod_{j=1}^{\lambda} \Phi\left(\frac{\varphi^j(u_{t-1}, x_t)}{c_t}\right) \prod_{j=1}^{\nu} \operatorname{sgn} \Psi(u_{t-1}, x_t), \qquad (16)$$

functions $\Phi(\cdot)$ and sequences c_t are the same as in (4), (5) and weight coefficients β_{jt}, $j=\overline{1,n}$ do not satisfy this time conditions, analogous to (5).

3. On the basis of the known value of $x_{t=1}=x_1 \in \Omega(x)$ and the system of stochastic equations (2) is resolved (one may find an approach to the solution of such sytems in [1,2]). As a result of that we find $q_{t=1}=(q_1[t=1], \ldots, q_n[t=1])$, $\hat{Q}_{t=1}=(\hat{Q}_1[t=1], \ldots, \hat{Q}_n[t=1])$, where $\hat{Q}_j[t=1] = \hat{Q}_j(q_j[t=1], q_j^*)$, $j=\overline{1,n}$, $\hat{Q}_j$ is an estimate of $M\{Q_j(q_j, q_j^*)\}$, $j=\overline{1,n}$.

4. PTD on the basis of the calculated value of $\hat{Q}_{t=1}$ chooses new values of parametres $\beta_{t=2}=(\beta_1[t=2], \ldots, \beta_n[t=2])$ and the computering process starts in the same way from the second stage and so on. As a result of described optimization process PTD indicates the set of unimprovable values (Pareto set) and chooses from it the most

preferable solution $u^* \in \Omega(u)$. Using non-parametric algorithms of optimization one must make fitting of the values of according to known sample $\{u_i, x_i, q_i\}$, $i=\overline{1,s}$. This problem is closely connected with the stochastic approximation of non-parametric type [2].

<u>Computer statistical simulation</u>. Investigation of the properties of optimization algorithms (12), (13) was carried out for minimization of scalar function $q=f(u)$, $u=(u_1, \ldots ,u_5)$. The equation of function of merit was as follows:

$$q = \begin{cases} \sum_{i=1}^{5} |u_i-0.5| + 1.5 , & 0 \leq u_i \leq 0.9, \\ \sum_{i=1}^{5} (u_i-2)^2 + 0.5 , & 0.9 < u_i \leq 2.7, \\ \sum_{i=1}^{5} 2(u_i-3.5)^2+1.5 , & 2.7 < u_i \leq 4.4, \\ \sum_{i=1}^{5} 2|u_i-5| +2.4 , & 4.4 < u_i \leq 5.9 , \\ \sum_{i=1}^{5} 0.5(u_i-0.5)^2 +4 , & 5.9 < u_i \leq 8.0 . \end{cases} \qquad i=\overline{1,5}.$$

Values of q were mixed with the additive noise ξ uniformly distributed on the interval $[-\alpha, \alpha]$ with zero mathematical expectation. For computer experiments c_t was taken as

$$c_t = (|q_t-q_{t-1}| -c_{t-1})* \mu , \quad 0 < \mu \leq 1.$$

Teaching sample of vector $u=(u_1, \ldots ,u_5)$ was generated in cube $[0,8]$ in correspondence with uniform distribution of random value $u=(u_1, \ldots ,u_5)$. In most number of cases algorithms of optimization find the point of global minimum. Fugure in the text shows the process of extremum for $s=320$, $\alpha=0.2$; point of global extremum is denoted as $q_э$.

Optimization algorithms offered here appeared to be sufficiently effective, and may be extremum. Results of various computer experiments proved possibility of application of non-parametric optimization algorithms for the control of complex objects of real nature.

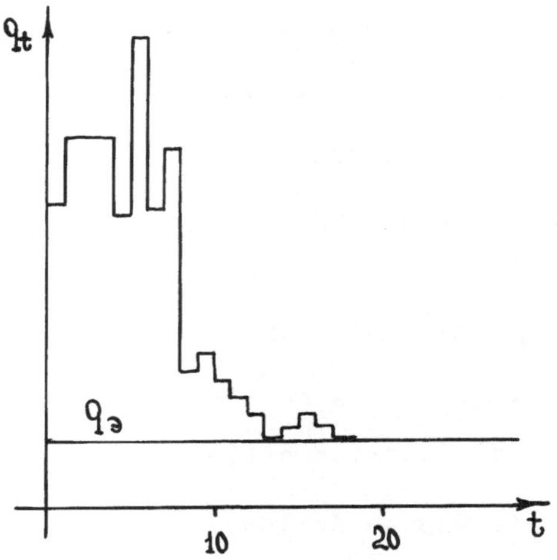

R e f e r e n c e s .

I. Медведев А.В. Оптимизация в условиях непараметрической неопределенности. В сб. "Численные методы нелинейного программирования". Тезисы II-го Всесоюзного семинара. Харьков, I976, с.229 - 232.

2. Медведев А.В. Адаптация в условиях непараметрической неопределенности. В сб. "Адаптивные системы и их приложения". Новосибирск, "Наука", I977, с.3 - 43.

3. Цыпкин Я.З. Адаптация и обучение в автоматических системах. М., "Наука", I968, с.399.

4. Дайер Дж. Многоцелевое программирование с использованием человеко - машинных процедур. В сб. "Вопросы анализа и процедуры принятия решений". М., "Мир", I976, с.I08-I26.

APPROXIMATE SOLUTIONS OF AN INTEGER LINEAR PROGRAMMING PROBLEM WITH RESOURCE VARIATIONS

M. Lucertini, A. Marchetti Spaccamela
Centro di Studio dei Sistemi di Controllo e Calcolo Automatici del CNR and Istituto di Automatica dell'Università di Roma, Via Eudossiana 18 - ROMA -ITALY

ABSTRACT

The problem analysed in this work is a particular parametric integer linear programming problem (PILP) and more precisely the problem to determine the behaviour of the optimal solution of an integer linear programming problem (ILP) when a resource varies in a given interval. The PILP is tackled with the following hypotheses:

- the ILP problem is solved via a classical branch and bound algorithm, by far the most common approach in integer linear programming;
- the interest is concentrated on approximate solutions of the PILP and on the set of ILP problems that can be usefully approached with approximate techniques.

INTRODUCTION

The problem analysed in this work is a paricular parametric integer linear programming problem (PILP). The most relevant results in the field concerning the possibility of redesigning branch and bound algorithms are in the works of Piper and Zoltners [9], who suggest to perform additional calculations solving each problem, of Marsten and Morin [6], who propose a generalization of branch and bound, and, finally, of Roodman [12] and [13] who has studied the possibility of recovering the standard termination conditions of the branch and bound tree. For a state-of-art survey and for conceptual foundations we refer to the work of Geoffrion and Nauss [4].

In this work the particular PILP analyzed is the problem to determine the behaviour of the optimal solution of an integer linear programming problem (ILP) when a resource varies in a given interval. It is well known [4] that this problem is one of the most hard to solve in integer programming and does not exist rigorous criteria to solve it (whereas there exists some criteria, for example, for cost variations [7] and [8]).

In this work we approach the PILP problem via a classical branch and bound algorithm, by far the most common approach in integer linear programming; our interest is concentrated on approximate solutions of the PILP and on the set of ILP problems that can be usefully approached with approximate techniques. With the expression "approximate techniques" we indicate algorithms that lead to a good solution, i.e. to a solution that differs from the optimal one for at most a given ε. In this aim we have pointed out a theoretical framework and an algorithmic procedure based on some approximate hypotheses in order to obtain this "good" solution.

The most relevant approximation hypotheses are:

i) given a suitable set of terminal subproblems we suppose that the optimal (or approximate) ILP solution can be found in the LP optimal subproblem.

ii) Given a subproblem we can approximate the optimal ILP solution utilizing some "continuous" considerations on the LP relaxation. If δ is the parameter of the PILP and $\delta = 0$ corresponds to the original ILP, the value ε can, in general, be a given function of $\delta(\varepsilon(\delta))$. In fact it is very usual that we pretend a greater precision for small values of δ and we are less interested to a solution close to the optimal one for large values of δ.

In section 2 we analyse the approximate behaviour of the objective function of a PILP as δ varies. The results can be utilized to analyze the nodes of the branch and bound tree.

In section 3 we analyse the approximate behaviour of the optimal parametric solution in the whole set of terminal nodes of a branch and bound tree.

2. SOLVING A PROBLEM WITH PARAMETRIC RESOURCE

Let a problem (P) be defined by suitable values of upper and lower bound of the variables ($\ell \leq x \leq u$):

$$(P) \qquad \min z = cx, \quad x \in F(P)$$

$$F(P) = \left\{ x \mid Ax \geq b,\ \alpha x \geq \beta,\ \ell \leq x \leq u,\ x \text{ integer} \right\}$$

with $A(m \times n)$, $\alpha(1 \times n)$, $x(n \times 1)$, $\ell(n \times 1)$, $u(n \times 1)$, $c(1 \times n)$, $b(m \times 1)$, β scalar.

Let (P_δ) be the PILP:

$$(P_\delta) \qquad \min z = cx, \quad x \in F(P_\delta),\ \delta \in \Delta$$

$$F(P_\delta) = \left\{ x \mid Ax \geq b,\ \alpha x \geq \beta + \delta,\ \ell \leq x \leq u,\ x \text{ integer} \right\}$$

where Δ is a dense or discrete subset of Q (set of all the rational numbers) containing the origin, obviously:

$$(\delta = 0) \Rightarrow (P_\delta) \overset{\Delta}{=} (P)$$

Let (PR_δ) be a relaxation of (P_δ) obtaining by dropping the integrity constraints on x; $z^*(R)$ be the optimal solution of the problem $R(R=P_\delta, PR_\delta)$.

PROPOSITION 1. $z^*(PR_\delta)$ *is a continuous, piecewise linear, non decreasing and convex function of* δ.

Transforming (PR_δ) by introducing the slack variables, we obtain:

$$\begin{bmatrix} A & \\ --- & -I \\ \alpha & \end{bmatrix} \begin{bmatrix} x \\ --- \\ s \end{bmatrix} = \begin{bmatrix} b \\ ---- \\ \beta + \delta \end{bmatrix}$$

with $s((m+1)\times 1)$; given the optimal PR basis, let (B_x, B_s) be the sets of the basis indexes of x and s respectively; let (N_x, N_s) be the corresponding sets of non basic indexes.

The optimal solution of (PR) can be expressed as

$$\begin{bmatrix} x^*_{B_x} \\ ----- \\ s^*_{B_s} \end{bmatrix} = \begin{bmatrix} G & g \\ F & f \end{bmatrix} \begin{bmatrix} b \\ --- \\ \beta \end{bmatrix}$$

where the previous matrix is the inverse of the optimal basic matrix of (PR).

Let us suppose that s_{m+1} is the slack variable of the parametric constraint. There are two possibilities.

<u>case a</u>) $(m+1) \in B_s$

PROPOSITION 2. *If* $(m+1) \in B_s$ (i.e. unless degenerancy $s^*_{m+1} > 0$) *then*:

(1) $(\delta \leq s^*_{m+1}) \Leftrightarrow (x^*(PR_\delta) = x^*(PR))$

(2) $(\delta \leq s^*_{m+1}) \Rightarrow (z^*(PR_\delta) = z^*(PR))$.

If, in addition, $x^*(PR)$ *is integer it follows*:

$$x^*(PR_\delta) = x^*(P_\delta) \quad , \quad z^*(PR_\delta) = z^*(P_\delta)$$

REMARK 1. In the (2) the converse is not true because the optimal solution of (SPR) can be not unique.

<u>case b</u>) $(m+1) \in N_s$ (i.e. $s^*_{m+1} = 0$).

Let $x_{B_x}(PR_\delta)$, $s_{B_s}(PR_\delta)$ and $z_B(PR_\delta)$ be the basic solution of (PR_δ) with the optimal basis of (PR):

(3) $x_{B_x}(PR_\delta) = x^*_{B_x} + g\delta$

(4) $s_{B_s}(PR_\delta) = s^*_{B_s} + f\delta$

(5) $z_B(PR_\delta) = z^*(PR) + c_{B_x} g\delta$

this solution remains (PR_δ) optimal for all the values of δ such that the constraints on the upper and lower bounds are satisfied.

Let us now define

$$\varphi_P = \left\{ i \mid g_i > 0 \right\} \qquad \varphi_N = \left\{ i \mid g_i < 0 \right\}$$

$$\psi_P = \left\{ i \mid f_i > 0 \right\} \qquad \psi_N = \left\{ i \mid f_i < 0 \right\}$$

and the following extreme points for the value of δ:

$$\bar{\delta}_\ell = \max\left\{ \max_{j \in \varphi_P} \frac{\ell_j - x_j^*}{g_j}, \max_{j \in \varphi_N} \frac{u_j - x_j^*}{g_j}, \max_{j \in \psi_P} \frac{-s_j^*}{f_j} \right\}$$

$$\bar{\delta}_u = \min\left\{ \min_{j \in \varphi_P} \frac{u_j - x_j^*}{g_j}, \min_{j \in \varphi_N} \frac{\ell_j - x_j^*}{g_j}, \min_{j \in \psi_N} \frac{-s_j^*}{f_j} \right\}$$

PROPOSITION 3. *The basic solution* (B_x, B_s), *optimal for* (PR), *is optimal for* (PR_δ) *iff* $\delta \in \gamma$ *with* $\gamma = \{\delta \mid \bar{\delta}_\ell \leq \delta \leq \bar{\delta}_u\}$.

If we consider the problem (P_δ) (i.e. the integrity constraint) the following theorem holds:

THEOREM 1. *The optimal solution of* (PR_δ) *is optimal solution of* (P_δ) *iff:*

$$\delta = k\hat{\delta} + \hat{\hat{\delta}}, \qquad k \textit{ integer}$$

with

$$\hat{\delta} = (\underset{i=1,2,\ldots,m-1}{\ell.c.m.} \left\{ \hat{d}_i \right\}) / g_m$$

$$(g_m \neq 0)$$

$$\hat{\hat{\delta}} = (\underset{i=1,2,\ldots,m-1}{\ell.c.m.} \left\{ \hat{\hat{d}}_i \right\}) / g_m$$

$$\hat{d}_i = \begin{cases} 1 \textit{ if } g_i = 0 \\ \textit{denominator of } (g_i/g_m) \textit{ if } g_i \neq 0 \end{cases}$$

$$\hat{\hat{d}} = \begin{cases} 1 \textit{ if } g_i = 0 \textit{ and } \left[-x^*_{B_x}\right]_i \equiv 0 \pmod 1 \text{ [1]} \\ \left[-x^*_{B_x}\right]_m \textit{denominator of } (\left[-x^*_{B_x}\right]_m \cdot g_i / \left[-x^*_{B_x}\right]_i \cdot g_m) \textit{ if } g_i \neq 0 \\ \infty \textit{ if } g_i = 0 \textit{ and } \left[-x^*_{B_x}\right]_i \not\equiv 0 \pmod 1 \end{cases}$$

PROOF. Obviously we can suppose $g_m \neq 0$ without loss of generality (the basis matrix is nonsingular). The theorem holds with $(\hat{\delta}, \hat{\hat{\delta}})$ defined as:

$$\hat{\delta} = \left\{ \min \delta \mid \delta g \equiv 0 \pmod 1,\ \delta > 0 \right\}$$

$$\hat{\hat{\delta}} = \left\{ \min \delta \mid \delta g \equiv -x^*_{B_x} \pmod 1,\ \delta \geq 0 \right\}$$

All the values δ satisfying the $\delta g_j \equiv 0 \pmod 1$ can be written as $\delta = h_j/g_j$ with $h_j \neq 0$ integer and $g_j \neq 0$ (if $g_j = 0$ the relation obviously holds for each value of δ); then it is possible to write:

$$\hat{\delta} = \left\{ \min h_m \mid h_m g_i / g_m \equiv 0 \pmod 1,\ i=1,2,\ldots,m-1,\ h_m \neq 0 \text{ integer} \right\} / g_m$$

(1) $\equiv$ indicates a congruence relation.

The same procedure can be easily extended to the definition of $\hat{\hat{\delta}}$, substituting g_j with $g_j/[-x^*_{B_x}]_j$. Remark that a necessary condition to have integer solutions is that $(\forall i, \exists \delta: \delta g_i \equiv [-x^*_{B_x}]_i \pmod 1)$. ◀

The case $(\hat{\hat{\delta}} = 0)$ is of particular interest: it happens when $x^*(PR)$ is integer and then the subproblem (PR) is a terminal problem of the branch and bound tree.

Remark that proposition 4 has been defined under the conditions of proposition 3 $(\delta \in \gamma)$ but its validity is more general. In fact it obviously holds also for values of δ outside of γ with different basic matrices (i.e. different values of g and $x^*_{B_x}$ in the definition of $\hat{\delta}$ and $\hat{\hat{\delta}}$).

In this way we can define a set of adjacent intervals $\{\gamma^i\}$ $((\delta' \in \gamma^i, \delta'' \in \gamma^{i+1}) \Rightarrow (\delta' \lneq \delta''))$ such that in each interval the basic matrix is constant (the values of $\hat{\delta}$ and $\hat{\hat{\delta}}$ can be indicated by $\hat{\delta}(\gamma^i)$ and $\hat{\hat{\delta}}(\gamma^i)$, the values of B_x and g by B^i_x and g^i). Following proposition 4 we can define the step function $\hat{z}(P_\delta)$ upper bound of the step function $z^*(P_\delta)$, obtained by taking into account only the values of $z^*(P_\delta)$ corresponding to the values of δ such that $z^*(P_\delta) = z^*(PR_\delta)$.

Let Λ be the following set:

$$\Lambda = \left\{\delta_k \,|\, z^*(P_{\delta_k}) = z^*(PR_{\delta_k}),\ \delta_{k-1} < \delta_k\right\}$$

we can now define the step function $\hat{z}(P_\delta)$ as:

$$\hat{z}(P_\delta) = z(PR_{\delta_k}),\ \delta_{k-1} < \delta \leq \delta_k \qquad \delta_k \in \Lambda \tag{6}$$

REMARK 2. Following (5) and (6) the maximum difference $\Delta z(\gamma^i)$ between $z^*(P_\delta)$ and $\hat{z}(P_\delta)$ is:

$$\Delta z(\gamma^i) = c_{B^i_x}\, g^i \hat{\delta}(\gamma^i)$$

REMARK 3. In proposition 4 it is possible that $\hat{\delta}(\gamma^i)$ for some i does not exist. In the interval containing the origin $(\delta=0)$ this is not a problem because we start in general from an integer solution (i.e. $\hat{\hat{\delta}}=0$). This is not true for the intervals associated with different optimal LP basis. In this case the upper bound $\hat{z}(P_\delta)$ that we can obtain is not a good approximation of $z^*(P_\delta)$.

Remark that given: two adjacent intervals (γ^i, γ^{i+1}) (let (B^i, B^{i+1}) be the associated basis), a point δ_h $(\delta_h \in \Lambda \cap \gamma^i)$, the half line r with the end point $(\delta_h, z^*(PR_{\delta_h}))$ and the same slope of $(z^*(PR_\delta),\ \delta \in \gamma^{i+1})$, we can find along r integer solutions spaced by $\hat{\delta}(\gamma^{i+1})$.

In fact the slope of r and $\hat{\delta}(\gamma^{i+1})$ depends only on B^{i+1}; it is easy to see that, in the given restriction of the admissible region, the basis B^{i+1} is admissible (and optimal if we assume the additional constraint $z \geq r$) for $\delta \geq \delta_h$, $\delta \in \gamma^i \cup \gamma^{i+1}$.

With this criteria we can construct new better step functions, based on a larger number of integer solutions.

A simple geometric interpretation of this fact can be found in fig.1,2.

If $\Delta z(\gamma^i)$ is, for some i, too large and the matrix A has special structures, it is possible to obtain other useful integer solutions, in order to construct a better approximation of $z^*(P_\delta)$.

Let:

A_j be the jth column of A

J be the set of column indexes of A

$\{J_i\}$ $(i=0,1,\ldots,k)$ be a (k+1)-partition of J

$\{\omega_j\}$ $(j=1,2,\ldots,|J|)$ be a set of integers such that:

$$\forall i \neq 0 \quad \sum_{j \in J_i} \omega_j A_j \geq 0$$

without loss of generality we can assume that the indexes of the variables are ordered so that

$$(j \in J_{i_1},\ \ell \in J_{i_2}) \Rightarrow (j < \ell)$$

The following result can now be stated:

THEOREM 2. *Given an integer solution* $\bar{x}$ *of* $(P_{\bar{\delta}})$ *a new integer feasible solution* $\tilde{x}$ *of* $(P_{\tilde{\delta}})$ *can be obtained as solution of the following Knapsack problem in the variables* y_i $(i=1,2,\ldots,k)$

$$(R_{\tilde{\delta}}) \quad \min z = \sum_{i=1}^{k} \Big(\sum_{j \in J_i} \omega_j c_j\Big) y_i$$

$$\sum_{i=1}^{k} \Big(\sum_{j \in J_i} \omega_j \alpha_j\Big) y_i \geq \beta + \tilde{\delta} - \sum_{j \in J} \alpha_j \bar{x}_j$$

with $\quad \omega_i^\ell \leq y_i \leq \omega_i^u$

$$\omega_i^\ell = \max\left\{ \max_{\substack{j \in J_i \\ \omega_j > 0}} \left\lceil \frac{\ell_j - \bar{x}_j}{\omega_j} \right\rceil,\ \max_{\substack{j \in J_i \\ \omega_j < 0}} \left\lceil \frac{u_j - \bar{x}_j}{\omega_j} \right\rceil \right\}$$

$$\omega_i^u = \min\left\{ \min_{\substack{j \in J_i \\ \omega_j > 0}} \left\lfloor \frac{u_j - \bar{x}_j}{\omega_j} \right\rfloor,\ \min_{\substack{j \in J_i \\ \omega_j < 0}} \left\lfloor \frac{\ell_j - \bar{x}_j}{\omega_j} \right\rfloor \right\}$$

Given a feasible solution $\tilde{y}$ *of the Knapsack problem we obtain a new solution* $\tilde{x}$ *as*

$$\tilde{x}_j = \bar{x}_j + \omega_j \tilde{y}_i \qquad j \in J_i \quad i=1,2,\ldots,k$$

$$\tilde{x}_j = \bar{x}_j \qquad j \in J_o$$

REMARK 4. In practice it is convenient to have the maximum number of variables y_i (i.e. the max number of subset of J).

In particular if there exists some columns of A such that $A_j \geq 0$ (or $A_j \leq 0$) it is convenient to have subsets J_i containing a single index.

REMARK 5. It is convenient to have $|\omega_j|$ as little as possible, because the range of y_i is strictly related to this choice (as large are $|\omega_j|$ as little is the range of y_i). In practice a good choice is $\omega_j = \pm 1\ \forall j$.

REMARK 6. If we analyze many nodes of a branch and bound tree (for example all the terminal nodes), the partition of J can be computed only once, at the beginning of the PILP solution.

COROLLARY 1. *If* $\bar{\delta} = \delta_h$ *(and then* $\bar{x} = x^*(P_{\delta_h})$*) and* $\delta_h < \gamma < \delta_{h+1}$ *the previous result can be utilized to construct a new step function* $\hat{z}(P_\delta)$ *better than the step function built up utilizing only* $\delta_i \in \Lambda$.

3. APPROXIMATE BEHAVIOUR OF THE OPTIMAL PARAMETRIC SOLUTION

The problem examined in this section consists in finding out among a suitable set of terminal subproblems of the branch and bound tree the one containing the optimal solution for each value of the resources. This will be done with the hypotheses that the optimal (or a good) integer solution can be found in the subproblem where exists the best continuous optimal solution (LP optimal).

In this aim we can procede in two different steps:

a) to find out some criteria in order to eliminate a set of the terminal subproblems; this can be done without approximation (i.e. to eliminate all the subproblems when cannot exist optimal solutions for every admissible values of the resources) or utilizing some approximation (in this case we can obviously eliminate a larger set of subproblems);
b) to analyse the behaviour of the optimal LP solution of all the remaining subproblems utilizing the solutions of a unique discrete mathematical programming problem (that can be considered an LP problem in a further approximation).

For an exposition of the results concerning step b we refer to [5].

3.1. *ELIMINATION CRITERIA*

In this section we give some elimination criteria that can be applied without approximation.

Given a particular subproblem k (indicated by a superscript), a first condition is based on two obvious points:

i) $(F(SPR^k_\delta) = \emptyset) \Rightarrow (F(SP^k_\delta) = \emptyset)$

ii) $(\delta' \geq \delta'') \Rightarrow (F(SPR^k_{\delta'}) \subseteq F(SPR^k_{\delta''})$

CONDITION 1. *If there exists a* $\bar{\delta}$ *such that* $F(SPR^k_{\bar{\delta}}) = \emptyset$ *we can eliminate the subproblem* k *for all* $\delta \geq \bar{\delta}$. *In particular if* $\bar{\delta} \leq \min_{\delta \in \Delta} \delta$ *we can eliminate* k *at the beginning of the analysis.*

A second condition can be obtained from the knowledge of an upper bound of the optimal solution $z^*(SP^k_\delta)$ for every $\delta \in \Delta$ (i.e. $\hat{z}(SP^k_\delta)$). This can be considered an obvious extension of the well known elimination methods of the branch and bound methods.

CONDITION 2. *If there exists a set* Γ *such that*

$$(7) \qquad z^*(SPR^k_\delta) \geq \min_{j \in \Gamma} \hat{z}(SP^j_\delta) \qquad \delta \in \Delta' \subseteq \Delta$$

we can eliminate the subproblem k *for every* $\delta \in \Delta'$.

If $\Delta' = \Delta$ *we can eliminate* k *at all.*

This condition can be hard to verify; in some cases can be useful to utilize different upper bounds of $z^*(SP^k_\delta)$ and more precisely linear upper bounds $\hat{z}_L(SP^k_\delta)$ calculated utilizing the results of Theorem 2.

Let:

$\bar{x}$ integer feasible solution of $(SP^k_{\bar{\delta}})$

$\tilde{x}$ integer feasible solution of (SP^k_{γ}) obtained from $\bar{x}$ via the solution of the Knapsack problem of Theorem 2 $(\gamma > \bar{\delta})$

$\bar{z}$ and $\tilde{z}$ the value of the objective functions of the solutions $\bar{x}$ and $\tilde{x}$ $(\tilde{z} > \bar{z})$

$$I = \left\{ i \mid \bar{x}_i \neq \tilde{x}_i \right\} \qquad \bar{\alpha} = \max_{i \in I} \{\alpha_i\} \qquad \bar{c} = \max_{i \in I} \{c_i\}$$

$$h = \min\{\bar{\alpha} r, \bar{c}\} \qquad r = (\tilde{z} - \bar{z})/(\gamma - \bar{\delta}).$$

THEOREM 3. *Given* $\bar{x}$ *and* $\tilde{x}$ *a linear upper bound of* $z^*(SP^k_\delta)$ *in the interval* $\Delta' = \{\delta \mid \bar{\delta} \leq \delta \leq \gamma\}$ *is:*

$$(8) \qquad \hat{z}_L(SP^k_\delta) = r\delta + h + \bar{z}.$$

PROOF. The proof is by construction. As the proof is simple but troublesome we give only an outline of it (see also fig.3). In particular we can take into account only the variable x_j such that $\bar{x}_j \neq \tilde{x}$; they are ordered such that $(c_i/\alpha_i \leq c_{i+1}/\alpha_{i+1}, \forall i)$ all the α_i are strictly positive and let k be the index such that $(c_k/\alpha_k \leq r \leq c_{k+1}/\alpha_{k+1})$. We can now construct new integer solutions in two different ways:

a) starting from $\bar{x}$ (and supposing $\bar{x}_i \neq \tilde{x}_i$, $i \leq k$) for $(\bar{\delta} < \delta \leq \bar{\delta} + \alpha_i)$ the integer solution $(x_i = \bar{x}_i + 1,\ x_j = \bar{x}_j,\ \forall j \neq i)$ is feasible and satisfies: $(c_i \leq \bar{c}$ and $c_i \leq r\bar{\alpha}) \Rightarrow (c_i \leq h)$ then $\hat{z}_L(SP^k_\delta)$ is, in the given interval, an upper bound of the step function defined by $\bar{x}$ and x. As the solution is under the line $z = r\delta$ (see fig. 3) the procedure can be iterated until all the variables x_j $(j \leq k)$ are at the upper (or lower) bounds

b) starting from $\tilde{x}$ (and supponing $\bar{x}_i \neq \tilde{x}_i$, $i > k$) for ($\delta \leq \gamma - \alpha_i$) the integer solution ($x_i = \tilde{x} - 1$, $x_j = \tilde{x}_j$, $\forall j \neq i$) is feasible and satisfies:
$(\alpha_i \leq \bar{\alpha}$ and $\alpha_i \leq \bar{c}/r) \Rightarrow (\alpha_i \leq h/r)$
then $\hat{z}_L(SP^k_\delta)$ is, in the interval $[\gamma - \alpha_i, \gamma]$, an upper bound of the step function defined by x and $\tilde{x}$. As before the solution is under the line $z = r\delta$ and so the procedure can be iterated.

It is easy to see that this construction can be extended to the case $\alpha_i < 0$ for some i. ◀

As conclusions we can remark that those criteria can be relaxed introducing a stronger elimination based on ε-optimality concepts. In particular, given a suitable $\varepsilon(\delta)$, (7) and (8) become:

(7') $z^*(SPR^k_\delta) \geq \min_{j \in \Gamma} \hat{z}(SP^j_\delta) - \varepsilon(\delta) \quad \delta \in \Delta'$

(8') $\hat{z}_L(SP^k_\delta) = r\delta + h - \varepsilon(\delta)$

obviously (8') remains linear only if $\varepsilon(\delta)$ is linear.

3.2. *SOME REMARKS ON THE COMPACT REPRESENTATION OF TERMINAL SUBPROBLEMS*

A compact representation of all the terminal subproblems can be pointed out [5], via a suitable translaction of the associated feasible regions, in order to obtain comparable values of the objective function and of the slack of the additional constraint. This compact representation is done in a parameter space (or variable space) whose dimensions are independent from the number of terminal subproblems (or equivalently from the number of branches) but depends only from the number of constraints. It is important to remark that the obtained results holds in a more general context than the PILP problems; in particular the procedure proposed can be utilized in order to reduce (under suitable hypotheses) the number of variables of a ILP problem, or to analyse the solutions of a suitable set of LP problems. The procedure reduce the computational complexity of the problem if there exist variables not constrained to be nonnegative, in particular if there exist (m+1) of such variables all the subproblems can be solved parametrically, solving a unique subproblem. The procedure is particularly useful when the integer variables are constrained to be binary.

3.3. *COMPARATIVE ANALYSIS OF SUBPROBLEMS*

The objective of the comparative analysis is to find out some criteria that, given two subproblems i and j, state if the follow inequality holds:

$$z(SP_\delta^i) \leq z(SP_\delta^j) \quad \delta \in \Delta_{ij} \subset \Delta.$$

Obviously if we are looking for "good solutions" it is sufficient to consider a relaxation of subproblems. A way of tackling the problem is to state an upper bound to the number of possible intersections between the solutions $z(SPR_\delta^i)$ and $z(SPR_\delta^j)$ of two nodes. Unfortunately we can see that, even in some very simple cases, the intersection between these two functions can be an increasing function of the number of different constraints.

EXAMPLE 1. min $z = x_2$ s.t. $-x_1 + x_2 \geq \beta+\delta$

$$A_1x_1 + A_2x_2 + A_3x_3 \geq b$$

$$x_1, x_2 \geq \text{integers}, \; x_3 = 0,1$$

Let us suppose to operate a branch on x_3. Now if we sketch the two sub problems we can have the situation of fig. 4. It is evident that, as δ varies, the optimal solution passes successively from one subproblem to the other one and viceversa.

REFERENCES

[1] U.J.JR.BOWMAN: *Sensitivity Analysis in Linear Integer Programming.* In AIIE Technical Papers (1972).

[2] J.M.FLEISHER, R.R.MEYER: *New Sufficient Conditions for Integer Programming and their Application.* Cpmputer Sciences Techical Report, University of Wisconsin, Madison (Jan. 1976).

[3] C.R.JR.FRANK: *Parametric Programming in Integers.* In operations Research Verfahren, vol. III (1967).

[4] A.M.GEOFFRION, R.NAUSS: *Parametric and Postoptimality Analysis in Integer Linear Programming.* In Management Science, vol. 23, n. 5 (1977).

[5] M.LUCERTINI, A.MARCHETTI SPACCAMELA: *Approximate Solutions of a Parametric Integer Linear Programming Problem: The Right-Hand-Side Case.* Rapporto Ist. di Automatica e CSSCCA del CNR, Roma, Aprile 1978.

[6] A.M.MARSTEN, T.L.MORIN: *Parametric Integer Programming: The Right-Hand-Side.Case.* In Hammer, Johnson, Korte and Nemhauser (eds), Studies in Integer Programming North-Holland Publishing Company.

[7] R.NAUSS: *Parametric Integer Programming.* Published as Working Paper n.226,Western Management Science Institute,UCLA(Jan.1975).

[8] H.NOLTEMEIER: *Sensitivitalsanalyse bei distreten linearen Optimierungsproblem*. In M.Beckman and H.P.Kunzi, eds. "Lecture Notes in Operations Research and Mathematical Systems, Springer-Verlag N.Y. (1970).

[9] C.J.PIPER, A.A.ZOTNERS: *Some easy Postoptimality Analysis for Zero-One Programming*. In Management Science, vol. 22 n.7 (1976).

[10] C.J.PIPER, A.A.ZOLTNERS: *Implicit Enumeration Based Algorithm for Postoptimizing Zero-One Programs*. In Management Sciences Research Report n. 313, Graduate School of Industrial Administration, Carnegie-Mellon University (March 1973).

[11] G.M.ROODMAN: *Postoptimality Analysis in Zero-One Programming by Implicit Enumeration*. In Naval Research Logistics Quarterly, vol. 19 (1972).

[12] G.M.ROODMAN: *Postoptimality Analysis by Implicit Enumeration: The Mixed Integer Case*. Report of the Amos Tuck School of Business Administration, Dartmouth College (Oct. 1973).

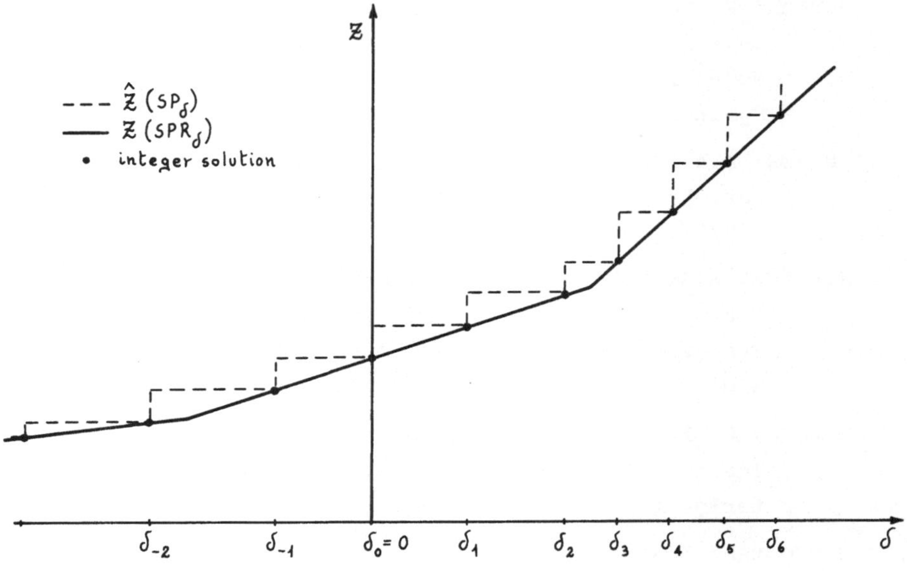
z
--- $\hat{z}(SP_\delta)$
— $z(SPR_\delta)$
• integer solution
δ_{-2}
δ_{-1}
$\delta_0 = 0$
δ_1
δ_2
δ_3
δ_4
δ_5
δ_6
δ

fig. 1

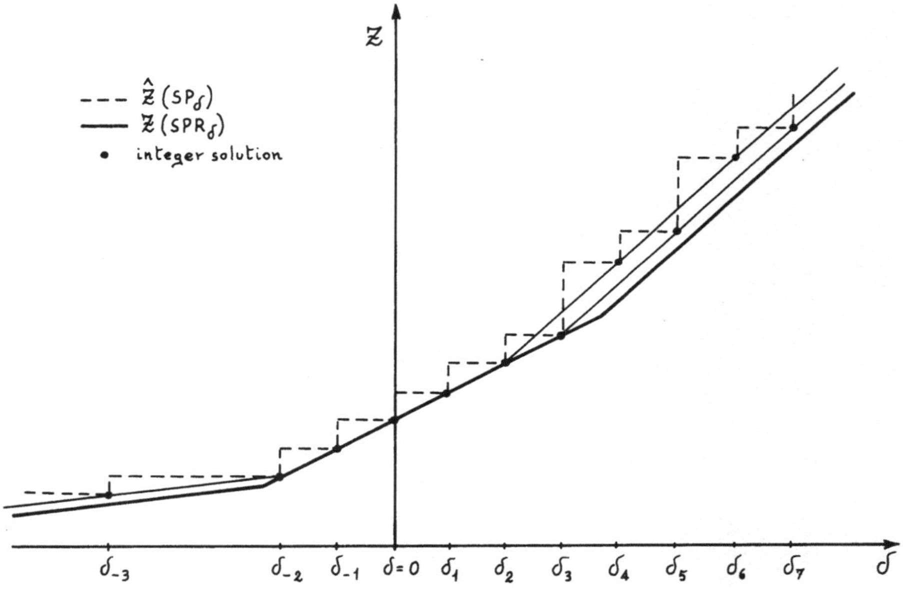
z
--- $\hat{z}(SP_\delta)$
— $z(SPR_\delta)$
• integer solution
δ_{-3}
δ_{-2}
δ_{-1}
$\delta = 0$
δ_1
δ_2
δ_3
δ_4
δ_5
δ_6
δ_7
δ

fig. 2

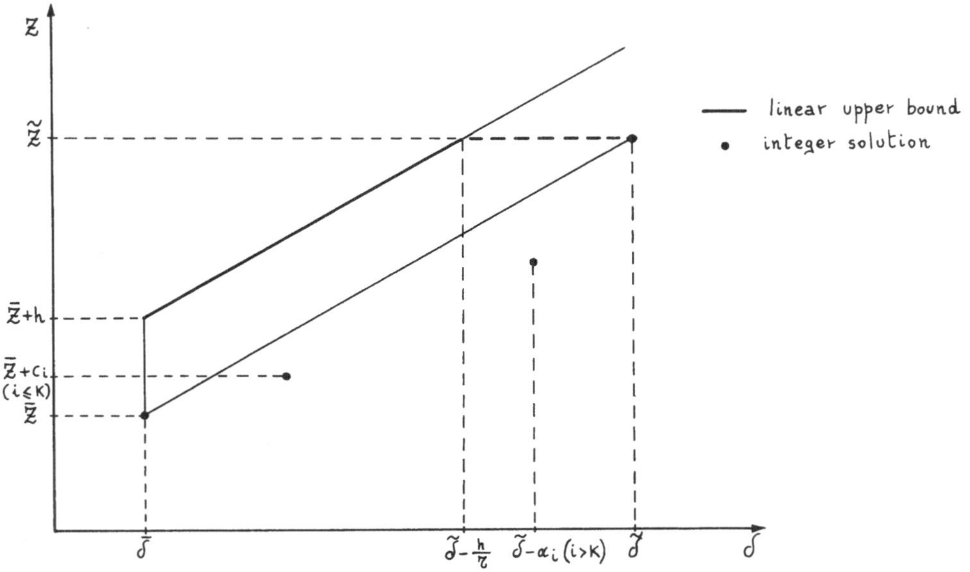
z
z̃
z̄+h
z̄+c_i
(i≤K)
z̄
δ̄
δ̃-h/η
δ̃-α_i (i>K)
δ̃
δ
linear upper bound
integer solution

fig. 3

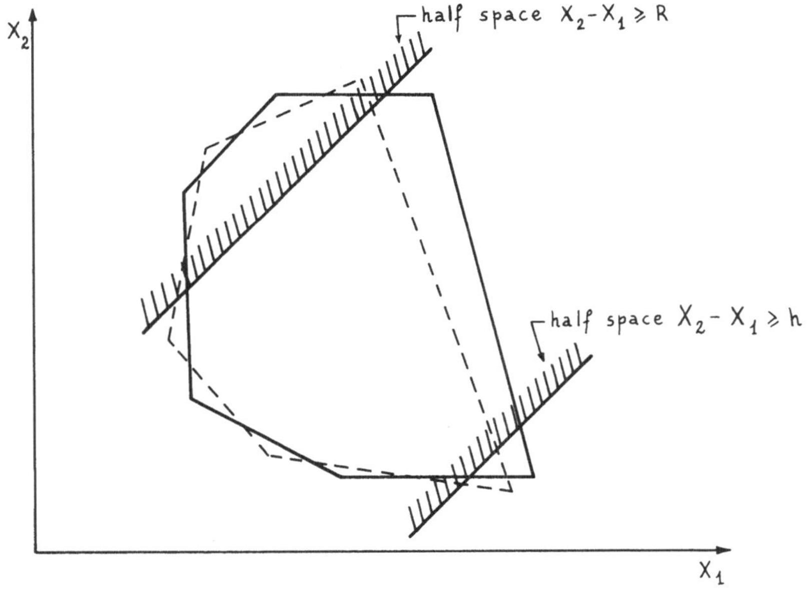
X_2
half space X_2-X_1 ≥ R
half space X_2-X_1 ≥ h
X_1

fig. 4

ON TECHNOLOGY OF MODELLING AND OPTIMIZATION OF COMPLEX SYSTEMS

V.M.Matrosov, S.N.Vassilyev, O.G.Divakov, A.I.Tyatushkin
The Siberian Power Institute SD AS USSR
Irkutsk,USSR.

This paper refers to the sphere of the mathematical technology (Janenko N.N.and others). The main results of the technology development of modelling and optimization of complex systems are presented. These results are obtained in the Department of the System Theory and cybernetics of the Siberian Power Institute of the Siberian Department of the USSR Academy of Sciences and based on the usage of systems analysis methodology, numerical methods of optimization, qualitative methods of dynamic properties analysis of solutions and ideas of artificial intelligence. These investigations of the Department are recommended and supported by G.I.Marchuk.

The actuality of the creation of the technology of modelling and optimization of complex systems which would involve the main algorithmical and heuristic procedures of the modelling and optimization of complex systems process and would foresee the high level of automatization using the computing technique in the interactive modes is connected with the necessity of increasing the efficiency of applied mathematical investigations and the computing technique usage, with the necessity of overcoming the existing difficulties of realization of study results of separate mathematical models and optimization problems in the planning and control processes for the real complex systems and in the concrete applied developments of technical systems.

I.Approach to the technology construction and structure of the system of the modelling and optimization of complex system.

The technology guarantees the modelling and optimization of complex systems in the form of a final iterative process including at every iteration the following procedures.

a)The formation of linguistic formulations of optimization problems,construction(and improvement) of mathematical models,restrictions and criteria; mathematical statement (correction) of optimization problems.

b) The analysis of problems of controllability, existence of optimal solutions and the possibility of their search; the determination of numerical solutions of given optimization problems.

c)The qualitative analysis of uniqueness,correction, stability, invariance,sensibility and other dynamic properties of optimal solutions; the construction of corresponding quantitative estimations.

d)The comparative estimation of obtained optimal solutions and decision-making(or conditions for further study).

For realization of the technology of the system of modelling and optimization of a complex system is being created. The developed system consists of main program complexes (moduli),realizing the enumerated procedures of main modelling and optimization of a complex system process, data bases for them, dialogue monitor and service programs. The structure of its first variant is shown in Fig.I. The modelling and optimization of complex systems technology and algorithmical software of its I variant oriented to the optimal control problems for finite-dimensional systems is completed.

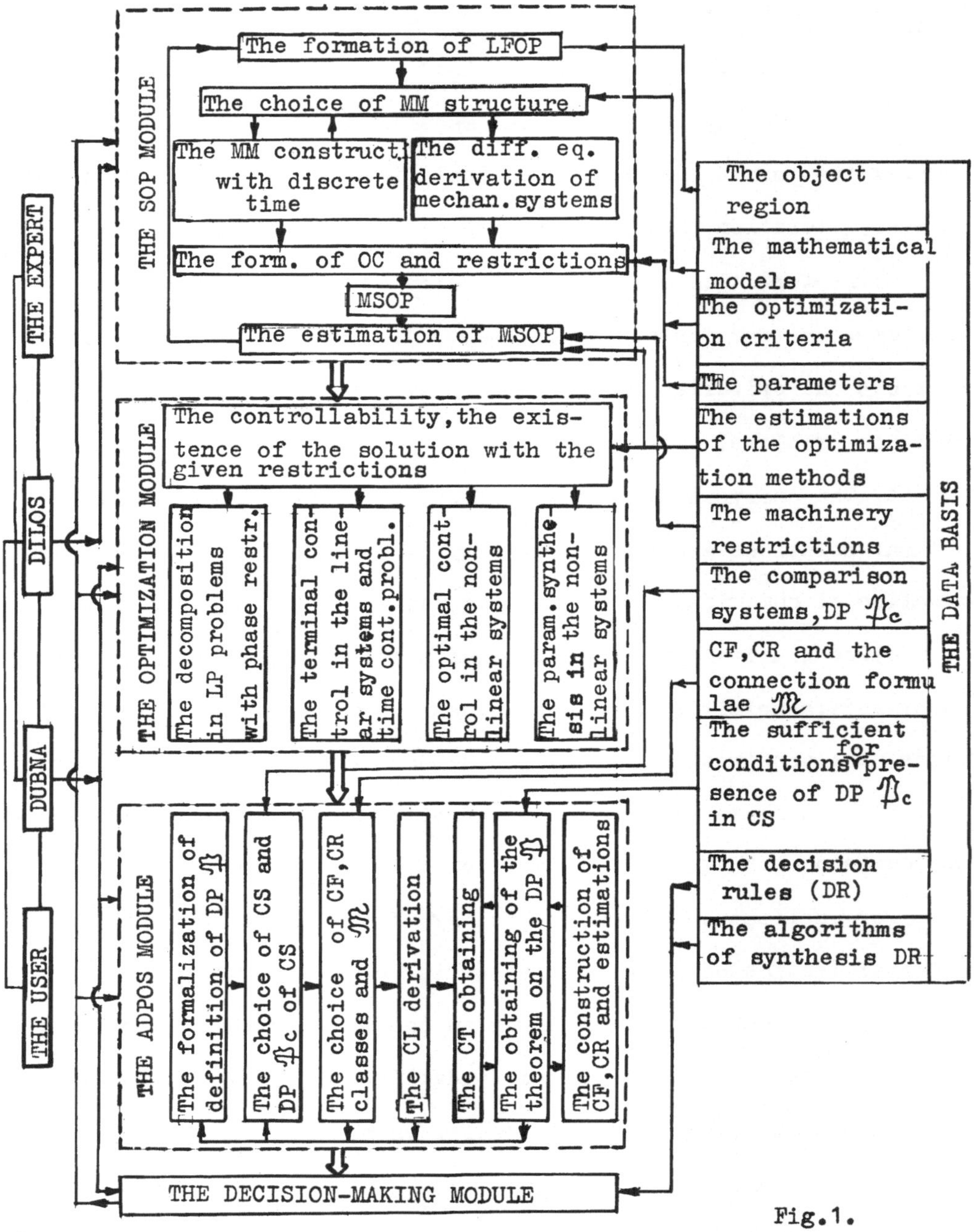

Fig.1.

ADPOS-analysis of the dynamical property(DP) of optimal solutions; OC-optimal criteria; LFOP-linguistic formulation of optimization problem(OP);MM-mathematical model;SOP-statement of OP; MSOP-mathematical statement of OP;LP-linear programming; CF,CS,CR,CL,CT-comparison function,system,relation,lemma,theorem,correspondingly.

The main algorithms are realized in the form of programs debugged by the computer BESM-6. The first variant of main moduli is being completed, the estimation of their efficiency is evaluated on the examples of optimal solutions of fuel and energy balance and precise electro-mechanical control systems. The DILOS (Bryabrin V.M. and others) system and DUBNA are used as a dialogue monitor.

2.The module of a mathematical model construction and formalization of optimization problems statements.

It is a dialogue system with the restricted natural language as an input one,realizing the procedures a), and consisting of three subsystems: the formation of linguistic formulations of optimization problems, the mathematical models construction, the obtaining of a mathematical statement of optimization problems. The system data bases: DB on the object region, containing the description of the object region in terms of concepts and relations between them are realized on the DILOS φ -language; data bases on the mathematical model containing the tree of 49 mathematical models descriptions on the system dynamics and the control theory, the program of these data manipulation based on their partial order; data bases on the optimization criteria that are used in the given object region; data bases on the provision of optimization methods containing a set of related to the concrete mathematical statement of optimization problems classes with estimations of their applicability; data bases on the computer restrictions on the used storage, the time of information processing and the accuracy of evaluation, etc.

In the first variant of linguistic formulation of optimization problems subsystem the following algorithms are realized for:

input from the user information recognition,representing in the formats of DILOS φ -language;

formation, representing the dialogue scheme with the user or the expert on the revealing and the characteristic of the object region, the goal of investigation, the essential factors, the criteria and the problem restrictions, the main functioning regularities of investigation object, etc. with the use of data bases on the object region, data bases on the optimization criteria;

allocation information in the positions of the fixed scheme of linguistic formulations of optimization problems;

completeness and consistency information verification in the linguistic formulations of optimization problems.

The subsystem of mathematical model construction is realized in the form of three blocks.

The block of the choice of the mathematical models structure represents a dialogue procedure of mathematical models structure estimation according to the linguistic formulations of optimization problems features and picking out the mathematical models classes having these features. In this block after the interpretation of picked classes one of these classes is chosen by the efficiency criterion, aggregating the modelling complication, adequacy, etc.

The blocks of mathematical model construction for the systems with continuous and discrete time.

Conformably to the finite-dimensional systems with continuous time the block of automatization of derivation of differential equations of mechanical systems in the Lagrangian form is realized, electric circuits and electro-mechanical systems in the Lagrangian--Maxwell form in letters form according to the given mechanical or electric scheme (Burlakova L.A.,and others), and their reducing to the Cauchy form (Oparin G.A.)

The block of mathematical models construction in the class of finite-difference equations is realized for the systems with discrete time; this block contains the algorithms:

of identification of mathematical models structure,representing a set of schemes of modelled regularities, the details of which are specified in the process of a dialogue with the user;

identification of mathematical models parameters using the calculated dependences or the expert estimations.

The subsystem of the mathematical statement of optimization problems obtaining consists of algorithms:

the formation of optimization criterion on the basis of chosen decision rule and a series of features; restrictions including the initial and boundary conditions, the control and phase coordinates restrictions;

the estimation of the mathematical statement of optimization problems quality according to the criterion including the features connected with the computer restrictions, with the software of optimization methods and the necessary information;

the choice of the mathematical statement of optimization problems on the basis of obtained estimations of its quality.

The mathematical statement of optimization problems represents the mathematical model of the object under investigation in the form

$$x(t) = X(t, x(t), u(t)), \quad x(t) \in R^n, \quad t \in [t_0, t_1], \quad u \in \mathcal{U} \tag{I}$$

or

$$x(t+1) = X(t, x(t), u(t)); \tag{Ia}$$

with restrictions of linear inequalities type $C(t)\,x(t) \leq b(t)$

$C(t) - m \times n$ matrix $b(t) \in R^m$ and the optimization criterion $J(x, u)$: for example , terminal criterion $J(x(t_1)), t_1, \ldots$

$$J_0 \triangleq \inf \{ J(x, u) : (x, u) \in D \}$$

where D is the set of admissible solutions.

3. <u>The optimization module</u> is oriented to the numerical methods of optimal control for the multi-dimensional systems taking into account the specificity of restrictions and a goal functional. The linear problems of the optimal control with the phase restrictions are reduced to the problems of linear programming of the quasi block structure.

The following blocks are included into the optimization module:

I) The block of controllability analysis, the existence of optimal solutions and the possibility of its obtaining. The optimal control problem for the linear systems with the absence of restrictions on the phase coordinates has the form:

$$\dot{x}(t) = A(t)x(t) + B(t)u(t) + f(t), \quad t \in [t_0, t_1], \quad x(t_0) = x_0 \tag{2}$$

or

$$x(t+1) = A(t)\,x(t) + B(t)\,u(t) + f(t), \quad t = 0, 1, 2, \ldots, \quad x(0) = x_0 \tag{2a}$$

with the terminal functional $J(x(t_1))$.

The following known condition (Kalman R. and others) in the linear problem of the optimal control is verified for the controllability analysis: the initial state x_0 is controllable (in the origin for the duration of time $t_1 - t_0$) , if and only if it belongs to the region of values of the linear transformation

$$W = \int_{t_0}^{t_1} F(t_1,\tau)\, B(\tau)\, B^T(\tau)\, F^T(t,\tau)\, d\tau, \quad F_\tau = -FA(\tau), \quad F(t_1,t_1) = E$$

or, in the stationary case,

$$W = \{ B, AB, A^2B, \dots, A^{n-1}B \} .$$

Otherwise, if exists such a vector y_0, that there is a representation $x_0 = Wy_0$, where $y_0 \in R^n$ in the non-stationary case and $y_0 \in R^{nm}$ in the stationary case.

This condition is verified by solving the problem

$$\min_y \rho(y) \triangleq \min_y \| x_0 - Wy \|^2 = \rho(y_0) .$$

If $\rho(y_0) = 0$, then the system is controllable and one can find the vector $y_0 \in R^n$ for the construction of the control with the minimal energy:

$$u^0(t) = -B^T(t) F^T(t_1,t)\, y_0 ; \quad \int_{t_0}^{t_1} u^{0T}(t)\, u^0(t)\, dt = \min \int_{t_0}^{t_1} u^T(t)\, u(t)\, dt.$$

If the restrictions on the controls are only of the type $|u_i(t)| \leq l_i, i=\overline{1,r}$, then considering the problem of control search with the minimal norm in L_∞ one can verify the existence of control transmitting the system from the given state to the origin.

$$\| u \| = \max_{1 \leq i \leq r} \ \mathrm{vrai} \max_{t_0 \leq t \leq t_1} | u_i(t) | .$$

With the L -problem of momenta, this problem is reduced to the search of a vector $y_0 \in R^n$, realizing the minimum of a function (the norm in L_1)

$$\varphi(y) = \int_{t_0}^{t_1} \sum_{i=1}^{r} | y^T F(t_1,\tau)\, B(\tau) |_i \, d\tau , \qquad C^T y = 1 .$$

The minimal modulo control will have the form

$$u^0(t) = \varphi(y_0)^{-1} \, \mathrm{sign} \, [y^T F(t_1,t)\, B(t)] .$$

These algorithms enable us to answer the question on the optimal solutions existence in the time control linear problem with the given restrictions.

For the non-linear systems (I),(Ia) with the terminal functional $J(x(t_1))$ one can use also the theorems with vector Lyapunov functions,in particular,the theorems obtained below.The auxiliary comparison system is considered according to the main idea of vector Lyapunov function method in the control theory(Matrosov V.M., Vassilyev S.N.,1977,1978)for (I)

$$\dot{x}_c(t)=f(t,x_c(t),u_c(t)),\quad x_c(t)\in R^k,\ t\in[t_0,t_1]\ u_c(t)\in R^r,\ u_c\in \mathcal{U}_c, \tag{3}$$

with the functional $J_c(x_c(t_1))$ and solutions space D_c ,and also the function $v:[t_0,t_1]\times H^*\to R^k$, $H^*\subseteq R^n$, for example,connected by the differential inequality of Chapligin Type $\dot{v}(t,x(t),u(t))\leq$ $\leq f(t,v(t,x(t)),u(t))$. Let for (3) the minimizing sequence is found $\{x_{sc},u_{sc}\}$, $J_{oc}=\inf\{J_c(x_c(t_1)):(x_c,u_c)\in D_c\}$, $\{x_s,u_s\}$-is any sequence of solutions(I).

T h e o r e m I. If for any $s=1,2,\ldots$ v is the vector comparison function (Matrosov V.M.,Vassilyev S.N.,1977)for (I),(3) with $u=u_s$, $u_c=u_{sc}$, $v(t_0,x_s(t_0))\leq x_{sc}(t)$,and either a) if

$$\dot{v}(t,x,u_s(t))=f(t,v(t,x),u_{sc}(t)),\quad v(t_0,x_s(t_0))=x_{sc}(t_0),$$

the upper semi-continuity condition of a function $(v^{-1}(\cdot))_{t_1}$ holds, or b)the condition of vector definite non-negativity of a function $v(t_1,\cdot)$ with respect to the sets $\{x\in R^n: J(x)-J_0<\varepsilon\}_{\varepsilon>0}$, $\{x_c\in R^k: J_c(x_c)-J_{oc}<\varepsilon_c\}_{\varepsilon_c>0}$ holds. Then the sequence $\{x_s,u_s\}$ minimizes J .

T h e o r e m 2. If exists the function v and the real positive(Matrosov V.M.,Vassilyev S.N.,1977) $k\times k$-matrix A and $k\times r$ -matrix B such that $\operatorname{rank}[B,AB,A^2B,\ldots,A^{k-1}B]=k$;

$$(\forall t \in [t_o, t_1])(\forall x \in H^* \setminus \{a\})\ \vartheta(t,x) \neq 0, \quad \vartheta(t,a) = 0 ;$$

$$(\forall x_o \in H^*)(\exists \tau \in [t_o, t_1])(\exists u \in \mathcal{U})\ \dot{\vartheta}(t,x,u) \leq A\vartheta(t,x) - BB^T e^{-A^T t} F$$

and $F(\tau, t_o, x_o)$ is any known real $r \times 1$ -matrix, then(I) is a-controllable (Matrosov V.M., Vassilyev S.N., 1977).

After establishing the controllability and the existence of problem optimization solutions the possibility of numerical solutions obtaining is analysed and the choice of algorithm of the numerical solution of the optimization problem finding is realized by one of the following blocks.

2)The block of decomposition algorithms of solving linear programming problems of large dimensionality. The time control linear problems with the phase restrictions are solved on the basis of these algorithms

$$\min\ (t_1 - t_o), \quad D(t)x(t) \leq \beta(t), \quad G(t)\, u(t) \leq \gamma(t),$$

$$LP:\ \min\ c^T \bar{u},\ W\bar{u} \leq b, \quad W = \begin{bmatrix} A_1 & A_2 \dots A_p \\ B_1 & & 0 \\ & B_2 & \\ 0 & & \ddots\ B_p \end{bmatrix} .$$

3)The block of optimal terminal control algorithms for the linear systems (2),(2a) without the restrictions on the phase coordinates in the class of piecewise-continuous controls at every t, taking the values from the convex compactum $U \subset R^m$.
The problem is effectively solved by the iterative procedure (Vassilyev O.V., Tyatushkin A.I.)

$$u^{k+1}(t) = \sum_{i=1}^{s} \alpha_i\, u^i(t), \quad \sum_{i=1}^{s} \alpha_i = 1, \ \alpha_i \geq 0, \ i = \overline{1,s}, \quad s \leq n+1. \quad (4)$$

The parameters α_i are determined from the solving of non-linear programming problem $\min\ \mathcal{J}\left(\sum_{i=1}^{s} \alpha_i\, x^i(t_1)\right)$ by

$\sum_{i=1}^{s} \alpha_i = 1,\ i=\overline{1,s}$, where $x^i(t)$ are the solutions of system (2) or (2a) by $u(t) = u^i(t)$ .As one of the controls in the convex hull (4) one takes the control obtained at the previous iteration and the rest are generated by the Pontryagin principle of maximum. In comparison with the single-parametric algorithms $(s = 2)$ the methods of (4) type converge considerably quicker and are applied to the systems with greater dimensionality.

The block of algorithms also contains the time control linear problems. The procedure (4) is applied with the sequential minimization of a function $\mathcal{J}(x(t_1)) = \| x(t_1) \|$ with the different values t_1 . The moment t_1 is verified by the formula

$$t^{k+1} = t^k + \frac{\rho(t)^k}{L}, \quad k = 1, 2, \dots, \ \rho(t) = \min_{u \in \mathcal{U}} \| x(t, u) \| .$$

4)The block of optimal control for non-linear systems (I),(Ia) (without the phase restrictions). The procedure (4) is also applied with the definition of parameters α_i from the condition

$$\min \mathcal{J}(x(t_1, \sum_{i=1}^{s} \alpha_i u^i))$$

by $\sum_{i=1}^{s} \alpha_i = 1,\ \alpha_i \geqslant 0,\ i = \overline{1,s}$.

If the system contains a great number of controlling influences then for the acceleration of the convergence the methods using the second variation of a functional are applied.

5)The block of dynamic analysis and parametric synthesis(Oparin G.A.)involves the optimization of parameters of non-linear precise controllable systems on some accuracy criterion with the use of procedures of numerical integration of a system.

<u>4.The module of analysis of dynamical properties of optimal solutions</u> is based on the use of vector Lyapunov function method for

the complex systems (Matrosov V.M.,Vassilyev S.N.,1977,1975,1978) and consists of blocks realizing the following man-machine procedures.

I)The revealing of necessary dynamical properties and quantitative estimations and the formalization of definitions of investigated dynamical properties of optimal solutions of the system $\mathcal{S}$ in the form of formulae $\mathfrak{P}$ on the base of the typical quantifiers language as it is illustrated in Fig 2. The following notations are used: $\mathfrak{m}_\nu \triangleq \hat{\mathfrak{m}}_\nu \triangleq \forall z_\nu\ (\mathcal{Z}_\nu \Rightarrow \sqcup)$ or $\mathfrak{m}_\nu \triangleq \check{\mathfrak{m}}_\nu \triangleq \exists z_\nu (\mathcal{Z}_\nu \wedge \sqcup)$.

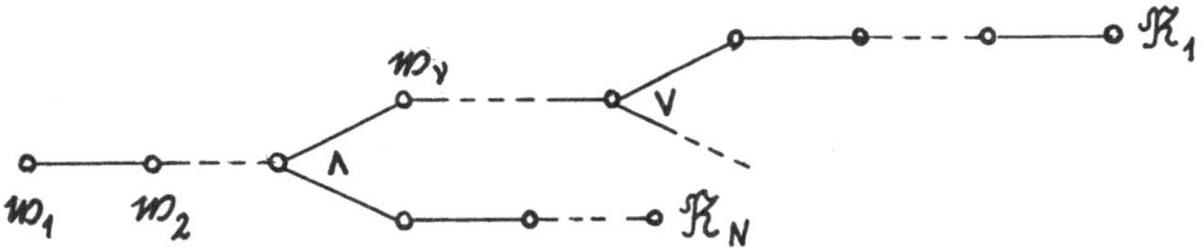

Fig.2.

For example, with the usage of vector functionals

$$\rho \triangleq (\rho^1,\ldots,\rho^\ell) : T \times X \to R^\ell_0,\ \rho_0 \triangleq (\rho^1_0,\ldots,\rho^{\ell_0}_0) : T^0 \times H^0 \to R^{\ell_0}_0 ,$$

when $R^\ell_0 \triangleq \{z \in R : z \geqslant 0\},\ R^\ell_+ = R^\ell_0 \setminus \{0\},\ \gamma \in R^\ell_+,\ H^0 \subseteq X$,

the formula of the important property of $\rho\rho_0$-exponential invariance (Matrosov V.M.,Vassilyev S.N.,1977) has the form

form $$\mathfrak{P} = (\forall t_0 \in T^0)(\exists \alpha \in R^1_+)(\exists \beta \in R^1_+)(\exists \delta \in R^{\ell_0}_+)$$
$$(\forall x_0 \in H^0 : \rho_0\ (t_0, x_0) < \delta)(\forall x \in \imath h)(\forall t \in T_{t_0}(x))$$
$$\rho(t, x(t)) \leq \gamma + \beta \,\|\rho_0\ (t_0, x_0)\|\, exp\,[-\alpha\ (t - t_0)]\ .$$

2)The choice of comparison system $\mathcal{S}_c$,for example, of the form

$$\dot{x}_c = f(t, x_c),\ x_c \in R^k,\ t \in T \triangleq [0,\tau],\ \tau \leq +\infty ,$$

or

$$x_c(t+1) = f(t, x_c(t))$$

and its comparison property $\mathfrak{P}_c$. In particular, for $\mathfrak{P}$ upper-exponential invariance property $\mathfrak{P}_c$ one may choose

$$(\forall t_{oc} \in T^\circ)(\exists \alpha_c \in R_+^1)(\exists \beta_c \in R_+^{l_c})(\exists \delta_c \in R_+^1)$$
$$(\forall x_{oc} : \| x_{oc} \| < \delta)(\forall x_c \in z_c h_c)(\forall t_c \in T_{t_0}(x_c))$$
$$x_c(t_c) \leq \gamma_c + \beta_c \| x_{oc} \| \exp[-\alpha_c (t - t_{oc})].$$

3)The choice of class of comparison functions or relations(of the type of direct and inverse vector Lyapunov functions,morphisms and the partial order relations) and of the formula $\mathfrak{M}$ connecting the systems $\mathfrak{J}$ and $\mathfrak{J}_c$ solutions behaviour. For example, one can choose the vector comparison function

$$\vartheta : T \times H^* \to R^k, \ H^* \subseteq X,$$

satisfying the connection formula

$$\mathfrak{M} = (\forall t_o \in T^\circ)(\forall x_o \in H^\circ)(\forall x_{oc} \in H_c^\circ : x_{oc} = \vartheta(t_o, x_o))$$
$$(\forall x \in zh)(\exists x_c \in z_c h_c)(\forall t \in T_{t_0}(x) \cap dom\ x_c)\ \vartheta(t, x(t)) \leq x_c(t).$$

4)The derivation of so-called comparison lemmas of the following structure

$$\mathfrak{M},\ c(\mathfrak{P}) \vdash \mathfrak{P}_c \Rightarrow \mathfrak{P}$$

with the use of algorithms of comparison principle (Matrosov V.M., Vassilyev S.N.,1975, 1977, 1978):

$$c(\mathfrak{P}) \triangleq \begin{cases} \hat{m}_i\ \check{m}''_{ic}\ c(\mathfrak{P}') \mid \mathfrak{P} = \hat{m}_i\ \mathfrak{P}' \\ \hat{m}_{ic}\ \check{m}''_i\ c(\mathfrak{P}') \mid \mathfrak{P} = \check{m}_i\ \mathfrak{P}' \\ c(\mathfrak{P}') \wedge c(\mathfrak{P}'') \mid \mathfrak{P} = \mathfrak{P}' \wedge \mathfrak{P}'' \text{ or } \mathfrak{P} = \mathfrak{P}' \vee \mathfrak{P}'', \end{cases}$$

$$c(\mathfrak{P}) \triangleq \; \rceil \mathcal{R}_q \wedge \mathcal{R}_{qc} \Rightarrow v(t,x) \notin x_c \mid \mathfrak{P} = \mathcal{R}_q ;$$
$$\check{m}''_{i(c)} \triangleq \check{m}_{i(c)} \mid z_i \neq t_o, x_o, t ;$$

$$\check{m}''_{i(c)} \triangleq \check{m}_{i(c)} \wedge \left\{ \begin{array}{l} t_{oc} = t_o \mid z_i = t_o \\ x_{oc} = v(t_o, x_o) \mid z_i = x_o \\ t_c = t \mid z_i = t \end{array} \right\} .$$

5) The obtaining of comparison theorem of the following formal-logical structure $\mathfrak{M}, \mathcal{B}, \bigwedge_i D_i, \bigwedge_\delta \mathcal{T}_\delta \vdash \mathfrak{P}_c \Rightarrow \mathfrak{P}$ by the algorithms (Matrosov V.M., Vassilyev S.N., 1975, 1978, 1977). Here $\mathcal{B}$, D_i, $\mathcal{T}_\delta$ are the conditions constructed by the formulae $c(\mathfrak{P})$ (for example, definite positivity of vector Lyapunov function v, the existence or continuability of solutions x_c , the existence of infinitely large inferior limit of vector Lyapunov function). The examples of comparison theorems are theorem I, and also the following comparison theorem for $\rho\rho_o$ -exponential invariance.

T h e o r e m 3. If exists vector comparison function v such that:

I° $(\forall h^o \in T^o \times H^o : \rho_o(h^o) = 0) \;\; v(h^o) \leq 0 ;$

2° $v(t_o, \cdot)$ is upper semi-continuous with respect to the sets

$$\{ x_o \in H^o : \rho_o(h^o) < \delta \in R_+^{\ell_o} \}_{\delta > 0} ,$$

$$\{ x_{oc} \in H_c^o : \| x_{oc} \| < \delta \in R_+^{\ell_{oc}} \}_{\delta > 0} ;$$

3° $(\forall t_o \in T^o)(\forall \alpha_c \in R_+^1)(\exists \alpha \in R_+^1)(\forall \beta_c \in R_+^{\ell_c})$

$$(\exists \beta \in R_+^{\ell})(\exists \delta \in R_+^{\ell_0})(\forall x_0 \in H^\circ : \rho_0(h^\circ) < \delta)(\forall t \in T_{t_0})$$
$$(\forall x \in X : \rho(t,x) \nleq \gamma + \beta \, \|\rho_0(h^\circ)\| \exp[-\alpha(t-t_0)])$$
$$\vartheta(t,x) \nleq \gamma_c + \beta_c \, \|\vartheta(h^\circ)\| \exp[-\alpha_c(t-t_0)];$$

4° $T_{t_0} \subseteq \operatorname{dom} x_c$,

then the upper exponential invariance of comparison system implies the $\rho\rho_0$ -exponential invariance of the system $\mathfrak{J}$.

6)The derivation of the theorem on dynamical properties by the substitution in the comparison theorem the sufficient conditions for $\mathfrak{M}$ and $\mathfrak{P}_c$ presence(from the theorems on differential and other inequalities and on the existence of $\mathfrak{P}_c$) contained in the data base. The examples are theorem 2 and the following theorem on the $\rho\rho_0$ -exponential invariance.

T h e o r e m 4. If exists comparison vector function ϑ , the matrix P , the function $\tilde{f} \in C[T \times R^k; R^k]$ and the vector $\gamma_c \in R_+^k$ such that

1° $(\forall (t,x) \in \Omega)\ \underline{\mu}\,(\max_{i=\overline{1,\ell}} \rho^i(t,x))^2 \leq \max_{s=\overline{1,k}} \vartheta^s(t,x);$

2° $(\forall h^\circ \in T^\circ \times H^\circ)\ \|\vartheta(h^\circ)\| \leq \bar{\mu}\, \|\rho_0(h^\circ)\|^2 \quad (\underline{\mu} \leq \bar{\mu});$

3° $\max_{s=\overline{1,k}} \gamma_c^s \leq \underline{\mu}\,(\min_{i=\overline{1,k}} \gamma^i)^2;$

4° $\dot{v}(t,x) \leq P(v(t,x)-\gamma_c) + \tilde{f}(t, v(t,x)-\gamma_c)$;

5° $p_{sj} \geq 0, \quad s \neq j \; ; \; (-1)^s \, | p_{ij} |_1^s > 0 \, , \quad s = \overline{1,k}$;

6° $\tilde{f}^s(t, x_c' - \gamma_c) \leq \tilde{f}^s(t, x_c'' - \gamma_c), \quad x_c'^s = x_c''^s ,$
$x_c'^j \neq x_c''^j, \quad j \neq s$;

7° $\tilde{f}^s(t, x_c - \gamma_c) / \| x_c - \gamma_c \| \overset{\rightarrow}{\underset{t}{\rightarrow}} 0, \quad x_c \rightarrow \gamma_c$,

then the studied system is $\rho\rho_0$ – exponentially invariant.

7)The vector Lyapunov function and estimations construction. In the first variant of module the numeriaal methods of vector Lyapunov functions construction are developed (Anapolsky L.J. and others, Vachonina V.S. and others, Abdullin R.Z.) and realized for the autonomous linear systems and the systems with polynomial right sides decomposed on the k interconnected subsystems and the construction of the quantitative estimations based on these functions is developed,too. The vector Lyapunov function components are the quadratic forms, the moduli of linear forms or polynomials, and comparison systems are chosen as the autonomous linear or vector Rikkati equation. Their choice is realized by solving the corresponding problems of the non-linear programming.

5.The decision-making module provides the optimal solutions estimation and contains the following blocks (Fig.3).

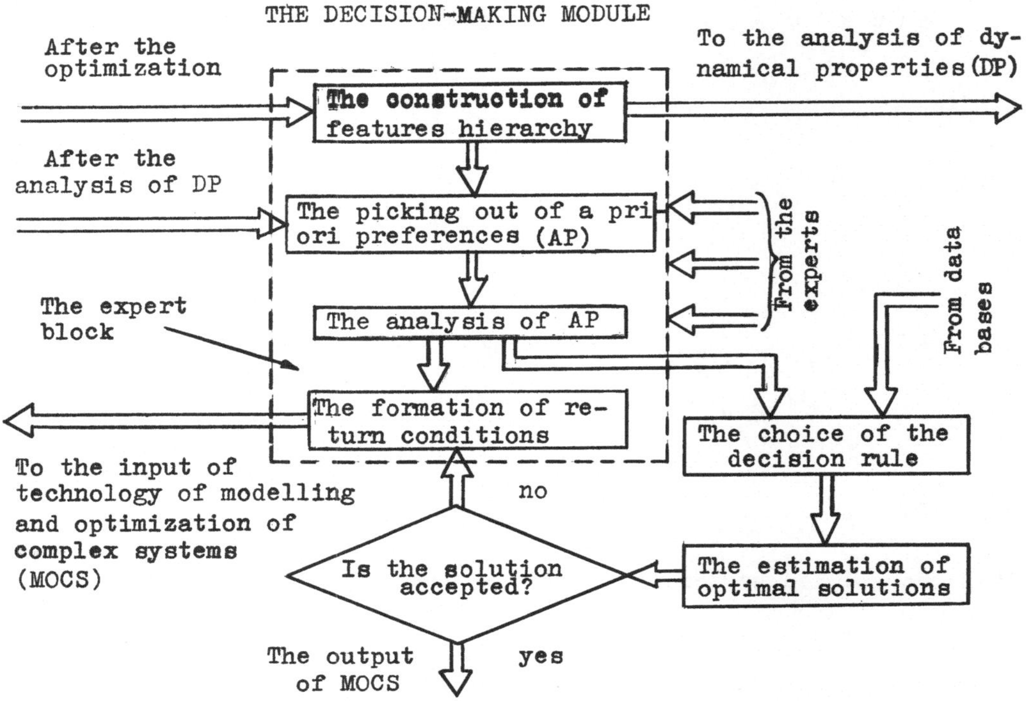

Fig.3.

I)The block of experts estimations obtaining and picking out the features and preferences (expert block). It realizes:

a)The construction and correction of features hierarchy $\mathcal{J}_i$ including the scalar optimization criteria,the features of the existence(or the absence) and the quantitative characteristics of dynamical properties of optimal solutions (for example, the stability storage, the parameters α, β, γ, δ from the definition of $\rho\rho_0$-exponential invariance characterizing the quality of the transition process,the accuracy, the estimations of the attraction region and others).

b)The revealing of a priori preferences on the sets of $\mathcal{J}_i$ features, their values ν_i , the used sources of information, and also in a series of cases on some set of optimal solutions

(x, u) from the obtained ones.

c)The analysis of a priori preferences properties. The revealed properties determine the applicability of these or other decision rules.

d)The formation of a condition of return to the original operations of technology MOCS.

2)The block of the choice of decision rules. It realizes the search of decision rules in the data bases by the picked out properties of a priori preferences. The absence of typical decision rules in the data bases initiates the procedure of the decision rule synthesis.

As one of such procedures the method of synthesis of the global scalar criterion is developed and realized in the class of quadratic polynomials :

$$\varphi(\nu) = \alpha_0 + \sum_{i=1}^{N} \alpha_i \nu_i + \sum_{\substack{i,j=1 \\ j \geq i}}^{N} \alpha_{ij} \nu_i \nu_j ,$$

where ν_i are the values of features $\mathcal{J}_i$ normed by the suitable manner. Besides the greater adequacy of the criterion to the investigator's intuitive preferences is achieved in comparison with the usually used additive or multiplicative structures. The finding of coefficients of the function φ is reduced to the linear programming problem solving

$$C^T \alpha \rightarrow max ,$$

where some restrictions

$$\alpha_i + (\delta^z, \alpha^i) \geq 0, \quad z = \overline{1, 2^n}, \quad i = \overline{1, n},$$

$$\alpha^i = (\alpha_{1i}, \alpha_{2i}, \ldots, \alpha_{i-1,i}, 2\alpha_{ii}, \alpha_{i+1,i}, \ldots, \alpha_{ni}),$$

provide the desirable monotony by ν_i and the others

$$\varphi(\nu_s^1) \leq \varphi(\nu_s^2), \quad s = \overline{1, p}$$

take into account the a priori pairwise estimations of alternatives.

3)The block of solutions estimation. It realizes the comparative estimation and the acceptance of optimal solutions (x, u) on the basis of the chosen decision rule. If the studied solutions do not provide the necessary values of the global criterion, by the procedure of the return condition formation one realizes the transition to the new iteration of modelling and optimization of complex systems.

L I T E R A T U R E:

Anapolski L.J .,Irtegov V.D.,Matrosov V.M. The methods of construction of Lyapunov functions. General mechanics,results of science, 1,2, M.,1975.

Abdullin R.Z. On one method of construction of VLF for investigation of practical stability. Theses of reports of the 3d All-Union Chetaev conference, Irkutsk,1977.

Bryabrin V.M. and others. DILOS-BESM-6. The preprint of Computer centre of AS USSR, M.,1976.

Burlakova L.A.,Irtegov V.D., Pochtarenko M.V. Computer usage for derivation and investigation of differential equations of mechanical systems.Theses of reports of the 3d All-Union Chetaev conference, Irkutsk,1977.

Kalman R.E.,Falb P.L., Arbib M.A. Topics in mathematical system theory. Mc Graw-Hill, New York,1969.

Matrosov V.M., Vassilyev S.N. Comparison principle in the dynamics of control systems. Theses of reports of the 7th All-Union conf.on control problems, Minsk,1977.

Matrosov V.M., Vassilyev S.N. Comparison principle for derivation of theorems of mathematical system theory. Proc. of the 4th Internat. United conference on artificial intelligence. Add. papers, M.,1975.

Oparin G.A. The program complex for parametric synthesis of the precise mechanical systems. Theses of reports of the 3d All-Union Chetaev conference,Irkutsk,1977.

Vassilyev O.V.,Tyatushkin A.I. On iterative procedure of the search of optimal control.Diff. and integr. equations,3,ISU,1975.

Vachonina G.S.,Kozlov R.I.,Malikov A.I. The algorithms of investigation of non-linear control systems by the method of VLF's. Theses of reports of the 3d All-Union Chetaev conference, Irkutsk,1977.

Yanenko N.N. and others. Problems of mathematical technology. The numerical methods of continuous environment mechanics, vol.8,issue 3, N.,1977.

APPLICATION OF OPTIMIZATION METHODS TO THE PROBLEM OF MATHEMATICAL SIMULATION OF ATMOSPHERIC PROCESSES AND ENVIRONMENT

G.I.Marchuk, V.V.Penenko

Computing Center, Novosibirsk, USSR

Modern models of the atmosphere and ocean dynamics are based on the laws of mass, momentum and energy conservation, which together with the thermodynamic laws describe atmospheric, oceanic and Earth's processes and their interaction. Mathematically, these are systems of multidimensional nonlinear partial differential equations which are solved under the assumption that the external source is solar energy. Initial conditions are determined according to the results of measurements in the real Atmosphere-Ocean-Earth climatic system. These systems include a set of parameters, which are assumed to be coefficients of equations, initial fields, characteristics of integration domain, external effects, etc. In solution of concrete problems some admissible set of input parameters can be described to some extent of reliability. The estimate of the range of variations of parameters is based on a priori data of the model, and the measured values of hydrometeorological fields. Solution of a concrete problem is determined not only as a function of space and time coordinates, but also as a function of input parameters of the model. To estimate the reliability of the solution obtained it is necessary to analyze its behaviour under variations of input parameters. This is a problem of a model's sensitivity to variations of the input data.

With the industrial development the man's influence on the climatic system becomes apparent in variations of basic parameters characterizing the atmospheric state and regime. This means that human impact should be interpreted as one of the factors in the climatic system and estimation of this factor is one of the applications of the sensitivity theory.

There is a wide range of problems connected with mathematical simulation of the atmosphere and ocean and with estimation of the industrial effect on the environment. To solve such problems a special mathematical method is needed. It should be based on variational principles, methods of perturbation, optimization and identification theory. Since we discuss here the behaviour of the model and its stability to variations of input data practical realization of numerical algorithms is of particular importance.

Variational principles together with splitting-up methods can serve as methodological basis of computational algorithms. Splitting-up methods provide economic and stable numerical algorithms for realization of the models and optimization theory. The variational principle guarantees mutual concordance of values at different steps of computation. It allows us to formulate methods for determining functions of the model's sensitivity and to consider them from the viewpoint of perturbation theory as methods of estimation of functional variations depending on variations of input data. Also important are the inverse problems, i.e. estimation of the input parameters by means of measured data about meteorological fields being simulated.

Perturbation and optimization methods as applied to numerical simulation of atmospheric and oceanic processes make it possible to qualitatively analyze the model, estimate relative contribution of various factors, rationally design numerical experiments, formulate a series of new problems of analysis and prediction of hydrometeorological fields, including inverse problems of identification of the model's parameters, estimate space and time scales of the domains of influence of parameter variations, etc.

1. Now, let us formulate problems and methods of their solution. Suppose that the structure of a mathematical model is given and defined by a system of nonlinear differential equations and relations describing fundamental hydrothermodynamic laws of processes being simulated. This assumption conforms to the present idea of the structure of mathematical models for the problems under consideration.

For convenience we write the mathematical model in the operator form:

$$B\frac{\partial\vec{\varphi}}{\partial t} + G(\vec{\varphi},\vec{Y}) = 0, \qquad \vec{\varphi} \in Q(D_t), \qquad \vec{Y} \in R(D_t), \tag{1}$$

Here the following notations are used

$\vec{\varphi}$ - vector of state of the system,

$\vec{Y}$ - vector of input parameters,

B - diagonal matrix, for a stationary problem - zero matrix,

$G(\vec{\varphi},\vec{Y})$ - nonlinear matrix operator, depending on the state vector and parameters,

D_t - range of space and time variables, $D_t \equiv \{D \times [0 \le t \le \bar{t}]\}$,

$Q(D_t)$ - space of functions satisfying boundary and initial conditions,

$R(D_t)$ - a set of admissible values of parameters.

The structure of operator $G(\vec{\varphi},\vec{Y})$ is determined by the system of model equations and boundary conditions. The functions $\vec{\varphi} \in Q(D_t)$ are assumed to be sufficiently smooth.

Mathematical simulation consists of several steps. These are: investigation of solvability of the system of equations (1), construction of discrete approximations and development of a computational algorithm, investigation of the model's behaviour in the domain $\{\vec{x} \in D_t, \vec{Y} \in R(D_t)\}$ and its sensitivity to variations of $\vec{Y}$, estimation of vector $\vec{Y}$ by a priori information of the model and measured data, etc. The numerical algorithm actually reduces to:

$$\vec{\varphi} = \vec{\varphi}(\vec{x},\vec{Y}), \qquad \vec{x} \in D_t, \qquad \vec{Y} \in R(D_t), \tag{2}$$

which expresses dependence of the state vector on independent variables and the input parameter vector.

A criterion of the model's quality and methods of its realization is some functional characterizing the behaviour of the state vector. An example of such a functional can be a deviation between measured and computed values of the state vector. We denote this functional by $J(\vec{\varphi}, \vec{\varphi}_m)$, where $\vec{\varphi}$ is value of the state vector computed by the model, $\vec{\varphi}_m$ is the value of the state vector obtained as a result of measurements. The components of vector $\vec{\varphi}_m$ are determined on a discrete set of points $D_t^m \in D_t$. In practice several criteria of the model's quality are used depending on the purpose of research.

The statement of optimization problems for partial differential equations requires that the discrete model and algorithms be of special structure because of the strict requirements to economy of computations and the necessity of strict formal concordance of discrete approximations of the basic and adjoint equations. To meet these requirements let us make use of the variational principle. Instead of the model of form (1), let us consider an integral identity and with the help of this identity define solution in a weak generalized form.

Let us represent the integral identity as

$$I(\vec{\varphi}, \vec{Y}, \vec{\varphi}^*) = 0, \qquad (3)$$

where $\vec{\varphi}^* \in Q^*(D_t)$ is an arbitrary, sufficiently smooth function. Its structure is assumed to coincide with that of vector $\vec{\varphi}$.

The functional in equation (3) is chosen so that on the class of sufficiently smooth functions $Q(D_t)$ and $Q^*(D_t)$ descriptions of the model (1) and (3) are equivalent, i.e. the functional is determined by inner product

$$I(\vec{\varphi}, \vec{Y}, \vec{\varphi}^*) = (B \frac{\partial \vec{\varphi}}{\partial t} + G(\vec{\varphi}, \vec{Y}), \vec{\varphi}^*)_{D_t}. \qquad (4)$$

On the other hand, for convenience let identity (3) be reduced so that

$$I(\vec{\varphi}, \vec{Y}, \vec{\varphi}^*) = 0 \qquad (5)$$

is an equation of the energy balance of the system without additional operations of differentiation and integration.

Identity (3) is a basis for constructing discrete approximations of the model. Let us discuss finite difference discretization. To this aim a grid domain D_t^h is introduced in the domain D_t. Integrals in (3) are approximated by quadrature formulas, integrands - by finite-difference relations. For approximation with respect to time we make use of the method of weak approximation with fractional steps. As a result we obtain the summation identity

$$I^h(\vec{\varphi}^h, \vec{Y}^h, \vec{\varphi}^{h*}) = 0. \qquad (6)$$

The system of finite-difference equations, approximating (1), is obtained from stationary conditions of the summation functional for arbitrary and independent variations of function $\vec{\varphi}^{h*}$, i.e.

$$\frac{\partial I^h(\vec{\varphi}^h, \vec{Y}^h, \vec{\varphi}^{h_*})}{\partial \vec{\varphi}^{*h}} = 0. \tag{7}$$

This is a system of basic equations. Similarly, the system of adjoint equations is obtained from stationary condition of the summation functional with respect to arbitrary and independent variations of the state vector in the vicinity of some given value

$$\frac{\partial}{\partial \vec{\varphi}^{1h}} \{\lim_{\xi \to o} \frac{\partial}{\partial \xi} I(\vec{\varphi}^h + \xi \vec{\varphi}^{1h}, \vec{Y}, \varphi^{h_*})\} = 0. \tag{8}$$

With the use of weak approximation and fractional step methods (7) and (8) become splitting-up schemes mutually concordant by means of the summation functional.

2. Let problem (1) be correct. Then the class of vector-functions $\vec{\varphi}$ determined by formula (2) continuously depends on $\vec{Y}$. This means that small perturbations $\partial \vec{Y}$ of vector $\vec{Y}$ correspond to small perturbations $\delta \vec{\varphi}$ of vector $\vec{\varphi}$. In a discrete finite-difference model all the vectors $\vec{\varphi}, \vec{Y}, \delta \vec{\varphi}, \delta \vec{Y}$ are given at points of grid D_t^h. The symbol δ denotes that at least one of the components $\vec{\varphi}$ or $\vec{Y}$ gets perturbation. From the physical sense of the problem it follows that vector $\vec{Y}$ has components of different dimension. Therefore for simplicity we renumber all components one by one and introduce the new notation

$$\vec{Y} = \{Y_i\} \text{ and } \delta \vec{Y} = \{\delta Y_i\} \qquad (i = \overline{1,N}), \tag{9}$$

where N is the number of components defined by the number of points in D_t^h and the number of different-in-sense functions constituting $\vec{Y}$.

Variations are assumed small if the following relations

$$|\delta Y_i| << |Y_i| \qquad (i = \overline{1,N}). \tag{10}$$

hold. By virtue of equation (2) variations $\delta \vec{Y}$ and $\delta \vec{\varphi}$ are related to one another. The task is to determine the effect of variations $\delta \vec{Y}$ on the state vector of the system and vice versa to determine vector $\vec{Y}$ by given values of the state vector.

Let us choose some functional as a measure for estimating the effect of perturbations $\delta \vec{Y}$ of the input parameters on vector $\vec{\varphi}$ and denote it by $\Phi(\vec{\varphi})$. Assume that it explicitly depends on $\vec{\varphi}$ and is continuous, bounded and differentiable on the set of functions $\vec{\varphi} \in Q(D_t)$ and $\vec{Y} \in R(D_t)$.

Variation of the functional $\Phi(\vec{\varphi})$ is determined by the two relations:

$$\delta \Phi(\vec{\varphi}) = (\text{grad}_{\vec{\varphi}} \Phi, \delta \vec{\varphi}) \tag{11}$$

and

$$\delta \Phi(\vec{\varphi}) = (\text{grad}_{\vec{Y}} \Phi, \delta \vec{Y}), \tag{12}$$

where

$$\text{grad}_{\vec{\varphi}} \Phi \equiv \frac{\partial \Phi(\vec{\varphi})}{\partial \vec{\varphi}} \text{ and } \text{grad}_{\vec{Y}} \Phi = \frac{\partial \Phi(\vec{\varphi})}{\partial \vec{Y}}. \tag{13}$$

The second expression is the basic relation of the model's sensitivity to variations of input parameters. The components of vector $\text{grad}_{\vec{Y}}\Phi$ are the functions of influence of variations $\delta\vec{Y}$ on variation of the functional $\delta\Phi(\vec{\varphi})$ or sensitivity functions of the model with respect to the functional $\Phi(\vec{\varphi})$. Expressions (11)-(13) are determined in the vicinity of the unperturbed values of vectors $\vec{\varphi}$ and $\vec{Y}$.

Let us write a scheme of the algorithm for computing functional variations by (12) and components of the vector $\text{grad}_{\vec{Y}}\Phi$, omitting intermediate transformations and following /6/.

1) An unperturbed value of vector $\vec{Y}$ is selected.

2) System of governing equations (7) is solved, with $\vec{Y}$ given. As a result we obtain an unperturbed value of state vector $\vec{\varphi}$.

3) System of adjoint equations (8) is solved with respect to function $\vec{\varphi}^*$ under the condition $\vec{\varphi}^*(t)=0$ and the source term $\text{grad}_{\vec{\varphi}}\Phi$. A discrete model of the adjoint problem is obtained from

$$\frac{\partial}{\partial\delta\vec{\varphi}}\{\lim_{\xi\to o}\frac{\partial}{\partial\xi}[\Phi^h(\vec{\varphi}+\xi\delta\vec{\varphi})+I^h(\vec{\varphi}+\xi\delta\vec{\varphi},\vec{Y},\vec{\varphi}^*)]\}=0, \tag{14}$$

where ξ is real parameter.

4) Components of vector $\text{grad}_{\vec{Y}}\Phi$ are calculated by

$$\text{grad}_{\vec{Y}}\Phi=\frac{\partial}{\partial\delta\vec{Y}}[\lim_{\xi\to o}\frac{\partial}{\partial\xi}I^h(\vec{\varphi},\vec{Y}+\xi\delta\vec{Y},\vec{\varphi}^*)]. \tag{15}$$

5) The variation $\delta\Phi(\vec{\varphi})$ is calculated by formula (12), which in this case is of the form

$$\delta\Phi(\vec{\varphi})=\lim_{\xi\to o}\frac{\partial}{\partial\xi}I^h(\vec{\varphi},\vec{Y}+\xi\delta\vec{Y},\vec{\varphi}^*). \tag{16}$$

From (16) it follows that the expressions of functionals in (7) and (8) determine the inner product in (12) which relates functional and parameter variations. In the above algorithm the function $\vec{\varphi}^*$ plays the role of the vector of Lagrangian multipliers for the account of the dependence of the functional on the parameter. Adjoint problem (14) is introduced so that the expression for variation becomes of the simplest form. The algorithm for solving problem (14) reduces to realization of the splitting-up scheme concordant with scheme (11) by the summation functional.

Thus, in addition to relation (12), we have formulated a numerical algorithm for finding the vector $\text{grad}_{\vec{Y}}\Phi$, essential to solution of multidimensional optimization problems.

3. Let us discuss an approach to determination of parameters according to this criterion. This approach is based on concepts of optimization and identification theory and realizes the feedback between variations of parameters and the criterion of the model's quality. For diagnostic studies, i.e. when measured data of the state vector components are available, we choose the quality criterion as a functional determining the mean quadratic deviation between computed and

measured values of the state vector. Let dimension of the state vector $\vec{\varphi}_m$ be specified on a discrete set of points $D_t^m \in D_t$. Define this functional as follows:

$$\Phi(\vec{\varphi}) = \|\vec{\varphi} - \vec{\varphi}_m\|_{D_t^m}. \tag{17}$$

The norm in (17) can be introduced taking account of a p r i o r i data about errors of measurement. When the problem is solved numerically the state vector φ is determined on a grid D_t^h. Therefore, in order to calculate functional (17), one must have an operator of data transformation from the grid D_t^h to the set D_t^m where the vector $\vec{\varphi}_m$ is specified. It is more convenient and justifiable to determine the model's quality functional on the state vector values, specified on the set D_t^m, than to determine it on the grid D_t^h.

To form the feedback between variations of the parameter vector and the quality criterion, let us take advantage of the concept of the steepest descent approach. Introduce in $R(D_t)$ the metric

$$ds^2 = \sum_{i=1}^{N} \eta_i dY_i^2, \tag{18}$$

where the η_i are scale factors, dY_i is variation of the i-th component of $\vec{Y}$. Derivative $ds/dt = U_p$ can be considered as the rate of change of the model in $R(D_t)$. Having assumed that U_p is proportional to the module of the functional gradient in the direction of vector $\vec{Y}$, i.e.

$$U_p = k\left[\sum_{i=1}^{N} \frac{1}{\eta_i}\left(\frac{\partial\Phi(\vec{\varphi})}{\partial Y_i}\right)^2\right]^{1/2}, \tag{19}$$

where k is the proportionality coefficient, we obtain the following system of differential equations:

$$\frac{dY_i}{dt} = -\frac{k}{\eta_i}\frac{\partial\Phi(\vec{\varphi})}{\partial Y_i} \quad (i = \overline{1,N}). \tag{20}$$

Any equation in (20) relates the rate of change of the i-th component of the parameter vector with respective component of vector $\mathrm{grad}_{\vec{Y}}\,\Phi$, computed in the vicinity of the unperturbed value of vector $\vec{Y}$.

Difference approximation of equations (20) is built as follows:

$$Y_i^{j+1} = Y_i^j - \left(\frac{k\Delta t}{\eta_i}\right)\frac{\partial\Phi(\vec{\varphi})}{\partial Y_i} \quad (i = \overline{1,N}), \tag{21}$$

where j is the number of time step and Δt is the time step of integration of basic and adjoint equations. The algorithm for vector $\mathrm{grad}_{\vec{Y}}\,\Phi$ was described earlier when we discussed the approach to estimation of functional variations. It is defined by formula (15).

We integrate equation (21) successively, together with integration of model equations (7) and adjoint equations (14). Solution of the adjoint problem is the necessary link between the change of the quality functional and that of vector $\vec{Y}$. It is reasonable to choose proportionality coefficient k in (20) at each time step with respect to the magnitude of the functional increment on the interval Δt or from the condition of the functional minimum in the direction of Y^{j+1} .

4. To illustrate application of the above approaches, let us discuss two formulations of concrete problems of mathematical simulation of atmospheric hydrothermodynamics and transport of atmospheric pollution.

As the first example, we consider a model of atmospheric hydrothermodynamics in diabatic approximation on a sphere in isobaric coordinates. Variational formulation of the problem is most convenient for constructing discrete approximations and computational algorithms. Therefore we do not represent the model as a system of differential equations. Let us define it as the integral identity /7/:

$$I(\vec{\varphi},\vec{Y},\vec{\varphi}^*) \equiv \int_{D_t} \{(\Lambda u,u^*) + (\Lambda v,v^*) + \sigma(\Lambda T,T^*) + (1 + \frac{\operatorname{ctg}\Theta}{a})(vu^* - v^*u) + (\vec{u}^* \operatorname{grad} H - \vec{u} \operatorname{grad} H^*) + \frac{R}{P}(T\tau^* - \frac{(\gamma_a - \gamma)\overline{T}}{g}\tau T^*) - \sigma\varepsilon T^*\} dD dt + \int_{S_t} \overline{\rho}(\frac{\partial H}{\partial t} H^* - \frac{\partial H^*}{\partial t} H)\Big|_{p=p_a} ds dt + \frac{1}{2}\Big[\int_D (uu^* + vv^* + \sigma TT^*) dD + \int_S \overline{\rho} HH^*\Big|_{p=p_a}\Big]\Big|_0^{\overline{t}} + I_D(\vec{\varphi},\vec{\varphi}^*) = 0, \tag{22}$$

where

$$I_D(\vec{\varphi},\vec{\varphi}^*) = \int_{D_t} \{\mu_1[D_T(\vec{u}_s)D_T(\vec{u}_s^*) + D_s(\vec{u}_s)D_s(\vec{u}_s^*)] + \chi_1(\frac{\partial u}{\partial p}\frac{\partial u^*}{\partial p} + \frac{\partial v}{\partial p}\frac{\partial v^*}{\partial p}) + \sigma[\mu_2(\frac{1}{a^2\sin^2\Theta}\frac{\partial T}{\partial\phi}\frac{\partial T^*}{\partial\phi} + \frac{1}{a^2}\frac{\partial T}{\partial\Theta}\frac{\partial T^*}{\partial\Theta}) + \chi_2\frac{\partial T}{\partial p}\frac{\partial T^*}{\partial p}]\} dD dt + \int_{S_t} (u^*\tau_\phi + v^*\tau_\Theta + \sigma T^* q_s)\Big|_{p=p_a} ds dt, \tag{23}$$

$$D_T(\vec{u}_s) = \frac{1}{a\sin\Theta}(\frac{\partial u}{\partial\phi} + \frac{\partial(v\sin\Theta)}{\partial\Theta}), D_s(\vec{u}_s) = \frac{1}{a\sin\Theta}(\frac{\partial v}{\partial\phi} - \frac{\partial(u\sin\Theta)}{\partial\Theta}),$$

$$(\Lambda\varphi,\varphi^*) \equiv \frac{1}{2}[(\frac{\partial\varphi}{\partial t}\varphi^* - \frac{\partial\varphi^*}{\partial t}\varphi) + (\varphi^*\vec{u} \operatorname{grad}\varphi - \varphi\vec{u} \operatorname{grad}\varphi^*)], \tag{24}$$

$$\vec{\varphi} = (u,v,T,H,\tau), \quad \vec{\varphi}^* = (u^*,v^*,T^*,H^*,\tau^*), \quad \vec{u}_s = (u,v), \quad \vec{u}_s^* = (u^*,v^*),$$

$$D_t = D \times [0,\bar{t}], \quad D = \{S \times [P_T,P_a)\}, \quad S = \{0 \le \psi \le 2\pi, 0 \le \Theta \le \pi\},$$

$$S_t = S \times (0,\bar{t}], \quad dS = a \sin \Theta d\Theta d\psi, \quad dD = dSdp.$$

The system of notations is as follows:

u, v, τ - components of the velocity vector in the direction of coordinates ψ, Θ, p, respectively;
t - time;
ψ - longitude;
Θ - supplement to latitude;
p - pressure ($p_T \le p \le p_a$, p_T, p_a - pressure at the upper and lower boundaries of air mass, respectively);
T and H - deviation of temperature and geopotential from their standard values $\bar{T}$ and $\bar{H}$, respectively;
$\bar{\rho}$ - standard density;
a - Earth's radius;
l - Coriolis parameter;
μ_i, χ_i ($i = 1,2$) - turbulence coefficients in horizontal and vertical directions;
ε - heat flux per unit volume;
R - universal gas constant;
g - acceleration due to gravity;
γ_a - adiabatic temperature gradient;
$\gamma = -\frac{\partial \bar{T}}{\partial z}$ - standard temperature gradient;

τ_ψ, τ_Θ - functions defining dynamic interaction of the atmosphere and the Earth's surface;
q_s - function of the heat flux from the Earth's surface;
σ - scale factor;
Components of vector function $\vec{\varphi}^*$ are arbitrary, sufficiently smooth functions.

The input parameter vector can be defined by

$$\vec{Y} = (\vec{\varphi}^0, \mu_1, \mu_2, \chi_1, \chi_2, \varepsilon, \tau_\psi, \tau_\Theta, q_s, \bar{\rho}, \bar{T}, \frac{(\gamma_a - \gamma)}{g}, a, l), \tag{25}$$

where $\vec{\varphi}^0$ is the initial value of the vector φ at $t = 0$. The integral identity (22) defines a generalized solution of the problem. It takes into consideration differential equations, external effects, boundary and initial conditions. Periodicity conditions of functions on a sphere are involved in the definition of a class of functions to which the generalized solution belongs.

Identity (22) is discretized as follows. At first we introduce in the domain D_t the grid domain D_t^h, then approximate integrals and integrands by quadrature and finite difference formulas, respectively. The fractional step approach is used for time approximation. Expressions of the same type in (22) must be approximated in a like manner. This ensures the energy balance of discrete approximations obtained from stationary conditions of the summation functional (7) and (8).

Principles of numerical methods for atmosphere and ocean dynamics problems are described in /1,2/ . Here we will discuss only the structure of the basic relation of sensitivity theory for the model under consideration and equation (20) for realization of the feedback between variations of functional and parameters.

We assume that some of the parameters get perturbations

$$\vec{Y} = (\delta\vec{\varphi}^{o}, \delta\mu_1, \delta\mu_2, \delta\chi_1, \delta\chi_2, \delta\varepsilon, \delta\tau_\psi, \delta\tau_\Theta, \delta q_s) \tag{26}$$

and sensitivity of the model is estimated by variations of a functional $\Phi(\vec{\varphi})$. Write down formula (12) to compute variations of the functional by variations of the parameter vector. Let $\vec{\varphi} = (u, v, T, H, \tau)$ be solution of problem (6) for unperturbed values of the parameters and $\vec{\varphi}^* = (u^*, v^*, T^*, H^*, \tau^*)$ be solution of the adjoint problem (7) provided that $\vec{\varphi}^* = 0$ at $t = \bar{t}$ and the source term is equal to

$$\text{grad}_{\vec{\varphi}}\Phi = \frac{\partial}{\partial\delta\vec{\varphi}} \lim_{\xi\to o} \frac{\partial}{\partial\xi} \Phi^h(\vec{\varphi} + \xi\delta\vec{\varphi}), \tag{27}$$

where the superscript h denotes discrete approximation of functional $\Phi(\vec{\varphi})$, ξ is real parameter, $\delta\vec{\varphi}$ is variation of the state vector in the vicinity of the unperturbed value $\vec{\varphi}$. With the above notations expression (16) is /6/

$$\begin{aligned}\delta\Phi(\vec{\varphi}) &= \int_{D_t} \{\sigma T^*\delta\varepsilon + \delta\mu_1(D_T(\vec{u}_s)D_T(\vec{u}_s^*) + D_s(\vec{u}_s)D_s(\vec{u}_s^*)) + \\ &+\delta\chi_1(\frac{\partial u}{\partial p}\frac{\partial u^*}{\partial p} + \frac{\partial v}{\partial p}\frac{\partial v^*}{\partial p}) + \sigma[\delta\mu_2(\frac{1}{a^2\sin^2\Theta}\frac{\partial T}{\partial\psi}\frac{\partial T^*}{\partial\psi} + \frac{1}{a^2}\frac{\partial T}{\partial\Theta}\frac{\partial T^*}{\partial\Theta}) + \\ &+ \delta\chi_2\frac{\partial T}{\partial p}\frac{\partial T^*}{\partial p}]\}dDdt + \int_{S_t}(u^*\delta\tau_\psi + v^*\delta\tau_\Theta + \sigma T^*\delta q_s)|_{p=p_a}dSdt + \\ &+ \frac{1}{2}[\int_D (u^*\delta u^o + v^*\delta v^o + \sigma T^*\delta T^o)dD + \int_S \bar{\rho}H^*\delta H^o dS|_{p=p_a}].\end{aligned} \tag{28}$$

Comparing expressions (12) and (28) we obtain formulas for computation of components of the vector $\text{grad}_{\vec{Y}}\Phi$, for example,

$$\begin{aligned}\frac{\partial\Phi}{\partial\mu_1} &= (D_T(\vec{u}_s)D_T(u_s^*) + D_s(\vec{u}_s)D_s(\vec{u}_s^*)),\\ \frac{\partial\Phi}{\partial\chi_1} &= (\frac{\partial u}{\partial p}\frac{\partial u^*}{\partial p} + \frac{\partial v}{\partial p}\frac{\partial v^*}{\partial p}),\\ \frac{\partial\Phi}{\partial\tau_\psi} &= u^*|_{p=p_a}, \quad \frac{\partial\Phi}{\partial u^o} = u^*|_{t=0}, \text{ etc.}\end{aligned} \tag{29}$$

Substituting expressions for the components of vector $\text{grad}_{\vec{Y}}\Phi$ into the right-hand side of (21), we arrive at the system of equations for finding the model's parameters with respect to variations of the functional $\Phi(\vec{\varphi})$.

Different application of the basic relation of the models' sensitivity to linear functionals for problems of the atmosphere and ocean dynamics are discussed in /2/. Identification algorithm for determination of meteorological fields on the grid D^h by the measured data is considered in /5/, where model (22), linearized in the vicinity of the state of rest, is used as a constraint. Application of optimization and identification methods is described in /8/ for a thermal regime atmospheric model.

The general structure of optimization and identification algorithms for problems of mathematical simulation of the atmosphere and ocean is based on the theory of optimization and identification of systems /4,9,10/. In concrete realization of these algorithms one must take account of the fact that this class of problems is defined by multidimensional nonlinear partial differential equations.

Simulation of the atmosphere and ocean dynamics is only part of the environmental problem. Of great importance in the study of human impact on the environment is the problem of simulation of pollution transport. Mathematically this problem is formulated as follows /3/. Let us find in $D_t^o \subseteq D_t$ solution of the pollution transport equation

$$\frac{\partial\varphi}{\partial t} + \vec{u}\ \mathrm{grad}\ \varphi + A\varphi - \frac{\partial}{\partial z}\nu\frac{\partial\varphi}{\partial z} - \mathrm{div}_s \mu\ \mathrm{grad}_s\varphi = q(\vec{x},t) \qquad (30)$$

under the conditions

$$\begin{aligned} \alpha\frac{\partial\varphi}{\partial z} + \beta\varphi + r_s &= 0 \qquad \text{at} \quad z = z_s(\vec{x}) \\ \nu\frac{\partial\varphi}{\partial z} &= 0 \qquad \text{at} \quad z = z_H, \end{aligned} \qquad (31)$$

where the following notations are used:

- φ - function of pollution distribution;
- $\vec{u}$ - velocity vector of air particles;
- ν, μ - turbulent exchange coefficients;
- $q(\vec{x},t)$ - distribution of pollution sources;
- α and β - functions defining conditions of interaction of pollution with the Earth's surface;
- r_s - distribution of surface sources;
- $z_s(\vec{x})$ - Earth's surface relief; z_H - upper boundary of air mass;
- A - operator describing local processes of interaction of aerosol particles and air.

Index S denotes the operators in horizontal directions. Initial conditions for problem (30) are determined from measured concentrations of pollution in D_t^o. The structure of this domain is similar to D_t in the atmosphere dynamics model. Therefore we will use the notation of (22) adding superscript o. Information about the state of the atmosphere is input for the pollution transport model. The gravity setting rate of pollution particles is included in the vertical component of vector $\vec{u}$.

To construct a numerical model, let us write a variational formulation of problem (30)-(31)

$$I(\varphi,\varphi^*) \equiv \int_{D_t^o} [(\Lambda\varphi,\varphi^*) + (A\varphi,\varphi^*) + \nu \frac{\partial\varphi}{\partial z}\frac{\partial\varphi^*}{\partial z} + $$
$$+ \mu \, \mathrm{grad}_s\varphi \, \mathrm{grad}_s\varphi^* - q\varphi^*]dDdt + \int_{S_t^o} \frac{\nu}{\alpha}(\beta\varphi\varphi^* + \qquad (32)$$
$$+ r_s\varphi^*)|_{z=z_s} dSdt + \frac{1}{2}\int_{D^o} \varphi\varphi^*|_o^{\bar{t}} dD = 0,$$

where φ^* is an arbitrary, sufficiently smooth function, and $(\Lambda\varphi,\varphi^*)$ is defined by expression (24). If D_t^o does not coincide with D_t, in (32) there appears integral of the side boundary of D^o. Function φ in its physical sense is non-negative. Therefore, in discretization of the model, besides ordinary requirements of approximation and stability, we must make sure that the condition of non-negative unknown function is met.

Below we give examples of some applications of model (30)-(32).

1) Estimation of pollution distribution in domain D^o at fixed time and identification of model parameters according to measured data.

This problem consists in minimization of functional (17) which determines the deviations between measured and computed values of pollution concentrations. The set of measurements depends on possibilities of measuring instruments and on their time-space disposition. Model (30)-(32) plays the role of constraints relating the set of parameters

$$\vec{Y} = (\vec{u}, \varphi^o, \mu_1, \mu_2, \alpha, \beta, q, r_s) \qquad (33)$$

with the function of pollution distribution.

2) The optimization problem with criteria determined by the norms of the pollution concentrations.

Let us introduce a set of functionals

$$\Phi_k(\varphi) = \int_{D_t^o} \varphi\eta_k dDdt \qquad (k = \overline{1,K}), \qquad (34)$$

where $\eta_k = \eta_k(\vec{x},t)$ are non-negative weight functions satisfying the normalization conditions

$$\int_{D_t^o} \eta_k dDdt = 1. \qquad (35)$$

The physical sense of the functional (34) depends on the choice of the weight function. For instance, function $\eta_k(\vec{x},t)$ can define distribution of detectors in D_t^o. Generally, function $\Phi_k(\varphi)$ is averaged-with-weight $\eta_k(\vec{x},t)$ concentration of particles in the domain determined by the support of function η_k.

If φ is the pollution concentration, then conditions

$$\Phi_k(\varphi) \leq N_k \qquad (k = \overline{1,K}), \qquad (36)$$

where the N_k, limiting admissible values of functionals $\Phi_k(\varphi)$, are criteria of the solution of practical environmental control problems. The natural question is: what parameters of the model will help fulfil conditions (36)? Analysis of the set of parameters (33) has shown that the distribution function and the pollution source strength can be regulated.

More concrete statements depend on purposes of research. If the pollution source distribution is fixed and meteorological situations, described by velocity field $\vec{u}$ are known, one must find the pollution source strength. This is a typical problem of forecasting of the state of the environment, which must be solved together with the weather forecasting problem.

One example of long-term planning is distribution of new industrial units whose construction and functioning will affect the environment. In this case conditions (36) determining the limiting admissible impact on the environment play the role of optimality criteria. In contrast to short-term forecasting problems, here one needs climatic data about atmospheric processes.

REFERENCES

1. Marchuk, G.I. Numerical methods of weather prediction. Academic Press, 495 (1974).

2. Marchuk, G.I. Numerical solution of problems of atmosphere and ocean dynamics. Leningrad, Gidrometeoizdat, 303(1974).

3. Marchuk, G.I. The Environment and Problems of Optimizing the Distribution of Businesses. Dokl.Akad.Nauk SSSR, 226, 5, 1056-1059 (1976).

4. Moiseev, N.N. Numerical methods in optimal system theory. Moskva, Nauka, 424 (1971).

5. Obraztsov, N.N,,and Penenko, V.V. Variational method of concordance of meteorological fields. Meteorologia i gidrologia, 11, 3-16 (1976).

6. Penenko, V.V. Computational aspects of simulation of atmospheric processes dynamics and estimations of the effect of various factors on the atmosphere dynamics. In: Nekotorie problemi vychislitelnoi i prikladnoi matematiki. Novosibirsk, Nauka, 61-77 (1975).

7. Penenko, V.V. Energo-balanced discrete models of the dynamics of atmospheric processes. Meteorologia i gidrologia, 10, 3-20 (1977).

8. Penenko, V.V. A numerical model of thermal regime of the atmosphere. Izv.AN SSSR, Fiz.Atm.Ocean, 13, 6, 571-580 (1977).

9. Eykhoff, P. System identification; parameter and state estimation. J.Willey and Sons, Ltd., N.Y., 1974.

10. Döös, B.R. Numerical experimentation related to GARP. GARP publication series, 6, 68 (1970).

11. Modelling for the first GARP global experiment. GARP publication series, VI, 14, 261 (1974).

12. Lions, J.L. Contrôle optimal de systèmes gouvernés par des équations aux derivées partielles. Dunod, Paris, 1968.

13. Tomovič, R., Vucobratovič, M. General sensitivity theory. AP, 258 (1972).

OPTIMUM DESIGN OF A MAGNET WITH FINITE ELEMENTS

A. MARROCCO - O. PIRONNEAU
IRIA-LABORIA
Domaine de Voluceau, Rocquencourt
78150 Le Chesnay, France

I - INTRODUCTION

In this paper we shall discuss some aspects related to the design of systems for which a good numerical simulation by partial differential equations can be done. The typical situation is the following : some engineers and numerical analysts have spent a great deal of time at making an efficient numerical simulation of a system. This numerical scheme is now currently used by the engineers in the design of new products. There, the "know how" of the engineers is used : he knows that is such and such parameters are changed, such behaviour is induced. The numerical analyst raise the following question ; can this be done automatically ? In general the answer is no ; indeed dialogues with engineers reveal that the criteria for optimal design are numerous and that the constraints are hundreds.

However the numerical analyst can be of great help to the engineer's intuition. With respect to one differentiable criteria, he can

1 - give the optimum design under certain constraints
2 - tell the direction of changes to be done to improve design.

The method proposed here operates in the physical plan and can be considered as a natural extension of the numerical study of the state equation. The method is the discrete analogue of the continuous case in O. PIRONNEAU [1]. The method is applied for the design of an electromagnet. The state equation is a non-linear equation considered for example in R. GLOWINSKI - A. MARROCCO [2], [3]. (The classical magnetostatic equation in potential vector form). We have looked for electromagnet with constant interpolar field but the technique can be adapted to other criteria and other P.D.E. The computations are done with triangular Lagrangian piecewise linear elements. The nodes are allowed to vary on prescribed curves (to avoid intercrossing, but it is not an obligation). The gradient of the criteria with respect to the coordinates of the moving nodes is computed analytically via an adjoint state equation and the criteria is then minimized by the method of steepest descent.

II - STATEMENT OF THE MAGNETOSTATIC PROBLEM

We consider the classical magnetostatic equation in potential vector form

(2.1) $\nabla\times(\nu\times\vec{A}) = \mu_o\vec{J}$

which can be in the two dimensional case written as

(2.2) $-\nabla\cdot(\nu\nabla A_3) = \mu_o j_3$

or

(2.3) $-\sum_{i=1}^{2}\frac{\partial}{\partial x_i}(\nu\frac{\partial A_3}{\partial x_i}) = \mu_o j_3$.

In these previous equations μ_o is a constant equal to $4\pi\ 10^{-7}$ in MKSA system, ν the relative magnetic reluctivity, which is constant in air and copper (ν=1) and is a non-linear function of $|\vec{B}|^2 = |\nabla\times\vec{A}|^2 = |\nabla A_3|^2$ in the iron ($\vec{B}$ is the flux density vector) the approximation of the relative reluctivity is made by a function of the family

$$\tilde{\nu}_{\varepsilon,\alpha,C,T}(x) = \varepsilon+(C-\varepsilon)\ \frac{x^\alpha}{x^\alpha+T}\ )$$

For the computation we take a bounded domain Ω, and the potential vector must satisfy suitable properties on the boundary of Ω (see fig. 1). On AD = Γ_1 we have natural symmetry condition, i.e. $\frac{\partial A_3}{\partial n} = 0$ (flux lines cross orthogonally this line), and on $\Gamma_o = \partial\Omega-\Gamma_1$ we have homogeneous Dirichlet condition (no flux lines cross this boundary Γ_o).

Let us define the functional space $\mathcal{V}$ by

(2.4) $\mathcal{V} = \{v, v\in L^2(\Omega), \frac{\partial v}{\partial x_i}\in L^2(\Omega), v|_{\Gamma_o} = 0\}$.

It is easy to see that with the norm

(2.5) $v \to \|v\|_{\mathcal{V}} = \int_\Omega |\nabla v|^2 dx$

$\mathcal{V}$ is an Hilbert space, and the magnetostatic problem can be formulated as an optimisation problem in the following way :

$$(2.6)\quad \begin{cases} \text{Find } A\in\mathcal{V} \text{ such that} \\ \mathfrak{J}(A) \le \mathfrak{J}(v) \text{ for every } v\in\mathcal{V} \\ \text{where } \mathfrak{J} \text{ is given by} \end{cases}$$

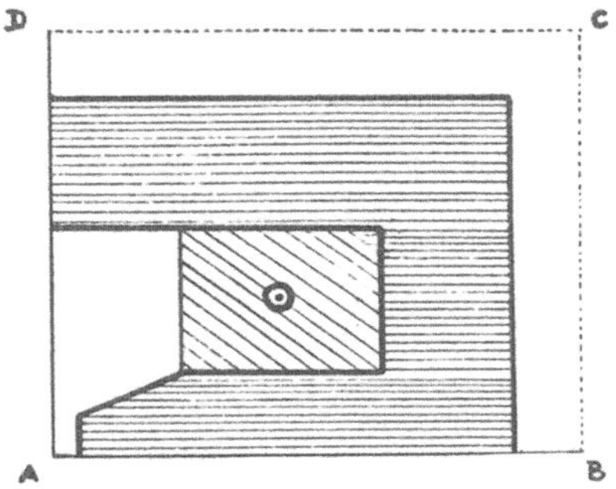

Figure 1

(2.7) $\mathcal{F}(v) = \frac{1}{2}\int_\Omega \Psi(x,|\nabla v|^2)dx - \int_\Omega \mu_o jv\ dx$

with Ψ defined by

(2.8) $\begin{cases} \dfrac{\partial\Psi}{\partial|\vec{B}|^2}(x,|\vec{B}|^2) = \nu(x,|\vec{B}|^2) \\ \Psi(x,o) = 0 \end{cases}$

The optimization problem (2.6) has a unique solution (see R. GLOWINSKI - A. MARROCCO [2]) characterized by the variational formulation

(2.9) $\begin{cases} \int_\Omega \nu(x,|\nabla A|^2)\nabla A\cdot\nabla v\ dx - \int_\Omega \mu_o jv\ dx = 0 \quad \forall v\in\mathcal{V} \\ A\in\mathcal{V} \end{cases}$

For the finite element approximation the variational formulation (2.9) is used. As usual we define a triangulation $\mathcal{T}_h$ on the set Ω (see for example fig. 2 for an initial triangulation).
The functional space $\mathcal{V}$ (2.4) is approximated by $\mathcal{V}_{oh}$

(2.10) $\mathcal{V}_{oh} = \{v_h | v_h \in \mathcal{C}^o(\Omega_h), d^o v_h \le 1 \text{ on } T, T\in\mathcal{T}_h, v_h = 0 \text{ on } \Gamma_{oh}\}$

where Γ_{oh} is the approximation of Γ_o
and we can express the approximated problem by

Find $A_h \in \mathcal{V}_{oh}$ such that

(2.11) $\mathcal{F}(A_h) \le \mathcal{F}(v_h)$ for every $v_h \in \mathcal{V}_{oh}$

where $\mathcal{F}$ is given by (2.7)

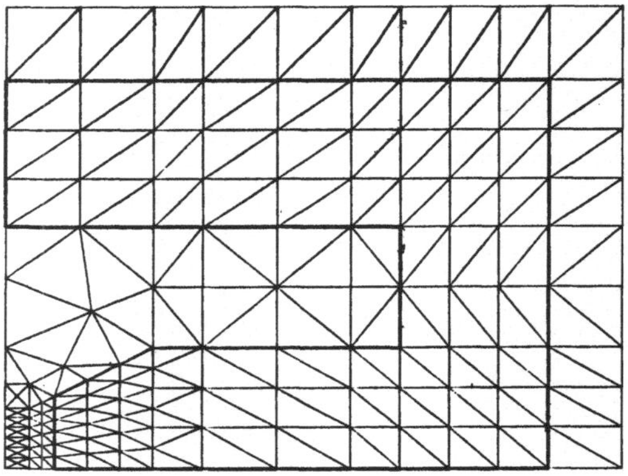

Figure 2

If $\omega_j(x)$, j=1,2...N is a basis of the finite dimensional space $\mathcal{V}_{oh}$, the discrete potential vector can be expressed as

$$(2.12) \qquad A_h(x) = \sum_{i=1}^{N} A_i \omega_i(x)$$

and is solution of the variational non-linear system

$$(2.13) \qquad \begin{cases} \int_\Omega \nu(x, |\nabla A_h|^2) \nabla A_h \cdot \nabla \omega_j \, dx - \int_\Omega \mu_o j \omega_j dx = 0 \\ j=1,2...N \end{cases}$$

II - STATEMENT OF THE OPTIMUM DESIGN PROBLEM (CONTINUOUS CASE)

Ω is an open set of $\mathbb{R}^n$ (n=2 in our case), and j and E_d are two given functions of $L^2(\Omega)$. Let F be the ferrous region, C the copper region and $G=\Omega-F\cup C$.
The potential vector A_F (which depends on the shape of ferrous region F), is solution of the non-linear elliptic variational equality

$$(3.1) \qquad \begin{cases} \int_\Omega \nu(x, |\nabla A_F|^2) \nabla A_F \cdot \nabla \omega \, dx = \int_\Omega \mu_o j \omega \quad dx \quad \forall \omega \in \mathcal{V} \\ A_F \in \mathcal{V} \end{cases}$$

If D is some open subset of G, we wish to solve the problem

$$(3.2) \qquad \min_{F \in \mathcal{F}} J(F)$$

where

(3.3) $J(F) = \int_D |\nabla A_F - E_d|^2 dx$

and $\mathfrak{F}$ is the set of admissible shapes for the ferrous region. For (3.2) to be well defined (with fixed copper region), we must have

(3.4) $\mathfrak{F} = \{F | F \subset \Omega,\ F \cap C = \emptyset\}$

Strictly speaking (3.2) is an optimal control problem for the distributed parameter system (3.1), where the control appears in the coefficient of the P.D.E. as a discontinuity of ν. Furthermore it should be pointed out that problem (3.2) is very similar to an optimum design problem (with Neumann condition on the unknown boundary). Now let us outline how such problems can be solved by gradient techniques. More details can be found in O. PIRONNEAU [1].
Let F' be obtained from F by

(3.5) $\partial F' = \{x+\alpha(x)\ | x \in \partial F\}$

where α is a given vector valued function (usually one takes $\vec{\alpha}(x) = \beta(x)\vec{n}(x)$, where $\vec{n}$ is the normal to ∂F).
We must be able to evaluate the first order term in α of the variation

$$\delta J = J(F') - J(F)$$

For the sake of clarity let us assume that D does not depend upon α from (3.3) with $\delta A_F = A_{F'} - A_F$

(3.6) $\delta J = 2\int_D (\nabla A_F - E_d)\nabla\delta A_F dx + o(\delta A_F)$

and from (3.1) with $\delta\nu = \nu(x,|\nabla A_{F'}|^2) - \nu(x,|\nabla A_F|^2)$

(3.7) $$\begin{cases} \int_\Omega [\nu(x,|\nabla A_F|^2)\nabla\delta A_F \cdot \nabla\omega + \delta\nu\nabla A_F \cdot \nabla\omega] dx = o(\delta A_F) \\ \forall \omega \in \mathcal{V} \end{cases}$$

Now let us give the first order term for $\delta\nu$ evaluation (see fig. 3)

in $F' \cap F$ $\delta\nu = 2\dot{\nu}(x,|\nabla A_F|^2)\nabla A_F \cdot \nabla\delta A_F$
in $G' \cap G$ $\delta\nu = 0$
in $F' \cap G$ $\delta\nu = \nu(x,|\nabla A_{F'}|^2) - 1$
in $F \cap G'$ $\delta\nu = 1 - \nu(x,|\nabla A_F|^2)$

where $\dot{\nu}(x,|\nabla A|^2 = \frac{\partial}{\partial|\nabla A|^2}(\nu(x,|\nabla A|^2)$

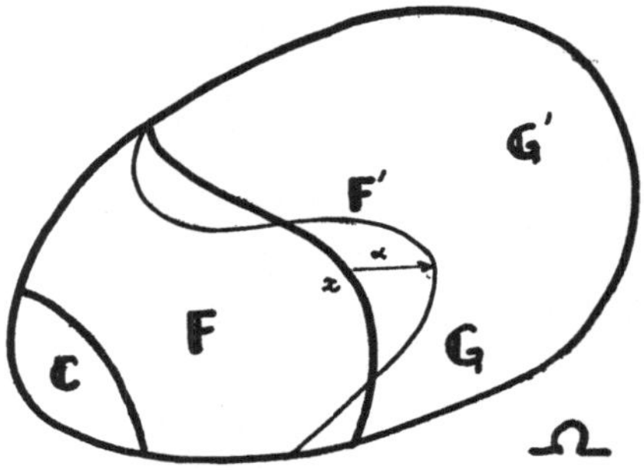

Figure 3

Therefore (3.7) becomes

$$
(3.8)\quad \begin{cases} \int_{\Omega} [\nu(x,|\nabla A_F|^2)\nabla\delta A_F\cdot\nabla\omega+2\dot{\nu}(x,|\nabla A_F|^2)\nabla A_F\cdot\nabla\delta A_F \nabla A_F\cdot\nabla\omega]dx \\ + \int_{F'\cap G} [\nu(x,|\nabla A_{F'}|^2)-1]\ \nabla A_F\cdot\nabla\omega\ dx \\ + \int_{F\cap G'} [1-\nu(x,|\nabla A_F|^2)]\nabla A_F\cdot\nabla\omega dx = o(\delta A_F) \qquad \forall\omega\in\mathcal{V} \end{cases}
$$

If $\alpha(x) \ll 1$ the last two integrals in (3.8) can be approximated by the surface integral

$$
(3.9)\quad \int_{\partial F} [\nu(x,|\nabla A_F|^2)-1]\ \nabla A_F\cdot\nabla\omega\vec{\alpha}(x)\cdot\vec{n}(x)ds + o(\alpha)
$$

Therefore if we define P_F as the solution in $\mathcal{V}$ of

$$
(3.10)\quad \begin{cases} \int_{\Omega} [\nu(x,|\nabla A_F|^2)\nabla P_F\cdot\nabla\omega+2\dot{\nu}(x,|\nabla A_F|^2)\nabla A_F\cdot\nabla P_F \nabla A_F\cdot\nabla\omega]\ dx = \\ 2\int_D (\nabla A_F-E_d)\cdot\nabla\omega dx \qquad , \forall\omega\in\mathcal{V} \end{cases}
$$

Then by letting $\omega = \delta A_F$ in (3.10) and $\omega = P_F$ in (3.8) we find from (3.6), (3.8), (3.9) that

$$
(3.11)\quad \delta J = \int_{\partial F} (\nu(x,|\nabla A_F|^2)-1)\nabla A_F\cdot\nabla P_F\vec{\alpha}(x)\cdot\vec{n}(x)dx + o(\alpha)
$$

Now it appears from (3.11) that by choosing $\alpha(x)$ such that

$$
(3.12)\quad \vec{\alpha}(x)\cdot\vec{n}(x) = -\rho(\nu(x,|\nabla A_F|^2)-1)\nabla A_F\cdot\nabla P_{F|\partial F}
$$

(where ρ is a small positive parameter), we can decrease the criterion J by

$$\delta J = -\rho \int_{\partial F} [\nu(x,|\nabla A_F|^2)-1]^2 \, [\nabla A_F \cdot \nabla P_F]^2 \, ds \tag{3.13}$$

This is the essence of the gradient method :

0 - choose F_o, ρ and set $i=0$

1 - compute A_{F_i}, P_{F_i} from (3.1), (3.10)

2 - compute $\beta_i = -[\nu(x,|\nabla A_{F_i}|^2)-1]\nabla A_{F_i} \cdot \nabla P_{F_i}\Big|_{\partial F_i}$

3 - set $\partial F_{i+1} = \{x+\rho\beta_i(x)n(x) \,|\, x \in \partial F_i\}$

set $i=i+1$ and go back to 1.

IV - OPTIMUM DESIGN WITH FINITE ELEMENTS

The discrete vector potential $A_h = \sum_{i=1}^{N} A_i \omega_i$ is solution of

$$\int_\Omega \nu(x,|\nabla A_h|^2)\nabla A_h \nabla \omega_\ell \, dx = \int_\Omega \mu_o j \omega_\ell \, dx \qquad \ell=1,2,\ldots N \tag{4.1}$$

As in the continuous case we search for Ω such that ∇A_h is as close as possible to E_d in a subdomain D of Ω. We define

$$J_h(\mathcal{T}_h) = \int_D |\nabla A_h - E_d|^2 dx \tag{4.2}$$

and we wish to find the coordinates of the nodes of $\mathcal{T}_h$ <u>such that</u> $J_h(\mathcal{T}_h)$ <u>is minimum</u>. Thus if χ is the set of admissible position of the nodes $X = \{x_k\}$, $k=1,2\ldots N$, then our problem is

$$\min_{X\in\chi} J_h(\mathcal{T}_h) \tag{4.3}$$

In order to apply a gradient method, we must compute

$$\begin{cases} \partial_{\alpha_k} J_h(\mathcal{T}_h) = \lim\limits_{\|\alpha_k\|\to 0} (J_h(\mathcal{T}_h') - J_h(\mathcal{T}_h)) / \|\alpha_k\| \\ \\ \text{for } k=1,2\ldots N \end{cases} \tag{4.4}$$

where $\mathcal{T}_h'$ is the triangulation obtained from $\mathcal{T}_h$ by <u>moving the</u> k^{th} <u>node</u> x_k <u>into the position</u> $x_k+\alpha_k$.

It is convenient to assume that

(4.5) $$D = \bigcup_{j \in J} T_j \ .$$

Applying the procedure used to derive descent direction vector in the continuous case, we obtain by working on the discrete formulation, the following proposition. Assuming that E_d is piecewise constant on $\mathcal{T}_h$ and that j=0 in T_j for all j such that $x_k \in T_j$, if $\mathcal{T}'_h$ is obtained from $\mathcal{T}_h$ by moving the kth node from x_k to $x_k+\alpha_k$, then we have

(4.6)
$$\left\{\begin{aligned} J_h(\mathcal{T}'_h)-J_h(\mathcal{T}_h) &= \int_\Omega \nu\nabla A_H\cdot\tilde{\alpha}_h\nabla\omega_k\cdot\nabla P_h dx + \int_\Omega \nu\nabla A_h\cdot\nabla\omega_k\nabla P_h\cdot\tilde{\alpha}_k dx \\ &- \int_\Omega \nu\nabla A_h\cdot\nabla P_h\nabla\omega_k\cdot\tilde{\alpha}_k dx + \int_\Omega 2\dot{\nu}\nabla A_h\cdot\nabla\omega_k\nabla A_h\cdot\tilde{\alpha}_k\nabla A_h\cdot\nabla P_h dx \\ &+ \int_D |\nabla A_h - E_d|^2\nabla\omega_k\cdot\tilde{\alpha}_k dx \\ &- \int_D 2(\nabla A_h - E_d)\cdot\nabla\omega_k\nabla A_h\cdot\tilde{\alpha}_k dx \quad + o(\alpha_k) \end{aligned}\right.$$

where P_h is the adjoint state and is given by (4.7).
$P_h \in \mathcal{V}_{oh}$ solution of

(4.7)
$$\left\{\begin{aligned} &\int_\Omega [\nu(x,|\nabla A_h|^2)\nabla\omega_\ell\cdot\nabla P_h + 2\dot{\nu}(x,|\nabla A_h|^2)\nabla A_h\cdot\nabla\omega_\ell\nabla A_h\cdot\nabla P_h]\, dx \\ &= \int_\Omega 2(\nabla A_h - E_d)\nabla\omega_\ell\, dx \qquad \ell=1,2\ldots N \end{aligned}\right.$$

V - NUMERICAL EXPERIMENT

5.1. Numerical experiment with fixed criterion domain

Example 1 : The current density j = 5×10^6 MKSA (even with this current density value the magnetostatic problem is non-linear).

The parameter E_d in the criterion is

E_d = (0,1.3)i.e. we want to have in D a uniform flux density B = (1.3,0) in a part D of the air gap (independent of the ferrous boundary F).

The starting value of the criterion is

$$J_o = 0.6116 \times 10^{-5}$$

and after 9 iterations in the optimization process (9 gradient steps) the criterion is

$$J_9 = 0.34 \times 10^{-5}.$$

In figure 4 we can see the initial magnetostatic state and in Fig. 5 the magnetostatic state and air gap shape after optimization.

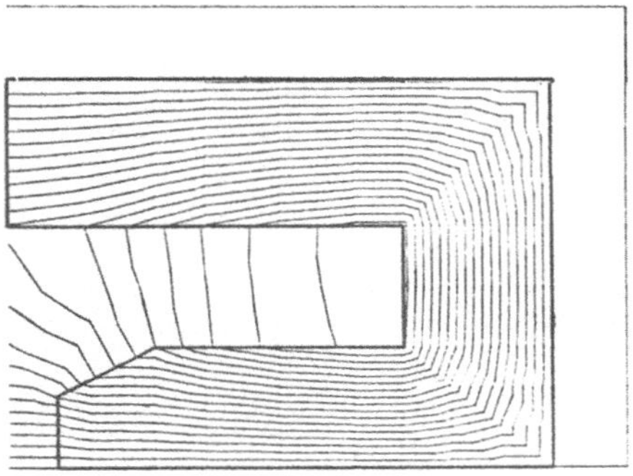

Figure 4

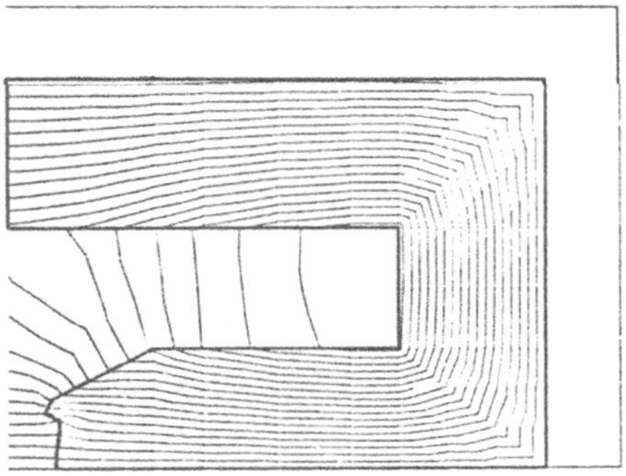

Figure 5

5.2. Numerical experiments with MOVING CRITERION DOMAIN

We can see in fig. 6 the initial domain D where the criterion J is evaluated. As the boundary between iron and air can move, the set D is a moving domain.

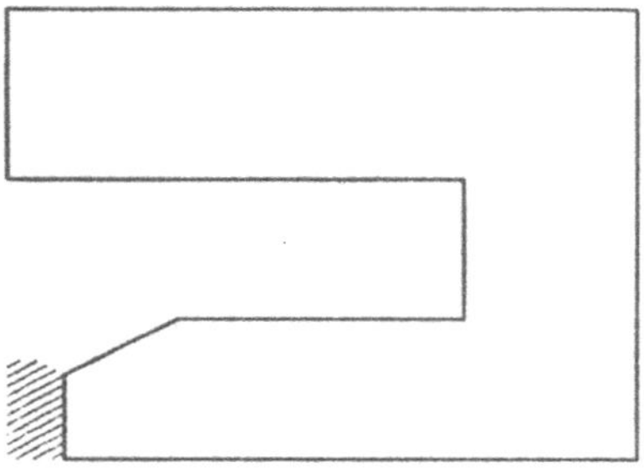

Figure 6

Example 2 : We take $j = 20 \times 10^6$ MKSA and

$$E_d = (0,\ 1.3)\ .$$

The initial value of the criterion is

$$J_o = 0.2724 \times 10^{-3}$$

and we can reduce the value to

$$J_{56} = 0.6785 \times 10^{-6}$$

For this example the result is obtained with 3 runs in the following way. The first run is made as in the previous examples. We perform 16 iterations and the final criterion value is

$$J_{16} = 0.1136 \times 10^{-4}$$

If we look at air-gap geometry, we observe an "oscillating" boundary (see fig. 7), for which we substitute a straight boundary and obtain a new geometry (fig. 8). The new value of the criterion after modification is

$$J_{16_*} = 0.9789 \times 10^{-5} \;;$$

in the second run we perform 20 more iterations starting with this last initial state, and we obtain

$$J_{36} = 0.18465 \times 10^{-5}$$

We make a new manual fitting of the oscillating boundary and obtain a new geometry. The criterion value is then

$$J_{36_*} = 0.3607 \times 10^{-5}$$

In the third run we make 20 new iterations and obtain

$$J_{56} = 0.6785 \times 10^{-6}$$

and the magnetostatic state is given in fig. 9

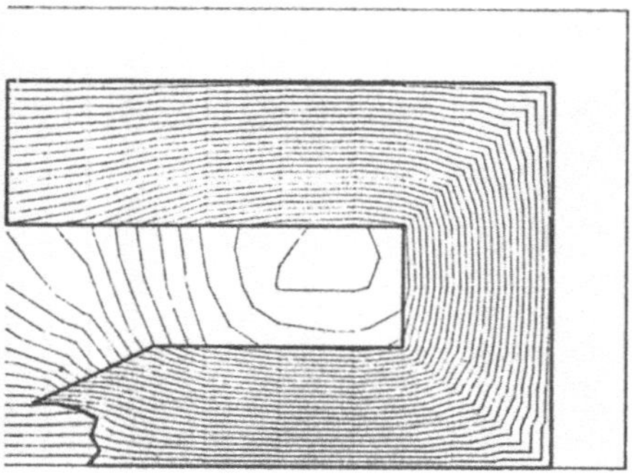

Figure 7

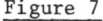

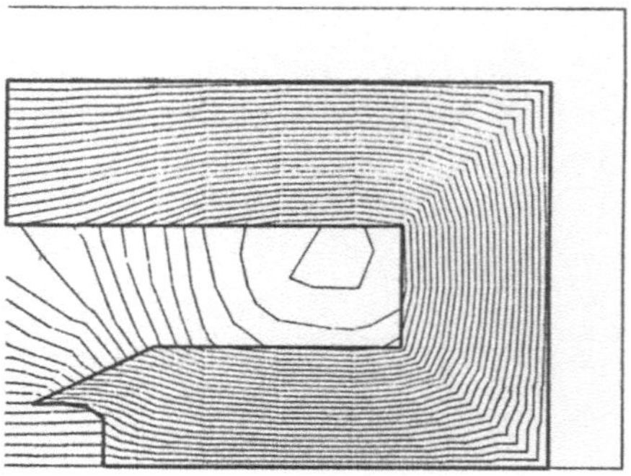

Figure 8

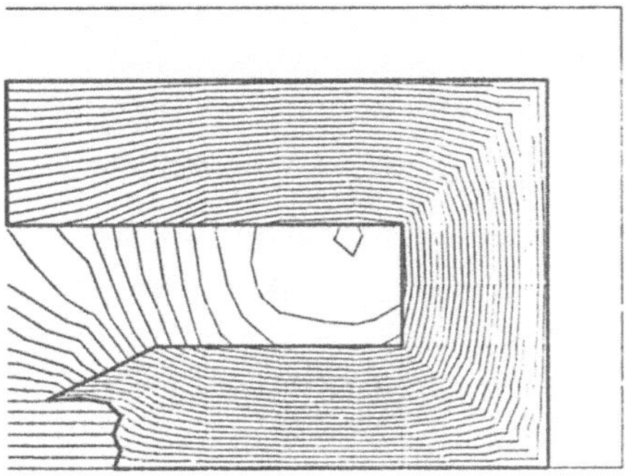

Figure 9

5.3. REMARKS

Thus, once the state equation is mastered, it takes only an additional "automatic" triangulation subroutine to optimize the design. However, it should be pointed out that the topology of the answer must be provided.

Let us also say that if the automatic triangulation subroutine is found to be too expensive to produce, one may compute the gradient vector only. Engineers find it to give very valuable information for the improvement of their design.

REFERENCES

[1] O. PIRONNEAU, Sur les problèmes d'optimisation de structure en mécanique des fluides. Thèse de Doctorat Paris VI, 1976.

[2] R. GLOWINSKI - A. MARROCCO, Analyse numérique du champ magnétique d'un alternateur par éléments finis et surrelaxation ponctuelle non linéaire, Computer methods in applied mechanics and engineering, Vol. 3, N° 1, Janvier 1974.

[3] R. GLOWINSKI - A. MARROCCO, Finite element approximation and iterative methods of solution for 2-D non linear magnetostatic problems. Proceedings of COMPUMAG conference, Oxford 1976, pp. 112-125.

[4] A. MARROCCO - O. PIRONNEAU, Optimum design with Lagrangian finite element : design of an electromagnet, Rapport Laboria N° 251, Août 1977.

FINITE ELEMENTS APPROXIMATION IN STATE IDENTIFICATION OF LARGE SCALE LINEAR SPACE-DISTRIBUTED SYSTEMS

Andrzej Masłowski

Institute of Applied Mathematics,
Physics & Chemistry
Technical University of Białystok
Białystok, Poland

1. INTRODUCTION

During the past decade considerable attention has been given the development of unified theoretical approach for state approximation of the systems in the case of incomplete information, particularly distributed parameter systems [1] ÷ [4] . This paper presents the investigational technique for state identification for some class of large-scale linear space-distributed system with the use finite elements theory, invariant imbedding and multilevel optimization techniques. Incomplete knowledge of the system is specified by unknown vectors which include uncertainty of the mathematical description as well as disturbance acting on the system and output observation. Disturbances can be considered in the spatial domain and on the its boundary, but no statistical assumptions are made concerning its characteristics. The error criterion utilized is the classical least squares formulation. It can be noted that under special hypothesis concerning the disturbances, namely, they be purely random with Gaussian probability density, above classical criterion coincides with the criterion results from extending of maximum-likelihood approach. Using the system dynamics, the output transformation, the error criterion and finite elements, the minimization of the weighted squared index is transformrd into large scale dynamic optimization problem in time domain. In the case of low dimensionality the sequential identification algorithm is generated by variational and invariant imbedding methods. In the case of very large dimensionality the problem is treated by multilevel optimization technique.

2. STATE IDENTIFICATION PROBLEM

We shall consider space-distributed system described by the following dynamic equation:

$$\frac{\partial}{\partial t}U(t,X) = \mathcal{L}(t,X)U(t,X) + F_D(t,X), \qquad X\in\Omega,\ t\in[t_0,T], \tag{1}$$

$$\mathcal{B}(t,X)U(t,X) + F_{DB}(t,X) = 0, \qquad X\in\partial\Omega,\ t\in[t_0,T], \tag{2}$$

$$U(t_0,X) = U_0(X) + F_0(X), \qquad X\in\bar{\Omega}, \tag{3}$$

and by the observation equation:

$$Z(t,X) = \mathcal{H}(t,X)U(t,X) + F_0(t,X), \qquad X\in\bar{\Omega},\ t\in[t_0,T] \tag{4}$$

where (t,X) - point in the space-time domain $[t_0,T]\times\bar{\Omega}$, $\bar{\Omega}=\Omega\cup\partial\Omega$, $U(t,X)$ - state vector, $\mathcal{L}(t,X)$, $\mathcal{B}(t,X)$ - linear partial differential space-time matrix operators, $U_0(X)$ - vector of the a priori estimate of the state at $t=t_0$, $Z(t,X)$ - observation vector, $\mathcal{H}(t,X)$ - linear space-time matrix operator which relates the state $U(t,X)$ to the observation $Z(t,X)$, and $F_D(t,X)$, $F_{DB}(t,X)$, $F_0(X)$, $F_0(t,X)$ - unknown error vectors, including uncertainty of the mathematical description of the system dynamics, boundary conditions, initial conditions and system observations, respectively.

The criterion used to the best state identification is choosen to be weighted least square quality index in the form:

$$\beta = \int_{\bar{\Omega}} \|F_0(X)\|^2_{P_0} dX + \int_{\Omega}\int_{t_0}^{T} \|F_D(t,X)\|^2_{Q_D} dt\,dX + \int_{\partial\Omega}\int_{t_0}^{T} \|F_{DB}(t,X)\|^2_{Q_{DB}} dt\,dX + \int_{\bar{\Omega}}\int_{t_0}^{T} \|F_0(t,X)\|^2_{R_0} dt\,dX, \tag{5}$$

where P_0, Q_D, Q_{DB}, R_0 are diagonal weighted matrices and $\|(\cdot)\|^2$ is appropriate squared metric.

Approximate state of the system, optimal in the sense of (5), we obtain minimizing β with respect to $U(t,X)$, subject to the constraints equations, Eq.(1) to Eq.(4). Because no statistical assumptions are made, this problem coincídes with deterministic optimization problem in space-time domain.

3. DECOMPOSITION BY FINITE ELEMENTS

The main question in effective solution of identification problem in question is mostly decomposition of the large scale space-distributed system into independent subsystems. Here, one can apply the decomposition method based on finite elements theory [5] . Making use of this theory, we will consider a finite element model of the domain $\bar{\Omega}$ which is now the union of E closed and bounded subdomains $\bar{\Omega}_e$, ($\bar{\Omega}_e = \Omega_e \cup \partial\Omega_e$, that is:

$$\bar{\Omega} = \bigcup_{e=1}^{E} \bar{\Omega}_e , \qquad \bar{\Omega}_e \cap \bar{\Omega}_f = \emptyset, \quad e \neq f \tag{6}$$

where $\emptyset$ is the null set. The finite elements $\bar{\Omega}_e$ are connected all together at a number G of nodal points labeled X^{Δ}, $\Delta = 1,2,\ldots G$. Locally, the nodal points belonging to $\bar{\Omega}_e$ are labeled by X_e^N, N=1, 2,...N_e, N_e is the number of all nodal points in $\bar{\Omega}_e$. Assuming the nodal compatibility conditions are satisfied, the connectivity and decomposition are established by respective mappings:

$$X^{\Delta} = \sum_{N=1}^{N_e} \overset{e}{\Lambda}{}_N^{\Delta} X_e^N , \quad (e \text{ fixed}), \quad X_e^N = \sum_{\Delta=1}^{G} \overset{e}{\Omega}{}_{\Delta}^{N} X^{\Delta} , \tag{7}$$

where

$$\overset{e}{\Lambda}{}_N^{\Delta} = \begin{cases} 1 & \text{if node } \Delta \text{ of the connected model } \bar{\Omega} \text{ is coincident with node N of elements } \bar{\Omega}_e , \\ 0 & \text{if otherwise,} \end{cases}$$

and $\overset{e}{\Omega}{}_{\Delta}^{N}$ is simply the transpose of $\overset{e}{\Lambda}{}_N^{\Delta}$.

Next we consider the construction of the semidiscrete model for the state vector i'th component $U_i(t,X)$, i=1,2,...p. If we used so called finite element first order representation of $U_i(t,X)$, then we obtain:

$$U_i(t,X) \cong \bigcup_{e=1}^{E} U_{ie}(t,X), \qquad U_{ie}(t,X) = \begin{cases} 0 & \text{if } X \notin \bar{\Omega}_e, \text{ for all t,} \\ \sum_{N=1}^{N_{ie}} a_{ie}^N(t) \psi_{iN}^{e}(X) & \text{in otherwise} \end{cases} \tag{8}$$

where $a_{ie}^N(t)$ are continuous time-dependent nodal coefficients and $\psi_{iN}^{e}(t)$ are local interpolation functions corresponding to the $\bar{\Omega}_e$, which are defined so as to have the properties:

$$\begin{aligned} \psi_{iN}^{e}(X) &\equiv 0, & X &\notin \bar{\Omega}_e, \\ \psi_{iN}^{e}(X^M) &= \delta_N^M, & X^M &\in \bar{\Omega}_e, \end{aligned} \qquad i=1,2,\ldots p \tag{9}$$

where δ_N^M is the Kronecker delta, M,N=1,2,...N_{ie}.
Globally, we can write:

$$U_i(t,X) \cong \sum_{\Delta=1}^{G} A_i^{\Delta}(t) \varphi_{i\Delta}(X) , \tag{10}$$

where the following relations are true:

$$\varphi_{i\Delta}(X)=\bigcup_{e=1}^{E}\sum_{N=1}^{N_{ie}}\overset{e}{\Omega}{}^{N}_{i\Delta}\,\overset{e}{\psi}_{iN}(X),\qquad \overset{e}{a}{}^{N}_{ie}(t)=\sum_{\Delta=1}^{G}\overset{e}{\Omega}{}^{N}_{i\Delta}A_i^{\Delta}(t),$$
$$U_i(t,X^{\Delta})=A_i^{\Delta}(t),\qquad U_i(t,X_e^N)=a^N_{ie}(t),\qquad \varphi_{i\Delta}(X^{\Gamma})=\delta_{\Delta}^{\Gamma}. \tag{11}$$

Making use of above properties of the finite element approximation we can formulate decomposed relations corresponding to the state identification problem. The quality index - functional β, Eq.(5) - can be now replaced by the sum of integrals as follows / taking into account Eq.(1) to Eq.(4) /:

$$\beta=\sum_{e=1}^{E}\Big\{\int_{\bar{\Omega}_e}\|U(t,X)-U_o(X)\|^2_{P_0}dX+\int_{\Omega_e}\int_{t_0}^{T}\|\frac{\partial}{\partial t}U(t,X)-\mathcal{L}(t,X)U(t,X)\|^2_{Q_D}dt\,dX+$$
$$+\int_{\partial\Omega_e}\int_{t_0}^{T}\|\mathcal{B}(t,X)U(t,X)\|^2_{Q_{DB}}dt\,dX+\int_{\bar{\Omega}_e}\int_{t_0}^{T}\|Z(t,X)-\mathcal{H}(t,X)U(t,X)\|^2_{R_0}dt\,dX\Big\}. \tag{12}$$

Substituting Eq. (10) into above equation, and integrating over spatial domains, we have:

$$\beta\cong\beta'=\|A(t_o)-\Gamma_o\|^2_{\alpha_o}+\int_{t_o}^{T}[\,\|f_D(t)\|^2_{\alpha_D}+\|\Gamma_R(t)-A(t)\|^2_{\xi_R}]dt+\varrho, \tag{13}$$

with:

$$f_D(t)=\frac{d}{dt}A(t)-\Gamma_D(t)A(t), \tag{14}$$

where global nodal coefficients vector is defined as:

$$A(t)=[\,A_1^{Tr}(t),\ldots A_i^{Tr}(t),\ldots A_p^{Tr}(t)]^{Tr},$$
$$A_i^{Tr}(t)=[\,A_i^{1}(t),\ldots A_i^{\Delta}(t),\ldots A_i^{G}(t)],$$

and other symbols are defined as:

$$\xi_R(t)=\gamma_D(t)+\gamma_{DB}(t)+\gamma_R(t)-\beta_D^{Tr}(t)[\alpha_D^{-1}(t)]^{Tr}\beta_D(t),$$

$$\Gamma_o=\alpha_o^{-1}\beta_o,\qquad \Gamma_D(t)=\alpha_D^{-1}(t)\beta_D(t),\qquad \Gamma_R(t)=\xi_R^{-1}(t)\beta_R(t),$$

$$\varrho=\gamma_o-\beta_o^{Tr}[\alpha_o^{-1}]^{Tr}\beta_o+\int_{t_o}^{T}[\alpha_R(t)-\beta_R^{Tr}(t)[\xi_R^{-1}(t)]^{Tr}\beta_R(t)]\,dt,$$

$$\alpha_0 = \sum_{e=1}^{E} \mathrm{diag}\Big[\overset{e}{\Omega}_1 \Big[\int_{\bar{\Omega}_e} \overset{e}{\phi}_1(X) P_{01} \overset{e}{\phi}{}_1^{Tr}(X)\,dX \Big] \overset{e}{\Lambda}_1, \ldots \overset{e}{\Omega}_p \Big[\int_{\bar{\Omega}_e} \overset{e}{\phi}_p(X) P_{0p} \overset{e}{\phi}{}_p^{Tr}(X)\,dX \Big] \overset{e}{\Lambda}_p \Big],$$

$$\beta_0 = \sum_{e=1}^{E} \Big[\overset{e}{\Lambda}_1 \Big[\int_{\bar{\Omega}_e} \overset{e}{\phi}{}_1^{Tr}(X) P_{01} U_{01}(X)\,dX \Big], \ldots \overset{e}{\Lambda}_p \Big[\int_{\bar{\Omega}_e} \overset{e}{\phi}{}_p^{Tr}(X) P_{0p} U_{0p}(X)\,dX \Big] \Big]^{Tr},$$

$$\gamma_0 = \sum_{e=1}^{E} \int_{\bar{\Omega}_e} U_0^{Tr}(X) P_0 U_0(X)\,dX ,$$

$$\alpha_D(t) = \sum_{e=1}^{E} \mathrm{diag}\Big[\overset{e}{\Omega}_1 \Big[\int_{\Omega_e} \overset{e}{\phi}_1(X) Q_{D1} \overset{e}{\phi}{}_1^{Tr}(X)\,dX \Big] \overset{e}{\Lambda}_1, \ldots \overset{e}{\Omega}_p \Big[\int_{\Omega_e} \overset{e}{\phi}_p(X) Q_{Dp} \overset{e}{\phi}{}_p^{Tr}(X)\,dX \Big] \overset{e}{\Lambda}_p \Big],$$

$$\beta_R(t) = \sum_{e=1}^{E} \sum_{i=1}^{r} \Big[\Big[\int_{\bar{\Omega}_e} Z_i(t,X) R_{0i} \mathcal{K}_{i1} \overset{e}{\phi}{}_1^{Tr}(X)\,dX \Big] \overset{e}{\Lambda}_1, \ldots \Big[\int_{\bar{\Omega}_e} Z_i(t,X) R_{0i} \mathcal{K}_{ip} \overset{e}{\phi}{}_p^{Tr}(X)\,dX \Big] \overset{e}{\Lambda}_p \Big],$$

$$\alpha_R(t) = \sum_{e=1}^{E} \int_{\bar{\Omega}_e} Z^{Tr}(t,X) R_0 Z(t,X)\,dX ,$$

$$\beta_D(t) = \sum_{e=1}^{E} \begin{bmatrix} \overset{e}{\Omega}_1 \Big[\int_{\Omega_e} \overset{e}{\phi}_1(X) Q_{D1} \mathcal{L}_{11} \overset{e}{\phi}{}_1^{Tr}(X)\,dX \Big] \overset{e}{\Lambda}_1, \ldots & \overset{e}{\Omega}_p \Big[\int_{\Omega_e} \overset{e}{\phi}_p(X) Q_{Dp} \mathcal{L}_{1p} \overset{e}{\phi}{}_p^{Tr}(X)\,dX \Big] \overset{e}{\Lambda}_p \\ \vdots & \vdots \\ \overset{e}{\Omega}_p \Big[\int_{\Omega_e} \overset{e}{\phi}_p(X) Q_{Dp} \mathcal{L}_{p1} \overset{e}{\phi}{}_1^{Tr}(X)\,dX \Big] \overset{e}{\Lambda}_1, \ldots & \overset{e}{\Omega}_p \Big[\int_{\Omega_e} \overset{e}{\phi}_p(X) Q_{Dp} \mathcal{L}_{pp} \overset{e}{\phi}{}_p^{Tr}(X)\,dX \Big] \overset{e}{\Lambda}_p \end{bmatrix}$$

$$\gamma_D(t) = \sum_{e=1}^{E} \sum_{i=1}^{p} \begin{bmatrix} \overset{e}{\Omega}_1 \left[\int_{\Omega_e} \mathcal{L}_{i1} \overset{e}{\phi}_1(X) Q_{Di} \mathcal{L}_{i1} \overset{e}{\phi}{}_1^{Tr}(X)\, dX \right] \overset{e}{\Lambda}_1, & \ldots & \overset{e}{\Omega}_1 \left[\int_{\Omega_e} \mathcal{L}_{i1} \overset{e}{\phi}_1(X) Q_{Di} \mathcal{L}_{ip} \overset{e}{\phi}{}_p^{Tr}(X)\, dX \right] \overset{e}{\Lambda}_p \\ \cdot & & \cdot \\ \cdot & & \cdot \\ \cdot & & \cdot \\ \overset{e}{\Omega}_p \left[\int_{\Omega_e} \mathcal{L}_{ip} \overset{e}{\phi}_p(X) Q_{Di} \mathcal{L}_{i1} \overset{e}{\phi}{}_1^{Tr}(X)\, dX \right] \overset{e}{\Lambda}_1, & \ldots & \overset{e}{\Omega}_p \left[\int_{\Omega_e} \mathcal{L}_{ip} \overset{e}{\phi}_p(X) Q_{Di} \mathcal{L}_{ip} \overset{e}{\phi}{}_p^{Tr}(X)\, dX \right] \overset{e}{\Lambda}_p \end{bmatrix}$$

$$\gamma_{DB}(t) = \sum_{e=1}^{E} \sum_{i=1}^{q} \begin{bmatrix} \overset{e}{\Omega}_1 \left[\int_{\partial\Omega_e} \mathcal{B}_{i1} \overset{e}{\phi}_1(X) Q_{DBi} \mathcal{B}_{i1} \overset{e}{\phi}{}_1^{Tr}(X)\, dX \right] \overset{e}{\Lambda}_1, & \ldots & \overset{e}{\Omega}_1 \left[\int_{\partial\Omega_e} \mathcal{B}_{i1} \overset{e}{\phi}_1(X) Q_{DBi} \mathcal{B}_{ip} \overset{e}{\phi}{}_p^{Tr}(X)\, dX \right] \overset{e}{\Lambda}_p \\ \cdot & & \cdot \\ \cdot & & \cdot \\ \cdot & & \cdot \\ \overset{e}{\Omega}_p \left[\int_{\partial\Omega_e} \mathcal{B}_{ip} \overset{e}{\phi}_p(X) Q_{DBi} \mathcal{B}_{i1} \overset{e}{\phi}{}_1^{Tr}(X)\, dX \right] \overset{e}{\Lambda}_1, & \ldots & \overset{e}{\Omega}_p \left[\int_{\partial\Omega_e} \mathcal{B}_{ip} \overset{e}{\phi}_p(X) Q_{DBi} \mathcal{B}_{ip} \overset{e}{\phi}{}_p^{Tr}(X)\, dX \right] \overset{e}{\Lambda}_p \end{bmatrix}$$

$$\gamma_R(t) = \sum_{e=1}^{E} \sum_{i=1}^{r} \begin{bmatrix} \overset{e}{\Omega}_1 \left[\int_{\bar{\Omega}_e} \mathcal{H}_{i1} \overset{e}{\phi}_1(X) R_{0i} \mathcal{H}_{i1} \overset{e}{\phi}{}_1^{Tr}(X)\, dX \right] \overset{e}{\Lambda}_1, & \ldots & \overset{e}{\Omega}_1 \left[\int_{\bar{\Omega}_e} \mathcal{H}_{i1} \overset{e}{\phi}_1(X) R_{0i} \mathcal{H}_{ip} \overset{e}{\phi}{}_p^{Tr}(X)\, dX \right] \overset{e}{\Lambda}_p \\ \cdot & & \cdot \\ \cdot & & \cdot \\ \cdot & & \cdot \\ \overset{e}{\Omega}_p \left[\int_{\bar{\Omega}_e} \mathcal{H}_{ip} \overset{e}{\phi}_p(X) R_{0i} \mathcal{H}_{i1} \overset{e}{\phi}{}_1^{Tr}(X)\, dX \right] \overset{e}{\Lambda}_1, & \ldots & \overset{e}{\Omega}_p \left[\int_{\bar{\Omega}_e} \mathcal{H}_{ip} \overset{e}{\phi}_p(X) R_{0i} \mathcal{H}_{ip} \overset{e}{\phi}{}_p^{Tr}(X)\, dX \right] \overset{e}{\Lambda}_p \end{bmatrix}$$

$$\overset{e}{\phi}_i(X) = [\, \overset{e}{\psi}_{i1}(X), \; \dots \; \overset{e}{\psi}_{iN}(X), \; \dots \; \overset{e}{\psi}_{iN_{ie}}(X) \,]^{Tr},$$

$$\overset{e}{\Omega}_i = \begin{bmatrix} \overset{e}{\Omega}{}^{1}_{i1} & \dots & \overset{e}{\Omega}{}^{N}_{i1} & \dots & \overset{e}{\Omega}{}^{N_{ie}}_{i1} \\ \vdots & & \vdots & & \vdots \\ \overset{e}{\Omega}{}^{1}_{i\Delta} & \dots & \overset{e}{\Omega}{}^{N}_{i\Delta} & \dots & \overset{e}{\Omega}{}^{N_{ie}}_{i\Delta} \\ \vdots & & \vdots & & \vdots \\ \overset{e}{\Omega}{}^{1}_{iG} & \dots & \overset{e}{\Omega}{}^{N}_{iG} & \dots & \overset{e}{\Omega}{}^{N_{ie}}_{iG} \end{bmatrix}, \qquad \overset{e}{\Lambda}_i = [\overset{e}{\Omega}_i]^{Tr},$$

$$i = 1, 2, \dots p.$$

In the above equations sign Tr denotes the transpose, and P_{oj}, U_{oj}, Q_{Dj}, Q_{DBj}, Q_{DBi_q}, R_{Oi_r}, Z_{i_r}, $\mathcal{L}_{i_pj}$, $\mathcal{B}_{i_qj}$, $\mathcal{H}_{i_rj}$, $j, i_p=1,2,\dots p$, $i_q=1,2,\dots q$, $i_r=1,2,\dots r$, are components of P_o, U_o, Q_D, Q_{BD}, R_O, Z, $\mathcal{L}$, $\mathcal{B}$, $\mathcal{H}$, respectively.

State identification problem, decomposed by semidiscrete approximation, can be now treated as large scale dynamic optimization problem, that is, minimization of the functional β', Eq. (13), with respect to A(t) and $f_D(t)$ and with equality constraint, Eq. (14).

4. SEQUENTIAL SOLUTION

In the case of low dimensionality of the vector A(t) we can use classical variational approach to finding minimum of β'. Employing results of calculus of variations and extending some results obtained by Bellman [6] we can find a sequential solution, prefered from on-line computing point of view. Depending on the instant at which the state identification is desired, the problem can be associated with finding of A(t) at a current time or past time which is contained in the interval of observations. In the first case the differential equations of sequential generating of nodal coefficients vector A(T) are obtained in the form:

$$\frac{d}{dt}P(T) = \Gamma_D(T)P(T) + P(T)\Gamma_D(T) + 2P(T)\xi_R(T)P(T) - \frac{1}{2}\alpha_D^{-1}(T), \tag{15}$$

$$\frac{d}{dt}A(T) = \Gamma_D(T)A(T) - 2P(T)\xi_R(T)[\Gamma_R(T) - A(T)], \tag{16}$$

with initial conditions:

$$P(t_o) = \frac{1}{2}\alpha_o^{-1}, \tag{17}$$

$$A(t_o) = \Gamma_o, \tag{18}$$

where P(T) is a matrix and T is now current time $T \geqslant t_o$.
In the case of past time state identification it is required to synthese the state at a fixed instant t_1, where $t_o \leqslant t_1 \leqslant T$. Determination of the nodal coefficients vector $A(t_1,T)$ can be now made in the following manner. At first we are solving Eq.(15) and Eq.(16) with initial conditions Eq.(17) and Eq.(18) till the fixed instant t_1. At this instant the following equations are adjoined to the above equations:

$$\frac{d}{dt}P(t_1,T) = P(t_1,T)\Gamma_D^{Tr}(T) + 2P(t_1,T)\xi_R(T)P(T), \tag{19}$$

$$\frac{d}{dt}A(t_1,T) = -2P(t_1,T)\xi_R(T)[\Gamma_R(T) - A(T)], \tag{20}$$

and solved simultaneously with the conditions:

$$P(t_1,t_1) = P(t_1), \tag{21}$$

$$A(t_1,t_1) = A(t_1). \tag{22}$$

The generalization of this solution when the state has to be identified at a finite set of fixed instants of time $t_1, t_2, \dots t_n$, where $t_o \leqslant t_1 \leqslant t_2 \leqslant \dots \leqslant t_n \leqslant \dots \leqslant T$ is straightforward.

5. LARGE SCALE OPTIMIZATION

In the case of very large dimensionality of vector A(t), in order to formulate a tracteable computational problem, we will assumed the vector A(t), consisting of all coefficients $A_i^\Delta(t)$, $\Delta=1,2,\dots G$, $i=1,2,\dots p$, will be splitting into smaller subvectors as following:

$$A(t) = [A_1^{Tr}(t), \dots A_l^{Tr}(t), \dots A_L^{Tr}(t)]^{Tr}, \tag{23}$$

Next we can express the problem as L independent subproblems introducing a new vectors $S_{ol}(t_o)$, $S_{1l}(t)$, $S_{2l}(t)$, $S_{3l}(t)$ in Eq.(13) and Eq.(14) to achive its independence as follows:

$$\beta' = \sum_{l=1}^{L} \beta'_l = \sum_{l=1}^{L} \Big\{ \| A_l(t_0) - \Gamma_{0l} \|^2_{\alpha_{0l}} + S^{Tr}_{0l}(t_0)[A_l(t_0) - \Gamma_{0l}] + \tag{24}$$

$$+ \int_{t_0}^{T} \Big\{ \| f_{Dl}(t) \|^2_{\alpha_{Dl}} + S^{Tr}_{1l}(t) f_{Dl}(t) + \| \Gamma_{Rl}(t) - A_l(t) \|^2_{\xi_{Rl}} + S^{Tr}_{2l}(t)[\Gamma_{Rl}(t) - A_l(t)] \Big\} dt \Big\}$$

and

$$f_{Dl}(t) = \frac{d}{dt} A_l(t) - \Gamma_{Dl}(t) A_l(t) - S_{3l}(t), \tag{25}$$

where:

$$S^{Tr}_{0l}(t_0) = \sum_{\substack{k=1 \\ k \neq l}}^{L} [A_k(t_0) - \Gamma_{0k}]^{Tr} \alpha_{0k}, \tag{26}$$

$$S^{Tr}_{1l}(t) = \sum_{\substack{k=1 \\ k \neq l}}^{L} f^{Tr}_{Dk}(t) \alpha_{Dk}(t), \tag{27}$$

$$S^{Tr}_{2l}(t) = \sum_{\substack{k=1 \\ k \neq l}}^{L} [\Gamma_{Rk}(t) - A_k(t)]^{Tr} \xi_{Rk}(t), \tag{28}$$

$$S_{3l}(t) = \sum_{\substack{k=1 \\ k = l}}^{L} \Gamma_{Dk}(t) A_k(t), \quad l = 1, 2, \dots L, \tag{29}$$

and where α_{0l}, $\alpha_{Dl}(t)$, $\xi_{Rl}(t)$, $\Gamma_{Dl}(t)$ are submatrices of α_0, $\alpha_D(t)$, ξ_R t , $\Gamma_D(t)$, respectively.

Above lower order mutually independent subproblems can be next solved separatelly if the second-level coordination constraints can be satisfied. With this in view, we can make use one of multilevel optimization technique, for example, Gauss-Seidel Controller method [7], which is in general well suited and fast convergent.

6. CONCLUSIONS

The problem considered here was concerned with the choice of the method of state identification for space-distributed systems. Presented approximate solution of the problem in question, involving partial differential equations, was studed by finite elements decomposition of the spatial domain and the state vector. This method appears particularly attractive and useful for irregular domains and mixed boundary conditions of the system. Sequential identification which is suitable in on-line computations can be obtained by variational approach to optimization and converting an associated two-point boundary value problem to an initial value problem using the method of invariant imbedding. In the case of large dimensionality the problem can be handled by multilevel optimization technique.

Effective realisation of the state identification algorithm is connected with the use of advanced software and hardware developed in classical finite elements technique, sequential as well as multilevel methods. Particularly useful will be application of the new computational techniques developed for main finite elements method, for example, microprogramming and multiprocessing [8] , [9] .

REFERENCES

[1] C.S. Kubrusly, Int. J. Control, Vol. 26, No. 4, 509-535, (1977)

[2] G.A. Philipson, Identification of Distributed Systems, American Elsevier, New York, 1971 .

[3] S.G. Tzafestas, J.M. Nightingale, Proc. IEE, Vol. 116, No. 6, 1085-1093, (1969) .

[4] G. Chavent, in Identification and System Parameter Estimation, / Edited by P. Eykhoff /, North-Holland Press, 1973 .

[5] J.T. Oden, Int. J. num. Meth. Engng, Vol. 1, 205-221, (1969) .

[6] R. Bellman, R. Kalaba, G. Wing, Proc. Nat. Acad. of Sc. of U.S.A., Vol. 46, 1646-1649, (1960) .

[7] D.A. Wismer / Editor /, Optimization Methods for Large Scale Systems, McGraw-Hill, New York, 1971 .

[8] E.I. Field, S.E. Johnson, H. Stralberg, in Structural Mechanics Computer Programs, University Press of Virginia, 1019-1042, (1974) .

[9] A.K. Noor, R.E. Fulton, J. Struct. Div. ASCE, 101, 731-750, (1975) .

MATHEMATICAL MODELLING OF SOCIO-ECONOMIC SYSTEM

A.A.Petrov, I.G.Pospelov

Computing Center of the USSR Academy of Sciences, Moscow

1°. The economic development of a country depends on the pattern of relations of production which determine the mechanism adjusting processes of production and social processes. Therefore it is necessary to develop mathematical description methods of not only the technological, demographical and other processes but the economic adjusting mechanism and the government control of these processes in a whole complex of models of the socio-economic system.

We mark out three levels of descriptions in this model complex.

The first level consists of the descriptions of the processes of production, exhaustion and regeneration of natural resources, technological innovations, the process of good consumption, labour resources forming and social mobility, the demographical processes and so on. These descriptions determine the processes states variable as function of time provided the control parameters are specified as time functions.

The second level consists of the descriptions of the economic mechanism adjusting the first level processes. The economic adjusting mechanism is a result of actions of many persons who control these processes. Within an acting legislation the economic adjusting mechanism operates automatically without any relief. The descriptions determine the control parameters of the processes as functions of their states and the government control parameters. If the control parameters have been fixed the first and the second levels descriptions generate a closed system of equations which describe the states of the processes (i.e. the economy state) at any instant provided the initial states are given.

The third level consists of the descriptions of the government control of the economy. In other words the descriptions determine the economic adjusting mechanism parameters as functions of time or the economy state. These functions simulate the government decisions which reflect interests of organized social groups.

2°. Let us use the above general scheme to develop a fragment of perfect market economy.

The first level. We consider the national economy divided into two sectors. The first sector produces homogeneous goods which are supplied as capital goods and consumer goods. Labour and raw materials are the sector inputs. The second sector produces the raw materials and uses labour and natural resources.

Each sector consists of units producing the homogeneous output. The units differ in the capacity m and the labour input coefficient λ. We assume for simplicity that all the units of the sector have the same capital stock per capacity unit coefficient b_i, material input coefficient a_1 ($a_2 = 0$), rate of capacity degeneration μ_i and natural resources stock per capacity unit coefficient ς_2 ($\varsigma_1 = 0$).

The technological pattern of the sector is described by the capacity distribution function $m_i(t, \lambda)$, $i = 1, 2$, with respect to technological parameter λ. The function is defined for $\lambda \geqslant \nu_i$. The value $\nu_i = \nu_i(t)$ characterizes the sector technical level. The derivative $\frac{d\nu_i}{dt} < 0$ due to the technical innovations process. The sector capacity is

$$M_i(t) = \int_{\nu_i}^{\infty} m_i(t,\lambda)\,d\lambda$$

and the sector total volume of employment is

$$\bar{R}_i^L(t) = \int_{\nu_i}^{\infty} \lambda m_i(t,\lambda)\,d\lambda \,.$$

The distribution function $m_i(t,\lambda)$ satisfies the equation

$$\frac{\partial m_i}{\partial t} = \eta_i(t,\lambda) - \mu_i m_i(t,\lambda) \tag{1}$$

where $\eta_i(t,\lambda)$ is the fresh capacity increment distribution function with respect to the technological parameter λ .

If $R_i^L \left(< \bar{R}_i^L\right)$ is the i -th sector labour demand then the gross output of the sector will be less then its capacity. Obviously, the maximal output will be

$$Y_i(t) = \int_{\nu_i}^{\xi_i} m_i(t,\lambda)\,d\lambda \tag{2}$$

where ξ_i satisfies the equation

$$R_i^L(t) = \int_{\nu_i}^{\xi_i} \lambda m_i(t,\lambda)\,d\lambda \,. \tag{3}$$

Let us introduce new variables

$$m_i(t,\lambda) = M_i(t) h_i(t,\lambda), \quad R_i^L(t) = M_i(t)\, x_i(t), \quad \eta_i(t,\lambda) = I_i(t)\psi_i(t,\lambda)$$

where

$$I_i(t) = \int_{\nu_i}^{\infty} \eta_i(t,\lambda)\,d\lambda$$

is the i -th sector capacity increment rate. Then the equations (1)-(3) lead to

$$\frac{\partial h_i}{\partial t} = \frac{I_i(t)}{M_i(t)}\psi_i(t,\lambda) - \left(\mu_i + \frac{1}{M_i(t)}\frac{dM_i}{dt}\right) h_i(t,\lambda) \tag{4}$$

$$\frac{dM_i}{dt} + h_i(t,\nu_i(t))\frac{d\nu_i}{dt} = I_i(t) - \mu_i M_i(t) \tag{5}$$

$$Y_i(t) = M_i(t) f_i(t, x_i) \tag{M.1}$$

where the function $f_i(t,x_i)$ is defined as

$$f_i(t,x_i) = \int_{\nu_i}^{\xi_i(t,x_i)} h_i(t,\lambda)\,d\lambda\,, \qquad x_i(t) = \int_{\nu_i}^{\xi_i} \lambda h_i(t,\lambda)\,d\lambda \tag{6}$$

The following equality holds

$$\frac{\partial f_i}{\partial x_i} = \frac{1}{\xi_i} \tag{7}$$

It is natural to assume that all the fresh capacity uses the best technology. Therefore $\psi_i(t,\lambda) = \delta_+(\nu_i(t) - \lambda)$ and the function $\delta_+(\cdot)$ is defined by the equations

$\int_{a+0}^{b} g(\theta)\delta_+(\gamma-\theta)\,d\theta = 0$ if $\gamma < a$ and $b \leq \gamma$; $\int_{a+0}^{b} g(\theta)\delta_+(\gamma-\theta)\,d\theta = g(\gamma+0)$ if $a \leq \gamma < b$

where $g(\theta)$ is a piecewise continuous function.

We assume in addition that $h_i(t, \nu_i(t)) = 0$ and

$$\frac{1}{\nu_i}\frac{d\nu_i}{dt} = -\varepsilon_i \frac{I_i(t)}{M_i(t)}, \tag{M.2}$$

with ε_i being a constant, and get from (4)-(6)

$$f_i(t, x_i) = 1 - \left[1 - \frac{1-\varepsilon_i}{\nu_i} x_i\right]^{\frac{1}{1-\varepsilon_i}}, \quad 0 \leq x_i \leq \frac{\nu_i}{1-\varepsilon_i} \tag{M.3}$$

$$\frac{dM_i}{dt} = I_i(t) - \mu_i M_i(t). \tag{M.4}$$

The sectors demand the capital goods amount

$$X_i^I = b_i I_i . \tag{M.5}$$

In addition the first sector demands the raw materials amount

$$X_1^A = a_1 Y_1 \tag{M.6}$$

and the second sector demands the natural resources amount

$$\Psi^N = \varrho_2 I_2 . \tag{M.7}$$

The total amount of natural resources which had been drawn into production is equal to

$$R^N = \varrho_2 M_2 . \tag{M.8}$$

The total volume of natural resources is assumed to be infinite and natural resources supply to be the increasing function of R^N :

$$\tilde{\Psi}^N = \beta\sqrt{R^N}, \tag{M.9}$$

with β being a constant.

Let us neglect the social mobility process and assume that the society consists of two groups - the workers' group and the capital and natural resources owners' group. The workers are wage earners. They use their income to buy the consumer goods. The owners draw interest and get rental. They divide their income into savings and consumer expenditures. The workers try to bring their per capita consumption into a proper correspondence with their per capita free time. As the result we get the following labour supply function

$$\tilde{R}^L = P^A U(\omega^L) \tag{M.10}$$

where P^A is the number of members of the workers' group capable of working,

$$\omega^L = \frac{\Phi^L}{p_1 P} \tag{M.11}$$

is the per capita consumption of the workers' group, P is the number of the worker' group members,

$$\Phi^L = s_1 R_1^L + s_2 R_2^L \tag{M.12}$$

is the income (i.e. the consumer expenditures) of the workers' group, p_i is the goods price, s_i is the wage rate, $i = 1,2$. The function $U(\omega^L)$ is shown in Fig. 1

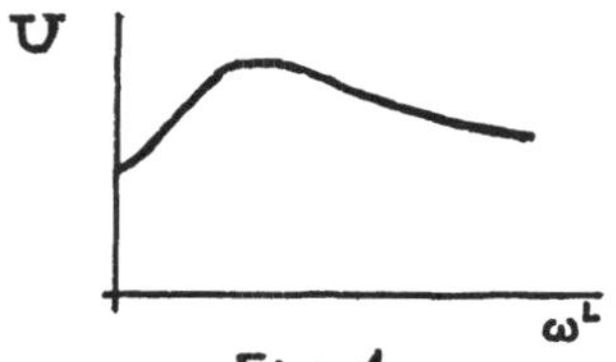

Fig. 1

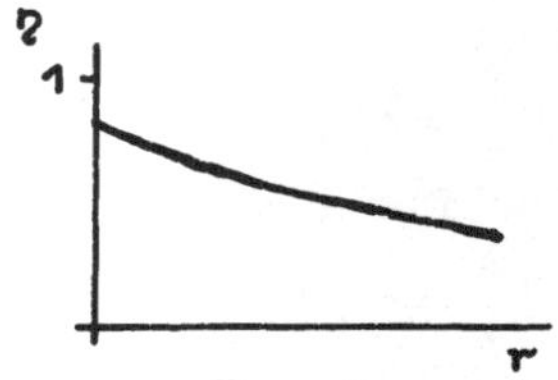

Fig. 2

The labour migration from one sector to another is described by the equations

$$\tilde{R}_i^L = x_i \tilde{R}^L, \quad \frac{dx_i}{dt} = \varkappa \sum_{i \neq j} (u_i - u_j), \quad u_i = \frac{R_i}{\tilde{R}_i^L}, \quad i = 1,2 \tag{M.13}$$

where $\varkappa$ is a constant.

The owners' consumer expenditures Φ^0 are proportional to their income estimated as $p_1 Y_1 + p_2 Y_2 + q \Psi^N$, with q being the rent and r being the interest rate. Hence

$$\Phi^0 = \eta(r)\,(p_1 Y_1 + p_2 Y_2 + q \Psi^N)\,. \tag{M.14}$$

The owners' propensity to consumption $\eta(r)$ depends on the interest rate. The function $\eta(r)$ is shown in Fig. 2.

Instead of considering demographical processes we assume now that

$$P = P_0 e^{\delta t}, \quad P^A = P_0^A e^{\delta t} \tag{M.15}$$

P_0 , P_0^A , δ being constants.

The functions R_i^L , I_i and economic variables p_i, s_i, r, q are the control parameters of the processes described.

<u>The second level</u>. First of all we consider the production management to determine R_i^L and I_i as functions of p_i , s_i , r , q. In the perfect market economy there are lots of small firms maximizing their short-termed profits. Therefore only the profitable firms will

operate at full capacity level in the sectors. In the first sector the profitability condition is $p_1 - a_1 p_2 - \lambda s_1 \geqslant 0$ and in the second sector: $p_2 - \lambda s_2 \geqslant 0$. It enables us to get the following equations of the sectors labour demands from the equation(7)

$$\frac{\partial f_1}{\partial x_1} = \frac{s_1}{p_1 - a_1 p_2}, \qquad \frac{\partial f_2}{\partial x_2} = \frac{s_2}{p_2}. \tag{M.16}$$

Thus R_i^L has been determined in terms of p_i , s_i .

We assume that the i -th sector firms get the short-run bank credit Φ_i^c ensured by their current gains $p_i Y_i$. The credit runs the period τ and the short-run interest rate is r . The whole credit is used to pay for the labour and raw materials inputs and to invest. Thus

$$\Phi_1^c = \frac{p_1 Y_1}{1+r} = s_1 R_1^L + p_2 X_1^A + p_1 X_1^I, \quad \Phi_2^c = \frac{p_2 Y_2}{1+r} = s_2 R_2^L + p_1 X_2^I + q \Psi^N. \tag{M.17}$$

We have determined I_i as the function of p_i , s_i , r , q.

The values of economic variables p_i, s_i, r, q are determined by an adjusting mechanism performance. A mechanism of supply and demand interaction regulates the prices, wage rate, interest and rent in the perfect market economy. Therefore we have to describe the labour market, the natural resources market, the goods market and the capital market. We don't believe that all the markets are in states of equilibrium constantly but we believe that the market prices are at such levels as to satisfy a paid demand.

In <u>the labour market</u> the wage rate s_i is fixed while $R_i^L \leqslant \tilde{R}_i^L$ and rises quickly during the short period Δ_i^s to an equilibrium state level when $R_i^L > \tilde{R}_i^L$. Mathematically, these conditions may be put in the form:

$$\frac{ds_1}{dt} = \frac{1}{\Delta_1^s} \max\left\{0, \left(\frac{\partial f_1}{\partial x_1}\right)_{x_1 = \tilde{x}_1} (p_1 - a_1 p_2) - s_1\right\} \tag{M.18}$$

$$\frac{ds_2}{dt} = \frac{1}{\Delta_2^s} \max\left\{0, \left(\frac{\partial f_2}{\partial x_2}\right)_{x_2 = \tilde{x}_2} p_2 - s_2\right\}, \quad \tilde{x}_i = \frac{\tilde{R}_i^L}{M_i}. \tag{M.19}$$

<u>The natural resources market</u> performs in the same manner:

$$\frac{dq}{dt} = \frac{1}{\Delta^q} \max\left\{0, \frac{\Phi_2^c - s_2 R_2^L}{\tilde{\Psi}^N} - \frac{b_2}{g_2} p_1 - q\right\}. \tag{M.20}$$

In the goods markets the prices oscillations follow the inventory oscillations about some standard level that may be expressed as

$$\frac{dQ_1}{dt}=Y_1-X_1^I-X_2^I-\frac{\Phi^L+\Phi^0}{p_1}, \quad \frac{dQ_2}{dt}=Y_2-X_1^A, \quad \frac{dp_i}{dt}=-\alpha_i Q_i \qquad (M.21)$$

where α_i is a constant.

The capital market is in a state of equilibrium constantly, i.e. the interest rate is at such a level as to equate the capital demand and supply. Consequently

$$\frac{p_1Y_1+p_2Y_2}{1+r}=\Phi-\Phi^0, \quad \Phi=p_1(X_1^I+X_2^I)+p_2X_1^A+q\Psi^N+\Phi^L+\Phi^0. \qquad (M.22)$$

Obviously, Φ is the monetary flow (i.e. the total payments per time unit) in the economy.

To determine Φ it is necessary to consider the monetary circulation. The equation of the bank reserve is

$$\frac{dV}{dt}=D^f(t)+D^0(t)+E.$$

The firms account change is

$$D^f(t)=\sum_{i=1}^{2}\Phi_i^c(t)+\Phi(t-\theta)-[1+r(t-\tau)]\sum_{i=1}^{2}\Phi_i^c(t-\tau)-\Phi^L(t)-p_2X_1^A(t)-p_1(X_1^I(t)+X_2^I(t))-q\Psi^N(t)$$

where θ is the period of monetary circulation. The owners' account change is

$$D^0(t)=[1+r(t-\tau)]\sum_{i=1}^{2}\Phi_i^c(t-\tau)-\sum_{i=1}^{2}\Phi_i^c(t)-\Phi^0(t).$$

The emission E is one of the government control parameters. We fix it by $E=\kappa_1Y_1+\kappa_2Y_2$, with κ_i being a constant.

We believe that the amount V corresponds to the reserve requirement for banks V_m. Assuming $V_m=\kappa\theta\Phi+\text{const}$, κ being a constant, and $\Phi(t-\theta)\approx\Phi(t)-\theta\frac{d\Phi}{dt}$ leads to the equation

$$\frac{d\Phi}{dt}=\pi_1Y_1+\pi_2Y_2, \quad \pi_i=\frac{\kappa_i}{(1+\kappa)\theta} \qquad (M.23)$$

The system of equations (M.1)-(M.23) is closed and enables us to know the economy state at any time if the initial state

$$\nu_i(t_0)=\nu_i^0,\ M_i(t_0)=M_i^0,\ x_i(t_0)=x_i^0,\ s_i(t_0)=s_i^0,\ q(t_0)=q^0,\ Q_i(t_0)=Q_i^0,\ p_i(t_0)=p_i^0,\ \Phi(t_0)=\Phi^0$$

is specified.

3°. Now we discuss some results of the model investigation.

1) If $R_i^L \leq \tilde{R}_i^L$, $\Psi^N < \tilde{\Psi}^N$ the system (M.1)-(M.23) has the characteristic particular solution - the balanced exponential growth in which $Q_i = 0$, M_i, Y_i, R_i^L, R^N, ... grow exponentially and x_i, p_i, s_i, r, q are constant. The growth rate γ is determined by the model structure : it is bounded by the technological parameters and depends on the emission rate π_i. The well-known Solow's "growth gold rule" follows from the balanced growth relations. If $\pi_i = 0$, so $\gamma = 0$ and the economy is in a state of equilibrium Having considered a transition of the economy to a neighbour state of equilibrium one gets the Keynesian multiplier relation.

2) If $R_i^L = \tilde{R}_i^L$, $\Psi^N < \tilde{\Psi}^N$ and $\delta = 0$, the system (M.1)-(M.23) has another characteristic particular solution - the inflationary stagnation in which M_i, Y_i, R_i^L, R^N, Q_i, r, q are constant and p_i, s_i, φ grow with a constant rate which is proportional to the emission rate π_i.

3) Some results of the simulation runs are plotted in Figs. 3-5. (ν_i = const in (M.3) and (M.2) omitted).

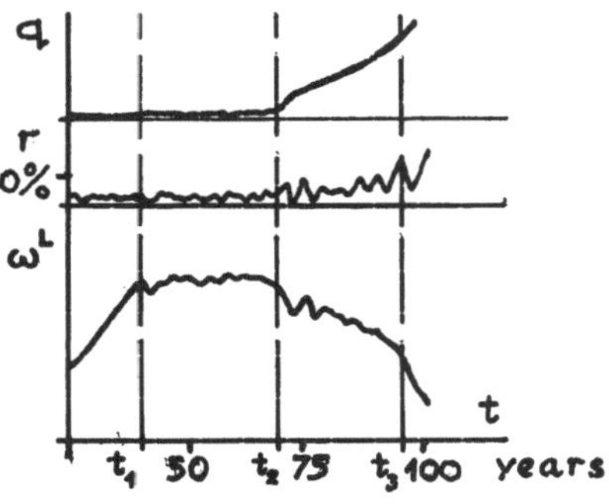

Fig.3

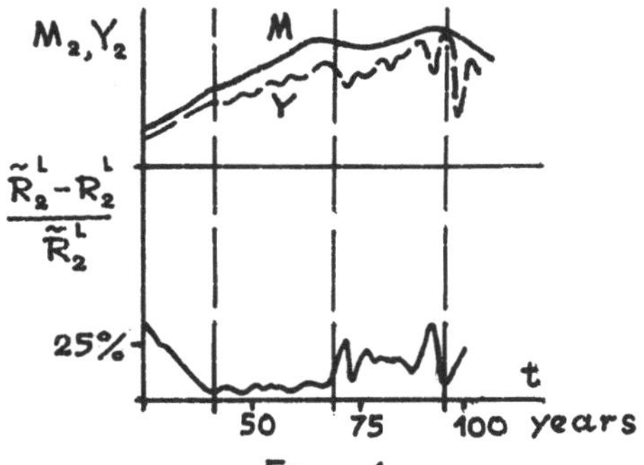

Fig.4

The economy exponentionally grows up to time t_1. The growth rate is $\gamma > \delta$. Starting from time t_1 the labour supply is restraining the economy growth. The average economy growth rate becomes equal to δ. The output and employment oscillations appear.

The output rise phase coincides with the high employment phase which is accompanied by the price and wage rate increases. The output fall phase coincides with the high unemployment phase and is accompanied by the price and wage rate stabilization. As a result the unemployment $\frac{\tilde{R}_i^L - R_i^L}{\tilde{R}_i^L}$ oscillates about some constant level and the price and wage rate increases slowly. The interest rate and per capita consumption of the workers also oscillate about constant levels. Putting $\delta = 0.02$ per annum and the other parameters being fitted so that $\gamma = 0.04$ per annum, the oscillations period is equal to 5-8 years. The unemployment value is oscillating about the 5% level. Therefore we can interpret these oscillations as the business cycles.

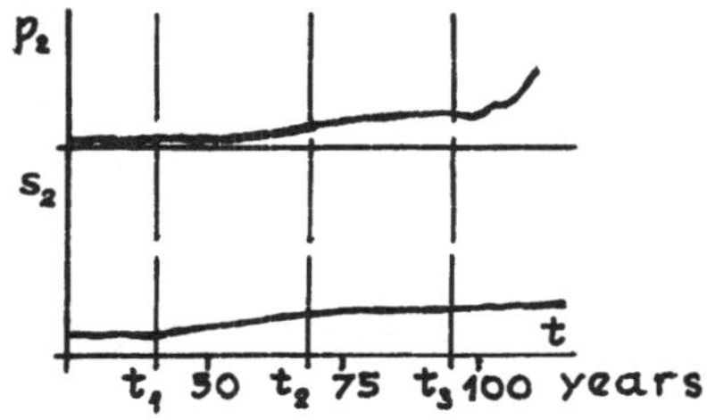

Fig. 5

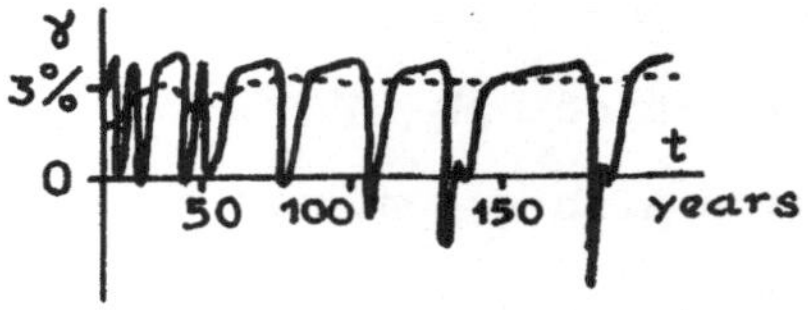

Fig. 6

Starting from time t_1 the natural resources supply is restraining the economy growth, the indication of this being the steep rise in the rent. The pattern of the economy growth changes greatly. The rise in the rent follows the rise in the interest rate. The investment falls so that the sector capacity even decreases. The output oscillations increase, the average level of unemployment and its oscillations increase too. The rise in the unemployment is accompanied by the rise in the price but the wage rate remaines fixed.

Consequently the per capita consumption of the workers falls. The crisis sets in the economy. Figs.3-5 show the growth pattern of the second sector. The first sector reveals the same pattern.

4) The results of simulation runs for $\Psi^N < \tilde{\Psi}^N$ constantly are plotted in Fig. 6. The dotted curve plots the growth rate γ as the function of time provided $\nu_i = const$ in (M.3) and (M.2) are omitted. The solid curve corresponds to the case when the technical innovations have been taken into considerations in form of (M.2), (M.3). One can recognize that the technological innovations not only increase the growth rate γ but also give rise to its oscillations with up to 50-70 years period. Probably these oscillations can be interpreted as the known "long-termed" cycles.

In conclusion we would like to mention that within the model described we were able to present a foreign trade of two economies and to analyse how the rates of economies growth are influenced by the rate of exchange.

ON ONE REPRESENTATION OF NECESSARY CONDITIONS OF OPTIMALITY FOR DISCRETE CONTROLLED SYSTEMS

V.M.Jakovlev,

Senior Researcher

Novosibirsk, Institute of Mathematics,

the USSR Academy of Sciences, Siberian Branch

1. Consider the following problem. A controlled system is given

$$x_i(t+1) = f_i(x(t), u(t)); \qquad x_i(0) = x_i^0; \quad (i = 1, 2, \ldots, n), \tag{1}$$

where $x(t) \in E^n$ are phase variables, $u(t) \in U \subset E^m$ are the controls. It is required to obtain the control $u^*(t)$, which gives the minimum to the value

$$J(u) = \sum_{i=1}^{n} c_i x_i(T), \tag{2}$$

where $c \in E^n$, T are prescribed.

For a fixed admissible control $u(t)$ we define the system

$$P_j(t) = \sum_{i=1}^{n} p_i(t+1) \frac{\partial f_i(x(t), u(t))}{\partial x_j} \qquad P_j(T) = -c_j \tag{3}$$

and the function

$$H(x(t), u(t), p(t+1)) = \sum_{i=1}^{n} p_i(t+1) f_i(x(t), u(t)). \tag{4}$$

DEFINITION 1. The relations

$$u_K(s) = u_K^* + \varphi_K(s) \qquad s \geq 0; \quad K = 1, 2, \ldots, m \tag{5}$$

define the regular arc $\varphi(s)$ which goes out of the point u^*, if the following conditions are satisfied

1) $\varphi_K(s) \in C^2$;

2) $\sum_{K=1}^{m} \left(\frac{d\varphi_K}{ds}\right)^2 \neq 0$;

3) $\left|\frac{d^2\varphi_K}{ds^2}\right| \leq K < \infty$; $K = 1, 2, \ldots, m$.

Here s is the arc length, $\varphi_K(0) = 0$.

DEFINITION 2. The set U has the property S, if for any $s > 0$ and any point $u \in U$, $\varepsilon > 0$ is found, such that any point $u' \in \mathcal{E}_\varepsilon(u)$, where

$$\mathcal{E}_\varepsilon(u) = \{u' : \|u - u'\| < \varepsilon ;\ u' \in U\} ,$$

can be connected to u by the regular arc which entirely lies in U and has the length not exceeding s .

THEOREM 1. Let $f_i(x, u)$ be continuously differentiable for u and for x in the system (1) and the set U have the property S . For the optimality of the control $u^*(t)$ and the solutions $x^*(t)$ and $p^*(t)$ of the systems (1) and (3) it is necessary to satisfy the inequality

$$\sum_{i=1}^{n} \sum_{j=1}^{m} p_i^*(t+1) \frac{\partial f_i(x^*(t), u(t))}{\partial u_K} \frac{d\varphi_K(0)}{ds} = \frac{dH}{ds_\varphi} \leq 0$$

for any regular arc $\varphi(s)$, which goes out of the point $u^*(t)$.

PROOF. By using specially, as in [1], the variation

$$\delta u(t) = \begin{cases} \delta u, & t = \tau \\ 0, & t \neq \tau \end{cases}$$

it is easy to obtain that the increment of the cost function (2) is

$$\Delta_\tau J = -\frac{dH}{ds_\varphi} \delta s + O(\delta s) + O_1(\|\Delta x\|) ,$$

where

$$O_1(\|\Delta x\|) = \sum_{t=\tau+1}^{T-1} o(\|\Delta x(t)\|).$$

It follows from the optimality condition $\Delta_\tau \mathcal{J} \geqslant 0$ and the condition $\delta s > 0$ of the theorem's assertion.

2. Let A be some constant, $\varphi(x)$ be an arbitrary twice continuously differentiable strictly convex function. Let us define the function for an arbitrary admissible control and the solutions $x(t)$ and $p(t)$ of the systems (1) and (3) corresponding to it

$$\tilde{H}(x(t), x(t+1), u(t), p(t+1)) = H(x(t), u(t), p(t+1)) +$$
$$+ A\left\{\sum_{i=1}^{n} \frac{\partial \varphi(x(t+1))}{\partial x_i} f_i(x(t), u(t)) - \varphi(f(x(t), u(t)))\right\}. \quad (6)$$

THEOREM 2. Let $u^*(t)$ be an optimal control in the problem (1), (2), $x^*(t)$, $p^*(t)$ be the corresponding solutions of systems (1) and (3). There exists the constant $A_0 \geq 0$ which is such that for any $A > A_0$ the function

$$\tilde{H}_u = \tilde{H}(x^*(t), x^*(t+1), u, p^*(t+1))$$

reaches the maximum for $u = u^*(t)$.

PROOF. Let us prove this theorem under the following conditions:

a) the set U has the property S ;

b) the functions $f_i(x, u)$ are continuously differentiable for x and twice continuously differentiable for u ;

c) not all the values $\dfrac{d f_i(x^*(t), u^*(t))}{d s_\varphi}$ are equal to zero for any regular arc $\varphi(s)$, which goes out of the point $u^*(t)$;

d) the solution of the system

$$f_i(x^*(t),\ u) = f_i(x^*(t),\ u^*(t))$$

is only $u = u^*(t)$.

Compose the difference

$$\Delta H(t) = \widetilde{H}(x^*(t),\ x^*(t+1),\ u^*(t),\ p^*(t+1)) -$$
$$- \widetilde{H}(x^*(t),\ x^*(t+1),\ u,\ p^*(t+1)) = \Delta H(t) + A\,\Delta_1(t)\ ,$$

where

$$\Delta H(t) = H(x^*(t),\ u^*(t),\ p^*(t+1)) - H(x^*(t),\ u,\ p^*(t+1)),$$
$$\Delta_1(t) = \sum_{i=1}^{n} \frac{\partial \Phi(x^*(t+1))}{\partial x_i} \cdot \left[f(x^*(t),\ u^*(t)) -\right.$$
$$\left. - f_i(x^*(t),\ u)\right] - \left[\Phi(x^*(t+1)) - \Phi(f(x^*(t),\ u))\right] .$$

Since $\Phi(x)$ is a strictly convex function, then due to the assumption (2)

$$\Delta_1(t) > 0$$

for any $u = u^*(t)$, $u \in U$.

Let $\varepsilon > 0$ be sufficiently small. Denote by $L(\mathcal{E})$ the set of regular arcs, connecting the points $u \in \mathcal{E}_\varepsilon(u^*(t))$ to the point $u^*(t)$ and let $\varphi(s) \in L(\mathcal{E})$ be such an arbitrary arc.

We have

$$\Delta H(t) = - \frac{dH}{ds_\varphi}\,\delta s_\varphi - \frac{1}{2}\,\frac{d^2H}{ds_\varphi^2}\,\delta s_\varphi^2 + 0(\delta s_\varphi^2)\,;$$

$$\Delta_1(t) = \frac{1}{2} \sum_{i=1}^{n} \sum_{j=1}^{n} \frac{\partial^2 \Phi(x^*(t+1))}{\partial x_i\ \partial x_j}\ \frac{df_i}{ds_\varphi}\ \frac{df_j}{ds_\varphi}\ \delta s_\varphi^2 + 0(\delta s_\varphi^2)\ .$$

Thus,

$$\Delta \widetilde{H}(t) = - \frac{dH}{ds_\varphi}\,\delta s_\varphi + \frac{1}{2}\left[A \cdot \mathcal{D}\left(\frac{df}{ds_\varphi}, \frac{df}{ds_\varphi}\right) - \frac{d^2H}{ds_\varphi^2}\right]\delta s_\varphi^2 + 0(\delta s_\varphi^2),$$

where $\mathcal{D}\left(\frac{df}{ds_\varphi}, \frac{df}{ds_\varphi}\right)$ is the square form with the matrix consisting of the elements

$$a_{ij} = \frac{\partial^2 \Phi(x^*(t+1))}{\partial x_i \, \partial x_j} .$$

Since $\Phi(x)$ is the strictly convex function and due to the assumption b) not all the values $\frac{df_i}{ds_\varphi}$ are equal to zero, then

$$\mathcal{D}\left(\frac{df}{ds_\varphi}, \frac{df}{ds_\varphi}\right) > 0 .$$

According to the definition of the regular arc and the continuity condition of the second derivatives for u of the functions $f_i(x,u)$ it follows that

$$\mathcal{A}_1(t) = \sup \frac{\frac{d^2H}{ds_\varphi^2}}{\mathcal{D}\left(\frac{df}{ds_\varphi}, \frac{df}{ds_\varphi}\right)} < \infty .$$

Since by Theorem 1 we have $\frac{dH}{ds_\varphi} \leq 0$, then

$$\Delta \tilde{H}(t) \geq \frac{1}{2}\left[A\mathcal{D}\left(\frac{df}{ds_\varphi}, \frac{df}{ds_\varphi}\right) - \frac{d^2H}{ds_\varphi^2}\right]\delta s_\varphi^2 + o(\delta s_\varphi^2) > 0$$

for $A > \mathcal{A}_1(t)$ and $\varepsilon > 0$ sufficiently small.

Denote

$$\mathcal{A}_2(t) = \max_{u \in U \setminus \mathcal{E}_\varepsilon(u^*(t))} \frac{|\Delta H(t)|}{\Delta_1(t)} .$$

Assuming that

$$A_0 = \max_{0 \leq t \leq T-1} \max \left\{\mathcal{A}_1(t), \mathcal{A}_2(t)\right\} ,$$

we obtain $\Delta \tilde{H}(t) > 0$ at $A > A_0$ for every $u \in U$. Q.E.D.

3. As an illustration consider the examples taken from [1].

EXAMPLE 1. $x(t+1) = \frac{1}{2} u(t)$; $\qquad x(0) = 0$;

$$y(t+1) = y(t) + x^2(t) - u^2(t); \quad y(0) = 0;$$

$$|u| \leq 1; \quad \min \; y(2).$$

The optimal control is

$$u^*(0) = 1; \quad u^*(1) = 1.$$

The function

$$H_u\left(x^*(0), u, p^*(1)\right) = -\frac{1}{2}u + u^2$$

at the point $u = 1$ has the local maximum. The function

$$\tilde{H}_u\left(x^*(0), x^*(1), u, p^*(1)\right) = -Au^4 + \left(1 + \frac{7}{4}A\right)u^2 + \frac{1}{2}(A-1)u$$

at $A \geqslant A_0 = 1$ reaches the maximum at the point $u = 1$.

EXAMPLE 2.

$$x(t+1) = 2u(t); \qquad x(0) = 0;$$

$$y(t+1) = y(t) + x^2(t) - u^2(t); \quad y(0) = 0;$$

$$|u| \leq 1; \quad \min \; y(2).$$

We have

$$u^*(0) = 0; \quad u^*(1) = 1;$$

$$H_u\left(x^*(0), u, p^*(1)\right) = u^2.$$

This function reaches the absolute minimum at $u = 0$.

$$\tilde{H}_u\left(x^*(0), x^*(1), u, p^*(1)\right) = -Au^4 - (4A-1)u^2.$$

This function at $A \geqslant A_0 = \frac{1}{4}$ has the maximum at the point $u = 0$.

EXAMPLE 3.

$$x(t+1) = v(t) \sin\frac{\pi}{2}u(t); \qquad x(0) = 0;$$

$$y(t+1) = v(t) \cos\frac{\pi}{2}u(t); \qquad y(0) = 0;$$

$$z(t+1) = z(t) + x^2(t) + y^2(t) + u^2(t) - v^2(t); \quad z(0) = 0;$$

$$|u| \leq 1; \quad \min \; z(2).$$

We obtain

$$u^*(0) = 0; \quad v^*(0) = 0; \quad u^*(1) = 0; \quad v^*(1) = 1.$$

$$H_u(x^*(0), u, p^*(1)) = -u^2 + v^2.$$

For this function the point (0,0) is a saddle one. It should be noted that the system considered here does not satisfy the conditions under which Theorem 2 has been proved. Indeed, for the point $u^*(0) = (0,0)$ the straight line segments

$$u = s \cos\alpha;$$

$$v = s \sin\alpha.$$

will be simple arcs connecting the point with the arcs of locality.

We have

$$\left.\frac{df_1}{ds}\right|_{s=0} = 0; \quad \left.\frac{df_2}{ds}\right|_{s=0} = \sin\alpha; \quad \left.\frac{df_3}{ds}\right|_{s=0} = 0.$$

There exist two arcs ($\alpha = 0$ and $\alpha = \pi$) for which all $\frac{df_i}{ds} = 0$.

Nevertheless, the function

$$\widetilde{H}_u(x^*(0), x^*(1), u, p^*(1)) = -A(u^4 + v^4) + 2A u^2 v^2 - -(A-1)v^2 - u^2$$

at $A \geqslant A_0 = 1$ reaches the maximum at point (0,0).

EXAMPLE 4.

$$x(t+1) = 2\sqrt{|u(t)|}; \qquad x(0) = 0;$$

$$y(t+1) = y(t) + x^2(t) - |u(t)|; \qquad y(0) = 0;$$

$$|u| \leq 1; \quad \min y(2)$$

We have

$$u^*(0) = 0; \quad u^*(1) = 1.$$

The function

$$H_u(x^*(0), u, p^*(1)) = |u|$$

is non-differentiable in the point $u = 0$ and reaches the absolute minimum at it.

For this example the conditions of Theorem 2 do not hold either. However, the function

$$\tilde{H}_u(x^*(0), x^*(1), u, p^*(1)) = -Au^2 - (4A-1)\cdot|u|$$

at $A \geq A_0 = \frac{1}{4}$ reaches the maximum at the point $u = 0$.

EXAMPLE 5.

$$x(t+1) = u(t); \qquad x(0) = 0;$$
$$y(t+1) = v(t) \qquad y(0) = 0;$$
$$z(t+1) = z(t) + x^2(t) + y^2(t); \qquad z(0) = 0;$$
$$U = \{u, v : (u-1)^2 + (v+1)^2 \geq 8;\ (u-2)^2 + (v+2)^2 \leq 18\};$$
$$\min z(2).$$

We have

$$u^*(0) = -1; \quad v^*(0) = 1;$$
$$H_u(x^*(0), u, p^*(1)) = 2(u-v).$$

This function at point (-1,1) reaches the minimum. Note that

$$\text{grad}_u H_u = (2,-2) \neq 0.$$

The arcs of the circles of the radius $r = (1+a)\sqrt{2}$, where $a \in [1,2]$ and with the center lying on the segment $x = 1+\lambda,\ y = -1-\lambda,\ \lambda \in [0,1]$, may serve as arcs φ in this case. If we introduce polar coordinates with the pole at a point $(a, -a)$, and read an angle ψ from the ray $[(2,-2),(1,-1))$, then we obtain

$$H_u = 4(a - (1+a)\cos\psi)$$

Since the length of the arc here is

$$s = a\psi,$$

then

$$\left.\frac{dH_u}{ds}\right|_{s=0} = \left.\frac{4(1+a)}{a}\sin\psi\right|_{\psi=0} = 0.$$

Hence, the point (-1,1) is quasistationary for the function H_u .

Further we obtain

$$\tilde{H}_u(x^*(0), x^*(1), u, p^*(1)) = -A(u^2+v^2) - 2(A-1)u + 2(A-1)v .$$

This function at $A \geq A_0 = \frac{1}{2}$ reaches the maximum at the point (-1,1).

EXAMPLE 6.

$$x(t+1) = x(t) + h\,u(t); \qquad x(0) = 0;$$

$$y(t+1) = y(t) + h\cdot(x^2(t) - u^2(t)); \qquad y(0) = 0;$$

$$|u| \leq 1; \quad \min\, y(2).$$

Let $h \in (0,1]$. Then

$$u^*(0) = 1; \quad u^*(1) = 1;$$

$$H_u(x^*(0), u, p^*(1)) = -2h^3u + hu^2.$$

This function fails to reach the maximum at the point $u = 1$ at any $h \in (0,1)$. At the same time the function

$$\tilde{H}_u(x^*(0), x^*(1), u, p^*(1)) = -Ah^2u^4 + (2Ah+1)hu^2 + 2(A-h)h^2u$$

at $A \geq A_0' = h$ has the maximum at the point $u = 1$.

Let $h > 1$. Then

$$u^*(0) = 0; \quad u^*(1) = 1;$$

$$H_u(x^*(0), u, p^*(1)) = hu^2.$$

This function at $u = 0$ reaches the minimum at any $h > 1$. At the same time the function

$$\tilde{H}_u(x^*(0), x^*(1), u, p^*(1)) = -Ah^2u^4 - (Ah-1)u^2h$$

at $A \geq A_0'' = \frac{1}{h}$ has the maximum at the point $u = 0$.

Having combined both the cases we obtain that at $A \geq A_0 = 1$ the function $\tilde{H}_u$ reaches the maximum at $u = u^*(0)$, whatever $h > 0$ can be. The examples considered above illustrate the universality of the proposed form of necessary optimality conditions for discrete systems. The fact that the approach also "works" in the cases when the conditions of Theorem 2 do not hold (Examples 3, 4), allows us to hope that the assertions of this theorem are valid for weaker assumptions than those it has been proved for in the present paper.

R e f e r e n c e

1 R.Gabasov, F.Kirillova. Quality theory of optimal processes. "Nauka", M., 1973.

Lecture Notes in Economics and Mathematical Systems

For information about Vols. 1–104 please contact your bookseller or Springer-Verlag

Vol. 105: Optimal Control Theory and its Applications. Part I. Proceedings 1973. Edited by B. J. Kirby. VI, 425 pages. 1974.

Vol. 106: Optimal Control Theory and its Applications. Part II. Proceedings 1973. Edited by B. J. Kirby. VI, 403 pages. 1974.

Vol. 107: Control Theory, Numerical Methods and Computer Systems Modeling. International Symposium, Rocquencourt, June 17–21, 1974. Edited by A. Bensoussan and J. L. Lions. VIII, 757 pages. 1975.

Vol. 108: F. Bauer et al., Supercritical Wing Sections II. A Handbook. V, 296 pages. 1975.

Vol. 109: R. von Randow, Introduction to the Theory of Matroids. IX, 102 pages. 1975.

Vol. 110: C. Striebel, Optimal Control of Discrete Time Stochastic Systems. III. 208 pages. 1975.

Vol. 111: Variable Structure Systems with Application to Economics and Biology. Proceedings 1974. Edited by A. Ruberti and R. R. Mohler. VI, 321 pages. 1975.

Vol. 112: J. Wilhlem, Objectives and Multi-Objective Decision Making Under Uncertainty. IV, 111 pages. 1975.

Vol. 113: G. A. Aschinger, Stabilitätsaussagen über Klassen von Matrizen mit verschwindenden Zeilensummen. V, 102 Seiten. 1975.

Vol. 114: G. Uebe, Produktionstheorie. XVII, 301 Seiten. 1976.

Vol. 115: Anderson et al., Foundations of System Theory: Finitary and Infinitary Conditions. VII, 93 pages. 1976

Vol. 116: K. Miyazawa, Input-Output Analysis and the Structure of Income Distribution. IX, 135 pages. 1976.

Vol. 117: Optimization and Operations Research. Proceedings 1975. Edited by W. Oettli and K. Ritter. IV, 316 pages. 1976.

Vol. 118: Traffic Equilibrium Methods, Proceedings 1974. Edited by M. A. Florian. XXIII, 432 pages. 1976.

Vol. 119: Inflation in Small Countries. Proceedings 1974. Edited by H. Frisch. VI, 356 pages. 1976.

Vol. 120: G. Hasenkamp, Specification and Estimation of Multiple-Output Production Functions. VII, 151 pages. 1976.

Vol. 121: J. W. Cohen, On Regenerative Processes in Queueing Theory. IX, 93 pages. 1976.

Vol. 122: M. S. Bazaraa, and C. M. Shetty, Foundations of Optimization VI. 193 pages. 1976

Vol. 123: Multiple Criteria Decision Making. Kyoto 1975. Edited by M. Zeleny. XXVII, 345 pages. 1976.

Vol. 124: M. J. Todd. The Computation of Fixed Points and Applications. VII, 129 pages. 1976.

Vol. 125: Karl C. Mosler. Optimale Transportnetze. Zur Bestimmung ihres kostengünstigsten Standorts bei gegebener Nachfrage. VI, 142 Seiten. 1976.

Vol. 126: Energy, Regional Science and Public Policy. Energy and Environment I. Proceedings 1975. Edited by M. Chatterji and P. Van Rompuy. VIII, 316 pages. 1976.

Vol. 127: Environment, Regional Science and Interregional Modeling. Energy and Environment II. Proceedings 1975. Edited by M. Chatterji and P. Van Rompuy. IX, 211 pages. 1976.

Vol. 128: Integer Programming and Related Areas. A Classified Bibliography. Edited by C. Kastning. XII, 495 pages. 1976.

Vol. 129: H.-J. Lüthi, Komplementaritäts- und Fixpunktalgorithmen in der mathematischen Programmierung. Spieltheorie und Ökonomie. VII, 145 Seiten. 1976.

Vol. 130: Multiple Criteria Decision Making, Jouy-en-Josas, France. Proceedings 1975. Edited by H. Thiriez and S. Zionts. VI, 409 pages. 1976.

Vol. 131: Mathematical Systems Theory. Proccedings 1975. Edited by G. Marchesini and S. K. Mitter. X, 408 pages. 1976.

Vol. 132: U. H. Funke, Mathematical Models in Marketing. A Coll tion of Abstracts. XX, 514 pages. 1976.

Vol. 133: Warsaw Fall Seminars in Mathematical Economics 19 Edited by M. W. Loś, J. Loś, and A. Wieczorek. V. 159 pages. 19

Vol. 134: Computing Methods in Applied Sciences and Engineeri Proceedings 1975. VIII, 390 pages. 1976.

Vol. 135: H. Haga, A Disequilibrium – Equilibrium Model with Mo and Bonds. A Keynesian – Walrasian Synthesis. VI, 119 pages. 19

Vol. 136: E. Kofler und G. Menges, Entscheidungen bei unvollständi Information. XII, 357 Seiten 1976.

Vol. 137: R. Wets, Grundlagen Konvexer Optimierung. VI, 146 Sei 1976.

Vol. 138: K. Okuguchi, Expectations and Stability in Oligopoly Mod VI, 103 pages. 1976.

Vol. 139: Production Theory and Its Applications. Proceedings. Ed by H. Albach and G. Bergendahl. VIII, 193 pages. 1977.

Vol. 140: W. Eichhorn and J. Voeller, Theory of the Price In Fisher's Test Approach and Generalizations. VII, 95 pages. 19

Vol. 141: Mathematical Economics and Game Theory. Essays in Hc of Oskar Morgenstern. Edited by R. Henn and O. Moeschlin. 703 pages. 1977.

Vol. 142: J. S. Lane, On Optimal Population Paths. V, 123 pages. 19

Vol. 143: B. Näslund, An Analysis of Economic Size Distributi XV, 100 pages. 1977.

Vol. 144: Convex Analysis and Its Applications. Proceedings 19 Edited by A. Auslender. VI, 219 pages. 1977.

Vol. 145: J. Rosenmüller, Extreme Games and Their Solutions 126 pages. 1977

Vol. 146: In Search of Economic Indicators. Edited by W. H. Str XVI, 198 pages. 1977.

Vol. 147: Resource Allocation and Division of Space. Proceedi Edited by T. Fujii and R. Sato. VIII, 184 pages. 1977.

Vol. 148: C. E. Mandl, Simulationstechnik und Simulationsmoc in den Sozial- und Wirtschaftswissenschaften. IX, 173 Seiten. 1

Vol. 149: Stationäre und schrumpfende Bevölkerungen: Demo phisches Null- und Negativwachstum in Österreich. Herausgege von G. Feichtinger. VI, 262 Seiten. 1977.

Vol. 150: Bauer et al., Supercritical Wing Sections III. VI, 179 pa 1977.

Vol. 151: C. A. Schneeweiß, Inventory-Production Theory. VI, 116 pa 1977.

Vol. 152: Kirsch et al., Notwendige Optimalitätsbedingungen ihre Anwendung. VI, 157 Seiten. 1978.

Vol. 153: Kombinatorische Entscheidungsprobleme: Methoden Anwendungen. Herausgegeben von T. M. Liebling und M. Rös VIII, 206 Seiten. 1978.

Vol. 154: Problems and Instruments of Business Cycle Anal Proceedings 1977. Edited by W. H. Strigel. VI, 442 pages. 1

Vol. 155: Multiple Criteria Problem Solving. Proceedings 1977. Ec by S. Zionts. VIII, 567 pages. 1978.

Vol. 156: B. Näslund and B. Sellstedt, Neo-Ricardian Theory. Applications to Some Current Economic Problems. VI, 165 pa 1978.

Vol. 157: Optimization and Operations Research. Proceedings 1 Edited by R. Henn, B. Korte, and W. Oettli. VI, 270 pages. 1

Vol. 158: L. J. Cherene, Set Valued Dynamical Systems and Econc Flow. VIII, 83 pages. 1978.

Vol. 159: Some Aspects of the Foundations of General Equilib Theory: The Posthumous Papers of Peter J. Kalman. Edited by J. Gr VI, 167 pages. 1978.

Vol. 160: Integer Programming and Related Areas. A Class Bibliography. Edited by D. Hausmann. XIV, 314 pages. 1978.